WHERE TO RETIRE America's
Best and Most Affordable Places

JOHN HOWELLS
FOURTH EDITION

D0111461

The
Globe
Pequot
Press

Guilford, Connecticut

About the Author

John Howells and his wife, Sherry, spent many months of travel by automobile, motor home, and airplane gathering information to produce this book. They interviewed retired folks in all sections of the country, collecting experiences, advice, and valuable insights into successful retirement lifestyles.

John has written and co-authored several other books about retirement locations. Among them are *Choose the South, Choose Mexico,* and *Choose Costa Rica.* He also writes about retirement and travel for mature Americans in magazines such as *Consumers Digest* and *Where to Retire Magazine.* He is a member of the board of directors of the American Association of Retirement Communities. John and his wife live in California and Costa Rica.

Cover design: Laura Augustine
Cover illustration: Jacqui Morgan/The Stock Illustration Source
Text design: Kevin Lynch

Library of Congress Cataloging-in-Publication Data

Howells, John Mack.
    Where to Retire : America's best and most affordable places / John Howells.—4th ed.
    p. cm.
  Includes indexes.
  ISBN 0-7627-0656-2
  1. Retirement, Places of—United States—Case studies. 2. Quality of life—United States—Case studies. 3. Social indicators—United States—Case studies. I. Title: America's best and most affordable places. II. Title.
HQ1063.2.U6 H68   2000
646.7'9'0973—dc21   00-021232

Manufactured in the United States of America
Fourth Edition/Second Printing

Table of Contents

Help Us Keep This Guide Up to Date

Every effort has been made by the author and editors to make this guide as accurate and useful as possible. However, many things can change after a guide is published—establishments close, phone numbers change, facilities come under new management, etc.

We would love to hear from you concerning your experiences with this guide and how you feel it could be made better and be kept up to date. While we may not be able to respond to all comments and suggestions, we'll take them to heart and we'll also make certain to share them with the author. Please send your comments and suggestions to the following address:

The Globe Pequot Press
Reader Response/Editorial Department
P.O. Box 480
Guilford, CT 06437

Or you may e-mail us at:

editorial@globe-pequot.com

Thanks for your input, and happy travels!

Introduction

THE PREVIOUS EDITION of *Where to Retire* reviewed some 200 communities as desirable places to retire. In this latest version we've added a few communities and deleted some. This is not because certain places have suddenly become undesirable. We've simply found other communities more deserving of mention. In any case, the listed cities and towns in this book are not to be taken as recommendations, but rather as suggestions, a sort of "menu" of interesting places where others have chosen to retire, with an emphasis on how it might be to live there. You'll need to do much research on your own to decide which place, if any, will become your dream retirement home.

As the title suggests, this book focuses more on *where* to retire than *how* to retire. It's designed for those who are approaching retirement with a vague notion that they should move away from their home towns after they retire, but aren't sure where.

Further, we hope to help you decide what could be an equally important question: Why should I move after retirement? Maybe you shouldn't. Many people assume that relocating is an obligatory part of retirement. Actually, the vast majority don't move away when they retire. For some, moving to a new town or a different state and starting over just doesn't make sense. But for others, finding a new home can be exciting and can contribute to a longer, happier life. Those living in places where recreational and cultural opportunities abound, the weather is nice, and where they have many friends see no reason to move from their neighborhoods when they retire. People who live in large cities are more likely to relocate than those who live in small towns. Depending on the state, as many as 25 percent of those leaving the workforce will move to another town, and between 1 to 10 percent will move to another state. This book is for that 1 to 10 percent who want to make a major change.

The *why* of moving to a new town or state when you retire requires a good deal of self-examination. You need to evaluate your goals, motives, and present lifestyle to be sure just where you need to relocate. People often think of retirement as a "permanent vacation." Nothing wrong with that. But before you pack up the proverbial lock, stock, and barrel to move to that beach town or mountain village where you've enjoyed spending your regular two-week vacations, ask yourself this question: Will I be happy living there year-round? Will you become bored with trout fishing after a couple of months? Will you enjoy the beach during the winter, when your summer-resident friends have left, the shops and restaurants are closed, and northern winds sweep in from a cold ocean?

Commonsense advice to those thinking about moving to another location upon retirement is to try it out for six months before deciding. You may discover drawbacks you never noticed before, items such as no intercity bus service, no air transportation, terrible restaurants, or unfriendly natives. The truth is, however, that most readers follow my recommendations about as faithfully as does my wife. Real estate folks tell me that couples often come to a place they've never seen before, fall in love with it, put down a deposit on a house, then return home to sell the old homestead.

After taking everything into consideration, you may find moving away is your best option. If you are like many people, your closest friends are those you work with. When you retire, you'll be leaving your friends at the office; you won't be part of the "gang" any more. You'll have to make new friends anyway, so why not try it in a more agreeable environment? Have your children grown up and moved away? If so, you have even less reason to stick around.

One of the few things my wife and I completely agree on is that you can't find an ideal retirement place by studying statistics. A computer can't swallow a bunch of numbers and then spit out the "ideal" place for you to spend the rest of your lives! It isn't that simple. You must look beyond statistics. You must see your new home through your own eyes.

Even if statistics are interpreted rationally and accurately, there remains the common fallacy that there is a "best" place for retirement. What is ideal for you could be excruciatingly boring for me. What I might consider a wonderful climate could be far too warm for you. The choice of a retirement location is as personal as the choice of an automobile or a vacation resort. Just as there is no one best car or ideal vacation, there is no perfect retirement spot. You'll need to give this decision a lot of thought.

Statistics can be useful, of course, but we use them for making comparisons, not for drawing conclusions. How many people live in a town, the number of people per square mile, and the cost of housing are interesting facts. But, more important than how many people, what *kind* of people are they? Will you find something in common with them? Will you fit in and make friends readily? Will you be in a religious or political minority? Will your friends and family be eager to visit you in your new location, or will they be appalled because they can't find good restaurants and the most exciting thing to do in your town is visit the bowling alley? Giving a locality a high rating because of good hunting and fishing means little to someone whose image of outdoor recreation is sitting in a beer garden. Museums, operas, and other cultural events would raise the ratings for some folks, but not for those who consider HBO or videocassettes their prime entertainment. A decision to move should be based on a thoughtful inventory of your likes and dislikes and the lifestyle you wish to achieve.

Research Methods

This book evaluates more than 150 communities, and by extension, hundreds more in surrounding localities. How are judgments made? Of course it would be impossible for one couple to visit all the potential retirement locations in the United States. What we've tried to do is select logical areas of the country where retirement is practical and illustrate a few cities, towns, or villages that are typical of that region. Our research has been ongoing for more than fifteen years. In each location, my wife and I try to picture ourselves living there. We visit neighborhoods and residential developments, senior citizens' centers, and chambers of commerce; we interview managers and residents of retirement complexes and we chat with retired couples. The last major research trip ended in November 1999.

In each location we visit at least one real estate office and interview salespeople. It turns out that many are retirees. They enjoy the sociability of their jobs, the chance to meet new people, and, of course, the opportunity to pick up a few commissions. They're especially helpful because they understand the problems involved in moving away for retirement.

We learn which neighborhoods retirees prefer, and we visit to see for ourselves. Sometimes we pose as buyers or renters looking for retirement property. This helps when looking at large retirement complexes, where potential customers tour in groups, since we find opportunities to talk with prospective buyers to find out what brings them to that particular place for retirement.

We use U.S. government publications, drawing statistics from the Bureau of the Census, Department of Labor, and National Oceanographic Administration weather charts. The FBI's crime statistics are carefully tabulated, and consultations are made with noted sociologists and police officials. The Consumer Price Index and the American Chamber of Commerce Research Association supply us with trends.

Over the years we've investigated hundreds of retirement areas and examined many different lifestyles before making the final selections for this book. However, because a town is *not* described here doesn't necessarily mean it wouldn't be a great place to retire.

Finding Your Shangri-La

MAGAZINE ARTICLES AND GUIDEBOOKS commonly grade retirement communities, ranking the top places from one to ten, as if they were rating major league baseball teams. With a baseball team, we can check the scores; can't argue with that. But cities and towns don't receive scores except in somebody's mind. The fact that a freelance writer likes a city and ranks it number one in his magazine article doesn't prove a thing. The writer's next article had better rank *another* city as number one, or the editor won't buy the article.

Favorable ratings are often awarded on the basis of conditions that don't affect retirees. For example: good schools, high employment, and a booming business climate will boost a town's popularity rating, while horrible weather and high taxes are often ignored. Quality grammar schools and juvenile recreational programs matter less to retirees than quality restaurants, continuing education programs, and safe neighborhoods. Full employment and thriving business conditions often spell high prices and expensive housing. Cultural amenities, such as museums and operas, receive high marks in retirement analysis. Yet, how many times a month will you be going to the opera? the museum? Would you rather live in a town with ten golf courses and no museums, or ten museums and *one* golf course? To find your ideal location, you're going to have to do your own ranking.

Ideally, you'll start your retirement analysis early. A great way to do this is by combining research with your vacations. Instead of visiting the same old place each year, try different parts of the country. Check out each location as a possible place to live. Look at real estate, medical care, and recreation. What about libraries? (An appalling number are closing because of lack of funds.) Does this town offer the types of cultural events you enjoy? Cultural events can be anything from concerts and stage plays to square-dance lessons and quilting bees to bowling tournaments and chili cookoffs. The point is, will you be happy there?

The local chamber of commerce office can be an excellent source of information. Although some offices hire minimum-wage employees who couldn't possibly care less if you moved there, the better ones are staffed by volunteers—often retirees—who will help any way they can, short of paying your moving expenses. Make sure to ask if the community has a "retiree attraction committee" or "retiree welcoming committee." This growing concept of welcoming retirees into a community is often coordinated by the chamber of commerce. A welcoming committee can be a marvelous way to make new friends and to adjust to your new surroundings.

If you can't or don't care to travel, you can do research at your local library. Almost all libraries subscribe to a variety of out-of-town newspapers; these are extremely valuable research tools. You'll learn much about a community by the news. If drunk-driving arrests are top news stories, you have one picture of crime. If murders and mutilations are so common that they are reported on page 27, you get another picture.

An important part of an out-of-town paper is the classified section. Check real estate prices, rentals, and mobile home parks; compare them with your hometown newspaper and you'll begin to get a picture of relative costs. Contrast help-wanted ads with work-wanted ads. This tells you wage rates, should you consider working part-time, and clues you in on what kind of competition you will have for jobs. An abundance of help-wanted ads might indicate an availability of part-time work. Even if you don't plan on working, you might be interested in local wages, so you'll know what you'll have to pay for help around your new home.

What to Look For

Following is a list of requirements my wife and I personally consider essential for a successful retirement relocation. Your needs may be different; feel free to add or subtract from the list, and then use the list to measure communities against your standards.

1. Safety.   Can you walk through your neighborhood without fearful glances over your shoulder? Can you leave your home for a few weeks without dreading a break-in?

2. Climate.   Will temperatures and weather patterns match your lifestyle? Will you be tempted to go outdoors and exercise year-round, or will harsh winters and suffocating summers confine you to an easy chair in front of the television set?

3. Housing.   Is quality housing available at a price you're willing and able to pay? Is the area visually pleasing, free of pollution and traffic snarls? Will you feel proud to live in the neighborhood?

4. Nourishment for your interests.   Does your retirement choice offer facilities for your favorite pastimes, cultural events, and hobbies, be they hunting, fishing, adult education, art centers, or whatever?

5. Social compatibility.   Will you find common interests with your neighbors? Will you fit in and make friends easily? Will there be folks with your own cultural, social, and political background?

6. Affordability.   Are goods and services reasonably priced? Will you be able to afford to hire help from time to time when you need to? Will your income be high enough to be significantly affected by state income taxes? Will taxes on your pension make a big difference?

7. Medical care.   Are local physicians accepting new patients? Does the area have an adequate hospital? (You needn't live next door to the Mayo Clinic; you can always go there if your hospital can't handle your problem.) Do you have a medical problem that requires a specialist?

8. Distance from family and friends.   Are you going to be too far away or in a location where nobody wants to visit? Would you rather they *don't* visit? (In that case, you'd do better even farther away.)

9. Transportation.   Does your new location enjoy intercity bus transportation? Many small towns have none, which makes you totally dependent on an automobile or taxis. How far is the nearest airport with airline connections? Can friends and family visit without driving?

10. Jobs and/or volunteer opportunities.   Will there be enough interesting volunteer jobs or paid jobs (if that's what you want) to satisfy your need for keeping busy? What about continuing education programs at the local college?

Private Retirement Communities

Year by year, retirement becomes more of a big business, prompting impressive corporate investment. Planned retirement communities, often of astounding size, are popping up all over the country. These complexes are often centered around a lake, golf course, or some natural attraction. Often these developments are "gated" communities; that is, to enter the property you must be a member of that development or have good reason to be there. Wanting to price property is usually a good enough reason to visit, although a few developments permit you to purchase only by invitation of other residents. Round-the-clock guards often staff the gates, scrutinizing everyone who enters.

Some private developments are "open" communities—without gates—yet are still age-restricted. Some are enormous. Arizona's Sun City West, for example, has more than 15,000 homes on 7,100 acres. (At this point in time, these units are almost all sold and a new development, Sun City Grand, is underway.)

Many complexes restrict buyers to those age fifty-five and older. Youngsters may visit but may not live there. This affects the community in two ways. Obviously, your lives will be more tranquil, without gangs of kids riding bikes, playing boom boxes, and knocking baseballs through your living room window. But more important than that, you'll enjoy a lower crime rate. Burglaries, vandalism, and theft usually occur in direct proportion to the number of teenagers in the neighborhood. The other side of the coin is that many retirees prefer living in mixed-age neighborhoods; they find young children and teenagers fun to be with.

Home buyers seem to be split into two groups when it comes to age restrictions. On the one hand, we often hear, "I can't imagine a more dreary and stifling situation—living in a same-age community! We prefer to socialize with a mixed-age group, with young people as well as those our own age and older." Personally, my wife and I tend to feel this way, at least to some degree. We often, however, visit friends living in those deluxe retirement complexes. They point out that in a mixed-generation community residents tend to segregate into age groups anyway. "Young couples are too busy with careers and their children's interests," they say. "When we want to play golf, we know our next-door neighbors won't be at work or hosting a Cub Scout meeting."

The bottom line is that age-restricted developments are selling a lifestyle as much as real estate. With organized activities and social groups ready to welcome new residents, transition to retirement is made painless and swift.

Moving to the Country

You might picture living in a rural or backwoods community as being the ultimate in get-away-from-it-all living. It's nice to enjoy an incredibly low cost of living, with housing at giveaway prices. I have mixed feelings about recommending retirement in some inexpensive areas—particularly rural, farming communities—to folks from big-city backgrounds. When you share few common interests with your neighbors, it's easy to feel left out. When almost everyone in the community is in some way involved in agriculture, conversations tend to dwell on the price of soybeans or the best way to deworm hogs. When your agricultural experience is limited to watering houseplants, you find you have few words of wisdom others care to hear. When your accent sounds funny to your neighbors, when your tastes in movies, politics, and food are different (or when you don't even own a pickup!), you could feel like an alien. Happily, situations like this are changing as more and more retirees from all over the nation are moving into small-town U.S.A. Nonetheless, it behooves you to look beyond the cost-of-living charts and real estate averages.

Cost of Living

The most comprehensive research on the cost of living in the United States is done by the American Chamber of Commerce Research Association (ACCRA). They tabulate the cost of groceries, real estate, utilities, and other everyday necessities and publish them quarterly. Although not all communities are indexed by ACCRA, it's possible to see regional patterns in the cost of living for various communities. Whenever statistics are available, they are mentioned at the end of each community description. You can be reasonably confident that nearby communities will have a similar price structure.

Local boosters too often place undue emphasis on low cost of living and cheap real estate as the prime attractions of their area. True, these items go hand in hand; that is, when you find low-cost housing, you'll also find economical living costs in general. In our travels, we've encountered places where $29,000 will buy a three-bedroom home; where carpenters will remodel for $6.00 per hour, where haircuts are still $3.50, and permanent waves cost $14.75. As I continually stress, however, *inexpensive* living isn't necessarily the same as *quality* living. Some low-cost areas are exceptional bargains, combining a high quality of life with welcoming neighbors and affordable living costs. Yet other low-cost areas are intensely dreary and boring.

Why is the cost of living and housing so much less in some localities? Basically, you'll find two reasons for cheap real estate and low rents. The most common reason: an undesirable place to live. These towns steadily lose population because they have absolutely nothing going for them—no jobs, no charm. Homes sell for rock-bottom prices because eager sellers outnumber reluctant buyers. Unless you are sincerely dedicated to boredom, bad weather, and cable TV, these are not places you would seek out for retirement.

The second situation deals with an unforeseen, disastrous business slump or trend that causes the job market to disintegrate. In this event, people don't necessarily *want* to leave and seek work elsewhere, they *have* to. Homes go on the real estate market at giveaway prices because sellers have no other choice. Although situations like this are personal tragedies for displaced families, they open windows of opportunity for retired folks. Since jobs and regular weekly paychecks aren't essential for most retired couples, bargain real estate is theirs for a fraction of what similar housing would cost elsewhere. As younger folks with growing children move away, older people move in and raise the ratio between retired and working people to impressive levels. Retirees become a majority and wield appreciable influence over local government and political processes.

We've visited a few of these towns and reported on them in earlier editions, places like the towns of Ajo and Bisbee in Arizona, where mines closed, and Colorado's Grand Junction, whose economy toppled when the shale oil industry collapsed. As you might imagine, opportunities like these don't last forever. As retirees move in and snap up the bargains, prices naturally rise. Yet they rarely rise to the level they were at before the problem occurred.

Military Base Closings

The newest bonanza for retirees: the closing and cutting back of a number of Army, Navy, and Air Force facilities. The closings were planned to do minimal local damage, but it's impossible to transfer thousands of military personnel and leave thousands of civilian workers jobless without some disruption.

A case in point was Fort Ord, near Monterey, California. When its closure was final, 14,000 military personnel had gone elsewhere. This affected 17,000 families, a considerable percentage of the county's population. Naturally, real estate brokers were flooded with homes, creating a buyer's market. Apartment rents dropped. Job competition became sharper. To make matters worse, the military administrators were offering to rent base housing to city and county employees at low rates, further depressing the rental market.

Before you pack your furniture and go speeding off to Monterey, Pebble Beach, or Carmel, however, realize that these reduced prices are bargains only when compared to original prices, which started off at a stratospheric level. When prices drop in an already expensive neighborhood, they have a long way to fall before they become as cheap as in Ajo, Arizona, where prices were reasonable even before the mine closing. Lower prices in this case simply mean that some folks who couldn't quite afford to buy in Monterey before could do so. The situation didn't last forever; the state converted the military base into a university campus, which will eventually have as many employees and students as Fort Ord's previous population. Before long the housing market returned to its normal, ridiculously high level.

Not all base closures will have a detrimental effect. For example, as the Air Force pulled its squadrons out of the base near Knob Noster, Missouri, a wing of Stealth bombers was scheduled to move in. The local chamber of commerce informed me that they expect more personnel there than *before* the base "closure." This will require some individual research, to see whether the areas will fit into your retirement place profile and whether the closure is for real or merely a cosmetic change.

A recent trend is to convert base housing into retirement neighborhoods. This works nicely, because there are usually plenty of facilities in place—such as golf courses, swimming pools, recreation complexes, as well as bike and hiking paths.

Working During Retirement

A few years ago, the question of working seemed out of place in a book on retirement. Most people eagerly looked forward to the day they no longer had to get up every morning, down a cup of coffee, and drag themselves off to work. If they merely changed jobs or went into business for themselves, how could they be *retired?*

Now the scene is changing dramatically. For one thing, the average age of those leaving the workplace is rapidly decreasing. Instead of holding on to age sixty-five, more and more people are now taking early retirement, voluntarily or otherwise. Still vigorous, these early retirees often like the challenge of a part-time job or, if the pay is good enough and the work interesting, maybe a full-time job.

The latest trend is millions of workers being "downsized" or given "golden handshakes." (In plain English: fired.) Whatever you call it, huge numbers of active, younger people are entering retirement whether they like it or not. Others, seeing the writing on the wall, cash in the equity in their homes, hang up their running shoes, and opt for early departure. Again, these people aren't looking for traditional retirement; they're too young to quit work entirely. Some opt for opening a business of some sort.

"Baby boomers" are now crossing the fifty-years-and-older bridge, and they are often the ones forced into early retirement. Those still working eagerly look forward to the time they can finally "drop out." According to a recent Del Webb survey of boomers, 30 percent have plans to retire in their fifties, and a large number plan on moving to another state.

Today's retirees are not only more youthful, but in general more affluent and clearly not ready to kick back with a cane fishing pole or watch soap operas all day long. They seek places where they can enjoy vigorous outdoor recreation and actively participate in community activities.

For these reasons many people today like to consider themselves "relocating" rather than "retiring." They often prefer to relocate within striking distance of the country's business concentrations because they want to keep their hand in the job market, at least, perhaps, on a consulting basis. This is why southern states are becoming so popular with those leaving jobs in the highly industrialized areas of New England and the Great Lakes states. That's where industry is relocating. Their former employers are moving south as well.

Many people just *think* they need part-time jobs. The real problem is that they've always worked and are horrified at the prospect of suddenly not having anything meaningful to do. The curse of the work ethic is all too real; after all those years of toil, folks tend to feel guilty and decadent when they no longer leap out of bed at 6:30 A.M. and scurry off to a job. Too often, those who don't really need the income end up working just for the sake of working.

This work ethic is understandable, and it is difficult to shake. Our recommendation is to get into volunteer pursuits should you not find enough to do around the house. As a volunteer, you will not only be doing meaningful work, but also you'll meet others in the community, widen your network of friends, and lay the groundwork for later years when *you* may need volunteers to help you. A special bonus is that your services will be sincerely appreciated and valued more highly than if you were to work in a fast-food restaurant or some other high-competition, low-paying job, trying to please an employer you don't like in the first place.

Let's take the case of Katharine, a retired librarian who lived in a tiny apartment in Monterey, California. Her rent was $700 a month. A part-time job in a bookstore paid $6.00 per hour for working 20 hours a week ($400 a month after taxes). When she moved to a small town in coastal Oregon, she found a larger apartment for $300 a month. This one had a view of the Pacific Ocean. Part-time jobs in a place like this pay minimum wages, but part-time jobs were all filled. However, Katharine discovered that the $400 she saved in rent made up for the $400 she had been earning at her bookstore job. In other words, she had been working half a day, five days a week just to pay higher rent. Now she devotes her time to art classes and satisfying volunteer work in the community.

Taxes

Property taxes vary from state to state and locality to locality, with states like Arkansas or Alabama taking less than Arizona or California. But choosing retirement in Alabama over Arizona simply to save a few dollars a year would be foolish unless Alabama has everything you want in the way of retirement and Arizona lacks something. Taxes are just one component of many. Just because a state has no individual income taxes or sales tax doesn't mean the total tax burden will be slight. States have ways of making up the difference. No income tax? Don't rejoice so quickly—higher property taxes and sales taxes will make up the deficit. No sales tax? You can be sure the state will figure out a way to tax you some way or another.

If you are like most retirees, your income will be lower; a lot of it will come from tax-deductible pensions and Social Security, so state income taxes may not be all that serious. (Of course, some states tax Social Security and pensions.) On the other hand, if you're in a high tax bracket, elevated tax rates could be significant, so you might consider a state that taxes income lightly or not at all. Those states without individual income taxes are Alaska, Florida, Nevada, South Dakota, Texas, Washington, and Wyoming.

Sales taxes are creeping up around the country as states try to scrounge funds for keeping their ships afloat. Rates vary from 8.5 percent in some states to no tax at all in Delaware, Montana, New Hampshire, and Oregon. Example: A $15,000 automobile will cost $1,125 more in Texas than in Oregon. The balancing factor is that in Oregon you pay state income tax, and in Texas you do not. One couple we interviewed in Vancouver, Washington, reported that since they live in Washington, they pay no state income tax, and when they shop across the river in Oregon they pay no sales tax!

Relative Tax Burdens

According to the Advisory Commission of Intergovernmental Relations, the tax burdens of the states discussed in this book are ranked as follows (from lowest to highest):

1. Alabama	7. Kentucky
2. Arkansas	8. Texas
3. Utah	9. Mississippi
4. Washington	10. South Carolina
5. Tennessee	11. Louisiana
6. Oklahoma	12. North Carolina

Choosing Your Climate

All your working life you've heroically put up with whatever inconveniences, insults, and misery your local weather dumped on you. The good news is, when you retire, you no longer have to take it; you can look for a perfect climate and live happily ever after. The bad news is, there is no perfect climate.

Folks in Maine love their summers, but say it's too cold in the winter. Their friends in Miami love Florida winters, but complain because summers are hot and muggy. Newcomers to Hawaii say they miss the change of seasons. Parts of California have what I consider the best overall climate—sunny, relatively bug-free and comfortable, with low humidity most of the year—yet folks here grumble when winter days drop below 50 degrees and winter rains keep them from walks along the beach or sunning beside the pool. (My friends in Michigan think we Californians are weather wimps!)

Even though you can't find the *perfect* climate, you certainly can find one that suits you best. And, chances are that you will find one far superior to the weather you've had to put up with all those working years. This is one of the exciting features about retirement: For the first time in your life, work doesn't dictate where you must live. You now have a choice in the matter!

Another advantage of retirement: You needn't lock yourself into one weather pattern. You can choose any combination of climates that fits your new lifestyle. Many people keep their hometowns as base camps, enjoying wonderful springs and summers there, and then head south to Florida, Texas, or Arizona and enjoy another summer. Some retirees choose Mexico or Costa Rica as an escape from the coldest winter months. It takes a little gumption to get started "following the sun," but thousands upon thousands do just that, and they love it!

Why Not My State?

Occasionally we receive letters from readers demanding to know why we didn't include their home states: Iowa or Indiana, for example. "What do you have against my state?" they inquire. "It's a wonderful place to retire." Other readers complain that we don't cover places in Idaho, Montana, or Maine that often receive retirement writers' praise.

Aside from the obvious explanation that it would be impossible to cover all communities in one book, there are other reasons for limiting coverage. Let's take Montana as an example. I've been there in the summer and can vouch for the fact that it's a delightful place in an exceptionally beautiful part of the country. Places like Glacier National Park make the Big Sky country a wonderful place to visit. Most folks who were born and raised in Montana will surely retire there when they leave their jobs, just as most retirees in Pittsburgh, Omaha, and Milwaukee probably will never move away from their hometowns.

However, I feel that it is irresponsible to encourage someone from Pittsburgh, Omaha, or Milwaukee to leave one cold climate to move to an even colder, bitterly frigid environment just for the sake of a few glorious summer months. If you're going to move, why not choose someplace comfortable? For those who love snow, surely the 40 to 45 total inches per season in Pittsburgh or Omaha should suffice. But in places like Montana or Idaho, winter effectively begins in October, often with an average 3-foot snowpack that remains until April. From my point of view, it's far better to retire in your hometown or move to a pleasantly warm winter climate and then make *summer* visits to glorious parts of the north.

True, some folks thrive on cold weather. They love to bundle up and tootle about the countryside in their snowmobiles, to race full-tilt down the ski slopes, or to chop holes through thick ice on the lake to drop in fishing lines. But most retired people, after a few days of outdoor fun, will find themselves lying on sofas in front of television sets when it becomes unbearably cold outside. Precious months of their lives are invested in *Family Feud* and *Jeopardy*. Their only outdoor activities are shoveling the driveway and trying to get the car started. Indoor exercise consists of opening and closing the refrigerator door. Had they moved to a warmer climate, they could be playing golf, taking brisk walks, or doing laps in the swimming pool throughout the winter.

I have to admit that after years of working in towns like Detroit, St. Louis, and Chicago, I've acquired a definite bias against winter. As I traveled around the country, I much preferred working in warmer places: Florida, Alabama, Texas, Arizona, and, finally, California.

It's interesting to note that while a large percentage of retirement questionnaires indicate a desire to move to a milder climate, many also show a preference for a *four-season* climate, with a certain amount of snowfall every winter. Therefore, you'll note that most locations discussed in this book have four distinct seasons, complete with snowfall and freezing Januarys. People living in places like Prescott, Arizona, or Hot Springs, Arkansas, boast of seasonal change as one of their attractions. If you look at the temperature charts with the place descriptions, however, you'll notice most places we endorse have mild midday winter temperatures. Ideally, during all but a few days of winter you can go outdoors for a walk wearing a sweater or light jacket. Although it may snow, a typical snowfall is but a few inches, making everything pretty, then generally melting away within a day or so. This contrasts with places like Montana, Minnesota, or Michigan, where snow is measured in feet rather than in inches, turning alternately from salty slush to ice and collecting soot and dirt until the next layer piles up, month after month, keeping people prisoners indoors.

I feel justified in my bias against harsh winters. Medical and health experts agree that inactivity is a threat to retired folks' health. In warm climates you'll tend to go outdoors more often to exercise and enjoy healthful activities, instead of huddling next to the heater and the television set. Swimming, golf, tennis, or brisk walks by the river are enjoyable, year-round activities in warmer climates.

If you absolutely can't stand the thought of hot summers, yet still want above-freezing winters, there are places (mostly on the West Coast) where air-conditioning would be a waste of money. In the California town I presently call home (1 block from the ocean), nobody uses air conditioners. Our furnace operates year-round. The same conditions apply in most coastal locations in California, Oregon, and Washington. But personally, I miss the yearly experience of a real summer! I dearly love backyard barbecues on warm summer evenings.

We're fortunate in North America, because we have a wider variety of climates to choose from than almost any other country in the world. We can decide how warm our summers should be or how cold we care to be in winter, and then we can find a town or city that matches our ideals.

Personal Safety

Many people agree that crime is one of the major problems in the United States. It's true that crime rates are dropping dramatically in most parts of the country, but there are still some neighborhoods where people are virtual prisoners in their own homes. Instead of criminals being behind bars, some law-abiding citizens find themselves hiding behind barred windows and chained doors. Meanwhile, outside the potential for criminal activity is strong.

There is little we, as private citizens, can do about any of this. The only solution is to look for safe places to live. Curiously, in neighborhoods not so very far away from high-crime areas, people can leave their doors unlocked and can walk home from a late movie without anxiety. There are still places where things are almost as calm as they used to be when we were children. Remember when kids used to play outside long after dark? Remember when nobody locked doors? In our research, we've come across many locations with almost that same safe feeling of those good old days. (I say *almost* because conditions have changed, even in the best of places.)

Not long ago my wife and I bought a summer home in a small town (population less than 100). When we inquired about safety there, we discovered some residents never lock their cars and some even leave their keys in the ignition so they won't lose them! On the other hand, residents in a nearby, much larger city also didn't lock their cars—but for another reason. Automobile break-ins were so common in their neighborhood that locking the car doors was an invitation for a thief to break the windows to see if something valuable might be inside. Yet, in the better neighborhoods of that same city, things are safe.

Finding a Safe Place to Live

Unfortunately, there is no such thing as a crime-free area. As long as people live in social groups, there will always be individuals who can't seem to distinguish between their belongings and those of their neighbors. It just stands to reason that the larger the social group, the more deviant individuals it produces. Thus, you find much higher crime rates in Washington, D.C., than in Walla Walla, Washington, and more crime in New Orleans than in New Madrid, Missouri.

Generally, the larger the city, the higher the crime rate. However, even among the larger cities, you'll find areas of relative tranquillity, sometimes not too far from the problem areas. These are usually stable, low-turnover neighborhoods where residents know each other and where most people are over the age of fifty. When the population of an area is largely composed of a younger age group, however, reports show that the tendency for crime to occur is greater. According to the FBI, about four-fifths of all arrests for property crimes or for violent offenses are males age twenty or younger.

As a rule, your best bet for finding a low-tension, low-crime area is to choose a small town or suburb. Not all small towns are idyllic islands of honest citizenship and peaceful tranquillity, however. Occasionally you'll run across one that is surprisingly violent and plagued by burglars and robbers. On the other hand, just because a town is peaceful doesn't mean that it is a great place to live. It could also be so boring that burglars and robbers can't stand working there. By way of contrast, most large cities have neighborhoods that are as safe as many smaller towns, particularly in the suburbs. For example, Hermosa Beach, an affluent suburb in the Los Angeles metropolitan area, ranks exceptionally high in safety, yet is twenty minutes away from one of the most crime-ridden areas in the country.

You can learn a great deal about a neighborhood by simply driving around and observing. Are the homes neat, with trimmed shrubbery and mowed lawns? Or are they shabby, obviously owned by absentee landlords? Are there old junkers parked around the neighborhood, with teenagers trying to get them started? Or do you see folks your own age working in the yard, walking the dog, or polishing the car? The best way to ascertain a neighborhood's safety is to simply ask. If folks feel safe living there, they're happy to tell you all about it. If they offer to lend you a weapon to protect yourself, it's not a safe neighborhood.

In this book, I've used the latest edition of the FBI's publication

Crime in the United States to discuss personal safety in a community. Unfortunately, the FBI doesn't publish statistics on places with less than 10,000 in population. Furthermore, not all towns submit reports to the FBI. For example, every police department in New Jersey, some 225 towns, report every crime to the FBI. Yet only four cities in the entire state of Illinois report! After all, the FBI statistics are based on what the police departments report. Some departments report thefts of comic books and tricycles; others report only major crimes. The FBI admits that sometimes a police department will not report all crimes in an effort to make their town look safe. Others exaggerate the crime situation in order to embarrass the city council into increasing police department budgets.

The FBI's list of criminal offenses for various communities is broken down by the type of crime committed: murder, forcible rape, robbery, aggravated assault, burglary, larceny-theft, and automobile theft. Therefore, when analyzing the FBI's statistics we tried to adjust our conclusions by giving more weight to offenses most likely to affect retirees, like burglary and assault, and less emphasis on crimes like shoplifting. Our analysis of personal safety for a community was also influenced by personal observations and interviews with folks living in the community.

The Southeast Coast States

FOR THOSE WHO LIVE in the Midwest or on the East Coast, the idea of a West Coast retirement is a pleasant thought, but it often seems too far away from friends and family. Florida, too, may be out of the question for any number of reasons. The search is then narrowed to an affordable location with a mild, four-season climate that isn't too far to return "home" periodically and where friends and family can reasonably be expected to visit from time to time. Of course, your retirement home should be in an attractive setting where friends and family will look upon visits with joyful anticipation rather than with dread. The southeastern part of the United States—Georgia, the Carolinas, and Virginia—fulfills all these requirements for a growing number of retired families.

From earliest times, Southern colonists who owned plantations in the warm coastal regions enjoyed the cool highlands as summer retreats. That Southern tradition continues, augmented by Florida residents who are discovering the high country in the nearby Carolinas and Georgia as sanctuaries from Florida's hot and humid summers.

Mountain sections of Georgia, the Carolinas, and Virginia are noted for a growing population of "part-time" retirees from Florida who come here to cool off in the summer. After spending a couple of seasons in the upland hill country, many visitors become *ex-*Florida retirees, choosing to settle here permanently. One North Carolina native said, "Northerners are discovering our part of the country by going to Florida first and then making a second retirement move here. We call that 'making a J turn.' "

The coastal Atlantic states offer a rich variety of retirement settings: sandy beaches, rolling green hills, and forested mountains brightened with azaleas, mountain laurel, and myrtle trees. From fertile agricultural lands with neat farms and white fences to rugged mountains where bears and herds of deer roam unmolested by humans, the Atlantic Coast region has it all. The ocean yields harvests of fish, crab, and oysters; inland streams offer superb sport opportunities for trout, bass, and other game fish. Modern cities with full conveniences and cultural attractions are but short drives from rural villages that are steeped in nineteenth-century atmosphere and country friendliness.

Any of these ecological worlds are within a few easy driving hours from almost anywhere in this area you might select as a home base. Florida is just next door and accessible for visits any time. Some Southeasterners take advantage of Florida's merciful winters by spending the coldest months there and returning to their mountain homes for the rest of the year.

Southern Hospitality

"Southern hospitality" is an oft-tossed-about phrase, but one with more than a kernel of truth. It's interesting to note how Southerners interact with one another as well as with strangers. You'll notice an open friendliness and sharing that differs from the general custom in other parts of the country. For example, when visiting friends or relatives in the South, I am always surprised how often people drop in unannounced for a visit. Sometimes it's a steady procession of acquaintances coming and going all day long. Close friends sometimes don't bother to knock. They'll just open the door and call out, "Anybody home?" They know they're always welcome for a chat. "Just passin' by," they'll explain, "Thought I'd stop in to say hello." An extra cup of coffee is usually on the kitchen table before they can pull out a chair.

In other parts of the country this would be unheard of. In my California neighborhood, before you visit someone other than a close friend, you telephone first and see if it's okay to come over. In still other parts of the country, you either wait for an invitation or you suggest meeting for lunch at a nearby restaurant. For some folks, Southern-style hospitality would take some getting used to. Some feel abused if casual acquaintances drop in and expect them to interrupt whatever they're doing to entertain them. Other folks love it.

Nonetheless, don't expect to move into a Southern neighborhood and immediately become friends with all the other kids on the block. It doesn't work that way in Southern communities any more than it does in your hometown. Although small-town Southerners are inclined to be more courteous and considerate than people from other parts of the country, you have to work at making friends just as you did back home. When asked whether residents of a small North Carolina town were friendly to outsider retirees, the local chamber of commerce representative thought for a moment and then replied, "Well, we tend to be friendly to everyone. But it's the *outsiders* who are most friendly to other outsiders." She added, "Outsiders have to learn to accept mountain people for who we are: sincere, hard-working folks who enjoy a simple life. We hate it when outsiders try to change things." They have a saying here, "You don't push mountain folks; you have to try and lead them."

A Geography Lesson   The Southeast Coast states are divided into three distinct regions. The first is a broad coastal plain that rises from the Atlantic, often in low, marshy ground studded with palmettos and scrub oak. Several hundred miles of beautiful white sand beaches are convenient for retirees who need to include the seashore in their retirement schemes. Farther inland, fertile fields and comfortable small towns offer a quieter, more introspective lifestyle.

These flat lowlands end at the fall line, where the foothills of the Blue Ridge and Great Smoky Mountains begin. Rivers, creeks, and streams flowing down from the mountains suddenly change into rapids and low waterfalls at this point, hence the name "fall line." This is the Piedmont or foothill region, a country of rolling hills covered with hardwood forests and dotted with more than 400,000 acres of lakes. Peach orchards, horse farms, neighborly small-town squares, and country lanes characterize the Piedmont country.

Finally, we come to the Blue Ridge and Great Smoky highlands, where the Appalachians lift to an elevation of nearly 3,000 feet. This mountain chain runs in a northeast-southwest direction from near the Canadian border to just north of Atlanta. Ancient, eroded mountains, sometimes scarcely touched by civilization, are richly cloaked with hardwoods and flowering trees, pines, beeches, poplars, and birch. Crystal-clear rivers and streams cascade through canyons and tumble over waterfalls into deep pools. This is a nature-lover's treat. More than 250 miles of trout streams run through

South Carolina, and there are probably at least that many in North Carolina. Northern Georgia also shares in this bounty.

Yet the mountain country isn't so high that it catches harsh winters. Snow is a regular winter visitor, but it seldom sticks around more than a day or two (except for a few higher elevations and skiing areas). Compared with Cleveland or Chicago weather, even the worst days of winter here seem gentle. The mountains have other functions besides being picturesque. They deflect or delay cold air masses approaching from the north and west and thus protect coastal areas from arctic blasts.

North Carolina

We're convinced that some of the most beautiful and scenic places in the world are found in the Blue Ridge and Great Smoky Mountains. October, when leaves are turning, is a marvelous time for a visit. Hardwood trees display a full explosion of color, with brilliant reds, yellows, purples, lavenders, and all colors in-between to dazzle the eye, while evergreens provide a conservative background of green. We've also made the rounds in the spring, when the dogwoods, azaleas, and mountain laurel trees were in full bloom. The sight and smell of spring make one forget winter.

Driving the Blue Ridge Parkway is an experience not soon forgotten. The parkway starts at the small town of Front Royal in northern Virginia and wends its way southwest

until it ends at Great Smoky Mountains National Park, which is partly in Tennessee and partly in North Carolina. The scenic highway winds through beautiful mountain terrain, past wild rivers and thick forests. Hikers and river rafters love this country. Golf is a top sport here, with more than twenty first-quality courses throughout the Great Smoky Mountains area alone.

Unless you are country bred and raised, you'll probably prefer to settle within striking distance of a city. Once in a while you'll get a hankering for a genuine supermarket or a department store. Even the bigger mountain towns—Asheville (pop. 85,000), Greenville (pop. 59,000), and Hendersonville (pop. 10,000) in the southern parts; Bristol (pop. 24,000) and Johnson City (pop. 41,000) up around the Tennessee border—aren't all that large. Each of these cities is large enough, however, for adequate medical care, heavy shopping, and services you might need from time to time.

NORTH CAROLINA TAX PROFILE
Sales tax: 4% to 6%, drugs exempt
State income tax: graduated, 6% to 7.75% over $60,000; can't deduct federal income tax
Property taxes: about 1.2%
Intangibles tax: 0.25%
Social security taxed: no
Pensions taxed: excludes $4,000 government, $2,000 private pensions
Gasoline tax: 22.3¢ per gallon

Asheville Asheville is the queen city of North Carolina's western region, residing in the finger-like projection of the state that forces its way between Tennessee and Georgia. Nestled in the mountains where the Great Smoky and Blue Ridge Mountains meet, Asheville sits 2,340 feet above sea level. This elevation accounts for the city's pleasant summer weather as well as its brisk, but not harsh, winters.

Three North Carolina towns in this region form a triangle, with Asheville as the apex and Hendersonville and Brevard forming the triangle's base. All three towns consistently receive praise as retirement locations in magazines, newspapers, and retirement guides. Since there's only about 20 miles or so between one city and the next, it would seem they could be treated as one subject, but we feel they are different enough to deserve separate consideration. We are starting with Asheville, the best known of the three.

As the largest city in western North Carolina, Asheville (pop. 85,000) is the region's cultural and commercial center. The region is characterized by prosperous farms and forest-covered foothills, rounded and green, growing steeper toward the north. Its natural setting, surrounded by a million acres of national forest, combines with the convenience of city living to make Asheville and its environs one of North Carolina's most desirable retirement destinations. Not surprisingly, Asheville was famous as a resort town, attracting tourists and retirees, long before Thomas Wolfe described his hometown in his novel *Look Homeward, Angel*; and even before George Vanderbilt thought about creating America's largest home here, the 255-room Biltmore House. Since the turn of the century, famous Americans such as Henry Ford, his friend Thomas Edison, F. Scott Fitzgerald, and William Jennings Bryan enjoyed summers here.

Many came for the summer and stayed on for retirement. They now come in ever-increasing numbers, with a surprising number of "second-chance retirees" moving here after having tried Florida, California, or Arizona.

Because of its distance from a truly large metropolitan center, Asheville enjoys many services and amenities normally absent in a small city. No less than sixteen shopping centers—four of them indoor malls—ensure wide selections of merchandise. Two interstate highways (I-40 and I-26) intersect in Asheville, as well as the Blue Ridge Parkway and ten other U.S. and state highways. This maze of freeways, plus an airport with daily flights and connections to several major cities, makes Asheville a transportation hub for this area.

The University of North Carolina at Asheville sponsors a unique resource for seniors living in the region. It's called the North Carolina Center for Creative Retirement. The Center consists of several programs designed to introduce retirement-age people to a wide variety of learning experiences as it integrates them into the community. The Center should be one of the first stops on your pre-retirement tour of Asheville, and, should you decide to move here, the Center should become part of your retirement scenario.

One of the Center's programs is called College for Seniors. Drawing on retirees' professional expertise and life experiences, curricula and classes are designed and taught by students as well as university faculty. Classes range from Chaucer to computers, from foreign affairs to opera. Another is the Senior Academy for Intergenerational Learning, which matches retired professionals with university students to work as research partners, tutors, and career mentors. The Leadership Asheville Seniors program brings seniors together to explore ways to link their talents and expertise with community needs. They work with civic leaders, social scientists, political activists, and other experts to learn about the community's past and present and confront future challenges. Lastly, the Seniors in the Schools program matches talented senior volunteers with public school students, where they tutor, present enrichment programs, and organize special projects.

A concentration of hospitals and related facilities firmly establishes the city as a medical center for the entire region. The claim is that Asheville has more doctors per capita than anywhere else in the world. Whether or not this is accurate, the fact remains that health care here is outstanding.

Outdoor recreation here is enhanced by Asheville's nearness to some of the prettiest Appalachian country imaginable. Always within view, the Blue Ridge and Great Smoky Mountains soar to heights of over 5,000 feet. Hiking, fishing, camping, and winter skiing make for year-round outdoor recreation within walking or driving distance. Several public and private golf courses challenge players with good weather in all but the two coldest months of the year.

A few years ago, Asheville was known for its low-cost, high-quality real estate market. But Asheville's popularity as a retirement destination has boosted prices until they are probably the highest in the state, at about 15 percent above the national average.

Brevard   The nearby towns of Hendersonville and Brevard are known for well-groomed residential districts and more-than-adequate shopping. Both towns routinely receive top recommendations as retirement destinations by retirement writers. Both are comfortable-looking places with picturesque settings (especially the country around Brevard). Unlike Asheville and Hendersonville, Brevard is in a dry county, so don't plan on Cabernet Sauvignon with your prime rib; it'll be Pepsi-Cola.

Real estate costs in Brevard range from above average to high, with one nearby private community on the extremely expensive side—many homes are priced well over $500,000. Homes in Brevard enjoy a natural setting of trees and mature shrubs, with 33 percent of the county in the Pisgah National Forest. Since much of the remaining land cannot be developed, land is expensive in comparison to surrounding counties.

Hendersonville   Many advantages accruing to Asheville can be matched in Hendersonville, although on a smaller scale. The population here is less than 10,000, although at first glance the city looks much larger. Its downtown has undergone a tremendous rehabilitation program. By making the main street one-way and adding lots of new parking spaces, they've slowed the pace and given the town center a pleasant, mall-like atmosphere. People of all ages with a wide variety of interests find the congenial surroundings the perfect place to raise a family or to get away from it all in their retirement years. The residential neighborhoods throughout the city and county offer quiet, traffic-free living with the advantage of being only minutes from shopping.

ASHEVILLE AREA WEATHER						
In degrees Fahrenheit						
	Jan.	April	July	Oct.	Rain	Snow
Daily Highs	48	69	84	69	48"	17"
Daily Lows	26	43	62	43		

ASHEVILLE AREA COST OF LIVING					
Percentage of	Overall	Housing	Medical	Groceries	Utilities
National Average	105	121	92	99	98

Blue Ridge Country

The rugged mountain country to the north of Asheville is appropriate for those demanding the best in Appalachian settings. This was Daniel Boone country. The famous pioneer was born and raised in Boone, one of the major towns in this area.

For more than a century wealthy families from all over the nation have traditionally used these mountains as summer hideaways, secluded places where they could slip away for quiet vacations. Industrialists from Chicago and Pittsburgh, socialites from New York and Boston, and southern aristocracy from Charleston, Charlotte, and other affluent cities maintained summer retreats deep in the mountains. Places like Linville, Banner Elk, and Blowing Rock are places unknown to most of the country, but quite familiar to the wealthy.

The first resorts and retirement homes appeared on the scene in the 1890s, but it wasn't until the advent of the automobile and good roads that retirement began in earnest. Then, anyone who could afford a Chevy could visit and settle in these formerly exclusive areas. And they did. This turned out to be a natural retirement haven, with inexpensive property, a mild climate, and gorgeous surroundings.

Today's latest retirement wave began around twenty or thirty years ago when a few developers bought small valleys of wooded land and built golf courses. Golf was the irresistible bait to entice Northern buyers to these parts. The ones with money built posh homes, at first for summer getaways, eventually for retirement.

Hound Ears   Despite its "down-home" name, Hound Ears is an example of an expensive development, one of the area's earliest. A developer visualized a golf course there, spreading over a valley floor. After laying out beautiful greens and fairways and an attractive clubhouse, he quickly sold the lots he had developed around the golf course. Buyers demanded more lots for retirement homes. He began cutting roads through the woods and into the hills that overlooked his valley golf course. As fast as he could lay out a new section of lots, it sold out. Each new house seemed to be more luxurious than the previous, with some homes valued well into six figures. We were told that one couple put $500,000 into construction, but before they could finish, someone offered them a million dollars for the house, as is.

Obviously, these places aren't for folks with ordinary pocketbooks. Security guards staff the entrances twenty-four hours a day, keeping out us riffraff. In fact, one development (Linville Ridge) is said to be so exclusive that one can buy into the development only by invitation! So far, the developers haven't invited me, so I suppose I won't buy. They probably wouldn't let me put it on my credit card, anyway.

However, all isn't for the rich. Enjoying the North Carolina mountains is practical because there are many affordable properties available. Although these dwellings may not be as costly, the view, the fresh air, and the delightful weather do not depend on our bank accounts. There are many small towns (and some not so small) where you can blend into the daily routine and live among friendly neighbors. The local folk, who proudly refer to themselves as "mountain people," are famous for their hospitality to "flatlanders." The number of such outsiders from various parts of the country is growing larger every day.

Newland and Blowing Rock   The roads in this area are not for high-speed driving; they meander lazily around hill and dale. Every few miles turns up another surprise, another lovely town for retirement-home seekers. Each has its own personality and charm. The little town of Newland, for example, is a quiet, country town, unpretentious and economical. A house set back from the road on several acres can be found for less than $100,000 and cozy little homes in a friendly in-town neighborhood for $80,000. The most popular restaurant has an old-fashioned soda fountain and sells a lunch special for under $4.00. A public golf course—just as beautiful as the exclusive, private ones—provides sport for the duffers in the crowd.

A contrasting town is nearby Blowing Rock, which is a tourist-oriented artist colony. Much older than Newland, Blowing Rock features antique, heirloom homes in the style of the last century, exquisite in design and construction. Many nice restaurants, boutiques, and antiques shops line the main street, and the town of Boone is nearby for heavy-duty shopping. Although Boone has a population of a little over 10,000, it seems larger because of its complete business district. Its crime rate is also very low.

When you ask people why they chose this part of the Blue Ridge Mountains to retire, a major reason (right after the area's beauty) is the mountain weather. Residents delight in contrasting seasons: mild summers, beautiful springs, honest-to-goodness autumns, and winters with soft blankets of snow create a wonderland of beauty. Skiing draws visitors from Florida and other parts of the South. Although Floridians visit here in the winter to enjoy winter sports, many mountain retirees head for Florida to *escape* the snow. We interviewed several retired residents who regularly go to Florida from December through March. Some take RVs; others rent condos or houses on the beach. The wealthier folks own a second home in Florida, with Vero Beach a popular destination for a winter reunion with their warm-weather neighbors.

Even though the region is somewhat isolated from Asheville (a long hour's drive away), a surprising array of cultural activities are available to residents. Mayland College, located in Spruce Pine, sponsors extension-class programs in many surrounding communities. This program, called Lifelong Learning, is associated with the Elderhostel Institute, which has as its purpose the fostering of continuing education among older people, regardless of their previous academic pursuits. Some classes offered are pottery, studio glass, traditional weaving, jewelry and iron working, and sculpture/bronze casting.

Jefferson/West Jefferson   We discovered Ashe County more or less by accident. The twin towns of Jefferson and West Jefferson are slightly off the beaten track for relocation—almost a "best-kept secret." During a recent research trip through the Blue Ridge Mountains, we decided to make a short detour and check the possibilities here. Jefferson sits a few miles off the Blue Ridge Parkway near the Virginia state line. Previously we had heard little about Jefferson as a potential place for Appalachian retirement, even though it's not far from some popular places like Boone and Banner Elk. We were pleasantly surprised to find Jefferson a good retirement possibility.

The town was established in 1803, the first in America named for Thomas Jefferson. For more than one hundred years, Jefferson remained the sole incorporated town in Ashe County. Of all the Blue Ridge country, Jefferson has probably changed the least since the Blue Ridge country was "discovered" by the outside world. The population boom hasn't struck as it has in other parts of the High Country. Since 1900 the populations of Jefferson and West Jefferson have risen and fallen but changed little overall. Combined, the twin towns muster a population of only 1,500, but this figure is misleading, since most retirees choose to live outside the town limits. Only about 10 percent of the county's residents live in town. The rest live on farms, in small crossroad communities, or in one of two newly developed golf-course subdivisions. Hardly a metropolis, the quaint downtown serves as the shopping center for the entire county of about 22,000 inhabitants, so all the facilities are in place, more so than in some other towns of this size. Jefferson's downtown, turn-of-the-century courthouse is a marvel of Victorian construction.

Local people say Jefferson reminds them of Boone, before Appalachian State University expanded and tourism took over to create traffic jams in the Appalachians. This northernmost region isn't quite as hilly, forested, or picturesque as some of the more popular places, but that's a matter of degree; it's still a beautiful place. One nice thing about Jefferson is that real estate prices haven't skyrocketed as they have in the Boone–Blowing Rock area. One couple told us, "When we retired from New Jersey, we wanted to live in North Carolina, in the mountains. But we realized we couldn't afford to buy property in Watauga County, where everybody wants to live. Then we discovered Ashe County and Jefferson." A home costing $110,000 near Boone might sell for $80,000 here.

Like all of North Carolina's Blue Ridge country, outdoor recreation is convenient and varied. Many miles of trout streams flow through the region, and the abundance of game such as wild turkey, squirrel, and deer can satisfy a hunter's dream. (One of the area's most famous hunters was the legendary Daniel Boone. In fact, Boone's descendants were among the first landowners in Ashe County.)

BLUE RIDGE COUNTRY WEATHER						
In degrees Fahrenheit						
	Jan.	April	July	Oct.	Rain	Snow
Daily Highs	45	68	84	68	49"	18"
Daily Lows	25	41	62	44		

BLUE RIDGE COUNTRY COST OF LIVING					
Percentage of	Overall	Housing	Medical	Groceries	Utilities
National Average	97	80	98	103	132

The North Carolina Midlands

Between the flat coastal regions and the Appalachians is a stretch of forested, gently rolling hills. Here you'll find a unique mix of Americana: from Beethoven to bluegrass, from stock-car racing to scholarly research, just about any kind of intellectual and recreational pursuit imaginable.

University Triangle   Unlike some sections of the South, where outsiders are rare curiosities, the area known as the "Triangle" attracts folks with academic interests and technical skills. People from all over North America and from all walks of life are represented. The Triangle consists of the cities of Chapel Hill, Durham, and Raleigh, containing three of the state's top universities, which explains why this area is called the "University Triangle." The University of North Carolina is based in Chapel Hill, Duke University in Durham, and North Carolina State in Raleigh. The universities—plus numerous research labs, think tanks, and other academic institutions—attract intellectuals and technicians from all over the world. Per capita, there are probably more academics, Ph.D.s, and scientists living in the Triangle than in any other part of the country. World-renowned Research Triangle Park employs some of the nation's top scientists and is located within easy driving distance of any of the Triangle cities. Besides the three major universities found here, there are five four-year colleges and eight two-year colleges grouped within a few miles of each other, with more than 64,000 students in attendance.

RALEIGH–DURHAM–CHAPEL HILL WEATHER

In degrees Fahrenheit

	Jan.	April	July	Oct.	Rain	Snow
Daily Highs	50	72	88	72	42"	2"
Daily Lows	30	47	67	48		

RALEIGH–DURHAM–CHAPEL HILL COST OF LIVING

Percentage of	Overall	Housing	Medical	Groceries	Utilities
National Average	101	106	101	99	108

Universities and colleges profoundly influence lifestyles here, with a large percentage of the community either working for or with educational institutions and others benefiting from the many stimulating events connected with academic life. Dramatic performances, lectures, sports, and a host of other presentations are open to the public as well as those involved with the schools.

Because of the schools, research, and related industries, academic and technician wages in the Triangle are higher than in most of the Carolinas. This means higher housing costs and fancier homes in the more elegant sections. Homes in the $200,000-plus price range have no trouble finding buyers. But homes in that price range seem like mansions compared to other parts of the country. We visited a couple who moved to Raleigh from New York City, from a small apartment into a spacious five-bedroom home on two acres of wooded grounds. "Our entire apartment could fit into our new dining room, living room, and kitchen," they said. "And never in our wildest dreams could we have afforded to buy an apartment there." Because they bought when interest rates bottomed out, the monthly payment on their $200,000 mansion is one-third what they paid in rent for a tiny apartment.

Home prices are predictably higher here than in other large North Carolina cities. Residential neighborhoods, such as the ones surrounding the university campuses, are absolutely upscale and lovely, but not cheap. This is not surprising in an area that is recession-resistant because of steady employment and high wage levels. This shouldn't put anyone off who is moving from a moderately expensive community in some other part of the country; chances are, they'll discover that prices are bargains compared to where they just left.

Pinehurst/Southern Pines/Aberdeen   The villages of Pinehurst, Southern Pines, and Aberdeen, in the central part of the state, have long enjoyed the distinction of being premier golf destinations. Located within minutes of each other, this triangle of towns contains thirty-five superb championship courses within a 16-mile radius, some of which are among the most highly rated in the world.

Before they considered retirement here, many people simply thought of Pinehurst and Southern Pines as convenient stopover places on their way to Florida vacations. This was the logical place to break up the trip—about halfway for many Easterners. Why not stay over a day or two and get in a few rounds of golf? As retirement time drew nearer, some folks naturally began thinking more about Pinehurst and less about Florida.

Of course, membership in Pinehurst Club was mandatory for those who bought lots in the many subdivisions ringing the golf-tennis complex. So today, new buyers automatically inherit their memberships as part of the purchase price of their lots or homes. (They inherit the monthly fees, as well.) This is an important feature, since some golf–club developments have a waiting list for membership.

Southern Pines is an offshoot development, separate from Pinehurst. Southern Pines is larger, with a population of 10,000 and a downtown area somewhat less touristy than Pinehurst's Village Center. Southern Pines is basically a residential community, liberally endowed with golf facilities and shopping malls and a quaint town center. The homes we looked at were superbly designed to fit into the Sandhills' pine and oak ambience.

Aberdeen, with 2,800 inhabitants, is the third village in this grouping. In its early days, Aberdeen was a bustling center of trade and commerce. Then came quieter years as the downtown saw businesses moving out. But Aberdeen has emerged from its slump, and Main Street is lively once more, with its fine antiques shops, boutiques, and other shopping. Our impression of Aberdeen is that it's

PINEHURST/SOUTHERN PINES/ABERDEEN WEATHER						
In degrees Fahrenheit						
	Jan.	April	July	Oct.	Rain	Snow
Daily Highs	55	68	91	71	41"	2"
Daily Lows	34	51	67	58		

a place for more affordable housing, but still in the golf–club circuit.

Because the elevation here is higher than most of Florida, summers aren't quite as warm or humid. Furthermore, the 55-degree January days permit plenty of outdoor activities. "Any day it's not raining, I can golf, hike, or ride horseback." said a retiree here. "When I lived in Florida, it was too damned muggy in the summer!"

More than adequate health care is covered by a 397-bed regional hospital with a medical staff of 112 physicians and 1,400 employees, assisted by 500 volunteers. A twenty-four-hour mobile intensive care unit provides up-to-date life support treatments.

The small-town atmosphere lends itself to a feeling of security, with an exceptionally low crime rate. Yet because of the large percentage of out-of-state retirees, newcomers don't feel that they stand out as they might in some other small Southern towns.

Carolina Trace   Although Pinehurst and Southern Pines are golf course communities, most of their neighborhoods aren't protected by gates and security guards. Basically, they're upscale residential areas with golf courses conveniently located next door or nearby. The neighborhoods are open; anyone can cruise through the streets without having to be a resident.

We decided to investigate another kind of retirement community that's become extraordinarily popular, not only in the South, but also in other parts of the country: a private country-club development. About 25 miles north of Pinehurst and Southern Pines, the Carolina Trace Country Club is an excellent example of this lifestyle.

For many, the term "private country club" carries the implication of elitism, snobbery, and expensive property. What we found was something entirely different. When interviewing people living in "closed" developments like Carolina Trace, we asked how it felt to be "locked in," in an "us against the world" mode, rather than an open community like Southern Pines. First of all, residents say they love the feeling of security that comes from having an armed guard at the gate to keep strangers from wandering through the neighborhoods. They also like having their own security patrols. After interviewing several couples, we began to understand why they felt that way. Many came from high-crime areas, places like New York, Detroit, and Chicago. These folks appreciate the meaning of the word "security," having been conscious of it all their lives. The second point is, residents have a real sense of belonging. People know their neighbors—they have dinner together at the clubhouse, they wave to each other as their pontoon boats pass on the lake, they play golf together. Since the club is a member-owned facility, they also sit down together and make decisions about how their community should function.

As for Carolina Trace being expensive, small lakefront homes often start at $75,000. For someone moving from Long Island, that's a gift. Granted, some of the more elaborate layouts have been known to sell in the $400,000 range, but you can imagine what you get for that price! As for being elitist, the folks we interviewed came from ordinary middle-class backgrounds. They were fugitives from northern cold weather, but were also fleeing crime, high taxes, and overpriced housing.

The centerpiece of the development is a sparkling lake that covers 300 acres, with 7 miles of shoreline stretching into every part of Carolina Trace's 2,500 acres. This means just about everybody has either a view of the lake or a place right on the water. In all there are seventeen small sections, or clusters, of homes. Each section has its own swimming pool and tennis courts. This creates a series of neighborhoods within the community. These quiet little groups of homes are separated from each other by expansive woods of live oak, southern pine, holly, and dogwood. In fact, half of the area is undisturbed forest.

South Carolina

Like the other Atlantic coastal states, South Carolina can be divided into three regions. The first is the Coastal Plain, bordered by South Carolina's 2,800 miles of tidal shoreline, barrier islands, and colonial cities. Next is the Piedmont region, whose rolling hills, rich farmlands, and foothills comprise about two-thirds of the state's land. The third division is the Appalachians, with the highest elevation in the Blue Ridge Mountains, in the northwestern part of the state.

SOUTH CAROLINA TAX PROFILE

Sales tax: 5% to 6%, food, drugs exempt
State income tax: graduated, 2.5% to 7% over $10,600; can't deduct federal income tax
Property taxes: about 2.5%, residents over 65 receive exemptions
Intangibles tax: no
Social security taxed: no
Pensions taxed: $3,000 exclusion
Gasoline tax: 16¢ per gallon

Columbia   Here in the heart of the South, on Columbia's coastal plain, there's a city that combines all the graces of a rich past with the vibrancy of the emerging sunbelt. Columbia, South Carolina, is a center for military, academic, government and business life. With a population of 110,000, Columbia is a city, yet small enough to feel like a small town.

Another educational center of the South, Columbia has the University of South Carolina as its focal point of cultural enrichment. A surprising number of Northerners have found this to be a great place for retirement. By the way, Columbia claims to have a higher percentage of retirees living here than anywhere else in the state.

Columbia is situated at the point where the coastal plain meets the beginning of the Piedmont. At the western edge of the city, rolling foothills begin, and at the opposite edge, the country is flat all the way to the ocean. This is a comfortable city, with the vast majority of the housing owner-occupied. The streets are shaded with tall trees, and there's a quiet charm that comes with ordinary people living in ordinary neighborhoods. Yet, Columbia has its sophisticated side as well, with a cosmopolitan feeling that goes with being a university town.

Most Old South cities grew haphazardly, with roads and streets going in random directions, without planning of any sort. But Columbia is different. The British needed a capital city for South Carolina, so in 1686 they designed the first planned city in the colonies. The city's broad boulevards and architectural gems attest to its early beauty. Robert Mills, one of the pioneers of U.S. architecture, designed several buildings here as well as many in Washington, D.C. (One of his more famous works is the Washington Monument.)

The university, with 28,000 students, is a major source of cultural enrichment. Along with a nearby two-year college, the school attracts academics from around the nation, many of whom later join the ranks of Columbia's retired. All South Carolina state colleges and technical institutes waive tuition for residents over sixty years of age (on a space-available basis). Retirees can also take full advantage of this benefit at regional campuses in Beaufort, Lancaster, Allendale, Sumter, Union, Aiken, Conway, and Spartanburg. Special low-cost spring and summer residential academic programs are also available for senior citizens.

This is a popular retirement location for many military families because of the town's proximity to Fort Jackson and the obvious advantages of retiring near a military installation. During World War II, thousands of GIs were stationed here, awaiting shipping orders to join their comrades in Europe. Many fondly recall the mild weather and friendly South Carolinians. These memories are bringing the ex-GIs back to Columbia for their retirement careers. These two out-of-state groups, academic and military, contribute toward making the Columbia area heterogeneous, with open, accepting feelings toward newcomers.

We found several retirees who had started out intending to retire elsewhere, but somehow wound up happily retiring in the Carolinas. For example, one retired couple admitted that they had always planned on retirement in Florida. "Every year, as we made our annual trip to Florida, we broke our trip up with a stopover in Columbia," they explained, "and again on the way back. Then, one day, just before retirement, we realized that we really liked Columbia better than Florida!" They decided to rent an apartment, just to "see how Columbia feels." They found low living costs and friendly, cultured neighbors. "We never made it to Florida," they said with satisfied smiles. "We still go there for vacations, though."

I asked him how he felt as a Yankee moving into a Deep South town. Did he find any prejudices? "To tell you the truth, I haven't noticed anything like that," he said. "My neighbors are just as nice as the ones we had back home, but they're definitely more friendly. Other Northerners warned us, 'They'll be neighborly, yes, but they'll never invite you to their daughter's debutante party unless you were born in Columbia.'" He shrugged his shoulders and said, "That's a relief to me, because the last place I'd want to be invited would be to some teenager's debutante party! I'd have to invent an excuse why I couldn't go."

Another advantage they pointed out—aside from the low cost of quality housing—is the excellent medical care available. (As a pharmacist, he was aware of such things.) About thirteen hospitals serve the area with more than 500 doctors to treat your ills.

COLUMBIA WEATHER						
In degrees Fahrenheit						
	Jan.	April	July	Oct.	Rain	Snow
Daily Highs	50	72	88	72	43"	5"
Daily Lows	32	50	69	50		

COLUMBIA COST OF LIVING					
Percentage of	Overall	Housing	Medical	Groceries	Utilities
National Average	97	91	92	98	122

Aiken   Aiken (pop. 25,000) is a genteel Old South town located in the western corner of South Carolina's Piedmont region, with the majestic Blue Ridge mountains a short drive away. Aiken's robust business district makes it look larger than it actually is, because it's the shopping and employment center for a large area. Aiken County has about 115,000 people.

One way Aiken differs from many other Southern towns is that so many out-of-state people have moved here that distinctions between natives and newcomers have blurred. Townspeople are used to different accents and other lifestyles; a cosmopolitan mix has broken through all but the most inbred social barriers. Where did these outsiders come from? Initially people came to work for the Department of Energy's high-tech, atomic-energy facility in Aiken. The department imported engineers, physicists, technicians, bricklayers—you name it—from all over the country.

When the energy project was finally up and running, many workers moved elsewhere to new jobs. Others—some nearing retirement anyway—elected to stay. The word soon got around about this beautiful little city with mild winters, friendly people, and low real estate prices. This brought even more outsiders into Aiken. The result is an eclectic collection of people from all over the country.

Aiken isn't all single-family homes, mansions, and honeysuckle. Modern condominiums, apartments, and gated communities are home to many families. Away from town, you'll find small farms and homes on acreages for horses or garden hobbies. Luxury communities—Kalmia Landing, Woodside Plantation, Midland

AIKEN WEATHER					
In degrees Fahrenheit					
	Jan.	April	July	Oct.	Rain	Snow
Daily Highs	57	77	91	77	43"	1"
Daily Lows	33	49	69	50		

AIKEN COST OF LIVING					
Percentage of	Overall	Housing	Medical	Groceries	Utilities
National Average	93	80	95	94	110

Valley, Cedar Creek, and Houndslake—offer country-club retirement accommodations and an atmosphere of studied elegance.

From its inception, Aiken was known as a health resort. Wealthy people from Charleston and the coastal plantations came here to escape the sultry, lowland summer heat and malaria-bearing mosquitoes. The Civil War and its aftermath of poverty put a temporary halt to Aiken's role as a summer health resort. But by the 1890s, Aiken entered a new golden age when wealthy Northerners, seeking pleasant, quiet places for their winter homes, "discovered" the town.

At an altitude of only 527 feet, the town had a climate mild enough to permit year-round grazing and was a perfect place to raise thoroughbred horses. Soon the ordinary rich, the filthy rich, and the disgustingly filthy rich bought old mansions and built new ones of their own designs. They bought farms for their racehorses and enclosed pastures with white fences. They established the Palmetto Golf Club in 1893 and were slicing drives into the lake by the time the first thoroughbred colts were frisking in the meadows.

These activities quickly established Aiken as a rich man's playground, mostly a haven for wealthy Yankees from New York and Connecticut. These newcomers brought prosperity to Aiken and, with it, a return to a genteel lifestyle that had disappeared with the Civil War. Aiken's old, aristocratic families quickly accepted the winter residents into local society despite different customs and accents. This established a tradition of openness and hospitality that has characterized Aiken ever since. Today, the super-rich Northerners have gone elsewhere, yet the legacy of hospitality and friendliness remains.

Aiken boasts a campus of the University of South Carolina and Aiken Technical College. This means free, or nearly free, courses for senior citizens and entry into the academic community of the town. There's a 190-bed medical facility that, we were told, has an excellent reputation. There are VA hospitals in both Columbia and Augusta for military retirees and their dependents.

Recreational choices abound; since the weather is generally mild, year-round outdoor activities are possible. Nineteen golf courses within a 20-mile radius of Aiken make this sport convenient; several feature senior citizens' clubs. The famous Masters Tournament is played every year in nearby Augusta. Each autumn on the shores of Lake Hartwell, Clemson University conducts a camping program for senior citizens. Fishing, swimming, even water-skiing for all those old-timers who go for that sort of nonsense, are available at any number of nearby ponds or lakes. Hunting and fishing permits are free to residents over age sixty-five.

Cheraw   Cheraw is one of South Carolina's oldest and most picturesque inland towns. Named for the Cheraw Indians, whose main town was nearby, the town began as a small trading post. Cheraw was as far upriver as steamboats could travel on the Great Pee Dee River and was the scene of busy steamboat traffic in the nineteenth century. The area of the original plan is now the nucleus of a 213-acre historic district, listed in the National Register of Historic Places, and is rich with gardens, trees, and parks and the architectural legacy of more than 200 years.

Cheraw is located on the edge of the Carolina Sandhills that stretch from Pinehurst, North Carolina to Warm Springs, Georgia. The town is located less than two hours from Columbia and Charlotte, three hours from the mountains, two hours from Myrtle Beach, and one hour from Pinehurst. Today Cheraw is a beautiful, prosperous town of close to 6,000 people who take pride in taking the best of the past and making it an important part of the future.

Citizens here have been involved in preservation efforts for almost a century. Well known for its trees for more than 150 years, Cheraw has been named a "Tree City" by the state tree-preservation program every year since the program's inception.

Cheraw is another of those towns that go out of the way to welcome newcomers. The head of Cheraw's welcoming committee says,

CHERAW WEATHER						
In degrees Fahrenheit						
	Jan.	April	July	Oct.	Rain	Snow
Daily Highs	52	74	90	74	43"	3"
Daily Lows	29	46	67	48		

"We are proud of our wonderful retirees who have become a vital part of our community. The town's people are committed to the arts, recreation, good schools, and government." She went on to point out that in Cheraw, as in many small Southern towns, the best way to immediately become involved in the community is by joining a church. Cheraw is home to almost all denominations, and any congregation is delighted to welcome new members. Joining Cheraw's chamber of commerce also provides a good chance to meet the community at the bimonthly Business After Hours.

Cheraw has beautiful antebellum neighborhoods as well as newer subdivisions. Prices here are about average for towns of similar size in South Carolina, about 10 percent under national averages.

On the Ocean

Most of South Carolina's Atlantic Ocean coastline is lowland country, suitable for rice cultivation and sparsely populated. Generally, the major roads and highways run far inland, with occasional roads meandering toward the ocean. Except for Hilton Head, the Charleston area, and a few isolated oceanfront towns, South Carolina's most logical beachfront retirement choices occupy a 60-mile stretch of spectacular coastline known as the "Grand Strand." It begins at Little River, on the North Carolina–South Carolina border, and stretches south to the Santee River, just beyond Georgetown.

Myrtle Beach   Myrtle Beach sits in the center of the accessible beach areas of the Grand Strand. With about 26,000 year-round habitants, Myrtle Beach doesn't sound like such a big town, but seasonal visitors can boost the population more than tenfold. The full length of the Grand Strand has a permanent population of about 58,000, a large percentage of whom are retired, but visitors expand the population to more than 300,000. Spring and fall have always lured golfers to enjoy the more than ninety golf courses along the Grand Strand. And summer traditionally draws crowds of vacationers to delight in beach sun and fun. Each summer seems to bring more and more tourists.

When we first researched Myrtle Beach about ten years ago, I described the town as South Carolina's equivalent of a Florida Panhandle resort: tourist-frenzied in the summer and somewhat relaxed in the winter. In fact, many restaurants and small businesses closed down when tourists deserted for the winter. Inexpensive homes were almost the rule and rentals were plentiful. I reported that after Labor Day, "the town drops its frantic, super-hero role and changes to its mild-mannered, sleepy identity for the rest of the year."

Since that time, the population of the Grand Strand has doubled. All seasons are busy. Myrtle Beach has become one of the South's premier golfing meccas, drawing visitors from all over the country. According to the chamber of commerce, Myrtle Beach has the greatest number of golf courses per square mile in the world! People who live in country-club developments in other parts of the South routinely organize excursions to play golf on the Grand Strand. Besides golf courses, you'll find an assortment of golf schools, golf shops, and a wide range of golf vacation packages, should you decide to come here to test the water (or the sand traps for that matter).

A proliferation of country-and-western entertainment centers, modeled after Missouri's Branson and Tennessee's Grand Ol' Opry, have joined golf to make full-tilt tourism a year-round business. Adding to the momentum are events like the annual Harley-Davidson motorcycle rally and the Sun Fun Festival. The increased tourism is nice for commerce, but it creates traffic congestion and additional strain on summer-season facilities already under pressure. With an increased workforce and long-term visitors competing for housing, bargain real estate is out of the picture today.

Despite the aforementioned drawbacks, folks are still coming here to retire. A look around tells why. Between Myrtle Beach's main thoroughfare (which used to be Highway 17) and the ocean, several blocks of beautiful homes on spacious, well-landscaped lots provide neighborhoods of gracious living, and other equally nice areas are found away from the business centers. Other choices are golf-course communities and upscale subdivisions as well as more modest homes between the main street and the Highway 17 bypass.

MYRTLE BEACH–GEORGETOWN WEATHER						
In degrees Fahrenheit						
	Jan.	April	July	Oct.	Rain	Snow
Daily Highs	60	75	89	75	51"	2"
Daily Lows	40	53	71	53		

MYRTLE BEACH COST OF LIVING					
	Overall	Housing	Medical	Groceries	Utilities
Percentage of National Average	94	85	92	100	105

Georgetown   At the end of the Grand Strand, halfway between Myrtle Beach and Charleston, the small city of Georgetown offers a fascinating snapshot of the colonial and antebellum past. Actually, Georgetown's rich history goes back even further than colonial times. Many readers will be surprised to know that Winyah Bay was the site of the earliest European settlement in North America. Colonists from Spain established a settlement at Winyah Bay in 1526, a century before the Pilgrims landed on Plymouth Rock. By 1729 Georgetown was a thriving shipping port for the highly successful indigo and rice plantations in the region. By the time of the American Revolution, Georgetown was an important city with a well-developed class of prominent and influential planter families. Thomas Lynch Jr., one of Georgetown's most vocal patriots, was a signer of the Declaration of Independence. Another area planter, Christopher Gadsen, is remembered for the flag he designed: "Don't Tread on Me." Georgetown resident Francis Marion was the legendary "Swamp Fox," who led a ragged band of followers to handily defeat the British in this area.

I hate to use the timeworn cliché "a town where time stood still," but the saying fits Georgetown perfectly. This is a virtual treasury of colonial, antebellum, and Victorian architecture. You can't help but feel humble as you tread silent, tree-shaded streets past historic homes, each one more ancient than the last, some more than 250 years old. It's easy to picture men wearing tri-cornered hats and ladies dressed in long skirts and petticoats ambling along the streets. You begin to wonder how life in South Carolina must have been before the American Revolution, before the Civil War, before the invention of automobiles, electricity, and miniature golf.

Georgetown is small and soft-spoken, yet immensely proud of its historic business district. The main street that faces the harbor has an Old World appearance, with ancient buildings in rows of pastel colors in the style of the colonies. The town clock tower sits atop the old Market Building, dating from 1842. Today the building houses a museum depicting the days of rice, indigo, and slavery.

Although Georgetown is technically located on the Grand Strand, it isn't on the ocean. The town's waterfront is Winyah Bay; the nearest ocean beaches are found at Pawley's Island, some 22 miles away. Pawley's Island is one of the oldest beach resorts in the country, having been used for recreation since the late 1700s. It also has the distinction of being one of the few South Carolina sea islands where original antebellum and Victorian beach homes have survived the occasional hurricanes that bruise the coast. Housing prices on Pawley's Island are well above average, whereas Georgetown has much more affordable places for sale, about 10 percent below the national average.

This is a place for people who used to like the old-time atmosphere of Myrtle Beach, but who are appalled at the changes in population density and proliferation of highway mall businesses. Folks who've relocated here from Ohio, Long Island, and elsewhere feel protective of their discovery; they don't want to spoil their piece of utopia. To protect the town from tourist clutter, Georgetown has some strictly enforced zoning laws that should guard against glitz and sleaze.

Charleston   After its settlement in 1670, Charleston quickly became one of the most prosperous cities in the thirteen colonies. Charleston was the standard against which people measured other cities in terms of beauty, culture, and riches. Located in what today is called the "Low Country," the land was rich and fertile. Planters, acquiring wealth from fantastically productive rice plantations, began designing mansions as lavish as money could provide. They built with such loving attention to detail and such devotion to quality and style that future generations of Charlestonians have resisted all temptations to exchange those prizes for new fashions. At least 240 homes are known to have been built before 1840 and 76 predate the American Revolution, with some dating back to the

1720s. Hundreds more date from the time of the Civil War and Reconstruction.

Today, Charleston vies with Savannah for the title of most beautiful city on the Atlantic Seaboard. Each scores high marks and each claims to be the "cultural center of the South." It's difficult to choose between them. Charleston is so steeped in history that a walk through its downtown streets is an adventure in time travel. It's easy to imagine fine carriages jaunting along the cobblestone streets or fashionably dressed women and nattily attired men strolling the sidewalks. A pause in front of a home built in 1720 evokes a feeling of humility as one mentally recreates the setting almost three centuries in the past. In California, where I live, any building more than 100 years old is considered a priceless antique.

Built on a narrow peninsula, the downtown section isn't very large. The peninsula is so narrow that it's almost an island between two rivers that empty into the ocean at the city's east end. The emphasis is on private homes rather than on commercial activity. The most important enterprise (from my standpoint as a lover of seafood) in this old section is the superb collection of fine restaurants. As major tourist attractions, Charleston's restaurants fully live up to their reputation for excellent seafood and Southern gourmet dishes of all descriptions. (We can never pass through town without a pause for our favorite culinary delight: she-crab soup.)

Charleston living isn't for everyone. It can be terribly formal, paced with the tempo of Southern society, intellectual pursuits, and traditional manners. We've been told that the social whirl is a closed affair, with few outsiders ever invited in.

Even even if you aren't into buying historic mansions and entering the social whirl, some alternatives might be an adventure for a part-time living arrangement. You can do as the old-time planters did: live in Charleston most of the year and somewhere else for the summer. Many old mansions in Charleston's Historic District were long ago converted to apartments, which at one time rented at unusually affordable rates, given the enchanted, historic atmosphere. Carriage houses behind the mansions were remodeled into studio apartments or charming cottages with lofts converted into upstairs bedrooms. However, as Historic District real estate becomes more and more valuable, more homes are being restored to their days of antiquity, and prices for rentals have risen to match the more expensive housing.

CHARLESTON WEATHER					
In degrees Fahrenheit					
	Jan.	April	July	Oct.	Rain	Snow
Daily Highs	61	78	90	77	49"	—
Daily Lows	38	54	71	55		

CHARLESTON COST OF LIVING					
	Overall	Housing	Medical	Groceries	Utilities
Percentage of National Average	104	103	101	103	115

All is not lace curtains and fresh paint in old Charleston. As in many cities, the curse of urban blight hovers. Not very far from the prosperous streets described here, you'll find rows of abandoned houses, so old and uncared-for that they look as if they might collapse from old age and decay. It's unfortunate that there's not some way to preserve these old mansions. Some stand three stories high, with beautifully crafted balconies and balustrades rising the full facade. Porches, high columns, and carved woodwork add to the impression of museum pieces from an irretrievable past. Within a decade these will probably all be gone. Most neighborhoods bordering the downtown area do not look to be appropriate retirement possibilities.

More than half of the city's population lives in West Ashley and James Island, which lie just to the west of the peninsula. These locations are a mixture of old and new; older neighborhoods with brick homes and graceful oak trees settle in with newer subdivisions and commercial centers.

If you don't care to live in or near a city center, or if you can't afford one of the historic places, you should check the outskirts of Charleston or one of the outlying towns, where you can live outside the city but visit Charleston for dinner or a play any time you feel like it. Nearby places where people choose to retire are Charleston's islands or nearby towns such as Summerville (described later).

Isle of Palms   Just east of Charleston, bordered by the Atlantic Ocean and the Intracoastal Waterway, two semitropical islands and one luxurious resort community are popular places for relocation. Miles of sandy beaches, pastel homes, and warm, friendly people make relocation pleasant. The Isle of Palms is a classic family-oriented beachfront community offering a wide variety of accommodations and recreation options. Wild Dunes, located on 1,600 acres at the northeastern end of the Isle of Palms, is a premier resort community with championship golf and tennis facilities, a full-service marina, and a full selection of homes and villas for sale.

Sullivan's Island   This is the Isle of Palms's sister island. More of a residential beach community, Sullivan's Island is located just south of the Isle of Palms, across Breach Inlet. There are beautiful beaches and an impressive selection of homes on this island. Natives describe the difference between the two islands this way: Isle of Palms is "more of a resort island," while Sullivan's Island is "more of a beach town."

Sullivan's Island offers much more, however, than a quiet beach-town atmosphere. Here you'll find a quaint restaurant area, historic Fort Moultrie, a working lighthouse, public tennis courts, and an old-fashioned community playground complete with a grandstand gazebo! Of course, Sullivan's Island offers all the natural amenities you could want: wide, sandy beaches, fishing, swimming, boating, sunning, and more.

Johns Island   More rural in character, Johns Island combines an intricate network of waterways with fertile farmland, residential property, and limited commercial development. Daniel Island and the Cainhoy Peninsula, which lie east and north of the peninsula, are among the most recently annexed areas of the city. The pristine Daniel Island, a full 4,500 acres in size, is just beginning to reflect the thoughtfully planned, environmentally sensitive community mapped out in the Daniel Island Master Plan. It is sure to be the future complement to Charleston's historic downtown.

Summerville   Summerville, a small city of 25,000 people, is about 20 miles from Charleston—near enough to take advantage of all that the Southern jewel offers, yet far enough away not to be bothered by the frenzy of the city. Located on a relatively high, pine-encrusted ridge, the town was first inhabited in the late 1700s. Traditionally, from May to September, families along the nearby Ashley

River and from coastal Charleston fled the malarial lowlands to enjoy their forest colony. Since they spent every summer here, what more logical name could it have than Summerville?

After the Civil War, the town gained a reputation as a health center and winter resort. Today it is gaining favor as a place for retirement. Much of its charm derives from the natural beauty of the historic architecture—with 700 buildings on the National Register of Historic Places—and the profusion of azaleas, camellias, and wisteria that line the streets and provide seasonal blooms. Its rambling streets, which deliberately wind around large pine trees to avoid destroying them, also add charm to Summerville.

Early on, Summerville realized that these pines were among the town's biggest assets. So when the village incorporated as a town in 1847, elected officials passed a law that prohibited the cutting of trees without permission and fined offenders severely. The town's motto was born, and still holds strong today: *Sacra Pinus Esto*—"*The Pine is Sacred.*" The ordinance is one of the oldest of its kind in the United States and is still on the books.

Summerville's special hometown feeling bubbles over during the Christmas holiday season. A special tree-lighting ceremony in the town square starts things off, and every Thursday until Christmas, the town enjoys strolling carolers, late evening shopping, free hot cider and cookies, free gift wrapping, Santa in the Square, and horse-drawn carriage rides through the historic district.

Hilton Head Island   Still in South Carolina, just 40 miles north of Savannah, Georgia, Hilton Head Island is the luxury retirement area. The island is divided into eight developments (called · "plantations") centered around active living—golf, tennis, boating, and 12 miles of white, sandy beach.

Golfers love the courses here and the 425 holes of golf spread over twelve locations on Hilton Head and nearby Daufuskie Island. For tennis buffs, there are more than 250 courts ranging from major complexes that host national championships to one or two courts adjoining a condo or apartment complex. Five hundred acres are reserved as a forest preserve with an astonishing 260 species of birds, alligators, deer, raccoon, and wild turkey. (A $3.00 gate pass is required to enter. Wild animals enter free of charge.) Hiking, shrimping from the shore, biking, and boating fill out the menu of outdoor activities. The list of gourmet restaurants is also impressive.

According to the chamber of commerce, about 200 restaurants, cafes, and fast-food emporiums serve everything from stand-up pizza and egg rolls to haute cuisine.

Hilton Head Island is a place for those who can afford it and who are willing to pay for a high-quality lifestyle. Be aware, however, that recently a new city administration was elected on a platform of shutting off the flow of retirees onto the island. Apparently many feel that "now that I'm here, we can lock the gates."

Georgia

The state of Georgia is trying hard to tempt out-of-state retirees into moving here rather than continuing on to Florida, and a growing number of folks discover that they like the state's varied menu of locations and its sunbelt climate. The largest state east of the Mississippi, Georgia stretches from the golden beaches of the Atlantic to the foothills of the Appalachians. The Blue Ridge Mountains taper off in the northern end of the state, but not before rewarding the region with rich valleys, forested hills, and scenic mountains. Another good prospect for retirement is Georgia's Atlantic coast, characterized by barrier islands with moss-draped oaks and magnificently preserved colonial towns, affordable retirement choices that once were domains of millionaires. To the south is the Plantation Trace with its early spring, delightful small cities, and nearness to both the Gulf and Atlantic. Another popular retirement area is around Augusta, which enjoys the benefits of two geographical areas: the Piedmont

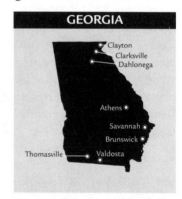

GEORGIA

Clayton
Clarksville
Dahlonega

Athens

Savannah
Brunswick
Thomasville   Valdosta

GEORGIA TAX PROFILE

Sales tax: 4% to 6%, drugs exempt
State income tax: graduated, 1% to 6% over $7,000; can't deduct federal income tax
Property taxes: taxed on 40% of market value minus $2,000 homestead exemption; typically 0.98%, plus variable local taxes
Intangibles tax: yes
Social security taxed: no
Pensions taxed: excludes first $10,000 for older taxpayers
Gasoline tax: 7.5¢ per gallon, plus 3% sales tax

Plateau and the Atlantic Coastal Plain. This is golf and thoroughbred country.

Valdosta   In their haste to get to Florida, many vacationers
zip right past the city of Valdosta (pop. 40,000), never suspecting
that a delightful little city sits undiscovered just a short skip away
from Interstate 75. Some tourists stay overnight in motels, maybe
getting in some shopping at the manufacturers' outlet stores before
steering their cars back onto the interstate to resume the high-speed
parade to the saltwater beaches a couple of hours down the cement
pavement.

Valdosta is set in Georgia's "Plantation Trace," a region
marked by fertile plains, bountiful woods, and hundreds of blue
lakes. Steeped in Victorian history and architecture as well as
modern subdivisions, Valdosta stands out as south Georgia's
dominant city. Featuring immaculately maintained neighborhoods shaded by enormous trees and enhanced by landscaping
that emphasizes flowering plants, Valdosta's residential sections
are exceptionally inviting. One retiree affirmed that this well-
groomed, upscale ambience influenced his decision to choose Valdosta as a place to settle, saying, "You can tell Valdostans respect
their town by the way they treat it. It's a joy to live among people
like that."

To be fair, I'll have to admit that my Valdosta research coincided with the first riotous days of spring in the midst of an
outrageous explosion of blossoms splashing color from every tree,
bush, and garden. It's no coincidence that Valdosta is called "the
Azalea City." Yet, the overall quality of these neighborhoods tran-
scends mere flower beds and magnolia trees. In Valdosta, the phrase
"quality living" is not a shopworn cliché; it's an apt description.

A glance at cost-of-living charts indicates that Valdosta is just a
little under the national averages, with housing costs 11 percent
below average. The region benefits from a recession-proof economy
based on military and university payrolls, which don't vary a great
deal. Because of a high turnover of Air Force families (mostly officers)
who are transferred in and out for training, there's a wealth of apartment complexes scattered about town—more than one hundred.

As I visited neighborhoods, noticing beautiful, quality brick
homes on half-acre lots, a theme kept recurring: This is a place
where a couple cashing in equity in overpriced sections of the

country could "move up" and live in a fabulous neighborhood, in a style never dreamed of—and probably still bank some of their profits from the sale of their house.

The downtown area, too, shows that Valdosta residents care. An ambitious renovation of an already nice-looking town center is going to make this one of the showplaces of the South. To finance this project, a special sales–tax measure passed with an overwhelming margin, a refreshing vote of confidence in Valdosta and its future.

An important consideration for those retiring from other parts of the nation is Valdosta's cosmopolitan retiree community; they come from everywhere! Large numbers of Air Force officers spent training time at Moody Air Force Base. Naturally, when retirement draws near, when military families begin discussing favorite towns, they remember this area with fondness.

This is a university town, too, and Valdosta State University's grounds and campus are in keeping with the upscale look of its surroundings. The university offers continuing education, with low-cost fees, in classes ranging from calligraphy to tai chi. Transportation is another strong point here.

The surrounding countryside's woodlands and numerous lakes make hunters and fishermen happy, particularly the federally owned Grand Bay Wildlife Area, which provides 5,900 acres of hunting preserve. With a wildlife management stamp firmly affixed to their state hunting licenses, sportsmen decimate ducks and geese as they make their way south each fall.

VALDOSTA WEATHER

In degrees Fahrenheit

	Jan.	April	July	Oct.	Rain	Snow
Daily Highs	70	80	94	83	49"	1"
Daily Lows	45	54	71	59		

VALDOSTA COST OF LIVING

	Overall	Housing	Medical	Groceries	Utilities
Percentage of National Average	93	84	94	97	101

Savannah Georgia was the last of England's thirteen colonies to be settled, and Savannah was the first British settlement in the state of Georgia. It all started in 1733, when England was anxious to secure her claim to the territory against Spanish encroachment from Florida. General James Edward Oglethorpe selected a spot to settle on the Savannah River, 10 miles from the Atlantic, on the edge of Yamacraw Bluff. Savannah's historic city hall now sits on the same bluff overlooking the Savannah River where Oglethorpe landed. Besides a military outpost, Oglethorpe hoped to create a planned city—a center of agriculture, manufacturing, and export. He was eminently successful. Instead of allowing a traditional, haphazard village layout to develop, Oglethorpe designed a system of street grids, broken by a series of public squares. From the beginning, Savannah was designed to be beautiful as well as defensible. This was the country's first planned city, a masterpiece of urban design.

Of the original twenty-four squares in the master plan, twenty-two still exist. Today, these squares—tastefully landscaped with live oak, azaleas, fountains, and statues—give Savannah that charming flavor that sets the city apart as a unique as well as beautiful city.

My first visit to Savannah was several decades ago, when the historic city center was in the first stages of renovation; at that point Savannah had a long way to go. The city looked somewhat seedy and in danger of succumbing to rampant decay. About fifteen years ago we passed through the city on a research trip; things had improved dramatically, but we remained unimpressed. I suppose this was because we had just left beautiful Charleston, and we were anticipating similar neighborhoods—that is, exotic, frilly mansions with Jamaica-style galleries and towering columns, each structure an individual creation, as different as possible from the next. When we didn't find what we were expecting, we assumed that General Sherman had struck again. Wrong assumption! When I wrote about Savannah, I should have remembered my Civil War history. Irate letters from Savannah lovers pointed out that Sherman did *not* harm Savannah, and that indeed Savannah has more antebellum homes than Charleston!

Puzzled at how we could have missed all of this, we returned for another visit. We were delighted to discover that my analysis of Savannah was totally wrong. Apparently, we had missed the forest by concentrating on the trees. It turns out that early architectural styles in Savannah were quite different from that of Charleston's Battery District. Instead of Charleston's ostentatious one-of-a-kind show-pieces, built as winter residences for inland planters, Savannah's antebellum mansions were owned by merchants, shippers, and townspeople. They preferred the dignified, formal expression of Italianate, English Regency, and Gothic Revival. They were designed to harmonize with each other, precisely arranged around park-like landscaped squares, instead of on narrow streets that tend to wander. Homes here are so well preserved and fit so perfectly in the scheme of things they look as if they were constructed yesterday. When appreciated in this context, I must admit that Savannah is every bit as beautiful as Charleston, if not more so (there's more of it). As one reader wrote in her letter, "France's publication *Le Monde* named Savannah the most beautiful city in America." To that, I might add that *Condé Nast Traveler* magazine nominated Savannah as one of the "Top Ten U.S. Cities."

Why didn't General Sherman destroy Savannah? Certainly he *threatened* to destroy the city. He wrote the defending General Hardee that if Savannah didn't surrender by December 17, "I shall feel justified in resorting to the harshest measures, and shall make little effort to restrain my army, burning to avenge the national wrong they attach to Savannah . . ."

General Hardee declined the offer to surrender, almost defying Sherman's burning veterans to destroy the city. Before he was forced to withdraw, he conceived a brilliant plan. He ordered 30,000 bales of valuable cotton to be stored in every home in Savannah—in garrets, cellars, and storehouses. If the city burned, the Union Army would destroy a fortune in badly needed cotton. Some people claim that Sherman didn't destroy the town because of gallantry, or because the city was just too beautiful, or because he had a mistress in Savannah. But I'm convinced that the bulldozer-hearted soldier grudgingly accepted the civilian surrender of Savannah for fiscal reasons rather than appreciation of fine architecture, gallantry, or a favorite mistress. Thank goodness he did.

With loving care and determined community action, Savannah's downtown historic district (the largest of its kind in the country) has been not only restored, but made exceptionally livable. It changed from an area of above-average crime to a safe place to be. In fact, *Walking Magazine* recently nominated downtown Savannah

SAVANNAH WEATHER					
In degrees Fahrenheit					
	Jan.	April	July	Oct.	Rain	Snow
Daily Highs	60	78	91	78	49"	—
Daily Lows	38	54	72	56		

SAVANNAH COST OF LIVING					
Percentage of	Overall	Housing	Medical	Groceries	Utilities
National Average	99	92	99	99	96

as one of "The Ten Top Walking Cities in the U.S." You can stroll the historic district, the cobblestone riverfront area, or City Market.

Four blocks in the heart of Savannah's historic district have been renovated to capture the authentic atmosphere and character of the old marketplace. Restaurants, open air cafes, jazz clubs, theme shops, and crafts and gift shops blend to create a pleasant place to pause during a walk, have lunch, and enjoy the scene. The market features artists working in their lofts and exhibiting their works for sale. Savannah's determination to protect and improve its historic sites presents a model for historic-preservation efforts.

For a flavor of Savannah, read John Berendt's book *Midnight in the Garden of Good and Evil*, which is set in the heart of the historic district. Tourism in Savannah increased more than 13 percent in 1996; folks wanted to see the places described in the novel. The motion-picture version of the book was filmed on location in Savannah, with lovely old masions as backgrounds.

Savannah has 150,000 inhabitants, which makes it too large for some tastes. But Savannah is surrounded by some very livable communities, probably more suitable for retirement than the city's historic center (as well as more affordable). The greater Savannah area comprises a 50-mile radius of Chatham County and has a total population of nearly 520,000. In the Savannah area the range of real estate varies from the very expensive properties on Skidaway Island, where building lots may run into six-figure prices, to livable neighborhoods in nearby towns where acceptable places can be purchased for less than $80,000.

One of Savannah's fastest-growing residential areas is on the fringes of the south side, only 6 miles from the historic district. A collection of attractive neighborhoods offer quality single-family housing as well as a number of apartment complexes, townhouses, and shopping centers. To zip downtown is a matter of minutes.

Garden City, the largest suburb, is on Savannah's northeast side, with 7,900 residents living in quiet neighborhoods. People here have a tradition of volunteerism. By working together, they've enabled Garden City to operate without property taxes since it incorporated as a city back in 1939. Pooler is smaller, with a population of 4,700, and it shares the hometown atmosphere of Garden City. One advantage is that Pooler sits on the intersection of two interstates, making it convenient to get into Savannah or to travel in any direction.

Savannah's Islands   Eighteen miles east of downtown Savannah, Tybee Island is the prototype of a summer beach community. People from Savannah and tourists from all over come here to enjoy sunning and shell collecting on the island's 2 miles of white sand beaches on the Atlantic. However, the 3,000 year-round residents enjoy the vacation atmosphere all year long. Accommodations are divided into short-term rentals of condos and apartments and permanent-resident housing, which tends to be older and not fancy. Other island communities on the way to Tybee Island are Wilmington, Whitemarsh, and Talahi. Like most Georgian islands, they are not crowded and have several nice-looking developments.

The ultimate in upscale living hereabouts can be found at Skidaway Island, the Isle of Hope, Southbridge, and a few other developments. Many of these are gated communities, very posh, and usually offer private golf–course membership as a part of ownership fees.

Brunswick and the Golden Isles   A hundred years ago—when being a millionaire meant more than having equity in an above-average Connecticut home—millionaires from all over the country converged upon the "Golden Isles" and encouraged their contractors and interior decorators to enter the competition for the fanciest homes possible. The objects of their affection were the islands of St. Simons and Jekyll on the south Georgia coast.

The mainland base camp and supply for the islands is the conservative old town of Brunswick. Compared to its rich island cousins, Brunswick is a rather ordinary community of about 20,000 inhabitants. But there's a charm about the place that money can't buy.

BRUNSWICK–GOLDEN ISLES WEATHER					
In degrees Fahrenheit					
	Jan.	April	July	Oct.	Rain	Snow
Daily Highs	61	78	91	78	49"	—
Daily Lows	38	54	71	56		

The town was founded before the American Revolution, with the names of streets and squares such as Prince, Gloucester, Norwich, and Newcastle honoring English nobility of the time. Property here is reasonable (if not downright cheap), and the homes are well kept. Streets are sheltered by overhanging oak trees hung with Spanish moss—quiet and peaceful. Some antebellum homes with columns and balconies grace the side streets, mixed in with more modern cottages. We saw a few mobile-home parks, but none had the class of Florida parks. These seem to be more for economical living, without extensive landscaping and organized clubhouse activities. All in all, Brunswick looks like the place to live for those who want to enjoy the fishing, beaches, and ambience of nearby Jekyll and St. Simons without paying the higher cost of actually living on the islands.

Development on the islands began in the 1880s when opulent families like the J. P. Morgans, Rockefellers, and Goulds formed the "Jekyll Island Club." Only club members were permitted to live on the island, making this one of the most exclusive resorts in the entire world. Historians estimate that at one time Jekyll Island Club members represented one-sixth of the world's wealth!

Nearby St. Simons imparts a pleasant small-town atmosphere, even though it's much more upscale than the average small town. An attractive pier and public park abut a low-key downtown—actually it is just a collection of tasteful shops. A quiet shopping center hides behind shrubbery on the main road that curves along the beach side of the island. Several miles of fine public beach provide excellent places for picnics. Good restaurants aren't scarce, with seafood the most popular fare.

Rabun, Lumpkin, and Habersham Counties This three-county region in the northeast corner of Georgia—where North and South Carolina join—has enjoyed much media publicity as one of Georgia's choice relocation areas. It's easy to see why. With lovely mountain scenery everywhere, you're never far from lakes, rivers, and state parks. The Chattooga Wild and Scenic River is nearby, with dramatic waterfalls and spectacular rapids and other natural beauties. Deep canyons like the 1,200-foot chasm of Tallulah Gorge, high peaks like the 3,600-foot Blue Ridge Crest, and the spectacular 729-foot plume of Amicalola Falls all combine to create some of the most dramatic and stirring scenery of the Appalachian chain. The famous Appalachian Trail traverses the counties. All this wilderness thrives here, yet is 90 miles or less from Atlanta. South of here, the Blue Ridge Mountains dwindle into foothills and finally change into gentle hill country as you approach the fringes of metropolitan Atlanta.

Successful publicity has taken its toll in northeast Georgia because of the number of people who've decided to relocate here. Although not overwhelming, the influx of newcomers to a sparsely settled area naturally pushed up real estate prices. Once at bargain basement levels, it's no longer a buyer's market here, especially in Rabun County. In fact, the campaign to attract retirees was so successful that the Clayton Chamber of Commerce was besieged with so many requests for relocation packets they had to start charging money to send them out—printing costs, postage, and handling got out of hand. But this doesn't mean homes are expensive; they're just not bargains any longer.

Rabun, Lumpkin, and Habersham counties have several delightful towns suitable for retirement. Clayton, in Rabun County, has attracted the most attention, probably because it's one of the more picturesque in Blue Ridge Mountain country. Other locations—such as Clarkesville, Demorest, Helen, and Dahlonega—haven't achieved quite the same popularity. To date, the demand for homes in these locales hasn't quite reached the level in Clayton. The terrain around these latter towns can be more accurately described as Blue Ridge foothills rather than Blue Ridge Mountains, but this doesn't detract from their charm.

None of the dozen locales that make up this region are very large. Clayton, with a population of 1,700, is the largest town in the high-mountain region of Chattahoochee National Forest. Dahlonega is the largest in the three-county area, with a population of 3,100. Many places here are mere villages. Helen, for example, has only 300 year-round residents. For this reason, folks hereabouts don't think in terms of towns; when you ask where they live, they'll reply "Rabun County" or "Habersham County" rather than mention a specific locality. But the commercial districts in these towns are larger than one would expect because they serve customers from the surrounding countryside. For example, Clayton is the commercial center for Rabun County's 11,648 residents; as such, it provides an unusually good selection of shopping, business, and medical services.

A natural getaway near the town of Clayton is an area called Sylvan Falls. Next to the Chattahoochee National Forest, about 600 homes are tucked away in the forest here, some with lookout vantage points from a 2,500-foot-high ridge. Not all homes are blessed with such breathtaking views, but each enjoys its own little natural paradise of rustic beauty. I once visited a couple, retired here from New Orleans, who live on the apex of the ridge. As we gazed out over the view, Marjorie said: "We feel like we're on the edge of Heaven here in the Blue Ridge Mountains of northeast Georgia. It has to be one of the most beautiful spots in the country!"

One feature all residents point out proudly is their four-season weather with gentle summers. As local boosters say, "This is where spring spends the summer." Flowering trees in the spring, delightful summers, and fall colors keep you aware of the seasons, yet comfortable enough to enjoy them.

Few communities the size of Clayton can support a senior citizens' center, and here is no exception. As an excellent substitute, the chamber of commerce organized a club called the Silver Eagles. About 200 enthusiastic members hold monthly meetings, elect officers, arrange social activities and tours, and share their expertise with others in the community. The camaraderie developed among the members is contagious. This is the place for newcomers to come and meet their new neighbors and forge all-important community connections. The program is such a success that it's being emulated in other parts of the country.

Clarkesville (pop. 1,400), the county seat of Habersham County, is another town often praised by retirement writers. A tourist brochure claims it is just an hour's drive from Atlanta, but I'd hesitate a long while before getting into a car with anyone who makes the 75-mile drive in an hour! The countryside here is made up of rolling hills rather than low mountains, and while not as picturesque as Clayton, it has a rural charm.

Another major retirement destination is Dahlonega, the location of the the first full-blown gold strike in the United States. Gold

RABUN COUNTY WEATHER						
In degrees Fahrenheit						
	Jan.	April	July	Oct.	Rain	Snow
Daily Highs	52	69	84	69	60"	10"
Daily Lows	32	45	65	46		

was discovered here in 1828 and can still be panned today. Dahlonega boomed until gold was discovered in California in 1849. Suddenly the local miners deserted their claims en masse and hot-footed it out West. The restored county courthouse now has a gold museum.

Virginia

As anyone who has traveled through Virginia can attest, it is a lovely state. The portion around Washington, D.C., however, is too heavily settled and business-oriented for our taste in retirement locations. Real estate prices reflect this orientation and so does traffic congestion. It's interesting to note that Virginia has one of the highest numbers of *outbound* retirees of any state. This is probably due to folks who move to the Washington, D.C., area to pursue careers and move away when they retire.

VIRGINIA
Charlottesville
Richmond
Hampton
Virginia Beach

VIRGINIA TAX PROFILE
Sales tax: 3.5% to 4%, drugs exempt
State income tax: graduated, 2% to 5.75% over $17,000; can't deduct federal income tax
Property taxes: average 1.2% of assessed value
Intangibles tax: no
Social security taxed: no
Pensions taxed: excludes $6,000 for people 62–64, $12,000 for 65 and older, minus Social Security and railroad retirement benefits
Gasoline tax: 17.5¢ per gallon, plus sales tax

The western portion of Virginia shares in the glory of the Appalachians, and the Blue Ridge Parkway runs diagonally from North Carolina almost to the upper edge of Virginia. Descriptions of North Carolina's

Great Smoky Mountains apply here as well, with small towns tucked away between wooded ridges and fast-running rivers. The one town here that struck us as having charm is Charlottesville, but it is so large that it seems to dwarf the university population.

The central portions of Virginia are similar to North Carolina's Midlands, with miles of rolling hills alternating between grassy pastures, woods and well-tended farms. Historic Charlottesville is an excellent example of this country. This was Thomas Jefferson's home, a place he called "the Eden of the United States." It's also the home of the University of Virginia, with its cultural and recreational activities, visiting dance troupes, and summer opera festival. Washington, D.C., and the Kennedy Center are just an hour away for additional entertainment.

But it's the eastern ("Tidewater") part of Virginia, the area that embraces Chesapeake Bay, that makes Virginia so different from the other Southeastern states. Wonderfully rural and sparsely settled, the land looks as it must have in colonial times. Some farmhouses indeed date from that period and appear to have remains of tobacco barns and old slave quarters falling into disrepair behind the large homes.

We combined our research with a visit to some good friends who live in this region. They live in a tiny crossroads community of about 150 people, an hour's commute from Richmond. They dearly love their new home, a hundred-year-old farmhouse sitting on five acres of partly wooded ground. The couple paid $90,000 for the property, which included a barn, a chicken house, and a rabbit hutch. One acre is cultivated as a truck garden, supplying veggies for their kitchen; there's even an asparagus patch.

The delightful part about where they live is their access to a nearby tidal inlet of the York River. The walk to the riverbank takes you through a wonderland of wildlife and unspoiled nature, with tidal waters swirling with fish, turtles, and who knows what else swimming beneath the surface. Ducks, herons, and songbirds go about their business unperturbed by human presence.

The downside of living in a Chesapeake Bay crossroads community is the total lack of services. Purchasing a can of tomato sauce or a roll of paper towels entails a 20-mile round-trip. The nearest doctor is 15 miles away, the same distance as the video-rental store. But as my friend Pam says, "It's worth it. We don't have many neighbors, but the ones we have are quality. They're more than neighbors, they're friends we can count on if we need them. We don't need a big city to be happy."

For saltwater retirement in more populated areas of Virginia, try Hampton or Virginia Beach. Both offer upscale living conditions, with the cultural and social benefits of a larger city. Hampton is top-heavy into educational institutions, with the College of William and Mary, Old Dominion University, and a satellite campus of George Washington University all contributing to the cultural and intellectual milieu.

CHAPTER 3

Florida:
A Retirement Tradition

WHEN DREAMING OF RETIREMENT, many people automatically picture Florida. They've vacationed there for years, so retirement there seems logical. Visions of warm weather, snow-free streets, and easy living dance temptingly through their retirement fantasies. Soft, sandy beaches with swaying palm trees and balmy January days complete the vision. Beginning in the 1920s, retirees moved south in such numbers that Florida retirement became almost a cliché.

Lately, some have started to question this traditional Florida dream. Attention-catching, negative publicity often sends waves of doubt throughout the nation. Magazines, newspapers, and television describe Florida as a place of violence, overcrowding, and general disrepair. Robberies of tourists, car-jackings, and drive-by shootings make Florida sound dangerous. Hurricanes, drugs, and illegal immigration would appear to foreclose Florida as a nice place to retire.

Does this mean we should write off Florida as a viable choice? Not by any means! From our research, we are convinced that of all the states, Florida still offers the best bargains in quality living and affordable retirement for the average retiree. Regardless of what you see on television, most Florida communities are as safe as other popular retirement destinations. If this book were to give ratings, many Florida towns would receive ratings far above towns of similar size elsewhere, both in livability and safety. Even though it isn't for everyone, Florida is still a great place to retire. That is precisely why so many retire here!

Recently I asked a Florida friend from Cape Coral how she felt about her own personal safety and her family's experiences with the crime problem. She replied, "The only crime I see is on television or newspaper front pages. It doesn't bother me, because most violent crimes happen in places I'd never go in the first place. I don't live in a high-crime area, so I feel safe."

Crime statistics confirm that many Florida places rank exceptionally high in safety. Cape Coral is a good example; it happens to have one of the state's lowest crime rates and compares well with other U.S. cities.

Another Florida retiree offered this observation: "The secret to avoiding problems in Florida is to stay away from tourist attractions. Criminals know that tourists have money, and wherever you find tourists and money, that's where criminals go. They don't hang around neighborhoods like mine." I visited this man and his wife in their rural community home in central Florida. It certainly seemed peaceful enough. The view from their living room picture window was across an expanse of wetlands to a distant meadow where three Holstein cows grazed.

FLORIDA TAX PROFILE
Sales tax: 6% to 7%, food, drugs exempt
State income tax: no
Property taxes: approximately 1.6%
Intangibles tax: yes
Social security taxed: no
Pensions taxed: no
Gasoline tax: 4¢ to 10¢ per gallon

Isn't Florida Overcrowded?

In 1999 Florida was the fourth-most-populous state in the Union. New residents move here at the rate of 900 a day, most of them retirees. Florida is expected to be third in population when statistics for 2000 become available, ranking only behind New York and California.

With all those retirees moving in, isn't Florida overcrowded? That depends upon which part of Florida we're talking about. Certainly, some parts of Florida are heavily populated, with high-rise apartments and condos clustered together with nothing but shopping centers and parking lots to break the monotony. Yet large sections of Florida are sparsely populated. Thousands of square miles have virtually no presence at all. Herons, egrets, ducks, storks, and wildfowl of all description share vast expanses of land with other wildlife ranging from panthers to rabbits and alligators to turtles. Deer abound in the open countryside and in the state's large system of national forests.

Lightly populated central Florida features rolling, wooded terrain dotted with small towns and crossroad communities comparable to those in small-town Ohio or Illinois. They are quiet, safe, and rural. Were it not for an occasional palm tree, you could easily forget this is Florida. These places are often overlooked in retirees' enthusiasm for living close to beaches and excitement. Surprisingly, most locations in the interior are less than an hour's drive from a beach. No place in the entire state is more than 70 miles from salt water. Some towns in the very center of the state give you a choice: A drive of an hour or so in either direction takes you to the Atlantic Ocean or to the Gulf of Mexico. You can spend a day playing in the sand and return home in time for dinner. And the state is well endowed with coastline—8,426 miles of it!

Florida offers a wide range of choices. You can select the convenience and excitement of a city, or you can choose a small-town atmosphere with slow traffic and rural tranquility. Florida has it all, except perhaps mountain climbing and downhill skiing.

Florida Weather

The near-tropical climate of Florida's peninsula has always been the main attraction for those in the North and Midwest who want something better to do with their winters than shoveling snow and staying indoors to watch television. January afternoon temperatures generally climb into the 60s or low 70s, with nights dropping to the 40s and 50s in some areas. Summers are hot, to be sure, but aren't summers in the Midwest and North scorchers, too? If you insist upon cool summers *and* mild winters, you need to think Pacific Coast—California, Oregon, or Washington. But that's in another chapter. In the summer, early-morning temperatures are usually in the 70s, giving you plenty of opportunity to exercise outdoors. Summer afternoons are why God gave Florida swimming pools and iced lemonade.

Florida's tropical setting is an accident created by a huge flow of warm water—a kind of oceanic river—known as the Gulf Stream. This balmy current sweeps up from the Caribbean, hooks around the Florida Keys, and then brushes across Florida's east coast. Its benevolent warmth flows close to shore, bestowing its blessings on the Atlantic coast until a point near Vero Beach, where it swerves out to sea.

The entire state benefits from the Gulf Stream, but the 80-mile stretch of southeastern coast known as the "Gold Coast" is the biggest beneficiary. Summers here aren't quite as hot because of the ocean's constant temperature and some cloud cover. The best part is winter; this part of Florida is warmer than anywhere else in the continental United States. This dreamy weather explains why you see several million people crowded together along the Gold Coast.

The rest of Florida experiences cooler winters and warmer summers than the Gold Coast, but not remarkably so, because the Gulf Stream—although offshore a distance in the northern parts and across the peninsula from the western shore—still influences the weather. All but Florida's coldest winter days are pleasant enough for golf or bicycling; rarely will you see frost in the morning. January lows average 52 degrees in Fort Myers (on the Gulf Coast side), compared with Miami's 60 degrees. Yet the average January high reaches 75 degrees in Fort Myers and 76 in Miami. Not bad for January!

Farther north along the Gulf, winters are cooler. Pensacola sees January highs averaging around 61 degrees and lows around 42. This is balmy to those who are used to below-zero windchill factors all winter long. Canadians are known to swim in the Gulf of Mexico throughout the winter (shudder).

Rainfall in Florida is generous. Most of the state rests on porous limestone covered with layers of sand and clay. This acts like a giant sponge, soaking up the rainfall and providing an almost unlimited water supply even in times of drought. During a drought, however, water problems can occur near the coast when ocean water seeps in and makes drinking water brackish. This is something you need to check on when buying beach property. Insist on a water-quality report before making an offer.

Thanks to its far-ranging ocean breezes, air pollution is all but nonexistent in Florida. Among the ten "cleanest" cities in the United States, three are in Florida: West Palm Beach, Orlando, and Jacksonville. The biggest industry here is tourism; tourists don't pollute the air, just the beaches.

Because of Florida's warm winters and balmy springs, many major-league baseball teams make their spring-training headquarters here. Every year more than a dozen ball clubs call Florida home, and residents all over the state enjoy the spring-training games. Many people retire here specifically for that purpose. Among the teams here:

Atlanta Braves (Kissimmee)
Baltimore Orioles (Ft. Lauderdale)
Boston Red Sox (Ft. Myers)
Cincinnati Reds (Sarasota)
Cleveland Indians (Winter Haven)
Detroit Tigers (Lakeland)
Florida Marlins (Melbourne)
Houston Astros (Kissimmee)
Kansas City Royals (Davenport)
Los Angeles Dodgers (Vero Beach)
Minnesota Twins (Ft. Myers)
Montreal Expos (Jupiter)
New York Mets (Port St. Lucie)
New York Yankees (Tampa)
Philadelphia Phillies (Clearwater)
Pittsburgh Pirates (Bradenton)
St. Louis Cardinals (Jupiter)
Tampa Bay Devil Rays (St. Petersburg)
Texas Rangers (Port Charlotte)
Toronto Blue Jays (Dunedin)

Florida Real Estate

If high-quality yet inexpensive real estate is an important consideration, then Florida should rank high, for dollar for dollar and feature
for feature you'll find the best bargains here of anywhere in the
country. True, you can find homes selling for less in Oklahoma or
Idaho, but as I continually stress, cheap housing should not govern
your retirement choices.

Florida offers virtually every kind of housing imaginable.
Condos, townhouses, and apartments are common along the
coasts or wherever land costs are high. Mobile homes and manufactured homes (mobile homes on foundations) allow for down-
scale, economical housing. Traditional subdivisions are common,
particularly away from the beaches, as are custom homes. A
common type of arrangement is a gated community, often reserved
for folks older than age fifty-five and built around a clubhouse and
tennis courts, sometimes with its own private golf course and other
facilities.

Coastal Retirement

For many folks, tourists and retirees alike, Florida's beaches are what it's all about. Condos rent by the day or week and motels, hotels, and glitzy restaurants abound, mostly catering to the needs of vacationers and weekend visitors. Yet, just a few miles away from the beachfront crush—sometimes just a few blocks away—a different world presents itself: the world of residents.

It's entirely possible to live in a quiet, normal neighborhood and then, whenever you choose, slip away to join the hedonistic, suntan-crazy world of the tourist just a few blocks away. When the sun starts to set, you can walk home to peace and quiet. With beaches on three sides of Florida—east, west, and south—no matter where you decide to settle, you can be near the coast.

Not all beachfront real estate is devoted to tourism; most coastal properties are residential. Some of the fanciest housing is found along sandy beaches, screened from the road by thick stands of palms and tropical shrubbery. Some areas are so exclusive that the only research we did was to drive past and sigh enviously. Yet, happily, there are beach areas where houses are definitely affordable.

Golf and Boating Properties

One of Florida's top retirement benefits is year-round outdoor recreation. Not surprisingly, some of the most successful retirement communities here are those focused on exercise and recreation. Thus we find country-club developments featuring Olympic-size pools, exercise rooms, jogging paths, and golf courses. The more desirable homes edge expanses of greens and fairways, giving a wide-open feeling as well as access to the game. In addition to the first tee sitting just a three-iron shot away from your back door, you probably won't have to wait long for a starting time, since residence in the development usually includes membership in the club.

The good part about some golf complexes is that membership is optional, so if you play golf as badly as I do, you don't have to pay for upkeep of the golf course and feel obligated to humiliate yourself on a regular basis. Often these courses are open to the public, with affordable green fees for nonmembers. A typical monthly fee (without golf) might be about $100, for which you receive cable TV, lawn maintenance, membership in the community club complete with tennis courts and swimming pool, social activities, hobbies, and dinners. Not only are houses and condominiums commonly bundled with a golf course, but some of the more expensive mobile-home communities often feature their own links.

Another Florida innovation is boat-canal living: homes built along a waterway, with sailboats, powerboats, and yachts tied up in their backyards. Residents of canal developments enjoy the ocean or gulf in ways that beachside folks cannot. Some boating communities are locked-in or gated arrangements, but most are in open neighborhoods. I'm continually surprised that homes backing up to a canal are often priced not much higher than similar places in "dry" neighborhoods.

Developing a boating community isn't as expensive or extravagant as it might seem. Since so much of Florida's real estate is low-lying—just a few feet above sea level—a practical way of reclaiming marshland is to dredge drainage canals and use the dredged material as fill to raise the level of the land. Since canals must be constructed anyway, boating access is a natural result of the preparation of the land for housing. All that remains is to place a wooden dock at the rear of each home and put up signs pointing the way to the salt water.

Although country club–type golf, tennis, and boating communities would appear to be expensive and luxurious, they can be surprisingly affordable. In fact, compared with some parts of the country, these houses can be downright cheap! To be sure, there are monthly maintenance fees, but because the golf courses, swimming pools, and tennis courts serve the entire country-club community, the costs and upkeep are spread among hundreds of families.

Ordinary Housing

Regular single-family homes, the kind you'll find in subdivisions and neighborhoods all over America, are priced quite reasonably. In most parts of Florida, two- or three-bedroom homes can usually be found well below national averages, many in the low $70,000 range. Locating property for less than that is difficult, but such homes can still be found. I visited the daughter of a friend in West Palm Beach, where she lives in a home valued at $60,000. The neighborhood was perfectly adequate, not far from the beach and good shopping, and most important, it was what she could afford. Yet, a half-mile away—

in Palm Beach—people were paying more than a million dollars for homes, mainly for the privilege of living right on—rather than just close to—the beach.

In Florida, a continuing difference of opinion exists between those who insist on retiring in a regular neighborhood, with neighbors of mixed ages and generations, and those who prefer the "same-age community" of a retirement development. Each has its advantages. The decision largely depends on your particular personality and lifestyle.

Those who make friends easily and tend to jump feet-first into community affairs will choose the mixed-generation neighborhoods. They'll soon know everyone on the block and will build a social life quickly. Other people have interests such as ocean fishing, college classes, or part-time businesses. They don't need or want organized activities to keep them busy; they already have too much to do. If they want a swimming pool, they'll buy a home with one already installed, and they won't have to share it with others. They don't see any point in paying extra money for something they won't use.

Those who prefer a retirement community love the idea of entering a neighborhood where everything is in place. Newcomers are immediately part of a social group and automatically invited to join bridge clubs, hobby groups, and all sorts of organized activities. They don't have to look for things to do and people to make friends with; this just happens. They won't feel like strangers in a new neighborhood; their neighbors come from somewhere else, too. Back in their hometowns, when they were younger, the neighborhood children were the focal point. Parents became friends of their children's friends; social life often focused around school activities. Now, they feel they would have little in common with younger neighbors in a traditional neighborhood.

To be perfectly honest, my wife and I can't decide which option we prefer. We have no recommendations one way or another.

The Mobile-Home Alternative

Those who are able to move to Florida and buy any property they choose with little regard for price are usually those fortunate people who bought a home in the 1960s for the going price, then in the 1990s sold it for many times their investment. Perhaps they realized a 1,000 percent profit; that's not unusual. These folks pay cash for their retirement homes and stash the rest of their profits in the bank, with the monthly interest helping to pay expenses.

But we all weren't that lucky or that far-seeing. If you've lived in an apartment or rented a house all these years, you'll probably be renting when you move to Florida. There is another option, however: a mobile home. Although you can pay as much for a Florida mobile home as you would for a conventional home, you can also buy one for the same price as a used car. At that price it won't be elegant, but it will be yours.

Mobile homes are a standard feature in most Florida communities. Unlike some other states, where mobile homes are considered low-income housing, many parks and developments in Florida are as spiffy (and as expensive) as some upscale traditional-home communities. So many families live in mobile homes that they have become an organized political force in the state. Lobbyists for mobile-homeowners' associations continually press for legislation protecting their rights.

Don't get the idea that the cheaper mobile homes are only for the impoverished. Other benefits accrue to this lifestyle besides low-cost living, not the least of which are friendly neighbors and park clubhouse social activities. Also, a great number of retirees who can afford more expensive housing would rather put even more of their home-sale profits into income-producing investments.

Mobile-home parks come in all levels of luxury, from the strictly utilitarian, with no amenities except a laundry room, to the ultra-luxurious, complete with eighteen-hole golf courses, Olympic-size pools, and deluxe country-club surroundings. Prices can be remarkably low or exorbitantly high, depending upon the level of park you choose. Most of the better ones also sell new mobile homes and will set one up to your specifications.

Following are several mobile-home scenarios we found during our last visit to the state. One was in Florida's interior, northwest of Tampa. We interviewed a couple from Clarksville, Tennessee, who purchased a new 14-foot wide, 70-foot long, two-bedroom, two-bath mobile home. The cost was $17,900, installed on a lot (all hookups, air-conditioning, etc., included). They bought their lot for $7,000 in a park with a nine-hole golf course. If the lot hadn't been next to the golf course, it would have cost only $3,000. The monthly membership fee: $125, which includes maintenance of their small lawn.

"We could have bought an acre lot away from town for $10,000," said the wife, "but since we plan on spending most summers in Tennessee, we feel better about having close neighbors to watch our home while we're gone." Her husband said, "We were coming here every winter and spending $900 a month for a small condo, so we decided to get our own place. And for $125 a month, we can afford to let it sit empty while we're traveling."

Another, even less expensive example is the case of an old friend who lives in a small mobile-home park on the Intracoastal Waterway north of Palm Beach. Ed is getting along in years, but is very much interested in fishing, betting on dog races, and playing the "penny" stock market. His park is definitely an economy affair, packed with trailers 45 feet long and under—mostly one-bedroom—showing unmistakable signs of age.

"Most folks who live here are from Canada," Ed said as he took me on a guided tour of his park. "Most of 'em go home about the first of April." He led the way onto a dock jutting into the Intracoastal Waterway, about 150 feet from his trailer door. "Couldn't get any closer to the water, not without owning one of those half-million-dollar houses on Palm Beach. This is where I catch fish. I could damn near have a fish dinner every evening if I wanted." He pointed out a well-kept trailer with a for-sale sign in the window. "Canadian lady owns that one," he said, "Wants $3,500 for it. It's bigger than mine, but I'm satisfied where I am."

How much does it cost to live here? "My rent just went up," he replied. "Now I pay $150 a month. With my Social Security and the money I win at the dog track, I put something in the bank every month." I thought he was joking, but when we went to the track that afternoon, Ed won $86 while I lost 18 bucks.

Over on the Gulf Coast, near Sarasota, we looked at three levels of park luxury in a single afternoon. The first was truly spiffy, with new double-wide, three-bedroom, two-bath units on large lots selling in excess of $65,000. This park had all the amenities, including a golf course, tennis courts, and a deluxe clubhouse. Park rent was about $395.

Nearby was a mid-range park, with units grouped around a small lake (no golf course, but some tennis courts and a large swimming pool). Used two-bedroom units were priced at $14,000 to $21,000, with new units starting at $27,000, all double-wide. The landscaping was elegant, and the clubhouse had a social director to organize activities. Park rent was $259 a month. In other, more rural areas, similar parks advertise a $150 rent, including water, sewer, and trash.

The third park was 2 miles closer to town and was full of older units, many twenty years old. The mobile homes here were spaced closely together, similar to conventional parks found in other parts of the country. The only facility was a laundry room, which served as a place to meet and gossip. According to residents, there was a level of social activity, but it was organized by residents on an informal basis rather than by the park management. It was quite pleasant and peaceful, with mature trees for shade. A few homes displayed for-sale signs, including a single-wide, two-bedroom place for under $8,000. Park rent was $200 a month.

Most parks we inspected included lawn maintenance in the rent. This makes it nice for those who spend the winter months in an inexpensive mobile home and then leave it for the rest of the year. But it isn't just snowbirds who live in the less-expensive units. The majority in the parks we visited were full-time Florida residents. It was comforting to realize that people of limited means have the opportunity to retire in their own homes in Florida so inexpensively.

Many developments sell mobile-home lots rather than simply renting them. This is usually a package deal; they sell you a mobile home as well as the land. One park we visited in Brooksville offered a $38,900 package (including taxes and fees) for a good-sized lot and a two-bedroom mobile home with carport, utility room, and screened patio. It had a twenty-four-hour guarded gate, a swimming pool, and tennis courts. This price seemed in line with others, although we've seen advertisements for mobile homes complete with land for much less. As with any community development, monthly membership and maintenance fees go on top of the original price.

Should You Rent or Buy?

Apartment rentals offer an interesting alternative. Not everyone is up to buying property. Even though prices are comparatively reasonable in Florida, home-buying still involves a considerable outlay of cash. Investing savings in a home means forgoing the interest or dividends that money would earn if invested in stocks or a money market fund. For example: an $80,000 investment at a 7 percent return would bring in $466 a month. That $466 a month you lose by not investing can pay most of the rent on a nice apartment in

Florida. In other words, the money you save by *not* buying a house allows you to live rent-free.

For example, a nice apartment complex in Daytona Beach offers two bedrooms, air-conditioning, two swimming pools, lighted tennis courts, and twenty-four-hour emergency service for $725 per month. A one-bedroom place rents for $610. Throughout the state, the local shopping centers usually have free, full-color booklets and brochures listing apartment complexes, complete with color photos of the grounds and facilities.

Almost anywhere you'll find an abundance of competing apartments, each trying to offer more than its neighbor to attract tenants. Swimming pools, hot tubs, and tennis courts are standard equipment, as are putting greens, exercise rooms, and billiards.

Why are apartments so high class and low priced? The answer is overbuilding: too many apartment buildings competing for too few tenants. It's the age-old law of supply and demand in action. You see, during the Wild West heyday of our savings-and-loan rodeo—when the supply of depositors' money was as unlimited as the demands of promoters—billions of dollars were spent building shopping centers, commercial buildings, and apartment buildings. Florida was considered an especially nice place to build. Since the supply of savings-and-loan dollars was virtually unlimited, we now have an overly generous supply of apartment complexes.

Wheeling and Dealing

Florida has long been famous for the land salesman with a glib tongue, fast pencils, and alligator shoes: the epitome of the wheeler-dealer. This tradition originated many years ago when a newcomer from Madrid—a guy named Ponce de Leon—purchased some land from a Seminole real estate salesman. At the time, it seemed like a good deal; after all, the property included a genuine Fountain of Youth. But it turned out the deed was faulty, and poor ol' Ponce ran himself ragged trying to locate the parcel on the tract map. Never did find it. The Fountain of Youth is still in escrow.

From that point on, Florida real estate ethics steadily slipped downhill. Promoters eagerly began subdividing swamps and selling lovely underwater lots by mail throughout the country. When they ran out of swamp, they made do with ocean bottom. Ironically, much of this property became valuable when the swamps were drained.

Because of a steady flow of buyers moving into the state and competition for their business, real estate people and developers have become masters at creative selling. Few if any of their methods are illegal, but some deals aren't exactly as they appear on the surface. There are so many ingenious ways to sell property, so many variables, that it behooves a buyer to be exceedingly careful. I'm not suggesting that salespeople or developers are dishonest, just that some are more forthcoming than others. In fact, it was a real estate salesman who pointed out the conditions described here. If you ask the right questions, you'll have a better chance of making the right decision. Situations like the following sketches are not unique to Florida, just more common.

Homeowners' Associations   Homes in retirement developments are commonly packaged with membership in a homeowners' association as a condition of sale. You're obligated to pay monthly dues and assessments for upkeep of the clubhouse, swimming pools, golf course, and things of that nature. This extra money must be considered when calculating the cost of your home. An additional $100 a month is the equivalent of $10,000 added to the mortgage. It may be well worth the extra money, but you should be reasonably sure it won't increase by another $100 later on.

It's important to know whether the association actually owns the clubhouse and other facilities you're supporting, or whether your association only has a contract or lease with the developer. There's a big difference. If the contract or lease agreement permits the owner to increase fees at will, you have to go along with it. Even worse, if the development is underfinanced and/or heavily mortgaged, there's always a danger of bankruptcy. The mortgage holder who takes over the facility may not be bound to honor the contract with your association, and you'll suddenly find yourself without the clubhouse, golf course, and Olympic-size pool that you thought were yours.

Another thing to find out is whether the association is incorporated and you are a shareholder, or whether it's a partnership and you are a "partner" with a lot more personal liability than you thought. Incorporation limits your liabilities. There's nothing wrong with the above arrangements, as long as you are aware of the conditions and are protected.

Condominium Associations   Condo owners own their individual portions of the development as well as having an interest in the facilities and common grounds. The condo owner also has a financial responsibility for maintenance of the grounds, recreation room, clubhouse, swimming pool, common hallways, and entryways, as well as the roof and exterior of the condominium. A condominium association is the equivalent of a homeowners' association. The same questions should be asked: "Who owns these common facilities and how are we protected?" After a project is completed, the developer may have little interest in keeping the facilities going. He could sell it to a third party, who may or may not have an obligation to honor the lease arrangement. Have a lawyer check these things out for you before you invest your bundle of cash.

Leaseholds   Mobile homes and modular homes (permanently attached units) are often sold on leased or rented ground. Again, if the development goes into foreclosure, the new owners may not have to honor the lease. If your investment is large, I suggest that you make sure of several things: one, that the lease is renewable in perpetuity; two, that monthly payments cannot go up more than the Consumer Price Index adjustment for inflation; and three, that the lease is transferable, just as a piece of property is transferable.

Less expensive mobile homes are usually placed on rented property rather than leased land. If someday, down the road, something happens to the park, you won't have as much to lose by moving to another mobile-home park. But an expensive development involves large investments in nonmovable items such as carports, screened rooms, utility and storage rooms, and landscaping.

Another item to consider is how difficult might it be to sell your home if or when the necessity arises. The buyer of a home on rented or leased land sometimes finds it difficult to obtain bank financing; you may have to self-finance in order to sell. With an inexpensive property this may not be a problem, but if you have a large mortgage, you may have to dig into your pocket to pay it off if you can't sell for top dollar. If you are in a limited-access park, potential buyers may be stopped from looking. Beware of rental or lease agreements that give the park managers an exclusive right to resell or to purchase your property. Don't count on them making any big effort to do so, not if they still have new properties of their own to sell.

With an exclusive right to purchase your property, they have a license to take you to the cleaners; they can pay you whatever they please. Perhaps the present management wouldn't do this, but who knows about the future?

Florida law prohibits forced removal of a mobile home for any other reason than unsafe or unsightly conditions. Don't hang your hat on this, however, because for all I know, a home's just being twenty years old could make it unsightly to some. You might feel more secure if you had something in your lease agreement to protect your home. We all know how age discrimination feels, don't we?

The Bottom Line   Don't get so starry-eyed about your lovely new home that you don't ask about the *total* cost. Let's say you've agreed upon a sales price plus the "usual hookup fees and closing costs," and eagerly sign the papers. Only after it's too late does the salesperson explain that "usual hookup fees" in this case means an extra $5,000.

"After all, ma'am, you didn't expect that sewer and water connections were free, did you? They cost money. Oh yes, will you be needing electricity? Well, that's additional, too. By the way, we'll be increasing the association fees once the developer finishes with this project, because he won't be subsidizing your clubhouse any longer. And then there's a few additional closing costs that we forgot to . . ."

The time to cover your backside is *before* you sign the papers! Get it all in writing.

North-Central Florida

Although attractive retirement places can be found all over the state, an area often overlooked for retirement possibilities is Florida's interior. The north-central part of Florida is a different world, as distinct from either coast as you can imagine. This is Florida with a four-seasons climate. Instead of being ironing–board flat, as is most of the state, central Florida sits at a higher elevation on rolling hills covered with dense woodlands, meadows, and hundreds of lakes. Forests of oak, pine and maple, flowering dogwood, and azalea make this a unique cosmos, a place where palm trees and other tropical flora seem out of place. Yet the fun beaches of either the Gulf or the Atlantic are within easy driving distance. Because of its slightly higher altitude and distance from the water, you'll find true changes of season, with cooler summer nights, even an occasional dusting of snow in the winter.

This part of Florida attracts more retirees from Midwestern and Northern states than from New York and New England (whose residents seem to prefer Florida's Gold Coast). Residents here tend to duplicate the ambience of their hometowns. By and large, the state's interior is more peaceful, more rural, and safer; it feels more like home to them than the hectic beachfront zones. Generous lawns and single-family homes make this a re-creation of small-town America, with a slight Florida flourish. Homes here come equipped with the pools, sun-

decks, and outdoor rooms so important for Florida outdoor lifestyles. Were it not for an occasional orange grove, many neighborhoods would look right at home in Peoria or Terre Haute, where their owners came from. Part of this openness is due to lower land costs that encourage large building lots, which are routinely measured in acreage rather than square feet.

The climate is different here, too. In this region, the weather-stabilizing Gulf Stream is far off Florida's coast, headed toward the open Atlantic. Consequently, summer days are hotter and winters are a few degrees colder. Slightly less rain falls as well. These temperature differences can be significant when you consider Florida's high humidity. Miami averages thirty days a year above 90 degrees, whereas inland it's more like 100 days over 90 degrees. This is enough to encourage many who retire in central and west coast Florida to return north for the summer.

Nevertheless, if you love warm weather (like me), 90-degree days aren't bad, even with the 75 percent humidity you find in most of Florida. As one person from Rochester, New York, pointed out, "Coping with hot weather is simply a matter of changing my living patterns. Back home in New York, I stayed indoors all winter. I only went outside to go to work or to shovel snow. Here, I stay indoors during the *summer,* yet every morning and evening it's comfortable outdoors for golf or bicycling."

Orlando Area   At one time I considered Orlando one of Florida's better retirement ideas. That was before it became so busy. In a short time, the city made a remarkable transition from a sleepy crossroads of citrus orchards and cattle ranches into a dynamic city, the fastest-growing in the state. Actually, for such a booming economy, Orlando managed to make this transition fairly painless by diversifying commerce and concentrating on clean, high-tech industry, gaining the nickname "Silicon Swamp." Another nickname for Orlando is "Hollywood East," because of the film industry's focus on this area. Disney, MGM, and Universal Studios invested millions in soundstages, production entities, and tourist attractions; apparently, this is just the beginning. There is much, much more to come!

Orlando's major problem, as far as retirement is concerned, is that it grew too much and too fast. With tourist super-attractions like Disney World and other Hollywood-style promotions, throngs of visitors create enormous traffic jams and encourage the proliferation of fast-food joints, souvenir stands, motels, and business areas, which can be depressing to those who live here year-round. This shouldn't detract from the fact that Orlando has many wonderful services and attractions that are worth a day visit for local residents. The secret to successful retirement living here is to settle *near* Orlando, not *in* Orlando.

The Orlando metropolitan area is surrounded by small, pleasant towns that are truly pastoral, yet close enough to down-

ORLANDO AREA WEATHER						
In degrees Fahrenheit						
	Jan.	April	July	Oct.	Rain	Snow
Daily Highs	72	84	92	84	48"	—
Daily Lows	49	60	73	65		

ORLANDO AREA COST OF LIVING					
	Overall	Housing	Medical	Groceries	Utilities
Percentage of National Average	98	94	111	100	102

town to take advantage of big-city offerings. The countryside is rolling, with orange groves and lemon blossoms to sweeten the air. More than fifty lakes dot the landscape, many with gorgeous, tropical shores edged with cypress, pines, and tall palm trees. Fish abound in the lakes, along with an occasional alligator.

Leesburg/De Land   The best retirement bets near Orlando are found north of the city in a fan-shaped area starting at Orlando's northern edge. A dozen small towns are scattered throughout this triangle, from De Land on the east to Leesburg on the west, places little publicized as retirement locations. Most towns are long settled, with established neighborhoods and mature shade trees along quiet streets, plus great real estate bargains. Shopping facilities are adequate, with Orlando a short drive away for heavy-duty shopping.

Most homes in these smaller towns are located in conventional neighborhoods, and larger retirement developments can be found in the surrounding countryside. We looked at a very impressive retirement complex near the comfortable little city of Leesburg. Since country property is inexpensive in this area, the developer was able to purchase a huge tract of land, a mixture of rolling hills, pastures, small lakes and marshland. Because homes can't be placed on wetlands, much of the land is open, giving most homes unobstructed views and privacy. The facilities (completely owned by the homeowners' association) are top quality, and include an Olympic-size pool, a huge clubhouse, tennis courts, and large areas of parkland. The development has a golf course, and you'll find half a dozen links within a 16-mile radius. Models of excellent design sell for $100,000 and up.

Winter Haven   Another possibility that shouldn't be neglected is the area southwest of Orlando and east of Tampa, a group of small communities centered around Winter Haven. Lakeland (pop. 72,000) is the largest and newest of the cities, and Frostproof (pop. 3,000) the smallest and probably the oldest. Winter Haven (pop. 25,000) is the best known, for it's received much positive publicity as a retirement center. Besides being the spring training camp of the Cleveland Indians and the home of Cypress Gardens, a famous tourist attraction, Winter Haven bills itself as the water-skiing capital of the world. For good reason: A series of eighteen spring-fed lakes known as Chain O' Lakes, interconnected by navigable canals, provides unlimited opportunities for water-skiing, boating, fishing, and swimming. Forty percent of the city is covered by lakes or canals, which contributes to cooling in the summer and warming in the winter.

Housing is affordable, with homes selling way below national averages, and Winter Haven ranks as the fortieth most-economical city in the nation and possibly the lowest in Florida with regard to real estate. Much lakefront is open and park-like, but boat access is almost unlimited. Lakes away from Winter Haven commonly have homes with private docks. Health care is a major industry, with seven hospitals and ten medical centers scattered about the county.

Interstate 4 hustles traffic to Tampa or Orlando for serious shopping in short order, but shopping is more than adequate in Winter Haven and environs, with a large mall just off the interstate that rivals those in larger cities. The area is lucky to have daily Greyhound bus service to Tampa, Orlando, Jacksonville, and Miami. Disney World is thirty-five minutes away, Sea World forty-five minutes away, and Busch Gardens sixty minutes away. Granted, these distractions are not nearly as far away as one might wish.

Gainesville The home of the University of Florida, Gainesville is one of the most culturally stimulating cities in the state. It's interesting how much one university town can resemble another, with the same kinds of businesses, services, students, even similar street names. Large, old homes on tree-shaded streets, some converted to fraternity houses, along with unobtrusive university construction, recall memories of my own college days. The city's official nickname, "The Tree City," is appropriate.

You needn't be a student to participate in the many activities connected with the university. Theater for all tastes is highlighted by the Hippodrome, one of only four state theaters for the performing arts. Miracle on 34th Street is a cultural complex with museums of art and natural history as well as an 1,800-seat performing-arts center. The university's ongoing program of public lectures and other cultural events entertains many retirees in the area.

Gainesville was originally planned as a health resort. Described as the "Eden of the South" by its founder, the town was visualized as

a community with a "regular body of skilled physicians in attendance." In a way, this dream was fulfilled, since Gainesville is
number one when it comes to Florida health care. Four full-service
hospitals serve the area, including the university's nationally
renowned Shands Hospital, a 548-bed nonprofit facility.

Nearby wildlife areas provide great pleasure to bird-watchers
and to those interested in ecology. About 65 percent of the county's
965 square miles is a wilderness of forests and wetlands dotted with
scenic lakes.

As in most college towns, rentals are at a premium, except for
the summer quarter, when many students leave town. If a town of
90,000 is too large for you, the nearby communities of High Springs
and Archer are a fifteen-minute drive away. Housing costs less there
and small farms are affordable. Haile Plantation, an upscale golf-
course development, offers miles of walking/bicycle trails, tennis
courts, swimming pools, and other recreational amenities in addition to a new eighteen-hole golf course. This is but one of several
such entities.

Besides the 35,000-student university, there's the two-year
Santa Fe College with a student body of about 7,500. A walk
through its pleasant campus reveals a large percentage of students
here with gray hair. Tuition is free under most circumstances to
those age 60 and older. The extensive curriculum covers classes such
as dog training, computers, and antiques collecting. If you're
looking for Florida retirement in an intellectual climate, Gainesville
is the place to investigate.

For outdoors people there's plenty to do. A dozen nearby lakes
invite anglers, six of them with boat ramps. For golf, Ironwood, an
eighteen-hole, par-seventy-two, public golf course, is one of four
public or semi-private links. Thirty parks, many with tennis courts,
are publicly maintained. And, of course, either the Gulf or the Atlantic is a short drive away. The closest saltwater fishing is in Cedar
Key, a 49-mile drive to the Gulf. Driving time on Interstate 75 is
about two hours to Tampa Bay. The University of Florida Gators
football team draws fans from all over the nation and creates great
excitement with local residents. If indoor shopping is your favorite
sport, there's the million-square-foot Oaks mall, an enclosed shopping facility with five department stores and 150 other shops and
boutiques.

Ocala   Another of Florida's fast-growing areas, Ocala comprises a rapidly expanding retiree population. About one in four adults is age sixty-five or older. Its quiet, laid-back lifestyle attracts those who hate Northern winters, yet want to avoid the traffic jams and insanity of the beach cities. The cost of living here is the lowest in Florida, and the average selling price of real estate is the third lowest. New-home subdivisions as well as conventional homes in comfortable-looking neighborhoods offer a range of housing choices.

Ocala's downtown business district is rather orthodox, looking very much like a typical Midwestern agricultural town, with a traditional downtown square. This isn't surprising, since Ocala is an agricultural center. Modern malls and chain stores haven't totally killed the town center, as they have in some small cities.

The countryside is checkered with farms, especially horse farms. The area around Ocala is one of the most important thoroughbred-breeding areas in the country. There are even "farm subdivisions," developments where you can buy a few acres, a barn, and a house, and do small-scale farming or horse raising as your retirement hobby.

One retiree told us that he chose to live here because Ocala reminded him of the countryside where he grew up in northern Illinois. "The only thing it lacks is the ice and snow in the wintertime," he added. When asked about northern Florida summers, he replied, "I don't believe they are any hotter than they were back home. Anyway, whenever we get the notion, the wife and I drive an hour and twenty minutes to Daytona Beach and cool off in the Atlantic

GAINESVILLE–OCALA WEATHER						
In degrees Fahrenheit						
	Jan.	April	July	Oct.	Rain	Snow
Daily Highs	66	81	90	81	52"	—
Daily Lows	42	55	71	59		

GAINESVILLE-OCALA AREA COST OF LIVING					
	Overall	Housing	Medical	Groceries	Utilities
Percentage of National Average	95	92	101	99	98

Ocean. We can get there by nine in the morning and be home with sunburns by suppertime!"

Several inviting mobile-home parks surround Ocala. We inspected one park just an eight-minute drive from the Ocala city limits that had a country setting worthy of the name, yet with a Florida accent. Shaded by spreading oak trees, the mobile homes rest on large parcels along paved drives that wind through the park. A radio-operated gate keeps out high-pressure salespeople. The park's ample clubhouse hosts senior citizens' activities plus a swimming pool and tennis courts, creating an atmosphere conducive to quiet, slow-paced retirement.

Not only do Ocala's mobile-home parks range from ordinary to deluxe, but it's also possible to buy a few acres, or just a small lot, and install your own mobile home. Many small farms of five to fifty acres dot the countryside, with nothing but a mobile home and a barn on the property.

The Atlantic Coast

Palm Coast   Let's take a look at one of those multiple-use communities, one with beach, golf, tennis, and boating facilities all in one. This is not to be considered an advertisement or an endorsement of this particular community, but rather an example of similar communities found all over the state. Some are much more expensive and most are smaller. Palm Coast is interesting in that it

FLORIDA — ATLANTIC COAST

Palm Coast
Daytona Beach
Cocoa Beach

Melbourne

evolved from a large-scale development into an actual city of almost 50,000 residents; it is now a conventional community with no ties to the original developer.

Palm Coast is located halfway between St. Augustine and Daytona Beach—22 miles each way. A private ocean beach club (open to residents) is an easy walk or bike ride across the Intracoastal Waterway bridge. The planned community was developed by ITT Community Development Corporation over a two-decade span and is still underway.

As you exit Interstate 95 to enter the Palm Coast development, you immediately feel as if you have entered a park. The landscaped, four-lane parkway through residential and commercial areas is bordered by lush forests of oak and native palms. Bicycle and jogging paths meander through the landscaped commons and are fully used by Palm Coast residents and visitors.

Great pains were taken to preserve the semitropical aspects of the Florida natureland, with its magnificent tall trees, tangled vines, and indigenous palm trees. Housing and businesses are skillfully hidden behind the vegetation so that it appears to the casual visitor that most of the developments are natural parklands. The business district and shopping centers are tastefully landscaped and surrounded by a buffer of trees to keep noise and traffic away from residential areas. Of the original 42,000 acres in the development, 5,000 acres are set aside as a nature reserve.

This development wasn't planned solely as a place for retirement. Provisions were made for business parks and light, technology-oriented industry to provide jobs for the residents of Palm Coast. These areas are located near the interstate and screened from the residential areas by nature preserves, yet close enough for workers to walk or ride bicycles to work. The infusion of young couples and children adds a freshness to the face of Palm Coast, taking it out of the category of a retirement center.

Scattered through the complex are five championship golf courses, two of them designed by Arnold Palmer. The community tennis club is one of only four clubs in the country with clay, grass, and hard surface within the same complex. Sixteen hard-surface

PALM COAST WEATHER						
In degrees Fahrenheit						
	Jan.	April	July	Oct.	Rain	Snow
Daily Highs	68	80	89	81	48"	—
Daily Lows	47	59	72	65		

PALM COAST AREA COST OF LIVING					
Percentage of	Overall	Housing	Medical	Groceries	Utilities
National Average	95	92	101	99	98

courts draw players of all skill levels. The club is complete with an aerobics room, lockers, and restaurant.

Boating enthusiasts have their own private marinas at their back doors. The canals vary from 60 to 125 feet wide and are about 8 feet deep. Houses here cost considerably more than houses on ordinary streets, but are still surprisingly inexpensive. Not long ago, several canal properties were being offered from $150,000 to $180,000. New model homes start from the mid $70,000s to the $150,000 range. Because the development is mature, many older places are now on the market.

All Florida retirement communities are not created equal. Across the Intracoastal Waterway is another development (also by ITT Community Development Corporation) called Hammock Dunes. It also features golf courses and natural Florida landscaping, but on a lavish scale, along 5 miles of oceanfront. An impressive 32,000-square-foot clubhouse overlooks the Atlantic and a spectacular golf course. Prices for homes start at the mid-$200,000 range. Building lots vary from $150,000 to $875,000. "Exclusive" is the appropriate description here.

Daytona Beach   Daytona Beach is about 65 miles south of St. Augustine and is situated partly on the peninsula and partly on the mainland. Daytona's main tourist section is on the peninsula's ocean side rather than on the mainland. The city population is 65,000, with 100,000 in the metropolitan area. The 23-mile-long white sand beach is perhaps its most famous feature, one of the few places in Florida where autos are permitted to drive along the beach.

DAYTONA BEACH WEATHER					
In degrees Fahrenheit					
	Jan.	April	July	Oct.	Rain	Snow
Daily Highs	68	80	90	81	48"	—
Daily Lows	47	59	73	65		

DAYTONA BEACH AREA COST OF LIVING					
Percentage of	Overall	Housing	Medical	Groceries	Utilities
National Average	95	89	101	99	104

The only time to drive it is during low or outgoing tide, when it is hard packed and pavement-like. Many speed records have been set on this beach. Overnight parking or camping is not allowed.

The famous tourist area—on the peninsula—has a wide promenade, an amusement park, and a fishing pier to entertain vacationers. To keep tourism alive during the slow tourist months, automobile and motorcycle racing were instituted. Over the years, these events have gained wide media recognition, bringing racing enthusiasts from all over the nation. During important races, the fans outnumber the residents. This creates welcome revenue for Daytona Beach and the surrounding communities, but also produces some marvelous traffic jams. Local people pay close attention to the schedules and avoid the peninsula during races.

Daytona Beach is one of Florida's nicer-looking Atlantic cities, with graceful buildings on both the peninsula side and on the mainland, where the commercial district is located. As you drive across the connecting causeway, rows of mature tropical trees outline a pleasant view of downtown in the distance. Housing prices are among the lowest in the state, about 14 percent below the national average.

The Halifax River is part of the Intracoastal Waterway that stretches from the Florida Keys north to Chesapeake Bay. It's wide and sheltered—a perfect place for learning how to handle a sailboat before venturing into open water. Everything from fishing dinghies to freighters uses this channel to follow the coast. You can make it to the Florida Keys with very little exposure to the open ocean. A new development in Daytona Beach is the recently completed Halifax Harbor Marina, which is now the largest marina between Baltimore and Fort Lauderdale.

Rents in the tourist sector vary widely, depending upon the season, the view, and access to the beach. When buying something near the beach, always make sure you aren't buying into a party pad. Any complex where most units are rented to tourists by the week is liable to mean trouble. A clean-cut college student can invite the whole fraternity house for an around-the-clock animal party. Retirement-type housing is available on the peninsula, but most retirees prefer to live in the comparative peace and quiet of the mainland.

Some nearby communities worth investigating are Ormond Beach—where the famous daredevils like Barney Oldfield raced automobiles in attempts to break the one-time 60-mile-an-hour speed barrier—and New Smyrna Beach, which is as far as autos can be driven on the sand. This is where Canaveral National Seashore wildlife preserve begins, the refuge of alligators, turtles, manatees, and a marvelous variety of birds.

Where the wildlife preserve ends, the Canaveral Peninsula and the John F. Kennedy Space Center begin. New Symrna Beach, by the way, is one of the oldest settlements in America. Historians believe Ponce de Leon landed here in 1513.

Cocoa Beach to Melbourne   The "Space Coast" derives its name from the John F. Kennedy Space Center on the Canaveral Peninsula. All along this section of coast, from Cocoa Beach down to Melbourne and Melbourne Beach, is an attractive group of towns just made for retirement.

Cocoa Beach's commercial center is much larger than its actual population of 13,000 might indicate. Its downtown streets are lined with flower boxes and old-time village shops where folks can watch potters at work, leathersmiths making belts and hats, and skilled craftsmen restoring antiques. Cocoa Beach serves as a focal point for nearby cities such as Cocoa, Merritt Island, and Rockledge. The Canaveral Pier at Cocoa Beach extends almost 800 feet into the ocean, a great place for fishing, dining, and nightlife.

Cocoa Beach is home to many space–center workers and military families from nearby Cape Canaveral and Patrick Air Force Base. Cocoa Beach and the nearby towns have attracted a large share of military retirees, folks who liked the area when stationed here.

According to the local chamber of commerce, a good percentage of the population are retirees, and they are very active in politics. The number of services available to senior citizens reflects this. Thirteen

COCOA BEACH–MELBOURNE WEATHER					
In degrees Fahrenheit					
	Jan.	April	July	Oct.	Rain	Snow
Daily Highs	72	81	89	83	51"	—
Daily Lows	52	62	72	67		

apartment and housing complexes are for senior citizens. A good public transportation system is augmented by the free van service for wheelchair-confined residents provided by a local surfing shop.

A community college and a state university are located here, with plenty of activities that involve retired residents. Hospitals are within 45 miles and air transportation is 45 miles away.

The area has an interesting mixture of very expensive and very ordinary homes. All in all, prices seemed a bit higher than in other sections of the state, probably because of the nearby air bases and space industries. Even so, plenty of inexpensive homes and condos are on the market. Some developments and mobile-home parks near the ocean are having problems with water; be sure to check for drinkability before buying on the beach.

Sitting at the lower end of this famous coast is the largest of the towns, Melbourne, with a population of 60,000. Palm Bay, Merritt Island, and Satellite Beach are also part of Melbourne's shopping area. This is a relatively quiet area, at least compared to the hectic, tourist-clogged pace of nearby Orlando.

Melbourne itself is on the mainland; a causeway takes you to the beach town of Indiatlantic. And what a beach it is, with 33 miles of sandy, uncrowded Atlantic shore! At one time this beach was nicknamed the "Treasure Coast"; when a hurricane shipwrecked a fleet of Spanish ships against the shore, millions of Spanish doubloons spilled into the sea. The survivors—some 1,500 men, women, and children—spent three years trying to recover the treasure. Today, divers still keep their eyes peeled for coins and bullion.

During the summer, from May until September, loggerhead turtles visit the beaches to dig nests and lay eggs. As many as 12,000 nests are dug each season. Retirees are invited to join the Sea Turtle Preservation Society. The elusive manatee is often sighted around here, as well.

This coast is liberally endowed with attractive apartments, complete with swimming pools, tennis courts, and social directors, starting at $450 and going up. Single-family housing and condos are comparably priced.

Florida's Gold Coast

It all started back in the 1880s when two starry-eyed promoters, John and James Lummus, bought a barren spit of sand that jutted offshore from the southern Florida mainland. Lying in the indigo waters between Biscayne Bay and the Atlantic Ocean, their new purchase inspired a dream. They were convinced they could turn this worthless piece of land into a fabulously productive coconut plantation. They planted thousands of trees and sat back, waiting for them to mature and for tropical winds to shake the harvest to the ground.

FLORIDA'S GOLD COAST

Palm Beach
Ft. Lauderdale
Miami Beach

Florida Keys

However, things didn't work out that way. Blight cut the harvest potential and tree rats harvested more than did the plantation owners. Mosquitoes and other insects drove workers away, and finally the dream died. But the coconut trees survived. Later promoters saw a different promise: tourism and retirement. They called their new development "Miami Beach."

The boom started in the 1920s and spilled from Key Biscayne north to Fort Lauderdale, Pompano Beach, Boca Raton, all the way to Palm Beach and beyond. By the 1930s it was in full swing as a winter retreat and retirement haven. This is Florida's famous Gold Coast. A drive along the coastal highway will explain how it received its name. It certainly took a lot of gold to build it, and more to maintain it.

Individually, the cities from West Palm Beach down to Coral Gables don't appear to be particularly large. Miami has only 350,000 people, Miami Beach about 97,000, West Palm Beach only about 67,000. But, together the more than forty towns comprise one long, enormous metropolitan area of about 2.8 million people. These many communities spread along the beach have no chance of having a central focus or a common "downtown" area. Broken into a string of suburbs without an urban area to be suburban to, each has its own shopping center, stores, businesses, and its own small political entity. In this unconsolidated way, Florida's Gold Coast resembles Los Angeles.

Except for the classy sections along the beaches, most housing is single-family bungalows, low-profile condominiums, and expansive apartment complexes. In some of the less intensely developed areas, where things aren't so tightly packed, it's easy to forget that

GOLD COAST WEATHER					
	In degrees Fahrenheit				
	Jan.	April	July	Oct.	Rain	Snow
Daily Highs	75	82	89	84	60"	—
Daily Lows	56	65	74	70		

you are part of an urban sprawl. People commonly don't go shopping away from their area; they have no need to.

Along the Gold Coast you'll find the biggest contrasts in all of Florida. From tall forests of condominiums and apartments that remind you of New York's Park Avenue, to rows of tract houses reminiscent of Los Angeles, you'll find almost every imaginable type of housing and neighborhood—all within miles or sometimes yards of each other. Then, just 10 to 20 miles to the west, the land is uninhabited, totally the domain of wildlife.

The Miami Complex   This is the Florida you usually read about in your newspaper's travel section, the Florida you see on television and in movies. For some folks, the thought of living in such a crowded area is a turnoff. But for others, the amenities of a metropolitan area—combined with a mild climate and gorgeous beaches—add up to ideal retirement living. They adore everything about the Gold Coast. They love the convenience of well-stocked shopping centers, good medical facilities, and a wide array of restaurants. Folks here enjoy apartment living, having someone else wash windows, mow lawns, and trim shrubs. As one lady put it, "We've lived all our lives in or near Manhattan. We couldn't survive in some dinky, one-horse town where they roll up the sidewalks after dark!"

Curiously, in the midst of this densely packed, tropical replica of Manhattan, distinct concepts of neighborhood and community emerge. We've visited several large condominium developments and are always fascinated by the way folks create their own islands of interests and community. A typical complex, this one in Pompano Beach, has a dozen eight-story buildings set apart in a park-like setting. Each building has complete laundry facilities and an exercise room. Jogging paths, swimming pools and tennis courts are strategically placed about the grounds, and a clubhouse dominates the center.

MIAMI AREA COST OF LIVING					
Percentage of National Average	Overall 106	Housing 109	Medical 115	Groceries 105	Utilities 104

In effect, the development corresponds to a small town, or an intimate neighborhood in a larger city. The condo owners' association substitutes for city politics back home. Residents have a great time voting for officers, running for election, lobbying for pet projects, or trying to recall those who aren't doing their job. "I feel like I have a helluva lot more control and say-so about my neighborhood now, than I ever could hope for back in New York," said one resident who was in the middle of a fight to redecorate the clubhouse and install more outdoor lighting.

Another example is a condo development in Deerfield Beach, a place called Century Village East. It seems to be populated primarily by former New Yorkers, many of whom knew one another back home. Century Village is not only large, but well organized, so much so that it puts out an impressive forty-eight-page newspaper every month to carry news of the development's activities to the 8,000 residential units in the development. Residents have their own shopping center, golf course, even buses and trolleys. They elect members to serve in positions analogous to mayor, city council, etc.

As in any metropolitan area, living in the Gold Coast area has drawbacks. Higher crime rates, traffic jams, and crowded stores are pretty much standard. However, the crime picture is somewhat distorted in the Miami area because of vigorous commerce in illegal drugs. Presumably, you are not into drug dealing and won't be participating in car chases, revenge killings, and Mafia shoot-outs as featured on television shows. Therefore, statistics on drug busts, drive-by shootings, and gang-related activities should not affect you significantly—as long as you stay away from the dangerous neighborhoods. Robberies of tourists obviously will occur in tourist-clogged areas, places you would avoid under normal circumstances.

One important point: What metropolitan areas lack in peace and quiet, they more than make up for in services and conveniences for retirees. The larger the population, the more and better senior citizen centers, health care facilities, libraries, educational opportunities, and other advantages.

Florida Keys, the End of the Line   Except for Hawaii, this jumbled string of islands and reefs is the most tropical part of the United States. A highway follows the route of an old railway line, an engineering marvel in itself, 110 miles to the last of the accessible islands, Key West. The highway skips from one coral atoll to another over numerous causeways and bridges, across islands festooned with palm trees, hibiscus, and bougainvillea and bearing such romantic names as Key Largo, Islamorada, and Matacumbre.

Substantial numbers of retirees, both snowbirds and regular residents, populate these islands. Boating and fishing are top attractions, with year-round tropical weather the frosting on the cake. When it comes to snorkeling and diving, these islands are a virtual paradise. Folks here boast of the longest living reef in the Western Hemisphere, crystal-clear waters with visibility up to 100 feet, and more than 500 wrecks to explore.

Yachts are "in" throughout the Keys, large ones and small ones. Resident sailors simply cut berths into the coral and limestone backyards of their homes and tie up. Other houses are set back against networks of canals, where their occupants can dock after a day's adventure of fishing or treasure hunting in the warm waters of the Gulf Stream. You'll even find mobile homes with sloops moored at their floating patios.

At one time, Key West developed a reputation as a retreat and retirement spot for writers and artists. Wallace Stevens fell in love with Key West back in 1922, and in his poem "The Idea of Order in Key West" he praised it as "a summer without end." Having let the cat out of the bag, Stevens soon found himself in the company of other intellectuals who wanted to participate in this "summer without end." Ernest Hemingway, John Dos Passos, and Tennessee Williams all maintained houses in Key West. Some of their homes are now major tourist attractions.

The tradition of an artist colony continues, but in a somewhat diminished form. Key West has become incredibly crowded and overrun with tourists and weekending college students. Finding a parking place becomes a treasure hunt. Key West's tolerant openness to varying lifestyles and its "live and let live" attitude has encouraged the establishment of a considerable gay community. Because it's such a long drive from the mainland, over a snail's-pace, two-lane highway, and because housing costs in Key West are hardly bargains, our recommendations lean toward retirement farther up the line, in places like Key Largo or Marathon.

A perpetual problem facing those living on the Keys is the threat of hurricane-driven tides—another reason for living closer to the mainland. Everywhere you look, you'll find some (not all) homes and businesses raised off the ground 10 or 12 feet. Storm tides are the obvious reason; they simply wash underneath the houses without causing much damage. Flood insurance rates are considerably less with this type of construction. That's good. But being up in the air raises the chances of wind damage, so storm insurance is higher. That's bad.

Although somewhat more expensive than the mainland, Keys real estate can be reasonable, considering the unique location and special circumstances. On both Key Largo and Marathon we checked out several homes, some with canals at their backs, where motorboats, launches, and yachts were tied to individual docks. Three-bedroom places can be found for $100,000; make it $150,000 if you want your own boat dock. You can also pay much, much more, with spiffy places going for more than $750,000. Older, fixer-upper homes can sometimes be located for $60,000. (I'm always worried about that term, "fixer-upper.")

Florida's West Coast

FLORIDA'S WEST COAST

Hudson
Tampa/St. Petersburg
Sarasota
Port Charlotte/Punta Gorda
Fort Myers/Cape Coral
Bonita Springs
Naples
Marco Island

Like Central Florida, Gulf Coast retirees tend to come from different parts of the country than the northern Atlantic Coast. Instead of drawing its newcomers from New York and New England, a higher percentage of residents emigrate from Midwestern and Northern states. Therefore, it isn't surprising that architecture and lifestyles are more disposed toward Midwestern values. Instead of tall condos and apartments, the preferred style is low-profile, informal, and conservative. Single-family homes are the norm, sitting on lots often measured in acres rather than in square feet, with generous areas of lawn and landscaping.

The climate is different here, too. The weather-stabilizing Gulf Stream misses Florida's west coast. The result: summers along the gulf are hotter and winters a few degrees cooler than along the Gold Coast. But the folks who've retired here say it's worth it, and they point out that the relative humidity is lower than on the other coast.

This southwestern part of the state is one of our favorites. From Fort Myers/Cape Coral on down to Naples and Marco Island you'll find a wide assortment of neighborhoods as inexpensive as any developed part of Florida, or as luxurious as you might wish. Cape Coral's average sales price for existing homes is one of the lowest in the country, while Naples and Marco Island are among the most expensive in Florida. Sanibel Island also ranks up there in expense and carries an added handicap of not having any place to park.

Fort Myers and its sister city of Cape Coral are separated by the Caloosahatchee River. (No, I'm not making that up.) Neighboring Pine Island lies across a saltwater pass from Cape Coral. Fort Myers Beach is also an island, one of a string of them that shelter the coastline all the way south to Naples. In the middle are Bonita Springs and Bonita Beach, two excellent choices for in-between expensive and affordable retirement.

Formerly a cattle-growing area, population growth here is nothing short of phenomenal, an astonishing 600 percent in the last twenty years! Good transportation accounts for some of this growth; Interstate 75 shoots through the area, making it a snap to drive east to the Gold Coast or north to the Tampa Bay area in two and a half hours. Fort Myers also boasts an international airport. Medical care is excellent with the new Gulf Coast Hospital's discounts for senior citizens. A half dozen other hospitals and several nursing facilities serve the area as well.

This is definitely a winter snowbird haven—the population doubles between the first of November and Easter week. Then, when summer's humidity and over-90-degree weather sets in, the comfort-loving snowbirds fly home to cooler northern climes. But year-round residents protest when I suggest that summer might be harsh. "Check it out; it's just a little bit warmer than Miami Beach," they point out, "and it's a lot safer living around here!"

In addition to the usual saltwater sports associated with Florida's west coast, those with a fondness for gambling will enjoy greyhound racing at the Naples–Fort Myers Greyhound Track.

Betting on the doggies is fun and not very expensive at two bucks a bet.

Fort Myers/Cape Coral   Discovered early in the century by Henry Ford and Thomas Edison, Fort Myers has been booming since. The city's landscaping is a unique heritage left by Thomas Edison. He loved to experiment with trees and shrubs, particularly palm trees. Older residential areas are full of them, grown tall and mature over the decades since the great inventor planted them around town. It's claimed that more than seventy varieties of palms grace the streets of Fort Myers. Some stand tall and stately; others are short, with bottle-like trunks. A few flaunt astonishing leaf patterns that look as if they were created by fashion designers.

The overall theme of this area is one of prosperity, with very few sections of town looking seedy. Well-manicured lawns, flowering bushes, and magnolia trees give residential areas of Fort Myers a quiet, homey look. Edison Community College offers a profusion of classes, almost free, in their Lifelong Learning Center. Naturally, landscaping is one of the more popular courses.

Fort Myers and North Fort Myers have a combined population of about 90,000, about the same as sister city Cape Coral. The island of Fort Myers Beach—population 14,000—fronts the city of Fort Myers and provides open access to the Gulf, making it a popular place for homes with boat docks. The 7-mile-long island is tightly packed with small homes, condos, and beachfront properties. It's only about three-quarters of a mile wide. For being close to such a popular beach, prices are affordable, but winter traffic on the island can be horrific and the number of tourists along the beachfront appalling. Be aware that Fort Myers Beach's population *triples* during the winter. A few blocks off the beach, confusion and noise greatly diminish, that's true, but this is a place for the young at heart and possibly the hard of hearing.

Throughout the area is a profusion of condos, some sitting on the edge of their own nine-hole golf courses. Condo styles seem quite practical: mostly two stories with bedrooms upstairs and no other families living overhead or underfoot. Condominium developers have been generous in providing spacious lawn areas between the condos, so you don't have the cramped, hemmed-in feeling that comes with east Florida multi-story skyscrapers and asphalt parking lots.

FORT MYERS–NAPLES WEATHER					
In degrees Fahrenheit					
	Jan.	April	July	Oct.	Rain	Snow
Daily Highs	74	85	91	85	54"	—
Daily Lows	53	62	74	68		

FORT MYERS-CAPE CORAL AREA COST OF LIVING					
Percentage of	Overall	Housing	Medical	Groceries	Utilities
National Average	96	87	98	99	120

Mobile home parks are plentiful. Most are beautifully land-scaped and offer organized activities in their clubhouses and recreational facilities. Some are downright luxurious, some super-expensive, and others quite affordable.

For quiet, rural island retirement, Pine Island is the place. Seventeen miles long and about two miles wide, this is the largest of the barrier islands in these parts. Its shores are almost completely ringed with mangrove estuaries, many in wildlife preserves. As its name implies, the island is rustic, covered with pines, and retirement housing is inexpensive. Approximately 8,000 year-round residents are joined by another 4,000 during the winter months.

Pine Island is accessed from Cape Coral via a fishing bridge that crosses over to Matlacha and Little Pine islands. This is known as "Florida's Fishingest Bridge," and at almost any time, day or night, you are apt to see fishermen dipping their lines into Matlacha Pass. This area is a throwback to the time when tiny fishing villages were the norm along the southwest coast. The western shore sits in the lee of Captiva Island, which makes the water safe for sailing and peaceful fishing.

Naples/Marco Island/Bonita Springs   Those accustomed to going first-class will want to check out Naples and nearby Marco Island. Naples dominates a stretch of public beaches 41 miles long. It's one of the fastest-growing upscale communities in Florida. One section of Naples, appropriately called Venice, is a modern-day re-creation of its Italian namesake, with luxury condos and some of the finest shops and boutiques on Florida's west coast built right down on the water line.

NAPLES/BONITA SPRINGS AREA COST OF LIVING

Percentage of National Average	Overall	Housing	Medical	Groceries	Utilities
	110	124	106	101	103

Naples has the reputation of being super-expensive, and it is if compared with nearby Florida communities. Yet many impressive neighborhoods of lovely landscaping, mature shade trees, and upscale housing look like bargains to folks from some parts of the country. A home costing $350,000 here couldn't be duplicated for twice that amount in the spiffy parts of California or New York.

This is the western terminus of the Tamiami Trail, a famous highway that cuts right through the Everglades. In addition to golf and the usual Florida pastimes, swamp–buggy racing is popular in the Marco Island–Naples area. Hopped-up swamp machines are run in special events in October to mark the beginning of the Everglades hunting season.

Bonita Springs, about fifteen minutes north of Naples and twenty minutes south of Fort Myers, is a mixed affordable/luxury community. The year-round population is around 25,000. Great beaches are about four minutes from town at Bonita Shores, which is a kind of "less expensive Naples." My impression is this beach is patronized more by local folks rather than tourists, which makes it much less zoo-like. The entire area is much more laid-back and quiet than the northern beaches. The water temperature of the Gulf is about 71 degrees in the winter and 84 in the summer, which translates into pleasant swimming.

Many homes are built on canals with open water access, thus making boating and yachting popular pastimes here. The average selling price of these places is about 50 percent higher than homes in conventional neighborhoods. Overall, home prices in this area are higher than Florida averages, higher than national averages as well.

Port Charlotte/Punta Gorda Not far north from Fort Myers, on expansive Charlotte Harbor, the cities of Punta Gorda and Port Charlotte display interests different from their neighbors. Beaches aren't the big deal here; instead, residents focus on the miles of man-made canals and waterways that cut through their neighborhoods like boulevards. More than 150 miles of these man-made waterways provide easy access to the Gulf for thousands of boating and fishing enthusiasts. As one resident pointed out, "The water is so clean and unpolluted here, we don't hesitate to swim or water-ski right here in town." The Myakka River and the harbor make possible some of the best fishing and boating in the state.

Having a boat tied up in the backyard is as common as having an automobile in the garage. Prices for these waterside residences are surprisingly affordable, probably because they are so common, and you'll notice some rather ordinary houses backed up to the waterways with more invested in the sailboats and yachts than in the homes. Boaters are quick to point out, however, that waterways in neighborhoods to the west of the Tamiami Trail—the main highway that bisects Port Charlotte—must pass under low bridges. Only boats with low profiles—motorboats or small sailboats with masts that can be lowered—can make their way to salt water. So, if you're a fan of tall-masted ships, better look on the saltwater side of the river, otherwise you'll never make it out to open water. Perhaps this is why some neighborhoods on Port Charlotte's west side benefit from such exceptionally low property prices. Everyone wants to be on the "saltwater side."

Port Charlotte is large, population about 95,000, but it doesn't have a city feeling. It spreads out along the Tamiami Trail (Highway 41), with businesses and malls scattered along the highway rather than concentrated in a downtown civic center. Just a block or so off the main thoroughfare, tranquil neighborhoods offer peaceful havens.

Punta Gorda, a smaller place with fewer than 20,000 inhabitants, sits just across the Peace River from Port Charlotte. It's older, more sedate, and housing can be fairly expensive. This is because most homes are built on one of Punta Gorda's 85 miles of navigable canals, all of which can provide access to the Gulf.

PORT CHARLOTTE WEATHER						
In degrees Fahrenheit						
	Jan.	April	July	Oct.	Rain	Snow
Daily Highs	74	85	91	85	54"	—
Daily Lows	53	62	74	68		

Every February, local people commemorate Ponce de Leon's reputed visit to Charlotte Harbor with a festival complete with conquistador costumes. They reenact the Spaniard's historic landing on the shore of Charlotte Harbor in his stubborn search for the Fountain of Youth.

From Port Charlotte, along the 30 miles of highway down to Fort Myers, are some most impressive mobile-home developments. Some parks are country clubs in every sense of the term. They aren't cheap, but they are well worth a visit even if you can't afford them, just to see how the other half lives. In some developments you purchase the lot your home sits on, in other places you lease, and in still others you rent. Each system has its own advantages and drawbacks, as explained earlier.

Tampa–St. Petersburg   Separated by Tampa Bay, the twin cities of St. Petersburg and Tampa are connected by three causeways. Interstate 275, the area's main link to southern Florida, crosses the wide mouth of Tampa Bay on yet another long causeway as it heads south to Bradenton. Together, the cities and their suburbs have about 1.6 million people, making it the second-largest metropolitan area in Florida. Although many retire here, the best places are nearby.

St. Petersburg (pop. 250,000) is famous for its proclaimed year-round sunshine; the local newspaper has a standing pledge to give away a newspaper every day the sun doesn't peek out at least some. On one visit it was overcast all day. I'm still waiting for my free newspaper. According to the U.S. Weather Bureau, the Tampa–St. Petersburg area can expect an average of 127 cloudy days a year and 107 days of rain. This surprised me, especially when I compared these figures to San Francisco, a place famous for foggy and overcast days. Turns out that San Francisco averages 100 cloudy days and only 67 days with rain.

St. Petersburg entered into the retirement business long ago, advertising in newspapers around the country, stressing its great climate and emphasizing the pleasant retirement possibilities here. It worked so well that the city soon became overrun with senior citizens. The city fathers then changed the advertising campaign to attract industry and younger people. The story goes that the city even removed park benches in an effort to discourage senior citizens from "hanging out." Perhaps they were concerned about gangs of

geriatric delinquents getting out of hand. That didn't discourage retirees; they kept on coming, probably bringing their own park
benches.

The emphasis on retirement here is not necessarily either St. Petersburg or Tampa, but surrounding, smaller locations, using the
metropolitan area as a central focus. The nearby towns of Sarasota
and Bradenton to the south and Clearwater, Indian Shores, Tarpon
Springs, and a dozen other communities north of St. Petersburg are
all pleasant places for retirement. Clearwater is famous for its
stretch of pure white sand beach. North of Tampa, along Interstate
75, you'll find another series of great prospects, particularly for inexpensive mobile-home living, in farming communities with affordable acreages and a down-home country atmosphere, yet minutes
from big-city life.

Sarasota is our particular favorite in this area. Apparently,
others agree with us, for *Money* magazine recently ranked Sarasota
among the "Top 20 Places to Retire" and fourteenth on its "Best
Places to Live in the U.S." list, and *Southern Living* named Sarasota
County "the nation's per capita arts capital."

With its own opera and symphony, bolstered by the Ringling
Museum and School of Art and the Asolo Theater, Sarasota can be
considered the culture capital of the state, attracting a population—
many of them retirees—that supports the arts. We have a friend who
resides here, a portrait artist, who has lived in and visited just about
every part of the country, including Hawaii, but chooses to live here
because of the city's comparatively low population density and
leisurely pace.

You'll find a wide selection of housing choices here, from small
cottages in renovated neighborhoods to luxury condominiums and
mansions on the Gulf, to smaller apartment complexes throughout
the city. Miles of beaches are within a few minutes of almost any residential area, and a protected bay and marina make boating and
fishing popular activities. Golfers and tennis enthusiasts enjoy the
city's many public and private golf courses and tennis courts.

Saltwater fishing is one of Tampa Bay's outdoor attractions.
Fishermen are out in early summer for silver king tarpon and then
kingfish in early fall. By the way, fishing licenses aren't required in
Florida for residents over age sixty. Baseball fans might be interested
to know that this coast is the winter home for the New York Yan-

TAMPA–ST. PETERSBURG WEATHER					
In degrees Fahrenheit					
	Jan.	April	July	Oct.	Rain	Snow
Daily Highs	70	82	90	84	47"	—
Daily Lows	49	61	74	65		

TAMPA–ST. PETERSBURG COST OF LIVING					
	Overall	Housing	Medical	Groceries	Utilities
Percentage of National Average	98	94	110	100	111

kees, Toronto Blue Jays, Tampa Bay Devil Rays, Pittsburgh Pirates, and the Philadelphia Phillies. Another popular sport in "St. Pete" is greyhound racing. Admission is reasonable; the track makes it up on the pari-mutuel (rabbits get in free). For golf addicts, about seventy golf courses dot the surrounding area.

For cultural balance the metropolitan area supports two theater groups, a ballet, and an opera company. Nine art museums, including two at the university and the Museum of Fine Arts, complete the schedule. Numerous hospitals and medical specialists ensure good health care.

Sun Coast North of Tampa–St. Petersburg is another area largely ignored by retirement writers. Local public relations folks call this area Florida's "Sun Coast." In our estimation, this is one of the more practical retirement areas in the state from several angles. Long stretches of Highway 19 are largely undeveloped, with many patches of affordable and quality housing. As Highway 19 goes north from Clearwater, it passes through several moderately settled areas and finally thins out into open farmland and untouched forest. Parts of it are as rural as you'll find in the state.

New housing developments and livable mobile-home parks spice up pleasant towns such as Hudson, Crystal Springs, and Homosassa. We especially liked the name of one town: Weeki Wachee. (As you've probably already guessed, Weeki Wachee is just south of the town of Chassahowitzka and is within easy striking distance of nearby Withlacoochee State Forest.)

Roadside signs and billboards clearly affirm the Sun Coast's

		In degrees Fahrenheit				
SUN COAST WEATHER						
	Jan.	April	July	Oct.	Rain	Snow
Daily Highs	70	82	90	84	47"	—
Daily Lows	49	61	74	65		

dedication to retirement services. Large billboards announce items of interest to senior citizens, services such as cataract surgery, arthritis clinics, hearing aids, and cardiac care. A billboard announces a large-print book fair, another advertises supplementary Medicare policies.

From Clearwater north, stores and businesses crowd the main route (U.S. Highway 19) and begin thinning out past New Port Richey. Even though much of this portion of the route sometimes seems to be one long shopping center, just a block off the highway in either direction you will find quiet residential areas.

But then, as you drive further north, population becomes sparse. Abandoned gift shops, motels, and restaurants give mute testimony that tourist traffic along this highway has fallen away drastically. My guess is that construction of Interstate 75, which parallels Highway 19, drew the flow of tourist traffic away onto its faster, 65-mile-an-hour route. For those entrepreneurs who hoped to make a killing from selling milkshakes and souvenirs to tourists, this must have been devastating, but for the retiree who hates heavy highway traffic, it is a boon. This is the lightest-traveled highway I've yet to drive in Florida—with divided pavement and few competing autos. The most important roadside signs caution motorists to watch for deer crossing the road.

Florida's Panhandle

Starting from Tallahassee, the state's capital, and stretching westward to Pensacola, Florida's Panhandle is different from most of the state. Pure white sand beaches and enterprising resort towns clearly remind you that you're in Florida, but the Panhandle also borrows from

nearby Georgia and Alabama. There's a "down-home" atmosphere here; the native accent is Deep South, the thinking is pure country. Many Southerners and Midwesterners feel especially comfortable with this combination of resort-country retirement living. Our research shows many Panhandle locations have personal safety statistics similar to those of Alabama and Georgia, which contrasts pleasantly with statistics for the Gold Coast.

It's the Gulf Coast beaches that draw outsiders for vacationing and tempt them to return later for retirement. Seeing the coast requires a drive over peaceful, slow-moving Highway 98. This lone highway follows the coast through many small towns, fishing villages, and an occasional town of size. The gulf's gentle waters lie just a few feet from the pavement's edge, and the northern side of the road is bordered by wilderness that sometimes extends 50 miles to the north without human habitation. You can drive for miles seeing nothing but a few cabins or an occasional mobile home set back into a clearing in the pines and moss-draped oaks.

Most towns and villages along the way are fishing centers. Fishermen unload their catches and sell them to wholesale and retail outlets. Tiny restaurants offer steamed crab, fresh oysters, fried mullet, and other seafood delicacies to eat there or to take with you. Trucks line up at a multitude of fish wholesalers to rush the produce of the sea to restaurants all over the South. And, of course, numerous bait shops and boat rentals take care of the amateur fisherman. Ninety percent of Florida's oysters come from this area, particularly from around Apalachicola, where 10,000 acres of oyster beds are maintained.

The main tourist and retiree attraction is a 100-mile length of beach that begins at the little town of Mexico Beach and runs westward to Pensacola. Many folks who eventually retire along this coast are those who regularly spent their summer vacations here with their families. They fondly remember summers on the white sand beaches and fishing expeditions far out on the gulf's blue waters.

Apalachicola   The stretch along Highway 98 from Lighthouse Point to Port St. Joe passes through some rather interesting and historical towns; the only one large enough to be called a small city is Apalachicola. Although most of Florida is new, with buildings

APALACHICOLA WEATHER					
In degrees Fahrenheit					
	Jan.	April	July	Oct.	Rain	Snow
Daily Highs	61	75	88	78	55"	—
Daily Lows	45	61	75	62		

from the 1920s considered antiques, Apalachicola is a fascinating treasure trove of pre–Civil War memorabilia, a quiet town steeped in the past. Homes built in the 1830s aren't unusual. Stately, two-story, wood-frame or brick mansions and churches seemingly imported from New England sit adjacent to a business district that looks as if it had been transported from a Mississippi River levee of a hundred years ago.

The downtown section slopes gently down to abandoned docks by the Apalachicola River. The old buildings were constructed of handmade brick at least 150 years ago. One gets the feeling that this could be Natchez, Vicksburg, or some other Deep South river town. Before the Civil War, this was one of the largest shipping ports on the Gulf, surpassed only by Mobile and New Orleans. When war broke out between North and South, the port was used to smuggle in supplies for the Confederates.

The town is full of historic buildings with selling prices the same as ordinary old houses. For anyone who is into restoring old homes, this would be a great place to pick up a piece of history at a bargain price.

Whether Apalachicola or any other place along this stretch of the Gulf would be a plausible retirement haven depends a lot on your personality. If you like quiet, with not too many tourists messing in your life, and if fishing and seafood are important, you might take a look here.

Panama City   About 20 miles west of Apalachicola the land ends abruptly at Cape San Blas, and the highway makes a right-angle turn north toward Port St. Joe. From here, all the way to the Alabama state line, two main features characterize this part of Florida's Panhandle: military bases and powder-white beaches.

From Port St. Joe to Pensacola are more than a dozen little towns that cater to tourists and retirees. Often no more than a few

EMERALD COAST AREA WEATHER					
In degrees Fahrenheit					
	Jan.	April	July	Oct.	Rain	Snow
Daily Highs	61	77	90	79	61"	—
Daily Lows	43	59	74	59		

PANAMA CITY AREA COST OF LIVING					
	Overall	Housing	Medical	Groceries	Utilities
Percentage of National Average	97	88	98	100	99

blocks wide, the towns string along the highway and beach in a very laid-back manner. Single-family homes, duplexes, and small apartments are available for either seasonal or year-round rental. Some stretches of high-rise construction would do justice to Florida's Gold Coast, however. During the winter months these little towns are quiet, but summers make up for this bustle deficit. The largest population center is Panama City (pop. 36,662). Like many towns in this area, Panama City has a dual personality. One side is that of a happy summer resort, the other a peaceful winter retreat. From November until March, the beaches are uncrowded and quiet. About the only tourists you'll see are speaking French with a Quebec accent. So many French Canadians congregate here in the winter that one begins to wonder who's tending to business in Montreal. But with warmer weather, the French Canadians go home just as Midwesterners arrive for their turn at the beaches.

An offshoot of the Gulf Stream known as the "Yucatan Current" moves close to Panama City. It tends to warm the water in the winter just a tad. This flow also brings nutrient-rich waters from the Caribbean and, with it, schools of sport fish. Fishermen haul in marlin, sailfish, tuna, and dolphin, as well as buckets of panfish. A fishing pier extends about 1,600 feet into the Gulf for the convenience of anglers. To a certain extent, the Yucatan Current moderates summer weather, but not to any appreciable amount. This doesn't deter the tourists, because as one of the natives pointed out, "It flat cain't get too hot for tourists!"

You needn't live on the beach to enjoy Gulf Coast living. Many folks reside in nearby towns just a twenty-minute drive from the sand and surf. Callaway, Springfield, Lynn Haven, and others are preferred by many retirees, particularly those who aren't captivated by the busy beach scene.

Part of the dual personality is the question of seasonal apartment and home rentals. In the off-season most rents drop rapidly, just as you would expect, but beach condos vary wildly, depending on season and demand. Housing prices along this coast are among the lowest in the nation, a good 12 percent below national averages.

The Emerald Coast   Between Panama City and Pensacola stretches a selection of towns ranging from ordinary to luxurious. A particularly interesting area circles a large body of water known as Choctawhatchee Bay. This is the self-styled "Emerald Coast." It includes the town of Navarre and a dozen other little towns, but does not include Seagrove Beach. Some places look very comfortable, and living isn't too expensive. Other towns look as if they coddle tourists to the *nth* degree. The skyscraper-type condo towers would look right at home on Miami Beach. Despite the tourist factor, the area enjoys an unusually low crime rate.

Major towns on the bay are Fort Walton Beach and Destin, which seem to blend together into one city with a combined population of around 40,000. Valparaiso is the second city across the bay. Personnel at Eglin Air Force Base account for much of the off-season business activity as well as the high numbers of retired military who live around Choctawhatchee Bay.

The long string of beaches here is famous for having some of the whitest, cleanest and softest sand in the world. According to geologists, the beaches are composed mainly of quartz washed down from the Appalachians via the Apalachicola River, some 130 miles east of Fort Walton Beach. By the time they get to Fort Walton Beach, the grains have been polished into tiny ovals that cause the sand to squeak when you walk along the dry part of the beach. Local residents are conservation-minded and are working hard to prevent erosion. Fishing is said to be wonderful both on the beach side and particularly good in the bay itself. A fishing pier at Navarre Beach, on Santa Rosa Island, is a popular loafing place for local retirees.

Okaloosa Island, where Fort Walton Beach and Destin are located, is one of several barrier islands that protect the mainland. The bay is sheltered and makes for great swimming, boating, and picnicking. This is the place to look if you insist on living within blocks of the water. Winter rentals are inexpensive and plentiful during the off-season, but expect to pay your dues during the rest of the year.

For the area's best bargains in housing and rentals, check around Niceville and other communities on the mainland side of the bay. About a 25-mile drive along a divided highway is Crestview, near Interstate 10. Real estate prices here are also favorable for retirees, and the interstate brings Pensacola's hospitals and services within a forty-five-minute drive.

Pensacola   The Spanish recognized Pensacola as an excellent seaport when they settled here in 1559. With both an offshore island and a peninsula barrier against storm-driven tides, the town is quite secure from the scourge of hurricanes.

Pensacola has a checkered history, its political allegiance changing thirteen times—among Spain, France, England, the Confederacy, and the United States. (Flag-making must have been a bustling cottage industry.) Its growth from when I worked here in 1952 has been phenomenal, changing from a small town into a modern city of more than 60,000.

Its beaches are extensive, with pretty white sand. But they're becoming covered with condos. Summer sees a greater influx of younger people than in other parts of the Panhandle coast. You'll find an emphasis on things like discos and bars that might be downplayed elsewhere. That shouldn't deter retirees, since they'll be living away from the hustle and bustle of the beach scene.

PENSACOLA AREA WEATHER						
In degrees Fahrenheit						
	Jan.	April	July	Oct.	Rain	Snow
Daily Highs	61	77	90	79	61"	—
Daily Lows	43	59	74	59		

PENSACOLA AREA COST OF LIVING					
Percentage of	Overall	Housing	Medical	Groceries	Utilities
National Average	96	85	104	103	94

Pensacola is the choice of many military retirees. Eglin Air Force Base, Whiting Field Naval Air Station, and the Pensacola Naval Air Academy ring the town. Upon retirement, pilots who've served here naturally recall the attraction of the Panhandle's "Riviera" beaches and the convenience of military medical and base-exchange privileges.

Other Panhandle towns also have military bases. Tyndall Air Force Base, with 6,300 personnel, starts just west of Mexico Beach and extends to Panama City. There's also a Naval Coastal Systems center in Panama City, with about 2,300 personnel. Next is Eglin Air Force Base, and finally Pensacola's Naval Air Station. The military presence is significant indeed, with large payrolls supporting the economy because many civilians work on the bases.

The Gulf Coast States

FIVE STATES CURVE AROUND the Gulf of Mexico's 2,000 miles of northern shoreline, forming a sort of private sea. Western Florida and the Panhandle account for more than a third of the gulf's coastline; the other states are Alabama, Mississippi, Louisiana, and Texas. Long strands of sparkling beaches alternate with miles of saltwater marsh, the home of egrets, herons, roseate spoonbills, and dozens of other shorebird species. Wildlife sanctuaries abound. Fishing ports, sheltered bays, and natural harbors protected by offshore islands make saltwater sports convenient and productive. Gulf waters teem with life: shrimp, pompano, flounder, speckled trout, plus weird specimens like blowfish, rays, and robbinfish. No telling what might attack your bait.

Sometimes a highway will run along the coast, just a few yards from the water. Other places are accessible only by boat or swamp buggy. Some towns are tourist-oriented, with large throngs of summer vacationers crowding the beaches. Other towns are quiet and reserved primarily for the enjoyment of residents. Not everyone chooses to live by the beach; more find their retirement inland, where other, non-marine attractions entice them to live.

Large, modern cities provide cultural and medical facilities prized by retirees. Quaint towns with friendly neighbors make transitions into retirement easy. Gracious old Southern mansions, moss-draped bayous and Southern hospitality are all part of the setting. To all of this add a four-season climate that varies from semitropical to warm-temperate, and you have a formula that spells successful retirement.

The cost of living in these states is as favorable as you'll find anywhere in the nation, and personal safety in the smaller towns is also gratifying. Some parts of the Gulf Coast states offer the most inexpensive housing we've ever seen. Wages are lower, to match the living costs. These economic benefits are offset somewhat by above-average utility costs in some locales.

Many people have images of the South that aren't so idyllic. The news media of thirty years ago highlighted a dramatic struggle for civil rights—complete with violence and tragedy—as citizens of color fought for the right to vote and to be treated with dignity, as equals under the law. These impressions of conflict, social injustice, and poverty were vivid and fade slowly.

This lingering bad press is unfortunate, because the South has undergone tremendous change over the past three decades, resulting in a 180-degree turnabout in the general conscience of the region. The younger generations often express difficulty understanding just what the fighting was all about. Few can imagine a world where people should be prevented from participating in society because of skin color, or where they should drink from separate water fountains or sit in designated sections of buses and theaters.

I don't believe that all Southerners have suddenly changed into color-blind liberals, totally free of racism and full of brotherly love. My point and opinion is that the overall Southern attitude toward race relations has taken a dramatic turn for the better. From my perspective, the South today harbors no more racism than the rest of the country. I'm convinced of this.

You might well accuse me of damning with faint praise, but as we know from media reports, some regions of our country harbor extremely racist organizations and militants dedicated to racial hatred. And in some northern states such as Michigan and Pennsylvania, extreme racist organizations stoke fires of hatred. According to the Southern Poverty Law Center, many regions in the United States harbor greater amounts of racial prejudice than most Southern locations.

Alabama

This is one of the nation's most active states when it comes to seeking out retirees and creating a welcoming environment for them. Over the past fifteen years, Alabama's share of retirement immigrants climbed from twentieth in the country to fifth. Part of this is due to a state-funded program called Alabama Advantage for Retirees, which works intensively at getting the news out about retirement opportunities within the state. Many Alabama communities participate in this program and deserve special mention as retirement destinations.

Alabama's convenient location midway between the northern states and Florida, its mild winter climate, and crime rates as much as 20 percent lower than the national average are important to many potential retirees, but there's much more. Among other enticements, Alabama combines quality living with one of the country's most favorable living costs. Tax burdens are lowest in the nation. For example, the property tax on a $100,000 home (way above the median sales price here) assesses out at about $300—often less, depending on the community. No, that isn't $300 each *quarter*, it's $300 for the *year!*

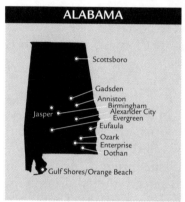

ALABAMA

Scottsboro
Gadsden
Anniston
Birmingham
Alexander City
Jasper
Evergreen
Eufaula
Ozark
Enterprise
Dothan
Gulf Shores/Orange Beach

Real estate is among the most affordable in the nation, with average new and resale home prices under $80,000. Other economic advantages for retirees include most pensions being exempt from taxes and free fishing and hunting licenses for residents sixty-five years of age and older. Alabama's colleges and universities offer free or reduced tuition to residents age sixty or over. Some private schools offer tuition discounts, special classes, and access to recreation and cultural programs for retirees.

ALABAMA TAX PROFILE

Sales tax: 4% to 9%, drugs exempt
State income tax: graduated, 2% to 5% over $3,000; deductible from federal income tax
Property taxes: average 0.3%, probably lowest in nation
Intangibles tax: no
Social security taxed: no
Pensions taxed: Most pensions exempt from taxes
Gasoline tax: 16¢ per gallon, plus possible local taxes

But Alabama's more than just a low-cost place to live; it's a state of multiple lifestyle choices and retirement opportunities. As more and more "outsiders" take up residence, the population becomes more cosmopolitan, making transition into the community easier.

Gulf Shores/Orange Beach   Because of the rude manner in which Florida's Panhandle elbows Alabama aside to hog the Gulf of Mexico shoreline, you wouldn't expect Alabama to have any beach at all. Look at a map and you'll see what I mean. Florida's Panhandle runs from the Georgia state line almost to Mobile in the west. However, visitors are flabbergasted at the quality and beauty of Alabama's 32-mile beach that fronts the Gulf between Pensacola and Mobile. It clearly matches anything Florida has to offer, and it's peaceful and relatively uncrowded.

Mobile—Alabama's only large Gulf Coast location—like most large cities, is best considered as a commercial center, a place for serious shopping and entertainment, with ideal retirement away from the metropolitan area. Traditional candidates for nearby retirement are Fairhope and Daphne. But because the city of Mobile is only about 15 miles distant, these towns have become "bedroom communities" for those working in the city. As such, property has become more costly and the percentage of retirees has fallen off in recent years.

On the other hand, the two small towns that comprise Alabama's Gulf Coast "Riviera" are fast becoming a choice destination for retirees, particularly with golf nuts and fishermen. Traditionally a roost for thousands of snowbirds each winter season, Gulf Shores (pop. 5,000) and Orange Beach (pop. 3,000) entice winter visitors to become permanent residents when they retire. White sand beaches, great fishing, and friendly neighbors are persuasive arguments that help retirees make up their minds about Alabama's Gulf Coast. Luxury retirement villages are making an appearance to accommodate newcomers.

GULF SHORES/ORANGE BEACH WEATHER						
In degrees Fahrenheit						
	Jan.	April	July	Oct.	Rain	Snow
Daily Highs	61	78	91	79	64"	—
Daily Lows	41	58	73	56		

GULF SHORES/ORANGE BEACH AREA COST OF LIVING					
Percentage of	Overall	Housing	Medical	Groceries	Utilities
National Average	92	85	83	95	107

World-class saltwater fishing is a strong drawing card. The largest charter-boat fleet on the Gulf Coast is located in Orange Beach, and seven golf courses are within a twenty-minute drive. There is an emphasis on golf communities, with seven golf courses nearby. As one resident put it, "We're becoming a mini-Myrtle Beach, minus the traffic, noise, and flash."

An interesting diversity of retirees gives Gulf Shores and Orange Beach a cosmopolitan flavor not common in smaller resort towns. Because retirees come from all parts of the country, they bring a rich mixture of interests and talents. Year-round residents love to participate in art shows, theater, concerts, and other cultural pursuits. Winter tourists bring a blessing to Gulf Coast businesses: This means seasonal part-time jobs are available for those who want them.

Even though the population is small, health care is adequate. Because of the number of elderly tourists each season, this area has an unusual number of paramedics, perhaps the highest per capita in the nation. A hospital is located in nearby Foley, just 5 miles from Gulf Shores. Foley, by the way, is a popular place because of its manufacturer's outlet stores of the "shop-till-you-drop" genre. For big-ticket items, Pensacola is just a 30-mile drive, and Mobile is about an hour away.

Dothan   Before we discovered some of Alabama's better retirement locations, we kept hearing about a town called Dothan (pronounced *DOE*-than). Readers would ask, "Why don't you mention Dothan in your books?" We checked our Alabama road map and were puzzled why a place in the corner of southeast Alabama should have something special going for it. We received so many inquiries that we decided to take a look for ourselves. We're glad we did.

Dothan (pop. 54,000) and its neighboring communities combine a pleasant Alabama location with an unusually diverse retiree population. Folks come from all over the world to settle here. This is partly due to nearby Fort Rucker, home of the world's largest international helicopter–training center; military families from around the world remember Dothan when making retirement plans. Post-exchange privileges and access to military medical services make it a natural.

But there's another interesting source of Dothan's unique diversity: a growing colony of civilian retirees from the Panama Canal Zone. Between 100 and 120 families have moved to Dothan to begin (or resume) their retirement careers. With the canal now having been transferred to Panama, more families are on the way.

How did such an unlikely place as southeast Alabama become a mecca for folks who lived most of their lives in tropical Panama? It started some years back when one canal zone employee convinced his wife to retire in his home state of Alabama instead of staying in Panama, as most others did. When they returned for visits, they talked so much about the charms and advantages of Dothan that others began visiting and eventually moving here. The treaty between Panama and the United States, which returned control over the canal to Panama, really started the ball rolling. With an unclear future ahead and no roots any place outside Panama, many decided to look more closely into Dothan.

The city and its businesses sensed a trend and, in an effort to draw as many retirees into the community as possible, sponsored emissaries to Panama to spread the word about the advantages of moving to Dothan. Obviously, it worked.

However, the influx of retirees here is more than just an accident. The biggest draw is the high quality of life, which is reflected in the lovely neighborhoods throughout the area. Quiet, tree-shaded streets with large lawns and elegant homes reflect well-kept neighborhoods and pride of ownership. The flowering trees in the spring and colorful leaves in the fall make changes of season a delight here. Visitors come every spring to follow the trail of pink along the Azalea–Dogwood Trail event.

As is the case in most of Alabama, housing is very affordable, with home prices from 10 to 20 percent below national averages. The cost of living is also way below average. Real estate taxes are almost ridiculous. Example: Taxes on an owner-occupied home valued at $65,000 amount to $152.50 a year, but if the occupant is over 65 years of age, taxes drop to $136.25.

For a town its size, Dothan has a surprising inventory of cultural events and establishments, including a symphony, ballet, community theater, and so forth. Health care is more than adequate, with three fine hospitals and two immediate-care facilities serving the area. The region also enjoys a low crime rate.

The Dothan area supports the usual outdoor recreational opportunities, including hunting, fishing, and golf. Golfers are pleased that one of the new Robert Trent Jones thirty-six-hole golf courses is located here. When I asked my chamber of commerce guide what her husband does, she replied, "He plays golf nine days a week." The city sponsors thirty-seven public tennis courts and many parks.

Ozark   Everything said about Dothan can be repeated about Enterprise (pop. 21,000) and Ozark (pop. 17,000). Of course, they are smaller, and those who value small-town qualities will adore Enterprise and Ozark. Why retire here? One retiree from Ozark put it this way: "This area is the best of all worlds. We live far enough south to avoid winter cold, far enough away from the ocean to escape destructive humidity. We enjoy a small-town atmosphere, yet we're close to the Gulf Coast and great fishing. We're only minutes from Dothan."

Ozark retirees appreciate the fact that they can drive around a charming city with no traffic jams and few stoplights. A relatively inexpensive, full-service country club with a challenging eighteen-hole golf course is only 2 miles from the courthouse square in the center of town.

Actually, our first visit to Ozark wasn't exactly fair, because it was in February, a time when flowering trees were exploding with color, birds were trilling songs of joy, and the world was turning emerald green. Our travels through the neighborhoods here and in nearby Enterprise were admittedly influenced by this early spring frenzy. Yet in neighborhood after neighborhood, even the more humble places, we found quality housing and pride of ownership.

Enterprise   The closest town to Fort Rucker, Enterprise is a favorite retirement location of ex-military families. They remember the town with favor and think about it when retirement plans are discussed.

A wide variety of housing is available in Enterprise, and the town is continually expanding its inventory of homes. A recent development is a group of "garden" homes and townhouses. These are smaller, maintenance-free places for folks wishing to downsize their house size and their house chores. Always moving ahead, Enterprise is in the process of building a new park with lots of walking trails and passive recreation.

Enterprise is also famous for an unusual landmark, a serious monument dedicated to an insect: the boll weevil. In the early part of this century, many parts of the South went from the height of afflu- ence to economic disaster because of the boll weevil. Within one season, the insects all but exterminated cotton, the crop responsible for the state's prosperity. But Enterprise/Ozark farmers didn't sur- render to despair, they plowed under cotton and planted peanuts. This change in tactics restored prosperity and then some. The relieved citizens decided to give credit where it was due, to the boll weevil, who forced them to make their communities even richer than before.

Enterprise is so proud of being a small town that one of their annual events is the "world's smallest St. Patrick's Day Parade." Pa- rade officials elect a "designated leprechaun" to march—only one marcher to a parade please, because more than one might permit some other town to stage a smaller procession and steal Enterprise's thunder! The parade's elected grand marshal is always absent; be- cause obviously, if he attended the event, there would be more than one marcher. When the long-anticipated Saint Patrick's Day arrives, celebrants rendezvous at Tops Restaurant and drink Irish coffee while they wait for the designated leprechaun to finish the journey. Since the parade route stretches only from Ouida Street to Tops's back door—a distance of approximately 50 feet—the wait isn't over- whelming. But the celebration is.

Eufaula   Not far north of Dothan, Eufaula is another place favored by military retirees as well as others seeking gracious Southern retirement. Both Ft. Benning and Ft. Rucker, with their hospitals, PXs, and clubs, are an hour's drive away. Its position on 45,000-acre Lake Eufaula makes it a great place for fishermen—with more than fifty fishing tournaments every year—and hunters find the surrounding woods and fields perfect for deer and wild turkey.

Before the Civil War, Eufaula was a prosperous river port and trading town for surrounding areas in Georgia and Alabama. Wealthy merchants and plantation owners created a showplace of beautiful homes in Eufaula that demonstrated their stature in the high society of the region.

DOTHAN/OZARK/ENTERPRISE/EUFALA WEATHER						
In degrees Fahrenheit						
	Jan.	April	July	Oct.	Rain	Snow
Daily Highs	57	77	91	77	49"	—
Daily Lows	36	53	72	53		

DOTHAN/OZARK/ENTERPRISE AREA COST OF LIVING					
Percentage of	Overall	Housing	Medical	Groceries	Utilities
National Average	92	87	85	100	96

Although Eufaula lost many soldiers during the Civil War struggle, the town was never threatened by the ravages of war until the closing stages of the conflict. Suddenly, on April 29, 1865, a messenger galloped into town. He carried the news that the city of Montgomery had fallen to Union troops. Four thousand cavalry were approaching. Fearing the worst, a delegation of citizens flying a flag of truce met the approaching troops, hoping to negotiate. At that same time, another message arrived: The war was over! Johnston had surrendered to General Sherman, and Robert E. Lee had presented his sword to General Grant at Appomattox.

Just in the nick of time, Eufala's antebellum homes were spared for their later role as a living museum of Southern aristocratic living. Shortly after the war Eufala regained much of its prosperity, whereupon another wave of extravagant building began in the 1880s, adding a collection of wonderful Victorians to mix with the prewar homes dating from the 1830s. Because of the mild climate, exquisite scenery, terrific fishing, and other recreational opportunities, Eufaula has become home to numerous "Winter Eufaulians" who visit here during the mild winters and return to their "summer homes" after they've enjoyed a glorious spring.

A modern hospital takes care of health-care needs, and three golf courses should help you improve your backswing. Housing, as usual in Alabama, is low-cost. Antebellum mansions sell here for the price of tract homes where I'm from.

Scottsboro   Sitting up in Alabama's northeast corner, Scottsboro is a picture-book version of a retirement town. An antique courthouse and old-fashioned town square, tree-graced neighborhoods of substantial brick homes, reasonable housing, and lakes ga-lore all contribute to making this a pleasant community for retire-ment. For those who enjoy fishing, boating, and other water sports, Scottsboro sits on one of the Southeast's largest lake complexes (Guntersville Lake), with over a thousand miles of shoreline, just in the county. Even though its population is only about 15,000, it is far enough away from the nearest large city to have ample shopping and facilities. Huntsville is forty-five minutes away by car, Chattanooga an hour, and it's three hours to Atlanta or Nashville.

Scottsboro is a city that believes in parks. Goosepond Colony, the largest of twenty-one parks and recreational areas in the county, is a complete recreational facility and is city-owned and -operated. Sitting on the edge of a gorgeous lake, Goosepond Colony boasts an eighteen-hole championship golf course, a lakeside restaurant, rental cottages, meeting rooms, marinas, and camping and picnic facilities.

Why should Scottsboro be described here, instead of one of a dozen other beautiful, economical, lakefront retirement areas that crowd northern Alabama? It was difficult to make this decision, but I submit two justifications. The first is the cosmopolitan makeup of Scottsboro's population. It seems that several years ago, Revere Cor-poration moved its plant down here from someplace in the North, transplanting hundreds of employees along with its manufacturing facilities. For some reason or another things didn't work out, and when Revere moved away, many employees liked Scottsboro so much, they refused to transfer away. They either took early retire-ment or found other jobs. Later on, other Northern companies se-lected Scottsboro as a place to move their operations and brought

SCOTTSBORO WEATHER						
In degrees Fahrenheit						
	Jan.	April	July	Oct.	Rain	Snow
Daily Highs	49	73	89	73	54"	—
Daily Lows	31	50	69	49		

SCOTTSBORO AREA COST OF LIVING					
Percentage of	Overall	Housing	Medical	Groceries	Utilities
National Average	93	82	90	92	86

along their employees, too. The result: a pleasant mixture of Northern and Southern neighbors.

My second reason is the community's dedication to betterment of their surroundings and quality of life. A case in point: an ultra-modern community recreation center, which serves a wide spectrum of citizens, from preschoolers to the elderly. Its construction came at a time when voters around the country were refusing to pass school bonds or fund libraries, yet Scottsboro voters didn't hesitate to allocate money for this impressive recreational and cultural facility. It comes complete with an Olympic-size pool that doubles as a training center for students as well as for senior citizen water aerobics, a gymnasium, an indoor walking track, racquetball courts, handball and a game room, plus meeting rooms and hobby shops. Another expensive project underway: An already substantial-looking hospital is undergoing an $11 million expansion, which will make Scottsboro a leading medical center of the region.

An example of an event that reinforces its small-city feeling: At a monthly happening called the "First Monday Trade Day," the courthouse lawn fills with residents selling arts and crafts, antiques, flea market items, locally-grown produce—anything that can be traded or sold. The first Monday in every September, the event grows so large they have to move it to a park.

This is an area that makes the most of its blend of mountains, forests, and lakes. Residential areas show taste and charm in this setting. Real estate selling at 18 percent below national average also makes retirement here affordable. Personal safety here is exceptionally high, ranking in the top 15 percent in the nation.

Evergreen   We would never have thought of visiting the little town of Evergreen, Alabama, were it not for a friend who was showing us the better retirement locations in the state. Since he's in charge of the state's Retirement Attraction program, we took him at his word that Evergreen would be worth a stopover. "It's a small place," he explained, "but they've put more effort into their Retirement Attraction program than some places ten times the size of Evergreen." We were pleased that we did visit.

A delightfully rural community of 4,000 people, Evergreen sits in the south-central part of Alabama, about 40 miles from the Florida state line. It's surrounded by hills and forests, broken by an occasional farm and rolling fields. This is probably the least-populated area in Alabama, yet the town is only a ninety-minute drive to the beaches of Pensacola or Gulf Shores for saltwater recreation. Evergreen is also about halfway between Mobile and Montgomery for big-city shopping, a seventy-five-minute drive in either direction.

Evergreen's business district is the essence of what small towns should be, and used to be. There's a thriving business section, with a traditional square, a railroad depot, and an old-fashioned county courthouse. This is a comfortable downtown, a place where you might enjoy sitting on a bench to chat with neighbors. The old railroad depot—now called "Ye Olde Railway Emporium"—has been converted to a cooperative where local artisans (some retired) display and sell their beautiful handiwork. As we visited various parts of town, we were delighted with the lovely homes sitting on generously sized lots with neat and well-cared-for landscaping, no matter the price range. Speaking of prices, we found no better values on quality real estate anywhere.

In order to ease the transition into retirement, Evergreen has a Hospitality Team to assist you. They offer free services to help you find a home as well as help with financial, legal, and health-care matters. Most important, the team will introduce you to your new neighbors. Folks we interviewed attest to the friendliness of the community. Al Burns said, "I'm from New Jersey but I worked in Boston and New York as a radio broadcaster. When I retired in New York, I couldn't afford to live there. Just the taxes were enough to drive me away. When I moved here, I decided I needed something to do, so now I'm doing a regular program for Radio WPGG. I love it here!"

With more than three-quarters of the countryside covered in woodland, outdoor recreation is popular here. Deer and turkey abound and bring hunters in from all over the region. (The nation's champion turkey caller lives here and operates a business in Evergreen's commercial district.) Many well-stocked ponds seem to be "well-kept secrets," but local folks are always happy to share their best fishing holes with you.

Evergreen has a private country club with a swimming pool and a nine-hole golf course. It isn't very fancy, but it isn't very expensive, either. This is a social center for clubs, dances, and meetings. Health care is provided by the Vaughan/Evergreen Medical Center, a

	Jan.	April	July	Oct.	Rain	Snow
EVERGREEN WEATHER						
In degrees Fahrenheit						
Daily Highs	57	77	92	78	54"	1"
Daily Lows	37	54	72	53		

forty-four-bed facility with coronary care, respiratory therapy, surgery, and physical therapy units.

Alexander City/Lake Martin   Back in the mid-1920s, the Alabama Power Company decided to place a dam across the Tallapoosa River. Residents at that time were devastated and totally convinced that the rising waters would create swamps and breeding grounds for flotillas of mosquitoes and armies of bugs. Resigned to disaster, they sold out at five dollars to the acre, feeling lucky to get anything at all for such worthless land. Little did they realize! Lakeshore lots now go for a minimum of $25,000, up to more than $500,000!

Today, travel writers describe Lake Martin as one of the most beautiful recreational lakes in the South. It's also become one of east-central Alabama's prime retirement destinations, having received numerous recommendation by retirement and relocation experts.

Scattered around the lake are nine or ten developments, which range from relatively inexpensive places nestled among the woods to elegant gated communities with private golf courses. Almost 22,000 people make their homes on the 750 miles of shoreline—on sandy beaches, in secluded coves or on rocky knolls with magnificent views. Officially designated one of Alabama's cleanest lakes, residents proudly refer to Lake Martin as "44,000 acres of pure drinking water." Golf, boating, water-skiing, and fishing, the lake has it all. Residents rave about the quality of their new surroundings.

With golf and water recreation the central focus, newcomers have a wide choice of lifestyles, from exclusive golf course developments, where homes cost a small fortune, to a mobile-home park with spaces that rent for as little as $100 a month. Don't expect super-bargains in real estate, however; after all if you live on a lake as pretty as this, you'll pay for the privilege. Strict building codes ensure that the housing is high quality—no shacks or fish shanties are permitted.

Nearby Alexander City is an alternative for those who would like to be near the lake, but prefer more inexpensive housing in town. Alex City (as people here call it) is a charming place in its own right. The town owes its prosperity to the Russell Corporation, a local company that made good as a Fortune 500 textile giant.

Just 50 miles from the state capital in Montgomery and 30 miles from Auburn University, the Alexander City–Lake Martin area is conveniently located for the occasional big-city shopping and cultural fixes. Birmingham is a 70-mile drive via a superhighway.

Quite naturally, recreation here centers around golf and water sports. Swimming, fishing, water-skiing, and boating are favorites. Many residents keep powered pontoon boats tied at their lakefront homes, ready for fishing, loafing, or a trip across the water to dine at a first-class restaurant. The original championship golf course at Willow Point has thirteen of its eighteen fairways edging the lakeshore. Two other courses are similarly located on the water. Alexander City also has an eighteen-hole municipal golf course.

The cultural and entertainment offerings of Montgomery and Birmingham are within an easy drive; however, Alexander City provides its own entertainment. There's a little theater group that stages several productions a year, and the Alexander City Arts Council uses the Central Alabama Community College facilities to bring plays, musicals, and concerts to the community. The college has special programs, free to students age 60 and over.

Russell Hospital, in Alexander City, has a modern, nonprofit

ALEXANDER CITY–LAKE MARTIN WEATHER

In degrees Fahrenheit

	Jan.	April	July	Oct.	Rain	Snow
Daily Highs	56	76	91	77	58"	—
Daily Lows	36	55	70	54		

ALEXANDER CITY–LAKE MARTIN AREA COST OF LIVING

	Overall	Housing	Medical	Groceries	Utilities
Percentage of National Average	97	93	89	95	101

seventy-five-bed hospital with twenty-four-hour, acute-care facilities. For military retirees there's a regional hospital at Maxwell Air Force Base in Montgomery, about an hour's drive.

Anniston   From the moment of its inception, Anniston was a planned model city. Back in 1879 two entrepreneurs decided this is where they would build their textile mills and blast furnaces. They needed a town and commercial center to go with their enterprises, so they hired a team of well-known architects to design a company town. They insisted that the new town must be modern as well as pleasing to the eye. Of course, "modern" in those days meant Victorian, and that's what we see today. Most of these historic structures are still in use, well preserved and reflecting Anniston's rich heritage.

Anniston, with of 27,000 inhabitants, is the population center of Calhoun County. Immediately adjacent, the city of Oxford has another 10,000 residents. The two cities form the major shopping center for the surrounding area's total population of 120,000. Thirteen miles away, not quite close enough to be considered an Anniston suburb, the town of Jacksonville provides a university setting. Including students, Jacksonville has a population of 11,000. The university has continuing-education programs as well as Elderhostel programs for folks from all over the country. Because the region is centrally located between Atlanta and Birmingham, the local slogan is: "Near Atlanta. Near Birmingham. Near Perfect."

We particularly liked Oxford as a retirement possibility. Originally it was called Lick Skillet, but when time came to incorporate into a town, residents wanted a more dignified name. Can you get

ANNISTON–SILVER LAKES–GADSDEN WEATHER

In degrees Fahrenheit

	Jan.	April	July	Oct.	Rain	Snow
Daily Highs	62	75	91	74	48"	2"
Daily Lows	33	51	70	51		

ANNISTON AREA COST OF LIVING

	Overall	Housing	Medical	Groceries	Utilities
Percentage of National Average	92	82	92	95	100

more dignified than "Oxford"? Essentially part of Anniston, Oxford has several unusually attractive neighborhoods that appear to be ideal for retirement living. The Calhoun County medical community includes more than one hundred physicians, forty-five dentists, and three hospitals.

Fort McClellan, an Army base occupying 15,000 acres of prime land, is one of the military installations that has been decommissioned. It's a beautiful place of woods and landscaped grounds. At the moment, the federal government, the state of Alabama, and the city officials of the surrounding cities are trying to decide what to do with the valuable land. One purpose, that seems fairly certain, is to devote a percentage of the surplus property to retirement housing.

Silver Lakes   Anniston and its neighboring city, Gadsden, both have enthusiastic retirement attraction committees ready to assist newcomers. The headquarters for the retirement committees is located at a golf development at Silver Lakes, between the two cities. Silver Lakes is a gorgeous setting of rolling terrain and lakes near the edge of Talladega National Forest. This is an experiment in retirement attraction because this is the first time one of Robert Trent Jones's Golf Trail courses has ever been placed within a private development. This is a 36-hole, world-class golf complex and it's always open for public play.

Gadsden   Gadsden (pop. 47,000) is located in the southern foothills of the Appalachian Mountains, where Lookout Mountain and the Coosa River meet. This is probably Alabama's most successful city when it comes to recruiting out-of-state retirees. A few years ago, Gadsden realized that it was losing its industrial base. It needed something to replace the disappearing factories, but didn't want to "chase smokestacks." Joining with several other cities in Etowah and Calhoun counties, Gadsden's retirement committee set a goal of attracting fifty retired couples a year. In 1994 they exceeded their goal; sixty-three couples moved to town that year. The next year forty-eight couples joined the party. In mid-1997, Gadsden was already fourteen couples ahead of schedule.

The impact of new residents on Gadsden's economy has been a dramatic textbook example of how communities benefit from out-of-state relocation. Because of the newcomers, jobs were created for health care specialists, construction workers, and retail businesses.

GADSDEN COST OF LIVING					
Percentage of National Average	Overall 92	Housing 75	Medical 91	Groceries 98	Utilities 105

Restaurants, motels, and service businesses blossomed. These new jobs were of a clean, non-polluting "smokeless-industry" nature. This helped the area to free itself of dependency on a handful of manufacturing facilities. Since the program began in 1991, more than 4,000 people have moved to Gadsden, with the strongest growth from 1994 to 1997.

The downtown's pride and joy is the huge 44,000-square-foot Gadsden Center for Cultural Arts. When a downtown department store closed its doors—a victim of strip mall syndrome—Gadsden decided to do something with the large multistory building. Rather than allow the edifice to disintegrate, they converted it into the Center for Cultural Arts, one of the most impressive downtown monuments to rehabilitation we've seen. Besides expansive rooms for community meetings, private parties, proms and dances, and concerts, the center has an experimental arts programs in which kids from a nearby housing project are paid to study art.

Two popular residential areas on Gadsden's outskirts are the towns of Rainbow City and Attalla. Attalla has a population of about 7,000 and a thriving commercial center. This was the bedroom community for employees of Gadsden's heavy industries before they closed some years ago. Much affordable housing is available here. For a while, Attalla's downtown section all but died. Then city officials encouraged the establishment of antiques shops and specialty boutiques. This seems to have turned the corner economically for Attalla, because folks come from miles around to shop, and storefronts are beginning to find tenants once again.

Rainbow City is slightly larger, with 8,000 inhabitants, and the residential areas are a bit more upscale. When Gadsden's industrial life was booming, this is where the white-collar and executive employees lived. Some exceptionally lovely homes are located here. Both towns are within minutes of downtown Gadsden.

Gadsden State Community College, Alabama's largest two-year college, and the University of Alabama–Gadsden Center provide educational opportunities. If that's not enough, Jacksonville State University is about 18 miles away.

Birmingham Area   Birmingham is the center of a large industrial and technical complex. Skilled technical and executive personnel are always in demand here, often as consultants or for part-time duties. It's also set in a lovely region of hills, forests, and lakes. For these reasons, many of those forced into early retirement look favorably toward the Birmingham area and its booming industrial environment. However, retirees today tend to prefer a smaller city rather than a big metropolis like Birmingham. Therefore, we'll focus on a couple of towns near enough to take advantage of what the city offers, yet far enough away to avoid big-city living.

On Birmingham's southern flank, the hustle and bustle of a large population center fades away into busy suburbs and finally disappears into a country-like atmosphere in Shelby County. Well, not really country, because you are within a half-hour drive to Birmingham, with all its cultural and commercial amenities. And it's rare you'll need to drive to the city: The suburbs of Hoover, Pelham, Helena, and Alabaster have shopping centers that would make most small cities envious. The crime rate in the county is one of the lowest in the state, and there are many middle- and upper-class neighborhoods to choose from.

A popular relocation choice here is Pelham, with a population of 15,000. The city of Hoover is of similar size and is also desirable as a place to live. Other nearby cities offer more or less the same attractions as Pelham. This is a place for those who want to live in an upscale suburb, yet close to a metropolitan center for the cultural and entertainment bonuses. In twenty years population has doubled, yet much of the growth isn't apparent. Many new homes are

BIRMINGHAM AREA WEATHER

In degrees Fahrenheit

	Jan.	April	July	Oct.	Rain	Snow
Daily Highs	52	75	91	43	52"	2"
Daily Lows	33	51	70	51		

BIRMINGHAM AREA COST OF LIVING

	Overall	Housing	Medical	Groceries	Utilities
Percentage of National Average	97	93	95	96	103

hidden in woodlands or on large lots with so many trees it's hard to see the houses.

Developers are busy carving fancy developments into the steep foothills adjoining Oak Mountain Park, and clearing enough trees to place attractive homes. Although you'll find all kinds of housing—"from cottages to castles," as the chamber of commerce puts it—this is not a place to expect an abundance of economical housing. In 1997 the average price of homes sold in Shelby County was more than double that of most other Alabama communities. That says something for the quality and amenities.

Jasper   A different retirement lifestyle option on the opposite side of Birmingham, the small city of Jasper (population 14,000), sits in a peaceful countryside of forested hills and small farms. Birmingham is a 40-mile drive over Highway 78, and a high-speed superhighway called Corridor X is under construction, which should trim the driving time to Birmingham to half an hour. Like Pelham, Jasper is sometimes described as a bedroom community for Birmingham, but on a more moderate scale. This has traditionally been a blue-collar city, where coal mining was king until the black gold mineral fell out of favor as an energy source. This turned the region into a real estate buyer's paradise.

Like most small cities, Jasper's downtown suffers from strip-mall syndrome; shoppers patronize large malls and stores on the town's outskirts. As a result, the town center is quaint, quiet, and laid back, a nice place to stroll.

Jasper is working hard to attract more residents. One of the community's efforts to lure retirees is the Newcomers' Club. The group invites new residents to join in cultural and service programs and make friendships through shared social gatherings. The Newcomers' Club holds monthly luncheon meetings to plan activities for the group. As an example of how out-of-state people are received: In a recent election for mayor of Jasper, voters chose Don Goetz, a Yankee who relocated here from Milwaukee.

JASPER AREA COST OF LIVING					
Percentage of	Overall	Housing	Medical	Groceries	Utilities
National Average	94	87	90	95	89

While Jasper does have some areas of expensive homes, most housing—located in quiet residential neighborhoods with lots of trees—is priced a bit lower than typical low Alabama prices. In town, as well as on the outskirts, you'll find a few neighborhoods of stately old homes—residences of mine owners and supervisory personnel. Just a few minutes from the town center, newer subdivisions and wooded acreages are for sale at affordable prices.

Mississippi

For most folks from outside the South, Mississippi comes as a pleasant surprise. They expect cotton fields and dreary farming communities where "outsiders" might not be welcome. These stereotypes will fade away upon your first visit to Mississippi. You'll find a delightful landscape of great diversity, from picturesque Appalachian foothills in the northeast to sandy beaches on the sunny Gulf of Mexico. In between are affluent towns and cities graced with lovely pre–Civil War mansions on landscaped grounds as well as contemporary houses, ranch-style homes in golf-course communities, and developments situated on fishing lakes or surrounded by forested hills.

MISSISSIPPI

Mississippi's cities jealously preserve their Old South heritage of lovely homes to complement modern subdivisions and tasteful commercial centers. Classic university campuses and medical centers are just as prominent as graceful residential districts and

MISSISSIPPI TAX PROFILE

Sales tax: 7%, drugs exempt
State income tax: graduated, 3% to 5% over $10,000; can't deduct federal income tax
Property taxes: average 1%, but for over age 65, homestead exemption could be as much as $700
Intangibles tax: no
Social security taxed: no
Pensions taxed: no
Gasoline tax: 18¢ to 10¢ per gallon, plus local taxes of from 2¢ to 3¢ per gallon

upscale restaurants and shopping. In short, the state of Mississippi has everything most retirees might need for a successful and pleasant retirement. I suppose you could find cotton fields if you look hard enough, but offhand, I don't recall seeing any.

The best part about Mississippi for retirement: It's the most welcoming state in the South, perhaps in the nation. From the governor's office down to the neighborhood level, the people of Mississippi are working hard to convince out-of-state folks to relocate here. The backbone of this campaign is a well-funded and professionally managed state program called Hometown Mississippi Retirement. The state allocates more than a half-million dollars a year for this program, spending more than any other state for retirement attraction. This money isn't spent on a mere propaganda barrage to lure warm bodies to the state. The message isn't just "Come to Mississippi" and leave the results up to chance. On the community level, hometown residents follow through with a well-considered program to welcome new individuals into each community.

I interviewed a wide range of retired couples who moved to Mississippi from places like California, New Jersey, Minnesota, and Florida. All attested to the genuine hospitality and friendliness of their new neighbors. Typical were comments such as, "We've only been here a year, but we have more friends now than we ever had in thirty years of living in our old neighborhood."

To further enhance Mississippi's status as a retiree-friendly place, the legislature voted to exempt retiree income from state income tax. Along with low property taxes and favorable living costs, this provides more dollars to be spent on recreation, travel, or investments. For those over age sixty-five or disabled, the exemption from the assessed value of their home is such that a home valued at $60,000 would owe no property taxes.

Mississippi Beach   Long a favored retirement destination for military personnel, the area around Gulfport and Biloxi combines a summer carnival atmosphere with sedate Old South values. The complex of beach towns stretching between Florida and Louisiana is known as Mississippi Beach. The total population here is around 90,000, and the cities are so closely connected that it's impossible to tell where one ends and the next begins.

It's obvious why this is such a tourist attraction. Vast stretches of sugary beach with gentle waves lapping at the sand are complemented by streets arched over by branches of majestic oak and magnolia trees, fine restaurants, and lots of sunshine. Large, formal

MISSISSIPPI GULF COAST WEATHER						
In degrees Fahrenheit						
	Jan.	April	July	Oct.	Rain	Snow
Daily Highs	61	77	90	79	61"	—
Daily Lows	43	59	74	60		

MISSISSIPPI BEACH COST OF LIVING					
Percentage of	Overall	Housing	Medical	Groceries	Utilities
National Average	94	90	90	97	105

estates survey the scene with Southern majesty. Here was—and is—the mansion where Jefferson Davis chose to live out his days, writing memoirs of his days of glory as president of the Confederacy.

A recent innovation is the appearance of eleven glittering gambling casinos that energize the coastline with bright lights, blackjack and roulette, and slot machines. Gambling provides tourists from surrounding states an additional excuse to congregate here; golfing and sunning on the beaches by day and shouting at the dice by night. In the winter, regular tourists are replaced by snowbirds, a large percentage of them Canadians, who don't mind the cooler water and occasional nippy days. Compared to Montreal or Moose Jaw winters, Gulf Coast's coldest days are tropical paradise.

Don't let gambling prevent you from considering Mississippi's Gulf Coast, because the way things are going, gaming palaces, riverboat casinos and even oceangoing gaming ships are popping up all over the Gulf Coast, Mississippi River towns, and Florida ports. You're not going to avoid them. Gambling's effect on the local economy brings a mixed bag of assets and deficits. On the one hand, gambling has created more than 5,000 jobs in the Gulfport–Biloxi area (including much part-time work for retirees) and has warmed the hearts of many local businesses. On the other hand, that old-fashioned Southern charm and honeysuckle neighborliness wears thin when trampled by herds of tourist-gamblers, traffic congestion, and inevitable increases in crime levels.

Housing prices used to drop drastically every winter after students went back to school and tourists went home to their jobs. That's no longer the case; gambling is putting more year-round pressure on housing.

Many military couples choose to retire here because of convenient medical and base-exchange privileges at Keesler Air Force Base. Most of these military retirees were stationed in the area at one time or another and developed a fondness for the beaches and the climate.

Long Beach   The best bets for retirement around here are towns *near* Gulfport–Biloxi. When most people talk of retirement on the Mississippi coast, they really mean the towns of Long Beach, Pass Christian, and Bay St. Louis. With the convenience of good hospitals and other emergency facilities in nearby Gulfport–Biloxi, many retirees look to the reasonably priced housing and pleasant neighborhoods away from the hustle-bustle and tourist world. A bonus is exceptionally low crime rates in these towns—among the lowest in the country, according to FBI statistics.

The quiet and peaceful atmosphere is one of the first qualities that local residents proudly point out. "Gulfport–Biloxi is too crowded and too honky-tonk," said several retirees in Pass Christian. "Here, we have 26 miles of quiet beach, all to ourselves."

Long Beach (pop. 22,000) is a former farming community to the west of Gulfport, whose quiet residential areas attract retirees who enjoy the quality neighborhoods. You'll find an interesting mixture of homes here, varying from extraordinarily inexpensive to amazingly extravagant. One home, facing the beach, carried a price tag of $350,000—which sounded overpriced for the area until we looked it over. It was a *Gone with the Wind*-type home: three stories, rooms with 10-foot ceilings, four bedrooms, four baths, fireplaces scattered throughout the place, and a swimming pool. Even the garage had two stories and its own bath. Then the price seemed reasonable. Old homes are treated like valuable jewels, continually polished and restored to yesterday's splendor. The city of Long Beach has strict local ordinances against cutting live oaks or magnolia trees without permission of the planning commission as well as approval of city officials.

Pass Christian   Pass Christian (pop. 6,500) is the elegant member of the retirement trio. Long a vacation center for wealthy New Orleans residents, Pass Christian is rich in history and past opulence. At one time steamboats regularly made the 55-mile voyage from New Orleans, bringing high-society families to their second homes. The original families are gone, but their homes remain, as do the gracious lifestyles of the last century. Mansions with manicured lawns line the beachfront and invitations for afternoon tea indicate social standing. But all is not tea and crumpets; there is another side to Pass Christian, just as there is to most gracious Southern towns. Fishermen, craftspeople, artists, and laborers make up the community's backbone. Their houses are smaller and located on streets away from the beach.

Twenty-two percent of the residents here are retired. Those with plenty of money live in the mansions while others live in modest cottages because they don't have money or don't care to put money into extravagant housing.

The town had its beginnings when a Frenchman from New Orleans named Nicholas Christianne settled here in 1745. The pass refers to the deep channel that passes through the oyster reefs, and the town became referred to as "the pass of Christianne." The French pronunciation was retained, becoming Pass ChristiAN. Its seafaring tradition continues to the present day, with shrimping, oystering, and fishing the major occupations and a colorful element of the economic life. The Pass Christian Yacht Club dates back to 1849 and is the second-oldest yacht club in the country.

In addition to fishing and boating, golf and tennis are popular. Twenty-two golf courses between Gulfport–Biloxi and Bay St. Louis encourage play. The beach is prominent in local recreational possibilities, with 7 of the 26 miles of Mississippi beach available for Pass Christian residents' enjoyment.

Bay St. Louis   Called "The Bay" by local residents, Bay St. Louis (pop. 8,500) is even older than neighboring Pass Christian. It was founded in 1699 by the French and named after their king. Its historical downtown, with palm-lined streets, Victorian mansions, and an old Catholic seminary, contrast with modern shopping and commercial centers.

One of the appealing aspects of living here—or anywhere in Mississippi, for that matter—is tax rates. The per capita tax burden in Mississippi is said to be only 57 percent of the national average. This is based on taxes from personal income, retail sales, residential property, gasoline, and auto registration. Compare this with taxes in Illinois of 98 percent; Wisconsin, 132 percent; and Michigan, 124 percent of the national average.

Oxford   Snuggled amid the forested hills of Northern Mississippi, Oxford is a picture-book example of a gracious Southern university town. Handsome antebellum mansions—partially concealed by flowering wisteria, redbud, and creeping ivy—hold court under ancient magnolias and magnificent oak trees. Oxford is positively saturated with history and Old South traditions. Quiet, tree-shaded streets, with silence broken only by the joyous song of a mockingbird and occasional barking of a dog in the distance, recall an era long forgotten in today's frantic rush toward urbanity.

Yet Oxford shows its modern side with a large shopping mall and all the usual businesses and home developments—mercifully located toward the outskirts of town. The outskirts, by the way, aren't all that far away. With a population of only 11,000, the town doesn't spread out to eternity.

Were I to rank places as to the "best place for retirement," Oxford, Mississippi, would surely rank in the top ten. I confess that as an author, I could be biased by a certain mystical literary connection between Oxford and the outside world. Oxford has fostered and developed writers from its very beginning as a university town—even before William Faulkner made his home base here—continuing today with several best-selling authors choosing to bask in Oxford's nurturing literary climate. It seems as if every third person we meet here has written a book!

The University of Mississippi's presence takes Oxford into another realm of being. Affectionately known nationwide as "Ole Miss," the school adds 11,000 students, to double Oxford's population. This unique mixture of students and retirees creates a unique consumer demand: quality shopping, restaurants, and entertainment at affordable prices.

Oxford's charming downtown square is a perfect illustration of how the presence of a university can preserve the character of a town. Commerce generated by students and residents keeps downtown enterprise alive and healthy instead of abandoning it to strip

OXFORD WEATHER						
In degrees Fahrenheit						
	Jan.	April	July	Oct.	Rain	Snow
Daily Highs	51	75	93	76	56"	2"
Daily Lows	31	50	69	49		

malls and shopping centers on the highways, as happens in many small towns across the nation. Downtown Oxford looks the way a downtown should look. A classic 120-year-old courthouse, with massive columns and centuries-old oak trees, dominates the scene, complete with the obligatory statue of a Confederate soldier standing guard.

Among the square's treasures are a department store dating from 1839, a wonderful art gallery, and enough shops and boutiques to make leisurely shopping a pleasure. The town square also supports several good-to-excellent little restaurants.

Across from the Confederate soldier's statue is a well-known Oxford tradition, the Square Book Store, which features a second-floor veranda that looks out over the square, where friends meet to sip capuccino and talk about books. The 25,000-volume collection, on every subject imaginable, makes you aware that the owner operates the store with a respect for books and literature rather than an eye for quick turnover and high profits—which seems to be the trend lately. On the staircase you'll find stacks of autographed copies of books by local authors. The Square Book Store's presentations by well-known authors who discuss their works and philosophical approaches in their literary accomplishments are favorite happenings.

Natchez   Stately Natchez sits on a scenic bluff overlooking the mighty Mississippi River on land that was originally a tribal center of the Natchez Indians. The French constructed a fort here in 1716 after chasing away the Indians, making Natchez one of the oldest European settlements on the Mississippi River.

Very early, the town blossomed as a prosperous cotton-raising and -exporting city. It became one of the South's wealthiest cities—possibly the richest in the entire nation. The large number of awesome homes and mansions testify to this. When war between North and South threatened, many Natchez plantation owners were staunchly opposed to secession. They fully realized that war would be a financial disaster as well as a tragic spilling of blood. Therefore, when the war descended upon the nation, Natchez's support was less than enthusiastic. When the first Yankee gunships drifted downriver, ready to bombard Natchez, they were greeted by a huge white flag of surrender fluttering on the bluff. The city of Natchez negotiated a peace that guaranteed the preservation of the magnificent mansions that graced the city.

NATCHEZ WEATHER						
In degrees Fahrenheit						
	Jan.	April	July	Oct.	Rain	Snow
Daily Highs	61	79	91	80	55"	—
Daily Lows	40	58	73	56		

After the war, its economy devastated, Natchez drifted into the doldrums. This had the further effect of preserving the antebellum homes from the catastrophe of modernization and urban renewal. Today, Natchez is a virtual museum of Southern aristocratic architecture. Approximately 500 antebellum homes grace the quiet streets of the city, some dating back to the eras of Spanish and French rule. Throughout the expansive historic district, lovely Victorian homes add to the feeling of stepping back in time. The South has numerous towns with proud antebellum homes, many of them for sale at what seem to be bargain prices, but few have as many beautiful places at such low asking prices as Natchez. (I once said something like that about Oxford, but at last visit, prices have risen dramatically.)

Today Natchez is a quiet town of 20,000 friendly people with well-cared-for neighborhoods and affordable quality housing. Newer subdivisions and apartments are found on the fringes of town and even in the thickly-forested surrounding countryside—some on acre-sized lots carved out of the woods.

The wealthy aristocrats had their homes on the high ground, but the rough-and-tumble steamboat crowd, rogues, and river pirates strutted their stuff down by the riverbank, at Natchez Under-the-Hill. This was a district of docks, saloons, and bordellos famous for gambling and illicit excitement. Today, at least some of the excitement has returned to Natchez Under-the-Hill in the form of riverboat gambling. In addition to a casino and gambling aboard the ship, several unique restaurants have been embellished to keep alive the wicked, 1800s decor.

The quickest way to make new friends here is to contact the very active Retire Partnership, a group specially dedicated to attracting retirees to the area and making them feel at home. Even if not your choice for retirement, Natchez with all its antebellum glory is well worth a visit.

Columbus   This is a city of comfortable size with a population of 28,000 (add 2,000 to the total if you count the military personnel on the air base). Columbus is known for its historic old
residences. Its antebellum homes were miraculously spared during
the Civil War. Although 238 battles were fought in Mississippi,
Columbus was never a prime military target and the city was never
invaded by Union troops. Today, the grand antebellum and Victorian mansions lining the old brick streets and tree-shaded lanes are
the pride of the region. Each April the town conducts a Pilgrimage
Tour of historic homes. Visitors are greeted by gracious hosts
dressed in authentic period costumes, who conduct the visitors
through their homes and proudly recite their histories.

The most famous of Columbus's historic homes is a wonderful
yellow-and-gray Victorian, the birthplace of playwright Tennessee
Williams. Some believe it was the setting of his play *Summer and
Smoke,* and I can envision it as the set for *The Glass Menagerie.* Once
when he returned to visit his boyhood home, he commented,
"Home is where you hang your childhood, and Mississippi to me is
the beauty spot of creation." The Tennessee Williams house is now
used as the Mississippi Welcome Center. Another famous home is
12 Gables, a Greek revival built in 1838. This is where the ladies of
Columbus met in 1866 to honor the fallen soldiers of the Civil War,
Union as well as Confederate, a meeting that was the origin of our
present-day Memorial Day commemoration.

It isn't surprising that many military families decide to relocate
in Columbus upon retirement. When service personnel leave the
military they naturally remember the more pleasant tours of duty
and long to return. Retirees can take advantage of the commissary,
base-exchange, and recreational opportunities on the post. This is
the home of Columbus Air Force Base, one of only three pilot-
training facilities in the United States. Although the base hires 1,500
civilian workers and pumps $2.5 million a week into the local
economy, Columbus it isn't just a "military gate" town. More than
fifty manufacturers, two universities, and a healthy agricultural
sector make for a diversified economy. For those who have reached
retirement age but aren't quite ready for the rocker, part-time work
is an option in Columbus. Skills are valued and expertise is welcomed in a variety of fields.

Like all Mississippi cities listed in this book, Columbus has a
welcoming committee for newcomers. Columbus has adopted a

"Silver Eagles" program for this purpose. The Silver Eagles are growing in popularity in other parts of the South as an organized social group bringing newcomers and residents together. They organize trips, potlucks, dances, and other congenial events. An important endeavor is offering visitors personally conducted tours of Columbus to help retirees make up their minds about relocation here. So, when you visit, expect to be met by Silver Eagles.

The recreational jewel of Columbus is the scenic Tennessee–Tombigbee Waterway. Part of 16,000 miles of inland waters, it eventually connects with the Gulf of Mexico in faraway Mobile. Unlimited water and natural woodlands encourage boating, hiking, and fishing as well as hunting and camping. Columbus is ideal for year-round golf, with eight public and private golf courses within a thirty-minute drive. You'll find plenty of tennis and handball at public and private facilities.

Hattiesburg   Hattiesburg, a lovely town of 48,000, is another of the many surprises Mississippi seems to be continually pulling on us. Our first experience with Hattiesburg was during a research trip to the rolling, piney woods of south Mississippi. Fortunately, our visit coincided with a dinner meeting of a group called the Hattiesburg Retirement Connectors. This is a group of retired volunteers whose main purpose is to make newcomers to Hattiesburg feel at home. Retirement Connection members are familiar with problems involved in relocating; all retired here from somewhere else. The Hattiesburg retirement relocation program is one of most successful in the state. It has welcomed 412 households from thirty-five states since the program began in 1993.

When newcomers visit the city, they understand why Hattiesburg was awarded the 1992 Livability Award for cities with population under 100,000 from the United States Conference of Mayors. Furthermore, as a college town, Hattiesburg reaps the benefits of the academic economy, which results in a lively and attractive downtown area.

Unlike some Mississippi cities listed in this book, Hattiesburg doesn't have a collection of antebellum homes. This is because the town's development didn't get underway until some years after the Civil War. But Hattiesburg's twenty-three-block area of lovely, turn-of-the-century homes in the Historic Neighborhood District truly compensates for the lack of pre–Civil War homes. Residents are

HATTIESBURG WEATHER						
In degrees Fahrenheit						
	Jan.	April	July	Oct.	Rain	Snow
Daily Highs	51	75	93	76	56"	5"
Daily Lows	31	50	69	49		

HATTIESBURG AREA COST OF LIVING					
	Overall	Housing	Medical	Groceries	Utilities
Percentage of National Average	94	90	90	97	105

proud of these perfectly restored Victorian, Queen Anne, and Greek Revival-style houses.

Hattiesburg calls itself the "Hub City" because of its convenient location. Saltwater fishing and gambling casinos on Mississippi's Gulf Coast playground are only a 70-mile drive through the DeSoto and Brooklyn national forests. The bright lights of New Orleans, with Bourbon Street fun and French Quarter restaurants, are less than an hour-and-half drive along Interstate 59. You can drive into New Orleans to watch an afternoon Saints football game, have dinner, and be home in time for bed. Mobile, Jackson, and Meridian are each about an hour and a half from Hattiesburg.

Hattiesburg is a golfer's paradise. Ten year-round golf courses are always ready for play, including a championship course described as one of the finest in the South, often hosting PGA events.

The University of Southern Mississippi and William Carey College enrich the community with theater, concerts, lectures, and exhibits. The university offers free auditing of classes for those age sixty-five and older. Of special interest is USM's Institute for Learning in Retirement. Located in a lovely, off-campus house, the program offers a relaxed setting for learning and sharing experiences. This is a great place to make new acquaintances in the community. No grades or exams take the stress out of the continuing educational process.

Although the cultural ambience of Jackson is within easy driving distance—with opera, museums, and such—Hattiesburg residents don't have to leave town to enjoy a rich cultural life. Musical, theatrical, concert, and other events that you'd expect from a big city are enjoyed right here. The Hattiesburg Civic Light Opera produces Broadway musicals; Just Over the Rainbow entertains with dinner–

theater productions. A gallery featuring works of Mississippi artists is maintained by the Hattiesburg Arts Council.

You'll find a wide variety of homes here to fit any lifestyle, and because Hattiesburg real estate is about 10 percent below national averages, prices are affordable. We looked at one very stylish development featuring large wooded lots arranged along the shore of a private lake. Amenities include tennis, boating, and trails for hikers, with homes selling for less than many California tract homes.

Hattiesburg is rightly proud of its two state-of-the-art hospitals, which serve as the health-care center for the southern Mississippi region.

Mississippi's Capital   Jackson is not only the capital of Mississippi, but it's also the state's cultural, financial, and population center. Jackson is a beautiful city in its own right, and for many folks, a good retirement choice. It is a large city, however, and when we find a place as nice as Jackson, we like to look for retirement places just outside the metropolitan center. In the course of our research, we discovered two delightful small towns, both within a few minutes' drive of Jackson's center—a compromise between living in the city of Jackson and living in the "country," yet close enough to enjoy all the cultural and civilized amenities to be found in the city.

These two communities are Clinton and Madison. Both have a lot to offer retirees, both communities have active welcoming committees, and both towns have women mayors. Since we couldn't decide which we liked best (both the towns and the mayors), we decided to include both places. Clinton sits beyond the western limits of Jackson, and Madison is to the northeast. We'll start (in alphabetical order) with Clinton.

Clinton   Clinton began as an Indian trading post back in 1805, when it was known as Mount Salus, meaning "mountain of health." The name was justified by the area's many refreshing, healthful springs. Located at the junction of the Natchez Trace and the road to Vicksburg, the settlement became an important stagecoach stop and the crossroads of the territory. Clinton almost became the capital of the newly formed state of Mississippi; it missed by one vote. Today it's one of the fastest-growing cities in the state, with a population nearing 25,000.

JACKSON–CLINTON AREA WEATHER						
In degrees Fahrenheit						
	Jan.	April	July	Oct.	Rain	Snow
Daily Highs	57	78	93	79	53"	1"
Daily Lows	35	53	71	52		

JACKSON AREA COST OF LIVING					
Percentage of National Average	Overall 92	Housing 94	Medical 80	Groceries 89	Utilities 97

Because Clinton is just a short commute from Jackson, its suburban quality is unmistakable. Quiet streets and quality neighborhoods make for tranquil living. Choosing a place like Clinton is like finding the best of two worlds: a place with a peaceful, small-town disposition, yet only minutes away from the convenience and action of the city. An example of the kinds of cultural advantages in living close to a city: When we visited Clinton for our research, we were privileged to take in an exposition at the Mississippi Arts Pavilion in Jackson. *The Palaces of St. Petersburg: Russian Imperial Style* was an exhibit never before displayed anywhere outside of Russia.

In keeping with its small-town image, the charming downtown area has been restored, complete with historic brick streets and tasteful shops, and named "Olde Towne." Clinton isn't strictly a bedroom community, however; several manufacturing facilities provide jobs and add to the overall feeling of prosperity. Clinton is also a college town. With the founding of Mississippi College in 1826, Clinton became known as the "Athens of Mississippi." One of the oldest universities in the country, the school prides itself on community involvement in a variety of activities, from collegiate sports to concerts and pageants.

Folks who've retired here swear by the small-town friendliness, yet they appreciate the nearby big-city conveniences. One retiree from Ohio said, "When my company moved us down here, we liked Clinton so well that I turned down promotions in order to stay. When retirement came around, we didn't even think of leaving."

Because Clinton is just a ten-minute drive from Jackson, residents here enjoy a rich, year-round source of cultural entertainment such as symphony concerts and chamber music recitals. There's always something going on at Jackson's Museum of Art and the Jackson Zoo, and there are even street parties with downtown stages for blues, rock, country, and gospel music. There's a full calendar of events year-round.

In Clinton, the city's arts council keeps cultural and fun events going. Among its activities is the Brick Streets Festival, which starts in April with a monthlong series of festivities. The brick streets of Clinton's restored "Olde Towne" are enlivened by music, food, and arts and crafts displays as well as a Shakespeare festival.

District and regional sporting events sponsored by Mississippi College draw athletes and fans from across the southeast. Hinds Community College also serves the community with continuing-education classes.

Because Jackson is just minutes away, Clinton residents have access to some of the finest medical care in the South. Six major medical facilities are located minutes away in the Jackson metropolitan area, with specialists in just about every medical field.

Madison   The second suburb of Jackson that caught our eye is the small city of Madison. Located about the same distance from Jackson as Clinton, where the Natchez Trace skirts to the north of Jackson, Madison is smaller than Clinton, with about 15,000 residents, and it has a totally different flavor. For one thing, Madison is definitely upscale; the homes and developments are tops in quality as well as price. Residents have the highest per capita income in the state. Shopping districts and outlying residential development clearly show this affluence.

Unlike other Mississippi towns and cities discussed in this book, Madison is not long established, with a history of gradual development. While the town has roots going back to pre–Civil War days, until about sixteen years ago Madison was little more than a farming crossroads community with about 1,000 residents. Since development started from scratch, residents seized the unique opportunity of planning, guiding, and shaping the way the town progressed.

One of the first things you'll notice about Madison is the lack of strip-mall clutter—no blinking signs, flashing lights, or bright plastic decor. Strict regulation of signs and business architecture should make Madison a model for other small cities—an example of how downtowns should be kept alive and well. (Unfortunately, it's too late for most towns; their depressed downtowns are filled with closed shops and painted-over display windows. Their shops, markets, and businesses were forced to go out of business or join the movement to the highway on the edge of town.) I urge city planners to visit Madison to see how it's done.

Much of the credit for Madison's success goes to Mary Hawkins, who has been mayor since she was first elected in 1981 at the age of twenty-six. Mary is extremely controversial with contractors and developers, upon whom she places stringent rules that she enforces with unrelenting vigor. (They're forever dragging her into court, accusing her of being dictatorial, but Mary is forever winning.) On the other hand, she is absolutely adored by voters and residents of Madison who desire to keep Madison from becoming just another bedroom community. (She ran unopposed in the most recent election.) A typical Mary Hawkins battle: The architectural design for a new post office conflicted with the general decor of Madison's downtown center, so the mayor took the U.S. government to task, and after a hard battle forced architects to redesign the post office and to build it in a more desirable locale. Another battle: When a new factory located in town, the mayor refused to connect the water until they agreed to landscape the grounds, to remodel the building's facade to match the downtown's architectural theme, and to replace the hurricane-and-barbed-wire fence with a nice-looking (but expensive) wrought-iron fence. "We probably have Mississippi's most beautiful factory building," Mary Hawkins said, with a satisfied grin.

The city complex now includes more than sixty carefully planned subdivisions, among the most upscale (and expensive) in Mississippi. As a planned community, Madison places emphasis on safety, comfort, and maintaining a quality small-town atmosphere.

Madison is also a favorite spot for antiques shoppers. Those in search of something special from a bygone era will fall in love with the pieces of antebellum and Victorian grandeur found in Madison's shops. Twice a year, 30,000 crazed antiques-shoppers descend upon the Madison area for the Canton Flea Market, which features 1,200 vendors of arts and crafts, antiques, and collectibles.

The inevitable result of restrictive zoning and building codes is plenty of high-quality homes but a dearth of low-cost housing. You won't find mobile–home parks or inexpensive tract homes here. Apartment rentals are all but nonexistent, and we saw no condominiums. The average price of houses sold here is about $25,000 to $50,000 higher than in most Mississippi communities. But if you can afford higher prices, you definitely get your money's worth. Madison has at least one lovely golf–course development, complete with a country club–type center for residents.

Tupelo   When Hernando DeSoto's expedition entered northeast Mississippi in the 1500s, present-day Tupelo was the site of a large Chickasaw Indian village. No longer a village, Tupelo has become a prosperous town of 34,000 inhabitants, where warm smiles and hometown hospitality are the rule, not the exception. This place has one of Mississippi's most enthusiastic retiree welcoming committees eagerly waiting to bring you into the fold, to make sure you get settled in your new home and are introduced all around. They'll have you working on a community project before you know what happened.

Nestled in the scenic beauty of northeastern Mississippi's rolling countryside, Tupelo sits on the Natchez Trace, about halfway between Natchez and Nashville. Memphis is an hour-and-a-half drive via Interstate 78, and Mississippi's lovely state capital at Jackson is a pleasant three-hour drive along the scenic Natchez Trace. The Trace, by the way, is a nature wonderland you'll not want to miss. You'll see wild turkeys, deer and birds, and enjoy light motor traffic (no trucks allowed). A leisurely drive along the Natchez Trace is truly a pleasure. We've driven this road many times, occasionally pausing for a picnic or a hike along one of the historic pathways that branch off from the Trace.

Twice named an All-American City by the National Civic League, Tupelo enjoys a prosperous base as a manufacturing, retail,

TUPELO WEATHER						
In degrees Fahrenheit						
	Jan.	April	July	Oct.	Rain	Snow
Daily Highs	57	78	93	78	53"	5"
Daily Lows	34	51	70	50		

and distribution center, and its furniture industry rivals that of North Carolina. Our impression is that this is an exceptionally pleasant place to live, with welcoming neighbors and plenty of opportunities for community participation. And in case you didn't already know it, residents will proudly inform you that Tupelo was the birthplace of Elvis Presley.

Five public and private golf courses and mild winters make for golfing pleasure year-round; there's also excellent golf at the Tupelo Country Club. The city has tennis courts in abundance, with instructors available to help you learn or sharpen your game. The 1,600-mile-long Tennessee–Tombigbee Waterway is minutes away from Tupelo, providing outdoor fun in the form of fishing, boating, picnicking, or camping.

Tupelo has two colleges, a branch of the University of Mississippi and the Itawamba Community College. Those over age sixty-five do not have to pay tuition! In addition to continuing-education opportunities at the colleges, the Lee County Library offers year-round lecture series and "brown bag luncheons" (informal presentations for workers on their lunch break and retirees on their shopping break).

Tupelo has a wide range of homes in a variety of comfortable neighborhoods. From stately, older homes to new residential construction, Tupelo provides choices for every budget and lifestyle. Neighborhoods are peaceful and tend to be closely knit, with residents benefiting from well-trained, professional fire and police protection.

Picayune   In the southern part of Mississippi, we made a surprising discovery in small-town retirement: Picayune. Conveniently situated an hour's drive from either New Orleans's French Quarter or the glittering casinos on the Gulf of Mexico, the town manages to hold onto an old-fashioned hometown atmosphere. Rolling, wooded hills and numerous lakes contribute to a high-quality retirement environment. The current population is 12,500 and growing.

We were impressed both by the comfortable, home-town feeling of Picayune's downtown and by the quality of its residential areas. From expensive and plush neighborhoods to more humble areas, you'll find good value for your housing dollar. Just a few minutes from downtown, the landscape becomes rural, dotted with homes on large, wooded lots commonly ten acres or more. Some places have acreage for horses, with part of the land in small farms. The surprising thing is that the cost of a quality home on a large piece of land is similar to that of a small subdivision home in many other areas of the country.

Picayune's name derives from that of the local newspaper, the *Picayune Item,* which in turn comes from the New Orleans paper of the same name. Both newspapers were owned by Eliza Jane Poitevent Nicholson, a local resident and probably the only woman publisher of a major daily newspaper in the country at that time. A picayune, by the way, was a tiny coin circulated in New Orleans when the territory belonged to the Spanish Empire. A picayune was the original cost of a copy of the newspaper.

To this day, women are unusually influential in the town of Picayune. The city manager, Kay Johnson, told us of some annoyance when she appointed another woman as city planner. The post of chief of police was already held by a woman, as was the job of city clerk. She told everyone that she planned on hiring a man soon. "We need another meter-reader," she assured them. (The mayor and city council, however, are all male.) The chief of police, by the way, is justifiably proud of Picayune's low crime rate. According to the latest FBI Uniform Crime Report, Picayune is in the top one-tenth in personal safety.

Recreation and entertainment are part of Picayune's heritage. Hunting and fishing in south Mississippi is said to be superb because of the pristine woodlands and numerous lakes, ponds, and streams. The countryside is heavily forested and filled with white-tailed deer, turkey, squirrel, dove, and other small game. For saltwater fishing, the Gulf beaches are 29 miles away. Golfers enjoy the Millbrook Country Club, with its eighteen holes of golf, tennis courts, and Olympic-sized pool. To enjoy the world-famous Mardi Gras, Picayune residents don't have to worry about finding a place to stay—New Orleans is only 40 miles away across Lake Pontchartrain. Similarly, Saints professional football is easily accessible to Picayune sports fans. Finally, the local community college offers a wide array of tuition-free classes to senior citizens on a space-available basis.

Louisiana

If you're looking for Gulf Coast beach property in Louisiana, you are out of luck. Except for a short stretch of sand in the western part of the state—humorously referred to as the Cajun Riviera—most of coastal Louisiana is swamps, mudflats, and bayous. People in Texas claim they can tell Louisianans by the high-water marks on their legs. Beaches start when you get to Texas, and Texans feel smug about that. Of course, Lousianans enjoy making snide remarks about Texans, so they're even.

Nowhere in the United States can you find such a rich diversity of people, customs, and worldviews as in Louisiana. These differences aren't imaginary. You can travel 50 miles in almost any direction and you'll hear distinct accents, slang, music, and possibly even different languages. The cuisine is different, too. With eight ethnic groups tracing their ancestors back through Louisiana's history, it isn't surprising that many people here are bilingual, sometimes with English as their second tongue. Visiting Louisiana is almost like visiting a foreign country.

LOUISIANA TAX PROFILE

Sales tax: 4% to 10%, drugs and some food exempt
State income tax: graduated from 2% to 6% over $50,000; federal income tax deductible
Property taxes: local taxes average of 1.15% of market value, with $75,000 exemption; no state property tax
Intangibles tax: no
Social security taxed: no
Pensions taxed: private pensions taxable, $6,000 exemption
Gasoline tax: 20¢ per gallon, plus sales tax

To truly understand Louisiana you need a background in the state's history. The region was first explored by the French in 1682. Twenty years later, French colonists arrived and replaced Indian villages with their own settlements. Before long the French were joined by the Spanish, who came to trade and decided to settle. The British tried to get a foothold here with small success. Then traders and merchants from the American colonies became regular visitors via flatboats from Pennsylvania. They drifted down the Ohio and Mississippi rivers to the Gulf of Mexico, sold their goods, and trekked back home via the Natchez Trace.

Hundreds of German families were recruited in 1719 by the Company of the West (which held the French royal charter for the development of Louisiana). These European pioneers settled up river from New Orleans along a section of the Mississippi River that is still called the *Côte des Allemands*, "German Coast."

Next, a wave of exiled French-speaking Acadians from Nova Scotia arrived to bolster the French personality of the region. West African slaves were imported to work the plantations, further adding exotic customs, cuisine, and languages to the mixture. More French influence was added by French aristocrats escaping the bloodbath of the French Revolution and those fleeing slave revolts in the West Indies. After the American Revolution, many of Lafayette's French and Italian mercenaries decided to stay instead of returning to Europe; many of them drifted to Louisiana.

In the mid-1800s, legions of Irish and Italians made Louisiana their New World destination when famine and depression drove them from their countries. These immigrants found ready employment in dangerous jobs; they constructed waterways and bridges, and cleared swamps. Slaves were too valuable to risk on such projects. A slave cost $2,000; an Irishman worked for a dollar a day.

Spanish influence never died out, even though France held Louisiana in its grip for most of its early years. You might be surprised to learn that many famous structures in New Orleans's French Quarter were actually built by the Spanish during the time Spain ruled Louisiana. Many old Louisiana families have Spanish surnames, and Spanish is still spoken in some communities, particularly in St. Bernard Parish, below New Orleans.

Prior to the Civil War, Louisiana was the most liberal-thinking state in the South regarding slavery. This was particularly so in New Orleans, where free blacks had many educational and professional opportunities. They became skillful carpenters, masons, blacksmiths, and artisans. Many became successful businessmen, even teachers and doctors. Free blacks amassed some of Louisiana's largest landholdings and made major contributions to the culture. Things changed after the Civil War, when the notorious Black Codes excluded people of color from certain occupations.

Other immigrant nationalities represented in Louisiana are Hungarians who became cultivators of strawberries and other crops in the Albany area. You'll notice that most of Louisiana's many local festivals are celebrations of particular ethnic contributions to the "cultural gumbo" of this unique state.

Suffice to say that Louisiana has an eclectic collection of nationalities and cultures. Of course, France quite naturally left the strongest influence, as evidenced by the widespread use of "Cajun French." Other artifacts of French influence are the concept of *parish* instead of "county" and Louisiana's legal procedures, which bear a stronger resemblance to the Napoleonic Code than British common law.

Louisiana's unique property tax system is highly praised by residents who relocate here from other states. Because the state derives most of its revenues from taxes on petroleum, there is no state property tax on residences. Furthermore, there's a $75,000 deduction from local property taxes. Since real estate prices are low, the generous tax exclusion is often higher than the value of the average home. Except for more expensive properties, the homeowner pays little or nothing in the way of property taxes.

Acadiana (Cajun Country)

Louisiana's most famous ethnic group is the Cajuns, those French Canadians who were evicted from the Canadian province of Acadia (today's Nova Scotia) back in 1755. The English authorities—with the typical British tact and understanding of the time—insisted that the Acadians not only swear allegiance to the Crown, but that they renounce their Roman Catholic faith and join the Church of England. Or get out. The mass exodus that followed was recounted in Henry Wadsworth Longfellow's *Evangeline.* (Somehow I always assumed the Acadians fled Canada rather than submit to English cooking. Ever notice how the Brits boil everything they can't fry?)

The exiles went through terribly difficult times. Some families were shipped to the West Indies, some to the New England colonies, others went back to France. Many wandered, homeless for twenty years, before finding a welcome in the French-speaking environs of Louisiana. They established small farms along the Mississippi River, Bayou Teche, Bayou Lafourche, and other streams and bayous in the territory's southwestern section. The word *Cajun* comes from a modification of the original French pronunciation of Acadian (*A-ca-jan*), describing their French Canadian origins.

At one time, Cajuns were noted for their closed society. As a defense mechanism, they jealously maintained their French language and their private way of living, excluding outsiders from their lives, referring to them as *les Americaines*. World War II and the Korean and Vietnam wars brought Cajuns into contact with the outside world. Television, radio, and movies added to the momentum of change. Acadian society is open today, with retirees from out of state trying retirement in Cajun country. Traditional Cajun hospitality now extends to all.

Occasionally, Cajun French can be heard today, the archaic French spoken by original settlers more than two centuries ago. Cajun music—played on the fiddle, accordion, and triangle—is still featured at dances. It's mostly older people who regularly speak French, however; the younger generation understands the language and still can converse if need be, but seems to prefer English.

This is particularly interesting country for those who love hunting and fishing. For more than two centuries, people living in these isolated and heavily wooded areas have hunted, not only for sport but to put meat on the table. Extensive networks of bayous, rivers, and streams provide fresh fish to supplement the diet, with hunting and fishing an integral part of every Cajun family's life. From almost any rural home, it is rarely more than a few minutes by foot or pickup to a "camp," which is what Cajuns call their favorite hunting or fishing places. Roast duck, venison, and wild boar perk up many Cajun menus.

Although we've traveled in Cajun country and love the people—with their quaint accents and spry sense of humor—we used to question whether out-of-state people might feel at home in such a different culture. During our last trip through Louisiana, we did some in-depth interviews and are now confident about recommending that people investigate Cajun country for retirement possibilities. Certainly, it is an option we personally favor (since we have friends there, we could be biased). Our experience is that Cajuns are exceptionally friendly.

An example of Cajun hospitality: One time, during a trip through Louisiana, we were invited to lunch at a Cajun couple's home. The meal was just being placed on the table when a stranger knocked on the kitchen door. Our friends were puzzled. They'd never seen this man before. It turns out he was a telephone repairman whose truck was stuck in the mud just down the road. Our host explained, "Can't help you right now. We're just sittin' down to eat. Why don't you have lunch with us? Got plenty of food. After we eat, we'll take my tractor and pull you out of that mud." Newcomers moving into this neighborhood won't be strangers for long.

From the perspective of someone who loves good food, a big plus for living in Cajun country is the connection with Cajun cuisine. A first cousin to the Creole cuisine of New Orleans, Cajun cooking is way ahead in terms of creativity of its dishes and the artistic inspiration of its seasonings. Favorite Cajun dishes include jambalaya, gumbo, *cochon du lait* (suckling pig), *boudin* (a blood, pork, and rice sausage), soft-shell crab, stuffed crab, crawfish étouffée, crawfish bisque, crawfish pie, and shrimp fixed every possible way a Cajun chef can imagine. That's just for starters.

Upscale restaurants all over the world are jumping on the Cajun cooking bandwagon. They've discovered that simply tacking the term *Cajun* to a menu item works miracles. Should the chef make a mistake and burn something, it's advertised as "Cajun Blackened Broccoli," or whatever. One Cajun, angry at worldwide plagiarism of cherished recipes, declares: "My Mama never blackened anything in her life and put it on the table. If my Mama ever blackened somethin' it was a pure mistake, and she wasn't ashamed to *call* it a mistake. She'd feed it to the *dogs!*"

Lafayette and Vicinity   Lafayette is often called the "Cajun Capital City," and it offers a full range of activities and services, anything seniors need for quality retirement. Housing of all kinds in all price ranges is available, including several specialized housing developments with independent and assisted living arrangements, such as Azalea Estates and Courtyard at South College. New developments are underway away from the center of the city, with some impressive "plantation manor" homes on half-acre lots.

For those who feel that Lafayette is too much like a city, there are several delightful choices away from town. Southwest of Lafayette the charming little city of Abbeville (pop. 12,000) is known for its two quaint town squares. Abbeville claims to be the "most Cajun place on Earth." Then, there's New Iberia (pop. 32,000) to the east, set among the breathtaking plantations and gardens of

LAFAYETTE WEATHER					
In degrees Fahrenheit					
	Jan.	April	July	Oct.	Rain	Snow
Daily Highs	62	79	91	79	54"	0.5"
Daily Lows	42	58	73	59		

LAFAYETTE AREA COST OF LIVING					
Percentage of	Overall	Housing	Medical	Groceries	Utilities
National Average	99	104	92	94	87

Shadows-on-the-Teche. Another major center of Cajun culture is Opelousas (pop. 18,500), the third oldest city in Louisiana, famous as the site of Jim Bowie's residence and well known for having produced many fine Creole and Cajun chefs. The nearby towns of Marksville, Bunkie, Simmesport, Bordelonville, and others are wonderfully steeped in history, yet lie quietly and unpretentiously as places for peaceful living.

Lafayette and the surrounding Cajun heartland offers horse racing, boat tours of the Atchafalaya Basin Swamp, and facilities for golf and tennis. Nearby Abbeville is known for excellent duck and goose hunting, hosting a duck festival every Labor Day. Golf courses, while not numerous, are scattered throughout Cajun country, so that you can play if you don't mind a thirty-minute or so drive.

Besides a branch of Louisiana State University, Lafayette has a local community college, affectionately known as "Gumbo U," that provides excellent adult education programs for cultural enrichment. Festivals are big here, with one taking place nearly every weekend. There's a crawfish festival in Breaux Bridge, a French music festival in Abbeville, a rice festival in Crowley, even a Boudin Festival. (Boudin is a special Cajun sausage.) Lafayette is host to the South's second-largest Mardi Gras, complete with parades, balls, masquerades, and more.

Lafayette has six hospitals, with a total of 1,134 beds. Opelousas General Hospital serves as a referral medical center and offers a comprehensive community health-care facility with a wide range of medical specialties and state-of-the-art technology.

Houma   French Acadians first settled Houma in 1765, when 250 exiles arrived from the Caribbean island of Santo Domingo. They were so delighted to finally have a homeland, the settlers christened the region *terre bonne,* which means "good earth." With fertile land and abundant fish and wildlife, their isolated geographic location ensured a minimum amount of governmental intervention. They lived in seclusion for generations and some continue their family traditions of living off the land today.

Houma is only an hour's drive from fabulous old New Orleans, less than two hours from the state capital of Baton Rouge, and a little more than two hours from Lafayette and the famed Evangeline country. This is an excellent location for the retiree who wishes to experience the unique sights and sounds, the *joie de vivre* so well known in Cajun country, and the "work hard and play hard" attitude of the people whose ancestors settled the bayou country so many years ago.

Crime in large cities like New Orleans is always high. When you leave the city, crime rates drop dramatically, no matter what part of the country. When we visited Houma a few years ago, it was ranked tenth in the nation in safety, according to FBI statistics. Occasionally it drops a few places, but that doesn't mean much. In a smaller city like Houma, a few isolated problems or a visiting burglar can magnify crime statistics, making it appear as if a crime wave had struck.

Its residential streets and homes are comfortable-looking: neatly mowed lawns, children roller-skating on sidewalks, and neighbors talking over backyard fences. If that's what you are looking for, you might investigate any number of towns like this

HOUMA WEATHER						
In degrees Fahrenheit						
	Jan.	April	July	Oct.	Rain	Snow
Daily Highs	62	79	92	79	57"	0.2"
Daily Lows	42	59	72	60		

HOUMA AREA COST OF LIVING					
Percentage of	Overall	Housing	Medical	Groceries	Utilities
National Average	96	90	87	94	111

within striking distance of New Orleans but far enough away not to be struck back.

Baton Rouge   Not really in Acadiana, Baton Rouge received its French name well before the Cajuns entered the bayou country. French explorer Pierre Le Moyne (Sieur d'Iberville) organized the first permanent European settlement here back in 1682. The site he selected for the village had a tall, bloodstained cypress tree on the riverbank that marked the hunting territory of two Indian tribes. The villagers christened the area *Baton Rouge*, "red stick."

As you might expect, Louisiana's state capital—Baton Rouge (pop. 225,000)—is a handsome city. With neat, prosperous-looking neighborhoods, attractive subdivisions, and one of the prettiest university campuses in the country, Baton Rouge fulfills its role as political and educational center of the state. Its distinctive blend of French, Creole, Cajun, and Old South traditions makes it as much a part of Louisiana as the great river on which it thrives.

Until the real estate market pushed up prices, Baton Rouge had one of the lowest costs of living of any city of its size in the country. Living costs and housing prices are now about average for the nation. But it's the quality of the setting that makes it a bargain.

Most university towns have lots to offer retirees. Baton Rouge's Louisiana State University (LSU) is no exception. Its cultural offerings and its enrichment of the intellectual aspect of the community are quite important, but additionally the school attracts scholars, professors, and university employees from all over the country. The narrow, conservative atmosphere of many Southern cities is absent in Baton Rouge. Students, faculty, support personnel, and families

BATON ROUGE WEATHER						
In degrees Fahrenheit						
	Jan.	April	July	Oct.	Rain	Snow
Daily Highs	61	79	91	80	55"	—
Daily Lows	41	58	73	56		

BATON ROUGE COST OF LIVING					
Percentage of National Average	Overall	Housing	Medical	Groceries	Utilities
	101	99	96	105	114

of these outside people nourish fresh views and lifestyles throughout the community.

My distinct impression is that most residents do *not* use the thick Southern accent one expects from such a deep South location. This shouldn't be surprising, since so many people come from places where Midwestern accents are the norm. I attribute the university's influence for this leveling of accents. Among the natives, a slight Cajun twist of pronunciation is common, but this is totally different from a conventional Southern accent.

The university touches the community in other ways, culturally as well as educationally. A slogan here is "Art is the Heart of Baton Rouge." Using the talent in theater, music, and fine arts that LSU attracts, the community has organized some commendable programs. Every year a 10-block stretch of downtown is blocked off so people can see potters at their wheels, musicians entertaining, and artists at their easels. Mimes entertain the crowds, and craftspeople of all kinds sell their wares. Two ballet groups bring stars from major companies to work with local students; the Baton Rouge Opera is in its tenth season. Two light opera companies, a symphony orchestra, and a professional theater company round out the cultural offerings. The city is quite proud of its historic past and is taking vigorous steps to preserve and restore two downtown neighborhoods, historic Beauregard Town and Spanish Town.

As a retirement location, Baton Rouge has a lot going for it. It's a cosmopolitan community, and it's centrally located. It's just 70 miles by interstate to New Orleans for those extra-special nights on the town or for the hilarity of Mardi Gras. You can reach the beaches at Pass Christian in two hours by car. Fifty miles to the north is the nineteenth-century atmosphere of historic Natchez. For riverboat gambling you don't have to go far. Baton Rouge has two riverboat casinos, The Belle of Baton Rouge and Casino Rouge.

Natchitoches   This is another place we would never have found had it not been for the state's retirement welcoming program: the town of Natchitoches in the north-central part of the state. Strangers always have problems pronouncing the name. We usually try to pronounce it as it's spelled, which brings polite smiles to the faces of natives, if not outright guffaws. It's pronounced *NAK-a-tish*.

NATCHITOCHES WEATHER					
In degrees Fahrenheit					
	Jan.	April	July	Oct.	Rain	Snow
Daily Highs	56	78	92	79	58"	0.7"
Daily Lows	36	55	73	55		

This is an Indian word meaning Place of the Paw Paw, or Chinquapin nut.

History buffs will find plenty to marvel at in this fascinating little city of 17,000 inhabitants. Natchitoches has one of the most picturesque and authentic downtown sections of any place we've yet seen in this region, reminiscent of the French Quarter in New Orleans. To get an idea of what the town looks like, rent the movie *Steel Magnolias* from your local video store. The picture was produced on location here, using homes in the downtown area as stages and local people as extras.

Natchitoches has the proud distinction of being the oldest settlement in the entire Louisiana Territory. French explorers first made contact with the Natchitoches Indians in 1700, and fourteen years later established a trading outpost on the Red River. Natchitoches soon became a bustling river port and an important crossroads. Wealthy planters not only built imposing plantation houses along the river; they also maintained elegant showplaces in town.

Sometime in the 1830s the U.S. government decided to clear the logjam so river barges could travel upstream to what is now Shreveport. Theoretically, this would make Natchitoches even more prosperous. But to the dismay of Natchitoches residents, the Red River changed its course, leaving the once-thriving river town high and dry, several miles from the new river course. The town's future as a bustling port town became history as the river became a spring-fed creek. Although this disaster isolated Natchitoches, it safeguarded its historic buildings from the curse of progress and urban renewal. It also preserved the deeply ingrained traditions of its residents.

Fortunately, Natchitoches came up with a great idea. Why not dam the old channel and create a lake? Today a 26-mile oxbow lake, called Cane River Lake, runs through upscale Natchitoches residential areas and is the showpiece of the downtown National Landmark

District. Cane River Lake looks very much like a river but aesthetically is much better. The lake-river doesn't flood or become silty in rainy weather. It doesn't have a current or carry flotsam and debris from upstream, and it provides a place for peaceful boating and good fishing in its clear, spring-fed waters. Best of all, it lends an air of Old South dignity to Natchitoches, with huge oak and magnolia trees arching over the lake's bank and weeping willows trailing branches into the still water.

Natchitoches's rich historical background encompasses French, Spanish, Native American, African, and Anglo-Saxon influences. Contemporary residents take pride in this colorful palette of tradition, and carefully maintain their ties with the past by preserving the older part of the city. Large antebellum "town homes" of cotton planters sit next to ornate Victorian houses and substantial homes dating from the early 1800s. Some have been converted to bed-and-breakfasts. (In all, Natchitoches has 21 bed-and-breakfasts.)

These historic buildings are more than museum pieces; they are homes of residents who enjoy being within a short walk of the fascinating downtown. At first we suspected that Natchitoches's commercial district might be a clever remodeling project. The brick streets, wrought-iron balconies, and storefronts—all in the style of the 1850s—looked too authentic to be real. But several stores display photographs taken of downtown businesses more than a century ago. They clearly show that, indeed, this is how Natchitoches looked in its prime.

Natchitoches's further claim to being a good retirement choice is enhanced by the presence of Northwestern State University. In addition to its symphony, dinner theater, ballet, and other entertainment, the school offers many interesting continuing-education programs for mature adults.

Compared to the national average, Natchitoches's housing prices seem low. Historic homes sell for half what similar places would fetch in Charleston or Savannah. But for this region, prices are probably $10,000 above average. This is understandable when the setting is considered.

Toledo Bend Lake   Toledo Bend, a 186,000-acre man-made reservoir created by damming the Sabine River, is the fifth-largest man-made lake in the country. The body of water stretches north-

TOLEDO BEND WEATHER					
In degrees Fahrenheit					
	Jan.	April	July	Oct.	Rain	Snow
Daily Highs	56	77	94	79	44"	0.7"
Daily Lows	36	55	73	54		

south for 70 miles, with 1,100 miles of irregular shoreline. Inlets and bays make great places for lakeshore homes and boat docks, though some sections have dead trees and stumps sticking out of the water. Apparently local fishermen prefer these areas because that's where the fish are. However, the Sabine Recreation Authority has three cutting barges working full time clearing stumps and trees in addition to improving existing boat lanes. Eventually most of the lake will be pristine.

The Toledo Bend region is in the first stages of development and is anticipating growth in the near future. In the meantime, the lake affords sports fun and excitement for tourists as well as low-keyed and quiet retirement living for residents.

Living in an isolated and rustic area like Toledo Bend has certain drawbacks. It's still sparsely populated, so, depending on where you live, you must travel to the nearby towns of Shreveport, Many, Leesville, or DeRidder for your medical services and major shopping. The way the area is developing, however, it may only be a matter of time until Wal–Mart, Walgreens, and Wendy's make their appearance. Residents hope not.

The real surprise in recreational facilities is the new public golf course at Cypress Bend. The $3-million, eighteen-hole championship layout fronts on the lake and was funded as a joint project by the federal and state governments. Plans are on the drawing board for a multi-million-dollar resort, complete with a 100-room hotel, condominiums, and a convention center at Cypress Bend. If this comes to pass, you can be sure there'll be a proliferation of jobs and new residents to swell the population.

The area surrounding Toledo Bend is home to many species of birds: pelicans, egrets, cranes, bald eagles, ducks, and a host of migratory species. Other wildlife in the area include white–tail deer, fox, armadillo, opossum, raccoon, coyote, beaver, and wild hog.

The lake is said to have a fish population of 300 pounds per square acre. Local residents swear that the lake is so full of bass, crappie, and catfish that the fish regularly engage in fistfights to see who gets to be next on your hook. In order to promote catch-and-release protocol, fiberglass replicas of lunker bass are awarded those sportsmen who catch and release the big guys. We've seen these fiberglass replicas; they look very natural, but local fishermen complain that they're difficult to clean, and you have to cook them a long time to make 'em tender.

Residential and business construction in the Toledo Bend area is on the increase. In the past few years there has been a significant increase in population, with more than 900 new homes constructed as well as almost 600 mobile homes to house new residents. Real estate offerings vary from rustic fish camps by the water's edge to gorgeous lakeview homes. Building costs here can be higher than in the larger towns, simply because workers and materials must be brought in from neighboring cities. This will change as the volume of building accelerates.

Leesville and DeRidder

When World War II exploded, the government hurriedly constructed a large Army post in an almost deserted part of western Louisiana. They called it Fort Polk. Generals Eisenhower, Patton, and Clark used the region to train several million soldiers. The first draftees pushed through Fort Polk for training retained bad memories of those rustic early days, so it's understandable that the installation acquired a poor reputation among the military. Over the years the government gradually improved conditions. They constructed quality off-post quarters in Leesville and DeRidder and added amenities to the post itself, such as a championship golf course,

LEESVILLE–DERIDDER WEATHER						
In degrees Fahrenheit						
	Jan.	April	July	Oct.	Rain	Snow
Daily Highs	56	77	93	79	44"	2"
Daily Lows	36	55	73	55		

park-like landscaping, and quality housing. Those who did tours of duty at Fort Polk in later years look back with fond memories of Leesville and DeRidder. One retiree from Klamath Falls, Oregon, said, "The first time I came to Fort Polk, the Army dragged me here kicking and screaming. But six years ago, I decided to retire here!"

Leesville   In line with recent Pentagon policy, Leesville's Fort Polk has been downsized. Local residents were delighted that the fort wasn't shut down entirely, something which would have been disastrous for the economy. As part of the cutbacks, however, the government ordered all enlisted men to live on base. This created a buyer's market for quality housing in Leesville and nearby DeRidder. These favorable real estate prices, along with the presence of a retirement welcoming committee in both Leesville and DeRidder, prompted our research for relocation opportunities here. Retirement committee volunteers are available to take visitors on a tour of their area and share their pride in the community.

A small city of about 12,000 residents, Leesville's homes were well designed, mostly of brick construction and set on generous plots of tree-shaded land. The historic downtown center, off the highway going through Leesville, is undergoing a dramatic renovation. An old theater has been beautifully restored as a special-events place for banquets, proms, parties, and meetings. Electric lines are now underground and attractive lighting has replaced old lightposts. Because of community efforts, Leesville won first place in the district's Cleanest City contest.

The older residential section immediately around the town center is stocked with prewar traditional white frame homes, mostly suitable for low-cost housing. There's a potential for restoration here, as well. These places would be suitable for people who like being within walking distance of downtown.

The golf course at Fort Polk is the local pride and joy, and its beautiful eighteen-hole layout is always open to the general public. With all the lakes, rivers, and forests nearby, outdoors people have plenty of opportunity for fishing and hunting or just enjoying a hike or boat ride. Leesville/Fort Polk is also blessed with a branch of Northwestern State University for adult education. The school offers courses in several professional fields in addition to leisure learning classes. Seniors may take one course per semester tuition-free, with an application fee of $15.

DeRidder   Down the highway 20 miles, DeRidder is slightly the smaller of the two towns, with an estimated population of around 10,000. DeRidder has a section of old, elegant homes, a legacy of the bounty the town realized through timber harvests in the early part of the century. These elaborate showplaces attest to the wealth of the timber barons and merchants. Several modern neighborhoods have more upscale housing, and some are showplaces in their own right.

Like Leesville, DeRidder is a home–buyer's market because of the downsizing at Fort Polk. The city is also in the process of revitalizing its historic downtown section. The center is starting to look as if it might make a comeback, with several businesses flourishing. The historic old railroad depot has been converted to a museum with a unique collection of antique dolls, bringing tourists to the downtown.

One of the absolute jewels of DeRidder's downtown renovation project is its new library. The library is fast becoming the heartbeat of the community. This is one of the first places newcomers should check in. An exciting part of the library is a program called the Cyberspace Launch Pad, an innovative approach to community involvement in computers and the Internet. Thanks to a generous grant from the state, a sophisticated computer network offers free computer connections to all county residents. The emphasis is on communications via the Internet. For retirees, this means staying in touch by e-mail with children and grandchildren anywhere in the world. Those seniors who don't have computers can use the library's equipment and are issued their own e-mail accounts. Those who don't know how to use computers are given lessons and hands-on training. An example of the library's innovative approach is the Cyber-Grandparent Program. This project links grandparents and grandchildren by e-mail and Web pages so they can work together to perform school projects. The cyber-grandparents help their grandkids with homework as they maintain close relationships.

DeRidder also has several upscale neighborhoods, with prices about the same as Leesville. Bargains are to be found in either community due to the present buyer's market.

Alexandria Between 1988 and 1995 the U.S. government closed down 536 military bases, handing over a total of six million acres to state and local control. This is the largest transfer of land since the Oklahoma Land Rush. From what we hear, this is just 30 percent of the planned closures; there are more to come. The big question is: What are we going to do with these multi-billion-dollar properties?

Of course, all military bases aren't exactly prime real estate. Many were constructed in deserts, swamps, or inaccessible back country. They'll probably sit and gather sagebrush until the next war. But many bases are ideally located for residential and industrial development. Over the years, the government spent untold billions on these bases, constructing homes for officers and enlisted men, building PX facilities resembling Wal-Mart, top-quality golf courses, swimming pools, and other amenities that made the bases resemble self-contained cities.

However, many localities feel highly threatened by these abandoned housing units. If sold to the public, these units could glut the open market, causing real estate values to plunge through the floor. Bad enough the military pulled many thousands of consumers from the region, without adding more chaos. Yet, it's a shame to let all of these expensive amenities go to waste.

The solution to this dilemma: convert base housing to senior housing, and bring in over-fifty-five folks (and their money) from

ALEXANDRIA WEATHER

In degrees Fahrenheit

	Jan.	April	July	Oct.	Rain	Snow
Daily Highs	56	79	93	79	42"	0.7"
Daily Lows	36	56	74	55		

ALEXANDRIA COST OF LIVING

Percentage of	Overall	Housing	Medical	Groceries	Utilities
National Average	96	93	84	89	114

outside the community to rejuvenate the local economy. The incoming retirees occupy homes that would otherwise be left to deteriorate and will be boosting the economy to boot.

When England Air Force Base, on the outskirts of Alexandria, was decommissioned, the city turned the airfield into its major commercial airport, re-naming it Alexandria International. Warehouses and repair facilities were leased to manufacturers, and some buildings were converted to offices and warehouses.

This left a large collection of housing, mostly two- and three-bedroom homes, in good shape and ready for occupancy. Since the redevelopment authority didn't want to damage the local real estate and rental markets, they decided to restrict the base housing to two categories of tenants: retirees and employees of businesses located on the former air-base property. They named the complex England Oaks, because of the live oak trees that abound here. As an experiment, it was decided that the homes should be leased, rather than sold (as is the case in most other senior developments).

Therefore, England Oaks is aimed at a distinct niche of retirement service: an independent living facility for middle-income seniors who don't care to invest a lot of money in their retirement homes. Additional advantages are the security and convenience that go with a maintenance-free lifestyle. Retirees combine suburban home life with group social and recreational activities, without sacrificing comfort, space, and privacy. Social life in England Oaks is centered around the development's clubhouse (the former officers' club) where regular meetings, potlucks, and social hours are held.

The two- and three-bedroom homes (formerly noncommissioned officers' housing) have been remodeled with a view to attracting active seniors whose health is such that assisted living is somewhere down the road. Homes are equipped with emergency-response systems, safety features for the elderly, and even telephones with large, easy-to-read pushbuttons and a voice that echoes back the number so that a person with poor eyesight can know he or she has made the right connection. This is a pleasant, secure neighborhood of homes shaded by oaks and pecan trees, with a golf course, hiking and bike trails, and a gated community that gives you a feeling of security.

An arrangement like this especially appeals to retired military because they're familiar with military retirement complexes like Air Force Village in San Antonio and elsewhere. The new concept here is that instead of large, nonrefundable deposits of many thousands of dollars, England Oaks requires only a $300 refundable deposit and $595 to $725 per month on a year's lease.

The Mid-southern Hills

IF YOU LOOK AT A MAP of the United States, you'll notice a curious east-west line that cuts the country almost in two. From the point where Nevada, Arizona, and Utah intersect, state boundaries form a line that runs eastward until it hits the Atlantic Ocean near Norfolk, Virginia. This line bisects the nation, separating Virginia from North Carolina, Kentucky from Tennessee, Missouri from Arkansas, Kansas from Oklahoma, Colorado from New Mexico, and Utah from Arizona. Except for a slight deviation around the southern edge of Missouri, the demarcation is almost perfectly straight.

Why the line runs as it does is something only historians or geographers can explain. A long stretch runs through what I call the "Mid-southern Hills"—through the heart of the Appalachians, the Tennessee-Kentucky hill country, the Ozark Mountains of Missouri and Arkansas, and into Oklahoma's Ozark section. Straddling this line is an interesting swathe of woodlands, hills, plains, and mountains, places that offer prime retirement conditions for those who like four seasons and a woodsy and slow-paced lifestyle. A low cost of living, inexpensive housing, and high personal safety are bonuses.

Industry and modern agriculture characterize the country to the north of this strip of semi-wilderness. Below is the Deep South. Life in the Mid-southern Hills moves at its own pace, always a little out of sync with the rest of the nation. Until World War II, this was one of the most poverty-stricken segments of the nation. Cartoonist Al Capp located his imaginary town of Dogpatch here, the home of indigent Lil' Abner, his family, and his girlfriend, Daisy Mae. Although the cartoon strip amused folks who didn't have to live in Dogpatch, real-life circumstances were anything but funny. Roads were often gravel and dirt. Subsistence farmers lived in flimsy shacks as they raised families and tried to coax a living from the rocky soil.

The change in living standards since the war years has been nothing less than miraculous. Change began with the government building dams and water–power projects to provide cheap electricity. Manufacturing industries and businesses relocated to take advantage of inexpensive power as well as low labor costs. Local people no longer had to move to the north to find employment.

Fortunately, progress didn't destroy the Mid-southern Hills's natural beauty; it actually improved things. With the dams came lakes, hundreds of them. The combination of Ozark and Appalachian scenery with new lakes—perfect for fishing, boating, water-skiing, and just plain looking—created an overnight tourist sensation. Vacationers brought money, and retirees brought even more dollars, which further contributed to economic growth. Today, small farms are more often a hobby or a sideline than a means of survival.

Because of its porous limestone base, the Ozark formation is honeycombed with underground caves, sometimes storing so much water that rivers gush from the cavernous depths as if by magic. One example: In Missouri's Big Spring Park, a full-fledged river surfaces at the rate of 286 million gallons a day! Ozark soil—typically rock-studded, rust-red in color, and nutrient-poor—doesn't lend itself easily to plows or farm machinery. For this reason large portions of this country escaped agricultural development; they remain rustic, unspoiled, and delightful places for retirement hideaways.

Climate

Every retiree we interview here emphasizes the four-season climate as a major plus. "I like to know what time of year it is," said one lady who had lived in California before retirement. "Here, I get the feeling of seasons. Summer is nice and hot, fall is beautiful and colorful, winter is short and merciful, and then comes spring!" She sighed in ecstasy.

Make no mistake: Winter does bring chilly winds, creeks ice over, and your furnace gets a workout. Still, it doesn't begin to compare with winters farther north. Summers are humid, but not unbearable, with 90-degree highs normal. Enough rain falls in the summer to keep the landscape looking green and fresh, streams flowing, and fishing good to excellent year-round.

Politics

Most Mid-southern Hills retirees come from Northern or Mid-western states. Besides bringing money, they often bring political know-how and a willingness to participate in local politics. This combination is tipping political scales throughout foothill and mountain communities. Since many retirees are well-to-do, they tend to think conservatively, and, as a consequence, traditionally Democratic states such as Arkansas, Kentucky, and Tennessee gain more Republican voters daily, much to the delight of Republican Party workers. One Republican Party official said, "When I started campaigning in north Arkansas in the 'sixties, it was like pulling teeth to find people to come out and help. This movement of new faces into the state has had a tremendous impact on Arkansas politics. People in the Republican Party are no longer considered carpetbaggers."

Regardless of political affiliation, retirees vote in much higher proportions than the younger set, and they tend to get involved in nonpartisan issues that affect community and state decision making. This new political power shows up clearly in the state legislature as well as in county and city partisan politics. Politicians are always sensitive to such a large bloc of voters. As an illustration: Arkansas spends more money per capita on services for the elderly than any other state in the nation. As you might imagine, Arkansas senior citizens' organizations are very active and take full advantage of state and federal allocations of funds.

Transportation

As mentioned earlier in this book, many small towns lack intercity bus service and air transportation. This is particularly common in the Mid-southern Hills area. Without intercity buses or passenger trains, you are totally dependent upon an automobile. The nearest airport could be 75 miles away. When the grandkids come to visit, how do they get to your place from the airport? If you don't drive, and if you're used to public transportation, don't take it for granted when looking for a retirement destination. Make it a point to determine the situation before locking yourself in.

Arkansas

Arkansas is a major beneficiary of today's retirement trends. Next to Florida, Arkansas is one of the fastest-growing states in number of new residents over age sixty-five. Throughout the state almost a fifth

of the population is over sixty, with percentages much higher in popular retirement locations.

Newcomers from Chicago or Indianapolis find it easy to make friends, because they find that many of their neighbors have come from the same part of the country, have similar interests, and have common things to talk about. This is convenient because, believe it or not, many Arkansas natives have never even *heard* of the Chicago Cubs, much less spent time discussing their pennant possibilities for the season.

What is the attraction here? Arkansas' mild, four-season climate, low taxes, and personal safety. Inexpensive housing and friendly people figure into the picture, but the catalyst for retirees settling in Arkansas is the glorious Ozark environment. These low, ancient, thickly forested mountains symbolize many retirement dreams. The Ozarks represent a rebirth of simplicity, a purging of city life, and a new mode of relaxation.

Besides clear-running streams, squeaky-clean air, and lakes swarming with fish, many retirement dreams also picture an isolated cabin with a boat dock at the back door and lazy days of casting for bigmouth bass or lake trout. True, the *wife* doesn't always picture things exactly that way, but even non-fishermen enjoy the Ozarks's beautiful surroundings.

The southern part of Arkansas, below the Ozarks, is rarely the choice of folks coming from other states. They prefer the northern half above Hot Springs and Little Rock. This is important to know. Without a substantial number of out-of-state retirees or other outsiders for neighbors, you could find yourself isolated among folks with whom you have little in common. Not that people would be anything but friendly and neighborly, but unless your cultural background is basically agricultural and small-town, you could have a difficult time adjusting.

Arkansas state policy on college education is to waive general student fees for credit courses to persons age sixty and older on a space-available basis. State vocational and technical schools also waive fees.

Following are some northern Arkansas towns we've visited and that we feel confident have potential for retirement. All have

ARKANSAS TAX PROFILE
Sales tax: 5.5%, plus 3.5% on fast food
State income tax: graduated, 1% on first $3,000 income to 7% on $25,000 and over
Property taxes: average 3.9% of assessed value, set at 20% of appraised value
Intangibles tax: no
Social security taxed: no
Pensions taxed: excludes $6,000 from government and private pensions
Gasoline tax: 18.5¢ per gallon

a significant number of non-natives living there. Some places are small, but none are isolated from medical and other important services. Intercity transportation is sometimes a problem, something you'll have to look at if you don't drive.

Fayetteville   Up in the northwest corner of Arkansas' Ozark Mountains, two great candidates for senior relocation await your consideration. On either side of 28,000-acre Beaver Lake, Eureka Springs and Fayetteville have both received favorable publicity as great places for relocation. Between them is the small city of Rogers, and to the north of Fayetteville is one of the earliest planned developments in Arkansas, Bella Vista.

Fayetteville is the largest, a city of about 50,000 people plus almost 15,000 students at the University of Arkansas. This part of Arkansas also shares in some of the most beautiful Ozark scenery in the entire region. It starts just a few miles from downtown Fayetteville.

One way you can tell you're in a college town: Look for a collection of offbeat gourmet restaurants. Fayetteville has 'em all. Besides a tempting selection of Japanese, Mexican, and barbecue restaurants, downtown Fayetteville offers esoteric eating establishments with names designed to grab your attention, such as: Gumbo Joe's Cajun Grill, Penguin Ed's, Armadillo Grill, and Schlegel's Bagels. I can't imagine a restaurant named "Penguin Ed's" in a farm town in flatland Arkansas. The chef would be arrested and handcuffed by the local sheriff before the first penguin-on-rye sandwich ever left the grill. (They might accept armadillo, however, if served with red-eye gravy and biscuits.) When Bill Clinton was first running for Congress back in 1974, he and his campaign committee used to meet at a popular place in Fayetteville called the D-Lux Café. (Now doesn't *D-Lux Café* sound more like down-home Arkansas?)

The University of Arkansas is Fayetteville's heart and soul. Without intentionally doing so, the school, its students, and professors add excitement and vigor to the city. To fully savor the magnetism of the resident student community, you must visit Dickson Street, near the campus. This colorful, entertaining street is filled with bistros, restaurants, and art galleries. It's a place to dance the night away to your favorite music. (Doesn't sound like Arkansas, does it?) Dickson Street is also home to the splendid Walton Arts Center.

Fayetteville's downtown is a delightful combination of a healthy business sector combined with a well-preserved historic district, which local residents refer to as "the Square." Commercial and residential buildings have been lovingly restored to their nineteenth-century glory. They contrast nicely with contemporary architecture containing shops and offices. Local farmers and craftspeople are encouraged to bring their wares to the laid-back farmers' market on the square, which takes place three times every week. A tourist trolley provides free transportation for shoppers and visitors to move around Fayetteville's downtown on their leisurely errands.

Homes around the Fayetteville historic district are very much in demand, with potential buyers asking to have their names placed on a waiting list. Most homes have been completely renovated, and are large, from 2,500 to 4,000 square feet. Downtown historic homes sell for as much as $300,000. By way of contrast, a few blocks away is Wilson Park, a safe, homey neighborhood with houses built in the

FAYETTEVILLE WEATHER

In degrees Fahrenheit

	Jan.	April	July	Oct.	Rain	Snow
Daily Highs	48	74	94	76	40"	7"
Daily Lows	27	49	71	49		

FAYETTEVILLE COST OF LIVING

	Overall	Housing	Medical	Groceries	Utilities
Percentage of National Average	88	79	89	91	88

1950s and 1960s, with much lower price tags starting in the $75,000 range. A dozen attractive areas around town, farther away from the city center, offer affordable housing in secure-feeling neighborhoods. Seven upscale developments are in place. One of these is a golf–course subdivision, with residents' back yards touching the greens. In short, the range of real estate is wide here, from Arkansas-inexpensive to more than you'd like to pay.

Bella Vista   About 20 miles north of Fayetteville is the planned community of Bella Vista. One of the earlier experiments in Ozark development, Bella Vista started thirty years ago and now has over 11,000 year-round residents and thousands of seasonal residents. It was created by the same developers as Hot Springs Village, employing the same concepts, although it's older. Originally intended as a retirement and vacation resort, it became popular with commuters to Fayetteville who didn't mind the drive over the new four-lane highway. When you buy into Bella Vista, you automatically belong to four country clubs and recreational complexes. Residents have access to tennis courts, swimming pools, eight lakes, and seven golf courses.

Eureka Springs   This delightful town in northwest Arkansas started with a retirement boom over a century ago. The word *eureka* means "I have found it," and this is how many visitors felt when they decided to convert their vacation visits into permanent retirement here.

People started coming to Eureka Springs around the turn of the century because of the "magical" healing qualities of the spring waters that gushed out of the canyon's grottoes. Perhaps the mineral water helped, but getting away from the crowds and squalor of the city, breathing the pure mountain air, and seeing the lovely Ozark surroundings probably had more than a little to do with the miracle cures.

Of course, the waters were known and appreciated by Native Americans long before the white man muscled into the region. The palefaced newcomers began arriving in large numbers in the 1880s, when the Frisco Railroad ran a line into town to carry visitors from Chicago, St. Louis, and Kansas City. Several large and luxurious hotels accommodated the crowds. Wealthy families built ambitious Victorian mansions that duplicated their big-city homes. Before long, the town's winding streets were lined with houses, hotels, and commercial buildings, many displaying the fancy gingerbread styles of that era.

During World War I, folks stopped coming to Eureka Springs. The town's bonanza was put on hold; its popularity declined as new residents moved away or died. Lovely homes were boarded up and forgotten as absentee owners lost interest in the town. The Great Depression was the final blow; Eureka Springs almost became a ghost town. At the time, townsfolk must have viewed this abandonment as extreme misfortune, but today's residents see it as a stroke of luck. Otherwise, Eureka Springs would have suffered from modernization, with the old buildings gradually replaced by modern structures. This temporary loss of popularity created a virtual time capsule of Victorian architecture.

Your first glimpse of Eureka Springs is a guaranteed surprise. Solid limestone and brick buildings, wrought-iron fancy work, and gracefully styled mansions with winding carriageways make the town a fascinating window into yesterday. Boutiques, restaurants, art galleries, and other businesses occupy the downtown's street-level stores with second- and third-floor apartments for those who live downtown.

Majestic residences line the streets that twist and climb the mountainside above the business district. This incredible collection of Victorians rivals and perhaps even surpasses the finest that San Francisco has to offer. Some have fluted columns rising three stories in front of dignified brick facades and wrought-iron balconies—homes that look as if they belong on the set of *Gone with the Wind*. It's difficult to describe Eureka Springs without slipping into clichés, because the entire town *is* a cliché, a magic peek at yesterday.

The town and environs offer all the amenities retirees seek: good medical facilities, a quaint, artistic cultural atmosphere, friendly neighbors, recreational opportunities, and inexpensive real

EUREKA SPRINGS WEATHER						
In degrees Fahrenheit						
	Jan.	April	July	Oct.	Rain	Snow
Daily Highs	48	73	90	76	44"	6"
Daily Lows	27	49	69	49		

estate. Eureka Springs has become both a retirement mecca and an artist colony.

An interesting aspect of Eureka Springs is that you often can buy a historic Victorian for about what you'd pay for an ordinary tract house in most parts of the country—even less. Several retired couples have converted their spacious old mansions into delightful bed-and-breakfasts. In the old days, not all Victorian homes were mansions, however. Ordinary folks lived in modest-sized houses just as they do today. These places are exceptional bargains, and conventional housing on the town's outskirts is similarly priced well below national averages.

Holiday Island   A half-hour's drive from Eureka Springs takes you to an ambitious golf/country-club resort known as Holiday Island. Located on Table Rock Lake, the resort is set on 5,000 acres of natural beauty. The lake is narrow at this point, following the twists and turns of an old riverbed, thus creating a large number of lakefront lots. Two golf courses (one a nine-hole layout), a number of tennis courts, two swimming pools, and most of the facilities expected of a resort community are in place. Ninety percent of the residents are from other states, mostly from Illinois, Missouri, and Texas.

Golf seems to be excellent here, so much so that enthusiastic golfers purchase inexpensive lots and pay the $283 annual assessment for unlimited use of the courses. Owners of lots also have the right to stay in the development's campground and use all the facilities.

Mena   Small towns have the reputation of being exceptionally low-crime areas. However, crime waves can strike anywhere, at any time. Recently, a serial auto thief struck the western Arkansas town of Mena. Faced with an emergency, Sheriff Mike Oglesby asked the local radio station to broadcast an emergency warning. The warning: "Don't leave your car keys in the ignition! Someone is stealing cars!" Fortunately, the culprit was quickly apprehended—and turned out to be a high school student who liked joyriding. A good thing, too, because Mena citizens aren't used to heavy-duty crime waves. They probably wouldn't remember to remove their keys.

Sitting in a valley surrounded by western Arkansas' Ouachita Mountains, Mena is a pleasant town of 5,500 in a county of 17,000.

It's near the Oklahoma border, about 77 miles west of Hot Springs, and 85 miles south of Fort Smith. Local boosters call their town "the pride of the Ouachitas." (Pronounce it this way: *WAH-shi-taw*!)

Mena is surprisingly prosperous looking, with several upscale neighborhoods where housing sells at scandalously low Arkansas prices. Another surprise: Mena is a college town. Students and faculty always brighten a community, adding a touch of energy and spirit. The college influence shows in the way the downtown is still alive and breathing: The old railroad station, refurbished and restored, is now a museum and chamber of commerce office. Stores, businesses, and restaurants are open and thriving, not boarded up and collecting cobwebs as in some small Arkansas towns.

Part of Mena's economic well-being is due to local industries that employ skilled workers and consequently pay better-than-average wages. U.S. Motors, a division of Emerson Electric, provides a large number of jobs. Another skilled-worker employer is a large facility that repairs and maintains aircraft for major U.S. and Canadian airlines. Its technicians are all FAA qualified, and can work just about anywhere in the world they choose. But they like it here in Mena. One man said, "We were looking for a good place to raise our children, and we couldn't find a better place than Mena."

Good wages have a multiplier effect on the economy in precisely the same way as retired people's incomes do. When spent in the community, wages and incomes turn into profits and wages for other residents. They, in turn, have more money to spend, which benefits still others. The money goes 'round and 'round. Mena's community leaders understand this very clearly. That's exactly why they are so enthused about sharing their community with retirees rather than going after marginal, minimum wage–paying industries as many other Arkansas cities have done.

Mena is surrounded by 1.5 million acres of the Ouachita National Forest, the South's oldest and largest national forest. There are thirty-two recreational areas in the forest where you can enjoy

MENA WEATHER						
In degrees Fahrenheit						
	Jan.	April	July	Oct.	Rain	Snow
Daily Highs	48	74	94	76	39"	7"
Daily Lows	26	49	70	49		

picnicking, camping, hiking, horseback riding, mountain biking, swimming, fishing, hunting, and boating.

A network of trails twists and turns through the forest from Talimena State Park in Oklahoma almost to Little Rock. Known as the Ouachita National Recreation Trails, they converge on Mena and are exceptionally popular throughout the region with ATV owners. (For those who don't know, an ATV is an all-terrain vehicle, one of those three- or four-wheel motorcycle-type contraptions that can practically climb walls.) From as far as Texas and Florida, ATV enthusiasts travel to Mena to participate in contests and off-road races along 50 miles of trails through breathtaking scenery. This is the country's only National Forest Service land where ATVs are permitted and encouraged.

For a small town, Mena surprised us by having two public golf courses as well as a private golf course at the local country club. Like most Arkansas small towns, Mena is in a dry county; however, for those who enjoy a glass of vintage grape with their steak, the local country club is allowed to serve. Also, the Oklahoma state line is less than 10 miles away. Ironically Oklahoma was one of the last states to permit legal sale of liquor, and now it's the first place people from neighboring states go to stock up their liquor cabinets.

Rich Mount, Mena's college, is a small school but has lots of get-up-and-go about it. The school's library has twenty computers, plus three computer labs, which the community is welcome to use between classes. Free tuition is offered to anyone over the age of sixty, for either credit or audit.

Housing costs in Mena are pretty much standard for Arkansas. (That means very low.) The difference between Mena and the average Arkansas small city is a higher number of affluent neighborhoods than you'd normally expect. One couple I interviewed (retirees from Wisconsin) were absolutely delighted with their home: a three-bedroom, two-bath, modern log cabin sitting on nine acres of wooded property with a stream flowing through it. "We always wanted to live in a log cabin," they said, "and we absolutely fell in love with this one. When the seller told us he was only asking $65,000 for everything, we didn't even think about making a counteroffer. Then we found out taxes were only $300 a year!"

Greers Ferry Lake Area   About 60 miles north of Little Rock, the Greers Ferry Lake area is one of Arkansas's retirement success stories. Three towns share in this success: Heber Springs, Greers Ferry, and Fairfield Bay. They sit on the shores of a 40,000-acre lake created by an Army Corps of Engineers dam. (One of President Kennedy's last official acts was to dedicate Greers Ferry Dam while on his way to Dallas.)

This 300 miles of wooded shoreline—encompassing a lake filled with bass, stripers, walleye, catfish, and lunker-size trout—soon caught the attention of folks considering an Ozark retirement. Inexpensive property, low taxes, a temperate climate, and an almost nonexistent crime rate added to the attraction of retirement here. Folks from Chicago and St. Louis paid particular attention, for the lake wasn't so far from their grandchildren and old friends that they couldn't go home for a visit whenever they pleased.

In a matter of twenty years, Heber Springs, the largest of the communities, zoomed from a population of 2,500 to well over 6,000. The vast majority of newcomers were retired couples. Their pension money and savings pumped up bank deposits more than twentyfold and the extra purchasing power boosted retail sales, created jobs, and generated tax money for local improvements. Home building activity continues today, with lovely new neighborhoods materializing in low-density clusters, hidden in wooded, lakeshore settings.

Actually, the area's population increased much more than the figures indicate. Many small neighborhoods are located *outside* town limits, nestled in wooded glades, often invisible from roads and highways. Typically, a development consists of a grouping of from ten to fifty homes, sometimes with lake views. This arrangement cuts the expense of utility installation as well as construction costs. There could be as many as 150 of these mini-neighborhoods scattered through the forests. Although building lots are usually half an acre or more, the setting creates a sense of closeness among the neighbors. "We never worry about leaving our home vacant during the winter," remarked one resident, "because our friends watch the place for us."

Construction quality is high, most homes are of brick, and low labor costs keep the selling prices affordable for retirees. Properties on the lake are priced higher, but not remarkably so. This is because the Army Corps of Engineers prohibits ownership of land directly on the water beyond a determined high-water line. This means no boat docks or direct access, and no immediate advantage to being

GREERS FERRY LAKE AREA WEATHER

In degrees Fahrenheit

	Jan.	April	July	Oct.	Rain	Snow
Daily Highs	50	74	96	75	49"	4"
Daily Lows	29	51	71	50		

next to the water. Lakeside homes enjoy the view, but so do places set farther back. Unlimited water access is provided by public docks, ramps, and marinas. A unique type of retirement development that appeals to those who fly small planes is Sky Point Estates, where you can build your home next to an airstrip.

For even smaller small-town retirement, Greers Ferry sits invitingly on the other side of the lake. The community provides all the basic services needed for day-to-day living, yet it's so small and uncongested that it doesn't require traffic lights. Greers Ferry has grocery stores, craft shops, and three branch banks. As a consideration for retirees' health care, the community has two full-time doctors and provides free ambulance service to Cleburne Hospital in Heber Springs.

Fairfield Bay, at the far end of the lake, is for those who prefer a more upscale setting where they can own a home near a golf course. This resort/retirement community features round-the-clock security and all the advantages of an exclusive, gated complex. Its parent company has built several other developments around the country.

One of the advantages of living in the Greers Ferry Lake area is its proximity to Little Rock, an hour's drive away. With a metropolitan area of nearly 250,000, Little Rock provides the health services that smaller towns cannot. Libraries, museums, and other cultural attractions fill a void for those who are used to larger cities. Little Rock is also the closest place to stock up on wine and beer to serve your guests, for like most smaller Arkansas areas, this is in a dry county.

Housing prices here have risen along with the improving economy, but prices and quality are remarkably better than where the retirees come from. A typical remark by new residents is, "Our new home is twice the size as the one we sold back home, and it cost half the money." Property taxes come as a pleasant shock when new residents receive tax bills just a fraction of what they paid back home.

Bull Shoals/Mountain Home   In the north-central part of Arkansas, along the Missouri border, a forested area of lakes and rivers has become a miniature melting pot, with retirees moving here from all over the country. Even traditional retirement areas like California and Florida are represented by former residents taking advantage of an exceptionally low crime rate, inexpensive living, and gorgeous scenery.

Surrounded on three sides by water, Bull Shoals and Lakeview sit on the shore of a lake that stretches for almost 100 miles. Its deep, blue waters are legend among bass fishermen, and the rivers and streams feeding the lake are considered premier spots for rainbow trout fishing, which in the spring and summer is done at night under lights. There are no closed seasons here; you can fish year-round. Sports aren't restricted to fishing or hunting; several challenging golf courses in the area will test your skills, whether you're a pro or a duffer.

The lake's shore is off-limits to construction up to the high-water mark, but the public has free access to both lake rivers. This restriction protects the lake's pristine quality, keeping it from being cluttered with sagging docks and scruffy-looking boats. The shoreline always looks clean and natural. Public marinas will house your boat for less than $400 a year, so you don't have to keep pulling your boat out of the water after every fishing trip.

Mountain Home is 15 miles from Bull Shoals and Lakeview, over a highway that winds through picturesque Ozark woods. This small city of about 10,000 is the commercial center for the lake communities and the surrounding county of nearly 30,000 inhabitants. Mountain Home has a real downtown area, including an archetypal, old-fashioned town square. Major shopping and consumer businesses are located on the highway and around the major crossroads. Stores here supply any consumer goods for which anyone could reasonably ask. A community college serves the area, and retiree organizations offer opportunities for volunteer work. A hospital

BULL SHOALS–MOUNTAIN HOME WEATHER						
In degrees Fahrenheit						
	Jan.	April	July	Oct.	Rain	Snow
Daily Highs	46	73	92	74	42"	8"
Daily Lows	25	47	67	48		

accommodates the area's population and an airport runs shuttle services to the nearest large cities. The Area Agency on Aging operates a local bus service.

The county in which Mountain Home is located allows the sale of package liquor, and cocktails are permitted to be served in at least one restaurant. Bull Shoals is dry except for one private club.

According to couples who retired in this area, major attractions are mild winters and low living costs. One couple from just north of Chicago said, "We cut our property taxes by $2,000 a year by coming here, and we cut our heating bills by more than half." They explained that they spend less than $100 a month for heat, whereas the colder Lake Michigan winters had whacked $250 out of their monthly budget during the coldest months. The husband said, "The money we save makes the difference between struggling to stay within our budget and having money to spend for luxuries."

Hot Springs   This fascinating little city, situated partially within Hot Springs National Park, is one of the more attractive retirement possibilities in Arkansas. Hot Springs combines the spirit of a 1920s resort with that of a 1990s city. It is as different from the previously described towns as can be, yet its rustic setting on the lower edge of the Ouachita Mountains lends it an Ozark feeling.

The old part of town sits in a canyon with buildings and homes clinging to the sloping-to-steep sides of the ravine. During the decades before, during, and shortly after World War II, Hot Springs maintained a reputation as a lively nightlife town. Roulette, blackjack, and slot machines were as much an attraction as the gushing hot springs. Nightclubs and fancy restaurants flourished in a kind of mid-country Monaco atmosphere. Wealthy and famous citizens rubbed elbows with ordinary workers and the elite of the crime syndicates. Gambling, drinking, and dancing the night away preceded health-restoring soakings in the hot springs the next morning. During its heyday, Hot Springs was considered as sumptuous a resort as Las Vegas or Palm Springs is today.

Casino gambling and nightclubs are just memories today. The action now is bathing in the soothing waters and enjoying the quiet atmosphere of the Ozark Mountains. After casino-style gambling was prohibited, the "old town," in the steepest part of the canyon, gradually fell into disrepair. When high rollers stopped visiting, money ceased flowing. Local folks preferred to shop in the malls away from downtown. But a new wave of retirees and a revival of tourist interest in the hot springs stirred a renewal of the downtown. Once-abandoned buildings now sport fine restaurants, art galleries, and quality shopping. The motif is turn of the century, with antique globe streetlamps, Victorian trim, even horse-drawn carriages for sightseeing. A new breed of visitors come to Hot Springs today, bringing retirement money instead of casino gambling money, and they tend to stay permanently.

Residential areas are located on higher levels, where the land is rolling and hilly but not steep. A good thing, too, because the canyon is subject to flash floods. Not long ago, newspapers reported that a 6-foot wall of water crashed its way down the main business street, flooding stores and wreaking havoc. Hot Springs business people are used to this. After cleaning out the mud, bathhouses, boutiques, and restaurants opened for business with little delay.

Volcanic springs pour steaming hot water from grottoes and crevices in the canyon floor. Neither drought nor rainy seasons affect the water's copious flow. For generations, the elderly and infirm praised the waters' healing and revivifying powers. The young and healthy (unaware of what revivification entails) simply enjoyed sitting in the hot water and relaxing. The bonus for all is the fresh mountain air and the smell of pines and sassafras trees. The bewitched waters are reputed to heal everything from rheumatism to dandruff.

Residential neighborhoods fall into two distinct categories: Victorian and modern. The older sections have ample yards and large homes—often with enormous lawns and large shade trees.

HOT SPRINGS AREA WEATHER

In degrees Fahrenheit

	Jan.	April	July	Oct.	Rain	Snow
Daily Highs	52	75	93	77	55"	3"
Daily Lows	31	52	71	53		

HOT SPRINGS COST OF LIVING

	Overall	Housing	Medical	Groceries	Utilities
Percentage of National Average	88	80	73	95	107

Other neighborhoods are more modern, with conventional bunga-lows, duplexes, and low-profile apartment buildings. There are sev-eral new, quality senior citizens' developments and some excellent mobile-home parks. Not only is the cost of living well below na-tional averages, but also homes sell for more than 20 percent below national average.

There appear to be more apartments than usual for a town of this size, probably because of the seasonal tourist invasions, which encourage temporary housing. Since the demise of gambling and the subsequent tourist scarcity, apartment owners have been forced to become competitive with rents.

Hot Springs Village   Fifteen miles from the city is one of the more impressive retirement complexes in Arkansas: Hot Springs Vil-lage, one of those Florida-style, self-contained, and guarded en-claves. The assurances and dreams of the promoters have been realized here; the promised improvements are in place, including a shopping center that would do justice to a good-sized town.

Property in Hot Springs Village is not inexpensive, at least not for Arkansas, but it is certainly first class and returns full value for the money. Condo prices start in the low $60,000 range, three-bed-room homes at $80,000. These compare favorably with similar de-velopments we've investigated in Florida, Arizona, and California.

Situated on 21,000 acres of rolling-to-steep Ozark foothill wilderness, the property is covered with a hardwood forest of oaks, hickories, and a scattering of evergreens. Roughly one-third of the property has been converted into lakes and golf courses. There are four par-seventy-two golf courses and one par-sixty-two layout, each with its own clubhouse, restaurant, and pro shop, each a separate "country club." Another third of the land is devoted to homesites, and the remaining third is natural forest.

Hot Springs Village is not exclusively a retirement complex; people who work in the nearby city of Hot Springs also buy houses here. But since there are no schools (residents voted down a school tax to avoid having schools), families with younger children rarely purchase property. According to the salespeople, the majority of the residents come from large Midwestern cities in Illinois, Missouri, and Kansas.

Missouri

Of course, Ozark hills and forests do not stop at the Arkansas border. They extend into Oklahoma on the west and about halfway up the state of Missouri before fading into plains and prairie country. Although the Ozarks indiscriminately bestow beauty upon all three states, Missouri's share is the largest, with 33,000 square miles of low mountains, verdant valleys, and rolling plateaus. The Missouri River marks the northern boundary of the Ozark range, Springfield the western edge, and the mountains taper out before they reach the Mississippi River in the east. Even in the midst of the mountains, plateaus can stretch for miles, with flat-to-rolling country reminiscent of the prairie to the north and west.

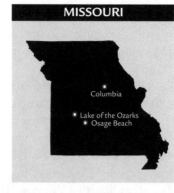

MISSOURI

Columbia

Lake of the Ozarks
Osage Beach

MISSOURI TAX PROFILE
Sales tax: 4.3% to 7.3%, drugs exempt
State income tax: graduated, 1.5% to 6% over $9,000; federal income tax deductible
Property taxes: average 1.1%
Intangibles tax: no
Social security taxed: half of benefits taxable for higher incomes
Pensions taxed: excludes $6,000
Gasoline tax: 15¢ per gallon

One of the more scenic areas is the 86,000-acre Current and Jacks Fork River country, set aside as the Ozark National Scenic Riverways. I cherish fond childhood memories of camping along the Current River and watching my father fly-fish for trout. Memories like this are probably why men dream of retiring in a fisherman's paradise like the Ozarks. (Perhaps a woman's memory of her mother cleaning fish influences her to dream of other locations.)

Most Missouri Ozark rivers have been impounded by dams, forming long chains of lakes. They sprawl and twist through wooded valleys, covering a great part of both Missouri and Arkansas with water. The largest lakes are the Lake of the Ozarks—in the middle of the Missouri mountain range—and the Table Rock–Bull Shoals–Lake Tane complex on the Missouri-Arkansas state line.

Lake of the Ozarks/Osage Beach The largest lake in the Ozarks originated with the construction of Bagnell Dam across the Osage River in the 1930s. Ninety-four miles long, the lake boasts more than 1,000 miles of shoreline for fishing and recreation. Ozark forests climb from the water's edge, up and over low mountains, as far as the eye can see.

Years ago, before World War II, most outsiders who owned Ozark property expected, and demanded, rustic accommodations. They preferred log cabins for use as summer retreats or as fall hunting lodges. Most cabin owners lived in St. Louis or Kansas City, occasionally coming from large cities as far away as Chicago. City folks prized their backwoods hideaways and wanted to keep things rustic. Ozark natives were few in number and culturally isolated from the outside world. Natives and outsiders had little in common and lived in separate worlds even though they might be next-door neighbors every summer.

Things have changed around the Lake of the Ozarks. The site of my family's vacation cabin, where we drew buckets of water from a well, cooked freshly caught fish on a woodstove, and ate dinner by the orange glow of a kerosene lantern, is now the site of a bustling motel complex complete with a gourmet restaurant and marina. Across the highway is a shopping mall. In contrast to sleepy lake towns in other parts of Missouri and Arkansas, Missouri's Lake of the Ozarks is jumping. Kerosene lamps are out, contemporary living is in.

Osage Beach is the largest town on the Lake of the Ozarks and by far the most commercialized, with shopping malls, classy restaurants, and all the other amenities that come with full development. Vacationers, weekenders, and retirees come from all over the Midwest. Newcomers spend dollars that attract more businesses and more employees in a circular growth pattern. Instead of a summer resort with businesses that close every winter, Osage Beach has become a year-round city of about 6,000, the commercial center for an unknown number of lakeside residents and cabin owners outside the city limits.

One couple, who retired to Osage Beach from St. Louis, said, "We're used to shopping malls, nice restaurants, and big-city conveniences. We couldn't stand living in a small, isolated village where we would have to settle for whatever the stores *have* rather than what we *want*. Yet we want to live on a lake and be away from it all." The

LAKE OF THE OZARKS WEATHER					
In degrees Fahrenheit					
	Jan.	April	July	Oct.	Rain	Snow
Daily Highs	42	68	90	71	40"	17"
Daily Lows	21	44	66	46		

LAKE OF THE OZARKS AREA COST OF LIVING					
Percentage of	Overall	Housing	Medical	Groceries	Utilities
National Average	94	88	88	95	100

couple's home is fifteen minutes from a shopping mall, but it couldn't be more private. It sits on a large lakefront lot surrounded by a forest of northern red oak, black oak, shagbark hickory, and basswood. They can't see a neighbor in any direction. Since this is not an Army Corps of Engineers lake, a private boat slip is permitted at the lake's edge. Roads follow the lake's twisted arms to reach large, luxurious homes, ordinary houses, and rustic, unsophisticated cabins, most within easy shopping distance of town.

A few years ago, a financial crisis in St. Louis's largest high-tech manufacturing firm caused a large number of employees—executives and factory workers alike—to seek employment elsewhere. This had a profound effect upon real estate prices around the Lake of the Ozarks. Weekend homes were unceremoniously dumped on the market. Bargains were legion, and the real estate market never fully recovered from the shock.

Of course, lakefront homes can be as expensive as you care to consider. Some areas are quite prestigious, with homes commonly approaching half a million bucks in price. We looked at one (briefly) for $379,000 in Hawk Island Estates that had five bedrooms, four baths, what seemed to be an acre of deck overlooking the water, and a four-car garage. In contrast, two-bedroom condos on the water were priced from around $50,000 up to $110,000 for deluxe models. Away from the lake prices drop dramatically.

Columbia   Although not exactly in the Ozarks, the small city of Columbia is just a short drive from the Ozarks' outdoor recreation and rustic mountain scenery. With a population of 70,000, Columbia is large enough to supply all the amenities and conveniences of a modern city, yet not so large that it suffers from the inherent congestion, crime, and pollution of the big cities.

As a place to retire, Columbia is popular with folks from large Midwestern cities such as St. Louis, Chicago, and Kansas City. Just as visiting the Ozarks is convenient from Columbia, so are visits to places like Kansas City or St. Louis. Either city is a two-hour interstate drive, giving Columbia residents access to major league professional sports, stage plays, and all the good things offered in a large city. Then they return to the refuge of a safe, quiet, clean hometown.

Making the decision to retire in Columbia is made easy by a unique program provided by Columbia's chamber of commerce. Volunteer retirees give newcomers an hour-and-a-half "windshield tour" of the city. The tour visits residential neighborhoods ranging from economical to deluxe. They drive you past the three colleges in town as well as by the golf courses and hospitals. You'll see the best shopping areas and visit Columbia's delightful downtown. This way, potential retirees check out neighborhoods, home styles, and amenities without being pressured by a real estate agent.

Despite Columbia's upscale appearance, housing costs are 16 percent below national averages. The most popular retiree housing choice here is the split-level ranch, usually of brick construction, with a large lawn. Condominiums are available for those who don't care for mowing lawns. Because of the college population, apartment rentals are often scarce. During the summer, however, temporary housing is easily found for those who want to savor the atmosphere of Columbia as a final test for livability. At least three developments are aimed at the retiree market. One development underway will feature golf–course living.

The economy here is solidly based on education, with three institutions of higher learning: the University of Missouri, Stephens College, and Columbia College, the city's major employers. This translates into a high level of prosperity, stability, and an almost recession-proof economy. The academic milieu enhances the city's cultural and social life with school activities that spill over into the community. It seems as if something is always happening for the public to participate in—lectures, concerts, sports events, or celebrations, some of which are free. The huge university library is open to the public for browsing and research, and although you can't check out books, the staff is very accommodating in helping you locate material. As you might guess, Columbia is a great place for continuing education. Many retirees choose Columbia specifically for that purpose; a myriad of adult education programs reaches out to mature residents and encourages them in their quest for lifetime learning.

Education flows through all sectors of the community, even in law enforcement; 90 percent of Columbia police officers are college graduates. That may have something to do with the city's low crime rate, which is 30 percent below national average.

The university, with its medical school, confers another blessing on the community by leading the way in health care. In addition to the university hospital, seven other hospitals serve the community along with so many health-care personnel that one in five workers in Columbia is employed in a health-related occupation. A unique service provided by the university is the Elder Care Center. Its major goal is to keep patients out of nursing homes by providing activities to help them maintain high functional levels. The daily fee is often covered by Medicaid—which is less than half the usual nursing–home cost in the area. University students in physical, occupational, and speech therapy benefit from their experience from the center while patients benefit from more robust health and postponement of nursing-home care.

Outdoor recreation is more than adequate. Besides two municipal golf courses and two private country clubs, there's the Twin Lakes Recreation Area, complete with boating, fishing, and swimming. A relatively new hiking and recreation trail follows the abandoned MKT Railroad line and will eventually connect up with hiking trails that cross the state. This 4.7-mile stretch invites jogging and biking through dense woods, past streambeds, rock cuts, and

COLUMBIA WEATHER						
	In degrees Fahrenheit					
	Jan.	April	July	Oct.	Rain	Snow
Daily Highs	36	65	89	68	36"	23"
Daily Lows	19	44	67	46		

COLUMBIA COST OF LIVING					
Percentage of	Overall	Housing	Medical	Groceries	Utilities
National Average	96	89	100	96	94

open meadows—a small escape to the country, yet just yards removed from the surrounding city. For inclement-weather exercise, the university hospital has organized a "mallwalker's" club. At six-thirty every morning, long before the huge indoor Columbia Mall opens for business, you'll find several hundred walkers working on their stamina and blood pressure. In thirty minutes you can do two full laps, equaling almost 2 miles of vigorous walking, and you don't get rained on.

Columbia consistently makes *Money* magazine's list of top places to live. According to this publication, "Columbia is not just inexpensive," it also is "clean and green," referring to the city's pioneering recycling/deposit law, enacted back in 1977. Columbia's dedication to improving its environment is furthered by Tree Power, an ongoing campaign to plant shade trees. The city-owned water and light department sponsored this program, providing shade trees free of charge. As a result of this awareness, Columbia neighborhoods show a pride of neatness, quality, and pride of ownership seldom surpassed anywhere.

Oklahoma

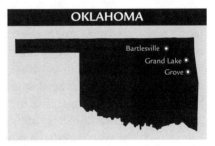

When people think of Oklahoma they imagine flat plains extending to the horizon, perhaps rolling hills studded with oil derricks or farm machinery, and cattle fenced in by barbed wire. True, parts of Oklahoma fit this description, for this is a state renowned for cattle, agriculture, and petroleum. But, just as New York State isn't all Manhattan, Oklahoma is not all flat farm country.

Parts of Oklahoma, particularly in the eastern and northern portions, are hilly and heavily forested, the tail end of the Ozark Mountains. Some places are even less populated than the Missouri and Arkansas Ozarks. You can drive for miles with barely a suggestion that anyone might be living behind the solid mask of forest that lines the highways. Several dams take advantage of the deep river valleys to create long, wide lakes that wiggle and squirm across the wooded landscape and through the hills. The largest, Eufala Reservoir, covers more than 100,000 surface acres. At least eighteen lakes, most of them built by the Army Corps of Engineers, provide recreation as well as irrigation and power. This huge complex of water storage changed forever the face of a state that once was in danger of drying up and blowing away during the 1930s.

OKLAHOMA TAX PROFILE

Sales tax: 4.5% to 8.5%, drugs exempt
State income tax: graduated, 0.5% to 7% over $9,950; federal income tax deductible
Property taxes: about 0.7%
Intangibles tax: no
Social security taxed: no
Pensions taxed: excludes up to $8,000, depending on income level
Gasoline tax: 16¢ per gallon, plus possible local taxes

The desolation of Oklahoma's Dust Bowl, drought, and depression is a well-known piece of history. Those dismal times are far behind as Oklahoma becomes a center for aerospace and aviation industries. The latest agricultural technology, conservation, and flood control protect the land from a repeat of the 1930s disaster. Wonder of wonders: A deep river channel utilizing a system of dams and locks links Tulsa with the Gulf of Mexico, making it an important seaport!

John Steinbeck's famous book, *The Grapes of Wrath*, dramatizes the desperate condition of life in Oklahoma during the Dust Bowl era. The book chronicles a dream of a good life in California and the Joad family's struggle to get there. (Of course, that was before California suffered from graffiti, drive-by shootings, and Madonna.)

Today, the children of those refugees who emigrated to California fifty to sixty years ago are old enough to retire. After suffering the hardships of freeway traffic, high taxes, and idiotic politicians, the Joad family dreams of a good life somewhere else. This time it's Oklahoma. Over the years, they've kept in touch with relatives and friends who didn't leave Oklahoma; visits between the two states were common. So it seems natural that the second generation, now affluent, is making the reverse trek from the West Coast's "land of milk and honey" to down-to-earth Oklahoma. Few have even a hint of an Oklahoma accent; they have no "country" mannerisms about them. Some don't even have relatives or family friends drawing them back here, yet Californians turn out to be Oklahoma's strongest boosters.

Grand Lake o' the Cherokees A series of lakes runs halfway down the state near the Missouri and Arkansas border. Each lake supports small towns that can be practical for retirement. One of the more popular areas is in the state's northeast corner, named after its largest lake, the Grand Lake o' the Chero-kees. Sometimes it's called the Pensacola Dam Project or simply Grand Lake. The contraction "o" does not mean *of,* but *over,* to commemorate the Cherokee burial grounds that lie at the bottom of the lake. Sixty-six miles long, with 1,300 miles of shoreline and 60,000 surface acres of water, this is one of the Ozarks' largest bodies of water. Unlike many reservoirs created by the govern-ment, workers cleared trees and stumps before impoundment, greatly improving both navigation and aesthetics. The country-side around these lakes is not as rugged as the true Ozark moun-tains to the east or to the south in the Tenkiller Lake area, but the charm of the Ozark foothills is still evident.

The lake's wide stretches of water encourage sailboats, even full-fledged yachts capable of cruising in all kinds of weather. Some marinas specialize in sailboat moorings. Fishing is great; bass are so abundant that there's no size limit. Countless coves throughout the many crooks and branches of the lake make great places for picnics, should you become tired of torturing worms by sticking them with fishhooks. The rivers that run into the lake are famous for canoeing, an important tourist activity, with "canoe trails" as part of the Ok-lahoma park system.

The Grand Lake area supports more population than most Ozark waterways, with houses all along the lakeshore. Also, unlike many man-made lakes in the Mid-southern Hills, lakefront owner-ship is not restricted and private docks are allowed. In addition to simple fishing piers, some folks build flat docks like floating patios; other boat docks are covered and enclosed floating cabins of sorts.

For years these lakes were considered the playground of Okla-homa oil patriarchs and big-city vacationers. They have long been popular weekend retreats for residents of northern Oklahoma, Mis-souri, Kansas, and Arkansas. Lately, however, the area is gaining prominence as a retirement destination.

Grand Lake even has a country club–type development. The 600-acre Coves of Bird Island (actually a peninsula) has a golf course, clubhouse, restaurant, and about 150 homes, mostly owned by retirees. The usual swimming pools, tennis courts, and twenty-four-hour security are provided, a plus for those who like to leave their homes and travel. Don't expect to see mobile homes or trailers here; they're not permitted. Residents do their shopping in nearby Grove or in Langley.

TYPICAL RURAL OKLAHOMA COST OF LIVING					
Percentage of	Overall	Housing	Medical	Groceries	Utilities
National Average	89	77	84	90	99

A number of little towns sit on the shore of Grand Lake, the largest being Grove, with a population of almost 5,000. About twice that number living nearby consider Grove to be their hometown as well. Without large industry to provide employment, most folks either work in service jobs or are retired. An estimated 30 percent of the total population are retired—a very high percentage. Heavy shopping is available in Joplin (Missouri), a forty-five-minute drive, or 75 miles away in Tulsa. Grove is fortunate to have its own hospital. Another hospital is located in Vinita, a half-hour drive away.

Several properties were listed for more than $300,000, but they were top quality, with four or more bedrooms and deluxe docks with multiple slips. Most lakefront property starts in the low $100,000 range, although some smaller homes on the lake sell for as low as $80,000. Homes within walking distance of the lakes can be had for $60,000 and sometimes even below this amount.

Bartlesville   Not everyone is enamored of the idea of living in Ozark small towns, and many retirees rank hunting and fishing low on their must-have list. Bartlesville is our idea of Oklahoma small-city living, a place consistently given high marks for quality of life by national publications. Located in the gently rolling grasslands of northern Oklahoma, Bartlesville is just forty-five minutes from Tulsa International Airport and a short drive to Ozark lake environs.

The city is small enough (pop. 34,000) that newcomers can make friends throughout the community, yet Bartlesville is sufficiently ample in size to afford amenities missing from more rustic sections of Oklahoma. In fact, the showcase entertainment events that Bartlesville stages each year would do honors to a much larger city. Its famous community center, designed by Frank Lloyd Wright, hosts the internationally acclaimed OK Mozart Festival. This occasion lasts ten days in mid-June, hosting guest artists from all over the world. The entire populace is invited to participate.

Bartlesville Community Center is not one of those public buildings that sits idle between big-time events. More than 200 community–service groups stage art shows, performances, exhibitions,

BARTLESVILLE WEATHER						
In degrees Fahrenheit						
	Jan.	April	July	Oct.	Rain	Snow
Daily Highs	46	72	93	75	38"	9"
Daily Lows	24	49	72	50		

BARTLESVILLE COST OF LIVING					
Percentage of	Overall	Housing	Medical	Groceries	Utilities
National Average	92	84	97	94	95

festivals, and parties. My wife and I attended a wedding dinner there—it was a fabulous evening! The seventy-five-piece Bartlesville Symphony is recognized as one of the best in the country. The Bartlesville Civic Ballet offers a mixed palette of music and dance, and the Theater Guild presents year-round entertainment. This is hardly what one would expect to find in small-town Oklahoma!

Bartlesville's overall cost of living is 8 percent below average. Housing costs fall 16 percent below national averages, making quality living in a nice neighborhood affordable.

Kentucky

The Mississippi River marks Kentucky's western border and the deep valleys and rugged gorges of the Appalachians delimits its eastern. In between you'll find a wide selection of countrysides from which to choose: from gently rolling farming country to magnificent panoramas of the Blue Ridge Mountains; from quiet, rural crossroad communities to sophisticated cities and university towns. The first region west of the Allegheny Mountains settled by American pioneers, Kentucky epitomizes America's rugged frontier heritage. This is the country of Daniel Boone, the Hatfields and McCoys, and good ol' mountain music. Today it's much more than that. With up-to-date services, neighborly people, and modern shopping everywhere, Kentucky is a great choice for retirement.

KENTUCKY

Bowling Green

Murray

Modern-day transportation, with paved highways crisscrossing the state, has opened the back country to the world. A robust economic development since the end of World War II boosted most rural areas out of Al Capp's Dogpatch past. No longer are large parts of the state isolated and populated with illiterate mountaineers and moonshiners. Kentucky today is too open for that.

KENTUCKY TAX PROFILE

Sales tax: 6%, food and drugs exempt
State income tax: graduated, 2% to 6% over $8,000; can't deduct federal income tax
Property taxes: average 1%
Intangibles tax: yes
Social security taxed: no
Pensions taxed: private pensions taxable
Gasoline tax: 15¢ per gallon

This opening of the state also created retirement opportunities that didn't exist previously. But the entire state certainly hasn't become a carbon copy of middle America. Many charming areas back in the hills are almost as rustic and unspoiled as ever. And since most Kentucky counties have opted for prohibition, you can bet some of those piney hills still contain moonshiners.

Kentucky is particularly attractive for Midwestern and Northern retirees who see advantages in retiring close to their prior homes, in inexpensive, low-crime surroundings. The relatively mild, four-season weather easily satisfies requirements for those who insist on colorful autumns, invigorating winters, and glorious springs.

Bowling Green   About an hour's drive north of Nashville (65 miles by Interstate 65) and the Nashville International Airport is the delightful little city of Bowling Green. Because of its central location (within one day's drive of three-fourths of the U.S. population), this is becoming a popular retirement location for fugitives from crowded Northern cities. The interstate, a major north-south artery, facilitates transportation and makes it easy for the grandchildren to visit.

Originally, the town was called The Barrens, after the Barren River that runs through the site, but in 1797 it was renamed something a bit more descriptive of the area: Bowling Green. The second name derived from the habit of court officials and visiting attorneys amusing themselves between trials by bowling on the lawn beside the old courthouse. The surrounding countryside is as green as its name—lush, with rolling meadows surrounded by white fences, with

BOWLING GREEN WEATHER					
In degrees Fahrenheit					
	Jan.	April	July	Oct.	Rain	Snow
Daily Highs	41	68	88	69	43"	14"
Daily Lows	24	46	67	46		

BOWLING GREEN AREA COST OF LIVING					
Percentage of	Overall	Housing	Medical	Groceries	Utilities
National Average	93	92	89	96	94

thoroughbred horses munching away at the Kentucky bluegrass. Bowling Green looks exactly as one imagines Kentucky should look.

Due to its location, Bowling Green serves as a regional hub for retail shopping and medical services. And, because this is the only place between Louisville and Nashville where alcohol is served, Bowling Green's higher-quality restaurants attract folks from miles around for celebrating that special occasion. According to a recent survey, Bowling Green has more restaurants per capita than any other U.S. city except San Francisco.

Another factor in maintaining an upscale atmosphere is the presence of Western Kentucky University, with 15,000 students adding intellectual warmth. The university maintains a symphony orchestra and two theater groups, and it hosts frequent visits from touring artists and entertainers. Other cultural offerings are presented by the Capitol Arts Center and the Public Theatre of Kentucky.

Participation in university affairs is made easy by Kentucky's policy of senior–citizen scholarships that pay the full cost of tuition. This is true for both full-time and part-time students and applies toward either graduate or undergraduate courses. Numerous continuing–education programs are also offered, ranging from History of American Presidents to motorcycle training.

Although Bowling Green is a fine example of a larger Kentucky town, it's not big enough to suffer from big-city problems. Crime rates here are low, pollution is almost nonexistent, and the cost of living is 7 percent below national average. Housing and utility costs are exceptionally low, with homes selling for 7 percent below average and utilities at 6 percent less than national averages.

Murray   Murray is a small city that consistently garners recommendations from retirement writers as a good place to relocate. It's also an excellent example of how good things can happen to a community when retirees move in. A few years ago Murray received a rash of national publicity when a popular retirement guide designated the town as the year's "top-rated" retirement location. This created an enormous amount of interest among folks planning retirement; before long, 250 couples made the move to Murray.

As you might expect, this had a snowball effect on the area's economy. The real estate market zoomed out of the doldrums and, before long, exhausted its inventory. Building construction increased to keep pace. At last report, five new housing developments were underway. In short, retiree immigration has proven to be an economic bonanza. Another positive side effect: These extra retirees were enough to push the city into enlarging the senior citizens' center and adding more services. The staff at the local center, by the way, is dedicated and enthusiastic about plans for the facility's future.

What were the bad effects? Apparently none. Real estate sells at 14 percent below national averages and while the cost of living may have gone up slightly, it is still 8 percent under most areas of the nation. People moving into the mid-South from most parts of the country feel like bandits as they sign the escrow papers. According to the FBI's last report, Murray came in very high in personal safety, with a record indicating that most criminals in Murray must have retired or moved away.

One of the volunteer workers at the Senior Center had retired from California and told of a special California Club com-

MURRAY WEATHER

In degrees Fahrenheit

	Jan.	April	July	Oct.	Rain	Snow
Daily Highs	42	68	88	71	47"	12"
Daily Lows	25	48	69	47		

MURRAY AREA COST OF LIVING

Percentage of	Overall	Housing	Medical	Groceries	Utilities
National Average	92	86	84	95	83

posed of others like her who had also chosen Kentucky for retirement. It turns out that a colleague of mine, who had lived in California for the past two decades, recently retired in Murray. When I asked why, he and his wife explained that with children living in St. Louis and Nashville, they were within a few hours' drive of either place. They also liked fishing in the nearby lake. What were the drawbacks? They had to admit that snow and ice took some getting used to, but since they were originally from Canada, no problem there. The lack of good restaurants (this being a dry county) was the only other thing they missed from their California experience.

Tennessee

Tennessee is somewhat of a mirror image of Kentucky to the north and Arkansas to the west. Eastward, the land slopes gradually upward until

the foothills finally become the Appalachian Mountains. They grow ever more rugged, reaching their highest peaks in eastern Tennessee, near the state's border with the Carolinas.

Near the Mississippi River, plains of fertile bottomlands alternate with dense hardwood forests. King Cotton once ruled this domain, a land steeped in the genteel traditions of the Old South. Flat-to-rolling land covers much of the eastern portions of Tennessee, rich agricultural fields hedged with rows of trees, neat and prosperous-looking farmhouses, barns, and silos. Most smaller towns here look pretty much like any in Middle America. Memphis and Nashville are the large cities.

TENNESSEE TAX PROFILE
Sales tax: 6% to 8.5%, food, drugs exempt
State income tax: 6% on interest and dividends; over 65, $9,000 exemption
Property taxes: vary from 1.46% to 2.37%
Intangibles tax: no
Social security taxed: no
Pensions taxed: no
Gasoline tax: 21¢ per gallon

As you move eastward you come upon Tennessee's heartland, a region of gently rolling hills and bluegrass meadows. Continuing east, the landscape grows more scenic with every mile. Before long you find yourselves in foothill country and finally in Tennessee's high country, rugged, tree-shrouded mountains that cross into the Carolinas and the Blue Ridge Mountains.

Clarksville   Located on the northern border, next to Kentucky, Clarksville sits conveniently on an interstate highway that whisks you to the big city of Nashville in less than 45 minutes. This is one of our favorite Mid-southern Hills locations. Clarksville combines an atmosphere of small-town living with city and urban conveniences.

Don't misunderstand, Clarksville is no small town. An estimated 76,000 population places it into the realm of a city, yet it somehow manages to maintain the flavor of small-town life. This a place where friends are constantly honking greetings to each other as they drive around town. Yet, shopping malls and complexes are as large and complete as you could hope for in a much bigger city.

For those who cannot live without hauling fish out of the water or killing ducks, this is a great place to be, with all the conveniences of a city plus great hunting and fishing nearby. The Land Between the Lakes recreational area is 35 miles away, with 170,000 acres of public lands for hiking, camping, fishing, and seasonal scheduled hunting. The peaceful Cumberland River flows through Clarksville; pleasure boats cruise where huge paddle-wheelers once carried tobacco and cotton for European ports. A half-hour drive from pleasant residential neighborhoods can take you to thick forests or rich farms and bluegrass meadows where horse breeding is a major industry. This is where the Tennessee Walking Horse breed was developed.

For big-city life, nearby Nashville offers fine restaurants, historical museums, and its famous Grand Ol' Opry. Seems as if every country and western star from Minnie Pearl to Conway Twitty has a museum dedicated to them. But to me, the most interesting museum is the home of President Andrew Jackson, where his original log cabin homestead still stands behind the stately Hermitage, the Greek Revival mansion he built during his more successful career.

A condition that makes Clarksville different from many Mid-southern Hills towns is the large number of out-of-state folks who retire here. This happens whenever you combine a pleasant area with a large military base like Fort Campbell, which straddles the Tennessee-Kentucky state line adjacent to Clarksville. The base covers 105,000 acres, mostly in Tennessee, but since the post office is in Kentucky, that state claims Fort Campbell as its own. Military retirees enjoy base PX privileges and medical benefits. The fort, almost a city in itself, has a population of 38,000, with a PX as large as a shopping center, plus seven on-post schools for military dependents.

The early-day prosperity of the tobacco plantations shows clearly in the beautiful antebellum mansions in town. Set back from the street among magnificent oaks and magnolia trees, surrounded by acres of lawn, these old homes are among the best preserved in the South. This notion of large lawns carries over into modern housing. Big lots are in. Even humble two-bedroom homes sit on enormous lots with awesome expanses of lawn—awesome because of the amount of energy spent in keeping the grass mowed. Yet folks tell you with straight faces, "I really enjoy yard work. Cutting grass is relaxing." Yes, of course it is. That's why rich people are so tense; they hire someone else to cut the grass.

Our previous research showed Clarksville to be one of the housing bargains of the nation. Median sales prices are about 7 percent below the national average. But conditions change here, depending upon what happens at Fort Campbell. When world conditions are peaceful, Fort Campbell operates with full staff and demand for housing is up. But when some military problems arise somewhere in the world, troops here are the first to go. When this happens, vacancies become easy to find and For Sale signs sprout on lawns.

Clarksville offers a large range of activities. Austin Peay State University is located here, complete with an active theater depart-

CLARKSVILLE WEATHER

	Jan.	April	July	Oct.	Rain	Snow
In degrees Fahrenheit						
Daily Highs	46	71	90	72	48"	11"
Daily Lows	28	48	69	48		

CLARKSVILLE COST OF LIVING

	Overall	Housing	Medical	Groceries	Utilities
Percentage of National Average	92	93	88	95	86

ment that produces five shows a season ranging from comedy to serious theater and even musicals. A jazz festival is held in March, and
a spring opera in May. Guest–artist recitals are offered throughout
the year, with free admission. Fort Campbell has an entertainment-
services office, and it produces seven theatrical productions a year,
open to the public.

Thirty miles to the west of Clarksville is the little town of
Dover. This is the gateway to the Land Between the Lakes, a
170,000-acre wilderness area that stretches over a narrow peninsula, 40 miles between Kentucky Lake and Lake Barkley. Almost
90 percent of this area is unspoiled forest, with just a few scattered
farms and some facilities for boat launching, hunting, and
fishing. Some retirees from Clarksville have moved into Dover, attracted by exceptionally low housing costs, peaceful living and
proximity to hunting and fishing in the Land Between the Lakes.
Dover is an interesting town, but verges on being provincial, with
fewer outsiders in residence. To retire here happily, you'll have to
love small-town living.

Crossville   East from Nashville along Interstate 40 or southeast on Interstate 24 brings you to the foothills of the Blue Ridge
Mountains and the town of Crossville. While doing research in
Crossville, we noticed that it looked somehow different from similar
Tennessee towns. Much of the downtown construction seemed to
be fairly recent, with fewer old buildings than one might expect.
Farms surrounding the town lacked older-looking houses and
barns, the kind built before the Civil War. When we asked about it,
a young lady who worked in a local business disagreed that the
buildings are new, saying, "No sir, Crossville is a very old town. Almost nothing hereabouts is new." When we asked, "How old?" She
replied, "Well, I understand that many buildings here date back to
the days of the Franklin D. Roosevelt Administration." We had to
agree that was indeed a long time ago.

It turns out that until the Great Depression Crossville was
pretty much woods and empty countryside. Despite rich soil and
abundant rainfall, the district had been all but ignored. FDR's New
Deal administration, searching for worthwhile projects to bootstrap
the country out of the depression, seized upon a plan to develop the
Crossville region as a model agricultural center. Government
workers cleared forests, and homesteaders were given loans and seed

CROSSVILLE WEATHER						
		In degrees Fahrenheit				
	Jan.	April	July	Oct.	Rain	Snow
Daily Highs	47	71	87	70	47"	12"
Daily Lows	29	48	68	48		

CROSSVILLE AREA COST OF LIVING					
Percentage of	Overall	Housing	Medical	Groceries	Utilities
National Average	96	94	88	97	91

money to get started. The plan evidently worked, because this is a very prosperous area today. Cheap electricity from the Tennessee Valley Authority Project lured industry into the area, adding jobs and even more prosperity.

As do most larger-sized towns in the South, Crossville enjoys friendly neighbors and inexpensive housing. The level of services for senior citizens is as good as anywhere in the state, with enthusiastic and imaginative folks running programs.

The town is dry, with residents routinely making the trek to Knoxville for alcohol—a 70-mile drive each way. When I expressed dismay that drunks should be free-wheeling down the interstate for their supplies, residents cheerfully assured me that bootleggers are plentiful in Crossville. "Why, you can buy anything you want, right here!" This weird custom of a community supporting prohibition and bootleggers at the same time never fails to puzzle me.

Property is quite affordable in Crossville and environs. Homes in town are usually on large lots with plenty of mature shade trees. On the town's outskirts, larger lots are the rule, with small farms commonly used as retirement homes.

Fairfield Glade   When retirement writers speak of Crossville, chances are they have one of the special country-club developments in mind. There are several. Fairfield Glade is the oldest and the largest in the area, possibly the largest in the entire state. It's about 15 miles from Crossville and has been under development for two decades. Its year-round population is between 4,500 and 5,000, but thousands more enjoy the facilities on a vacation and part-time retirement basis. The corporation that put the package together has lots of experience—they have similar operations throughout the retirement areas of the nation.

Over the years, Fairfield Glade has matured gracefully. It has changed from a glitzy promotion into a series of stable, pleasant neighborhoods scattered throughout the 12,000 acres. Eleven lakes and four championship golf courses with all the adjuncts—such as tennis, swimming pools, and restaurants—uphold the original country-club tradition.

Unlike some developments, all promised facilities seem to have materialized. A large gymnasium offers everything from basketball to billiards to bicycle rentals. A riding stable presents complete equestrian facilities and miles of hiking and riding trails. Finally, there is a fully functional shopping mall (20,000 square feet under one roof) and a range of good-quality restaurants. Of course, the better establishments serve cocktails to members of Fairfield Glade. A bus service takes residents into Crossville.

Homes surrounding this lake/golf course complex are well built, attractively priced, and architecturally pleasing. Acres of wooded and green space separate the various tracts. The closer to the golf course, the more expensive the homes.

Holiday Hills   Closer to Crossville, just a few miles from the downtown section, is the retirement development of Holiday Hills. It spreads over 1,200 acres of prime land around a lake and a golf course. Apparently, this one also started as a time-share resort, but retirement homes have become the style. The tennis and clubhouse facilities are excellent.

Holiday Hills is newer than Fairfield Glade and more convenient to town. Homes are priced comparably to those in Fairfield Glade, and its natural setting is just as beautiful. An interesting feature is the Cumberland County Playhouse, located just outside the development's main gate. Dramas, musicals, and ballets draw visitors from all over the nation.

Nearby is another retirement development, a no-frills place called the Orchards. In recognition of retirees' propensity for recreational–vehicle travel, they build carports high enough to accommodate RVs. The Crossville area attracts retirees from Indiana, Ohio, and Illinois, but the hottest place of origin is Michigan, particularly from the Detroit area, which is an especially popular place to be *from.*

CHAPTER 6

Texas, the B-i-i-g State

YOU DON'T HAVE TO BE TOLD that Texas is one enormous state. Give a Texan half a chance and he'll tell you all about it. Don't give him a chance and he'll tell you anyway. The truth is, Texas is almost as large as Texans claim, and that's pretty darn big. It's bigger than any country in Europe except for Russia, and ten times larger than many European countries. Not only is Texas spacious, but it boasts some of the prettiest scenery you can imagine, as well as some of the most boring. This wide range of climate, scenery, and elevation presents a broad menu of retirement options, something for almost every taste.

Texas's range of climates varies wildly. The subtropical southern tip of the state never sees snow and thinks any temperature below 60 degrees is downright chilly. At the other extreme, the high plains of the northern Panhandle region can be one of the coldest conceivable places in the winter, yet it can also be one of the hottest places this side of Death Valley in the summer. The Gulf Coast is as humid as Florida, and west Texas is dry as the proverbial bone. You'll encounter large cities and small villages and medium-size places perfect for retirement. Landscapes vary from plains to deserts to seashores to mountains. Variety is the spice of Texas retirement choices!

TEXAS TAX PROFILE

Sales tax: 6.25% to 8.25%, food, drugs exempt
State income tax: no
Property taxes: about 2.2%
Intangibles tax: no
Social security taxed: no
Pensions taxed: no
Gasoline tax: 20¢ per gallon

The Texas Gulf Coast

With more than 600 miles of the Texas coast facing the Gulf of Mexico, one would expect beachfront developments galore. The fact is, most of the Texas waterfront is uninhabited. Furthermore, almost all the mainland faces not the Gulf, but offshore islands and narrow peninsulas that effectively shut off the open gulf waters. For the most part, these islands are long and narrow, composed of sand dunes and unexplored beaches. Much of the actual coast is little changed from the days in the early 1800s when the French pirate Jean Lafitte used the islands as a base.

Long stretches of these islands, as well as parts of the mainland, are designated as wildlife refuges. Whooping cranes and Kemp's Ridley sea turtles are making a comeback after what once seemed almost certain extinction. Turtle eggs from Mexico planted on the Padre Islands about twenty years ago are beginning to show wonderful results. The hatchlings from the experiment have grown into adult turtles and are returning to their beach of origin to nest in a protected environment. When the new batches of eggs hatch and the baby turtles start for the sea, they are quickly captured and cared for in special pens until they're old enough to have a good chance for survival.

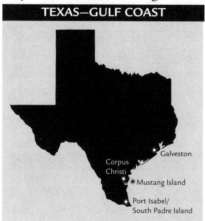

TEXAS—GULF COAST

Galveston
Corpus Christi
Mustang Island
Port Isabel/ South Padre Island

This is a fisherman's paradise. Both the channel and Gulf sides of the long islands teem with fish. From beaches and piers you can expect to catch redfish, speckled and sand trout, flounder, sheepshead, skipjack, croakers, and drum. Group boats offer bay and deep-sea fishing, with charter cruisers available for individual or small-party sport. The offshore game includes tarpon, sailfish, kingfish, marlin, mackerel, pompano, ling cod, bonito, and red snapper, among others. By far, fishing is the major sport attraction for retirees who have chosen the Texas Gulf Coast for their home.

Galveston   On the entire Texas coast only one city actually faces the open gulf: Galveston. With a population of almost 60,000, it occupies one of those long islands and is reached via a lengthy causeway across Galveston Bay. Except for this 32-mile stretch of beach—not all of which is developed—there is little residential construction on the gulf, just a tiny portion around Corpus Christi and farther south on Padre Island.

Many years ago Galveston was one of our favorite weekend resorts; we visited as often as we could, swimming in the surf, crabbing off the jetties, and driving along the beach with the waves playing at our car wheels. Upon returning, after an interval of almost thirty years, we expected change. To our surprise, we discovered that Galveston had changed very little.

This shouldn't have been so surprising, because limited space on Galveston Island long ago filled to capacity with homes and businesses. The only new construction possible is replacing old buildings with new, something the local people are reluctant to permit. The old downtown section, instead of being replaced by slick new glass-and-steel monsters, has been preserved and restored to a charming, turn-of-the-century state. Old brick and cast-iron fronts with wrought-iron balconies give the area a New Orleans French Quarter feeling. One street has been turned into a pedestrian mall, complete with restaurants, smart shops, and park benches for sunning and people-watching.

True, along the beachfront some older homes and buildings slowly give way to newer, more profitable construction focused on tourist dollars. But change is slow in coming. Most of the town is still the same: old-fashioned and comparatively inexpensive. Surf fishermen can try their luck almost anywhere along the beach. There are free municipal jetties and rock groin piers at regular intervals. If you fail to catch anything, markets sell the freshest catch found anywhere—right out of the Gulf into your frying pan.

Galveston has few high-rise buildings, either on the beach or in town. Fascinating Victorian homes—some in a poor state of repair, most in fine shape, some positively gorgeous—grace quiet, tree-lined streets away from the bustle of the seashore. When you leave the honky-tonk atmosphere of Seawall Boulevard, it is hard to believe you are in one of the major tourist attractions on the Texas coast—it is too residential and calm.

People who don't live here think of Galveston as a weekend or vacation hot spot, a convention site, a place to go and blow off steam. However, there is a surprisingly intellectual air about Galve-

GALVESTON WEATHER					
In degrees Fahrenheit					
	Jan.	April	July	Oct.	Rain	Snow
Daily Highs	59	73	87	78	40"	—
Daily Lows	48	65	79	68		

GALVESTON COST OF LIVING					
Percentage of	Overall	Housing	Medical	Groceries	Utilities
National Average	92	89	93	87	99

ston. The University of Texas medical school is in downtown Galveston, as well as a branch of Texas A&M and a community college. These are serious students, some interested in art and literature to the exclusion of fishing (heaven forbid).

In the old days, we could drive for at least 20 miles on hard-packed sand, but today the beach is no longer open to automobile traffic. There are plenty of access points, however, where fishermen can surf cast, and there are piers for easier fishing. I fondly remember blissful days and large catches of blue crab, later made into a seafood gumbo at the home of a displaced Cajun who lived in Houston.

Today, the beach outside town is no longer deserted and wild, but is often lined with ugly, unpainted summer homes that are built on 15-foot stilts to avoid high waves during hurricane weather. (All along the Gulf Coast, from Key West to the tip of Texas, you find this stilt construction. Insurance companies insist on new buildings having stilts; it cuts their losses considerably.) Some owners successfully disguise the stilts by screening the lower portions of their houses, turning them into garages and storage spaces. This disguise makes the houses look like attractive two-story homes. But others don't bother, making stretches of beach look as if they had been invaded by spindly-legged monsters. Since the beach area is pure tourist and most popular during the spring and summer, it turns into a ghostly place in winter. Few homes are lived in year-round.

Corpus Christi   The only other major city on the Texas coast is Corpus Christi, a fast-growing metropolis of 264,000 inhabitants. It's actually not on the Gulf, but on a large bay, sheltered from open water by 30-mile-long Mustang Island. A major deepwater port, Corpus is large enough to mask the tourist crowds in all but the most hectic times (college semester breaks). For the most part, it looks like an ordinary, contemporary city—pleasant and unusually neat. It even has a modern, high-rise downtown. A seawall runs along the downtown area, with stairs that lead down to the water and a yacht basin. Palm-lined boulevards and cosmopolitan hotels and office buildings complete the picture.

Unlike Galveston, which sits exposed to the whims of hurricane-driven tides, Corpus Christi enjoys the protection of offshore islands. Thus construction work isn't impeded by the constant threat of flood. The town as a whole has a relaxed look about it.

Medical services are excellent here, with eleven hospitals as well as the military medical facilities serving the local naval air station. (Numerous retired military families live here.) Educational and cultural needs are met by a two-year college as well as a state university. A new aquarium is becoming one of the major tourist attractions, with its 132,000-gallon deepwater exhibit.

Since the Corpus Christi area offers the only beach access along many miles of coastline, it has become quite popular as a resort. Not only are there beaches along the bay, but also there are 110 miles of sand and surf on the islands that shelter the mainland. Corpus has become almost as famous as Fort Lauderdale, Florida, for its assemblage of frolicking college students during semester break. As many as 100,000 tourists—an uncounted number of them college students—flock to Corpus Christi and Mustang Island to celebrate every spring.

Because of these sporadic visits by enthusiastic, youthful celebrants, local crime statistics can become distorted. The police are kept busy arresting drunks, breaking up fistfights, and stopping exuberant youngsters from destroying motel rooms. These offenses show up in the FBI's crime reports even though they are crimes that don't really affect ordinary residents or retirees, who neither live in nor frequent the tourist areas during the wild days.

CORPUS CHRISTI WEATHER						
In degrees Fahrenheit						
	Jan.	April	July	Oct.	Rain	Snow
Daily Highs	69	82	90	82	28"	—
Daily Lows	52	67	75	66		

Mustang Island   So many families from San Antonio and Austin traditionally vacation and maintain summer homes across the Laguna Madre, on Mustang Island, that it is referred to as an annex of San Antonio. There is only one town on the island: Port Aransas, a small community with a year-round population of about 2,000. Summer tourism doubles and triples this figure.

Since the island is unprotected from open water and the possibility of hurricane-driven tides, many homes stand high on the familiar pilings and stilts of Gulf Coast construction. We did our research there in the winter and saw Port Aransas at its quietest time of year. Real estate activity was also at its lowest ebb, with properties rather inexpensive. Some of the low-cost homes had a kind of temporary air about them. They looked as if their owners were hesitant to put much maintenance into them, just in case a hurricane might make it a waste of time.

Mustang Islanders brag about their low crime rate. "With only two ways off the island," they point out, "either by ferry to the mainland or by the bridge to Corpus at the other end of the island, no one expects to commit a serious crime and make a getaway." When a crime is committed, the police immediately shut down the ferry and place a roadblock at the bridge. Our own trip by ferry involved an annoying hour of waiting in line for our turn at boarding. I can just imagine how annoyed and nervous I would have been had I been driving a getaway car with the police chasing after me.

Islanders also love to brag about the fishing, claiming that Mustang Island is a place "where the fish bite every day." This is fortunate for the retiree who loves to fish, because there is very little else to do on Mustang or North Padre Island. Boats are available for rent, and deep-sea charters take you out for the big ones. Many people use the conventional rod and reel, but sail fishing is becoming popular. This is done by attaching a trolling line to a sail that moves with the wind, said to be very effective and requiring no work on the part of the fisherman.

When you leave Port Aransas, the island becomes very sparsely populated on the drive south. Long stretches of dunes and beach line the Gulf side, with lagoons and marsh facing the mainland. Except for a few tourist condos and some dispersed private homes, the lower part of the island is the domain of sea turtles and birds. If you keep driving south you find yourself on North Padre Island, where the road abruptly ends, with no more pavement for another 80 miles.

South Padre Island   From time to time travel writers describe the coast between Corpus Christi and the tip of Texas—where it touches the Mexican border—as Texas's Riviera. Nothing could be further from the truth; this is one of the most deserted and unpopulated places in the United States. But that's its charm. Except for one solitary highway approaching the shore, Texas maps show a blank: no roads, no towns, nothing but beach wilderness. A Texas Riviera, it is not.

Pavement penetrates North Padre Island for 5 miles; from then on you're looking at untouched dunes and deserted beaches for 75 glorious miles. Picnicking, camping, and driving are permitted on the seashore, except for a 5-mile stretch reserved for pedestrians. Four-wheel drives are almost essential here, but they can't be used anywhere except on the beach. (No dune-running, please.) No bridge connects North Padre Island with South Padre Island. When the island terminates, that's it. The wilderness area continues on this neighboring island for many more miles until a highway heads south to the town of South Padre Island.

Approximately the same latitude as Miami Beach, the southern tip of South Padre Island has always stirred the imagination of developers and promoters as the next tourist and retirement bonanza. So far, their optimism has been greater than their successes. To be sure, a wealth of condos, hotels, and rental units compete for space with restaurants and souvenir shops, but the expected mass immigration just hasn't happened yet. Not long ago, luxury condos that had been built to sell for $400,000 were going at auction for $70,000 and less. This has changed, of course, with the real estate market leveling out. Real estate brokers say there are still bargains on the market, but few distress sales at this time.

Although the town of South Padre Island looks like a city when first viewed from the causeway that crosses the Laguna Madre from Port Isabel, only about 1,200 residents live here year-round. That figure increases impressively during the season, because over 3,000 condo units are rented out to tourists and visitors, and even in the off-season, a good percentage of the rentals are occupied. Unlike nearby Lower Rio Grande Valley, the peak season is summer, rather

than winter. At the crescendo of the tourist crush, during spring semester break, an unbelievable number squeeze into town. Fortunately, miles and miles of camping on the beaches handle the
overflow.

The developed portion of the island covers 6 miles of the southernmost tip, with the remaining 34 miles in deserted dunes and
beaches inhabited by RVs, campers, and fishermen. The beaches
seem endless and gently sloping—great for swimming and surf
fishing. By the way, driving the beach is permitted (four-wheel drive
recommended) as far as Mansfield Pass. This artificial ship channel
created two islands out of one. Local people will argue that an artificial channel doesn't make two islands out of one, but in 1964 the
state of Texas officially pronounced it to be two islands, so that set-
tles that. All along the beach fishermen camp and cast bait into the
surf for some really great sport fishing.

The Laguna Madre—those bay waters between the mainland
and South Padre Island—is said to be jumping with fish such as
sand trout, flounder, sheepshead, redfish, and croakers. In the town
of South Padre Island and also in Port Isabel, you can find charter
fishing for sailfish, marlin, tarpon, kingfish, and pompano. For
those who don't fish, there is plenty to do in the built-up, modern
town. Several commercial RV parks accommodate visitors and there
is a county park, Isla Blanca, where you can park your rig while you
beachcomb for lost pirate treasures.

Since South Padre Island lies at the most southern latitude of
anywhere in the continental United States except for the Florida
Keys, you might expect it to have a Florida-like climate, particularly
since it enjoys a lower summer humidity. But, because the Gulf
Stream, the secret to Miami Beach's climate, misses the Texas coast,
summers are hotter here and winters cooler. This is more than com-
pensated for by the calm and peaceful atmosphere (except during semester break).

Port Isabel   On the mainland across a short causeway is Port
Isabel (pop. 5,000). Most retirees choose to live here and make the
2.6-mile drive across the causeway to enjoy South Padre Island
without paying premium prices for property. Another advantage to
living in Port Isabel is that the island acts as a barrier against storm-
driven seas, so stilt construction isn't necessary.

SOUTH PADRE ISLAND–PORT ISABEL WEATHER						
In degrees Fahrenheit						
	Jan.	April	July	Oct.	Rain	Snow
Daily Highs	69	82	90	82	28"	—
Daily Lows	52	67	75	66		

BROWNSVILLE COST OF LIVING					
Percentage of	Overall	Housing	Medical	Groceries	Utilities
National Average	93	81	97	95	109

Like all South Texas towns that attract "Winter Texans," Port Isabel's population rises in proportion to the thermometer's fall in the colder sections of the United States and Canada. RV parks begin filling the last of October and stay packed until spring thaw lures the snowbirds back home. Because this is a year-round resort area, several large parks don't empty as they do in the winter resort areas. Those with self-contained rigs often prefer to boondock on the island beaches since they don't need electric or water hookups. Just north of town, and for miles up the coast, pristine beaches, all but deserted, invite campers and RV boondockers, offering good surf fishing and quiet times for reading or just sitting and contemplating whitecaps on the Gulf's blue waters.

In addition to the climate and beach location, local people point out the low crime rate, lack of rush-hour traffic, and serene living as reasons for retirement here. For traffic jams, people need to travel elsewhere.

The Rio Grande Valley

After flowing 2,000 miles through Colorado, New Mexico, and Texas, the Rio Grande, the state's most famous river, finally empties into the Gulf of Mexico just below South Padre Island. This, the lower Rio Grande Valley, is the domain of motor homes, trailers, and campers. It is also the yearly destination of the "Winter Texans," those warmth-loving folks who follow the sun south when arctic winds start blowing up north. Their winter target is a 90-mile stretch of valley starting at the Gulf of Mexico and westward to Rio Grande City. RV travelers and snowbirds from the United States and

Canada who make the yearly migration, call this place the "Poor Man's Florida." In many ways, this part of Texas does resemble Florida. Lines of palm trees, fragrant citrus blossoms, bougainvillea, and other flowering shrubs provide a distinctly tropical flavor. Temperatures can drop, however, suddenly and dramatically.

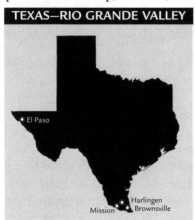

TEXAS–RIO GRANDE VALLEY

El Paso

Mission   Harlingen
Brownsville

The lower Rio Grande Valley would seem to be an unlikely place to become a popular retirement location because of its stifling summer heat. Many feel that it's all but unlivable from June through August. As evidence, witness the retirees leaving en masse every spring, not to return until summer has faded into late fall. In the coolest part of a summer evening, the temperature here rarely falls below 75 degrees, while it generally climbs into the high 90s during the day. Because of humidity, evaporative coolers are worthless; you must depend on refrigeration units. Yet, despite the hot summers, many retirees are choosing to adopt full-time retirement along the Rio Grande. For them, the pleasant winters make it all worthwhile, and they avoid the hassle of moving twice each year.

A Retirement Tradition

Winter is why folks come to the lower Rio Grande Valley. With seemingly endless sunshine, palm trees, and other tropical plants gracing the city streets, the ambience is unmistakably subtropical. Balmy breezes from the Gulf of Mexico caress the countryside, perfuming the air with the scent of orange and grapefruit blossoms. Meanwhile, back on the ranch, winds are whipping snowdrifts and dropping the chill factor to subzero records.

Although most retirees here start off as part-timers, or "Winter Texans," more and more are making their stays permanent and becoming "Year-round Texans." According to the U.S. government, the number of Social Security checks being sent to the lower Rio Grande Valley went up by 16 percent over a three-year period. RV and mobile-home parks report twice as many spaces being occupied year-round as ten years ago.

South Texas winter retirement isn't a new concept, not by any means. Midwestern farmers have known about it for years. When snow and ice gripped their fields with bitter winter cold, they arranged for someone to feed the cows and hogs, hooked a house trailer behind the old pickup, and headed for the Rio Grande for a winter of leisure and sunshine. Orange groves, palm trees, and 80-degree afternoons made for pleasant living while winter paralyzed farming country back home.

The bonus: Lower Rio Grande living was (and is) cheap. Local people used to joke that "farmers come down here with a five-dollar bill and a pair of overalls, and don't change either one the whole winter." You don't hear that joke nowadays. Winter retirement means big cash business in South Texas. Social Security, pension checks, and millions of outside dollars—American and Canadian— pump well over half a billion dollars into what could otherwise be a sagging economy. Alongside main highways, roadside signs proclaim, WE LOVE WINTER TEXANS!

Farmers are no longer a majority today; retirees come from all walks of life and all parts of the continent. More come each year, mostly in RVs. A few years ago, 50,000 snowbirds wintering in the Brownsville–Harlingen–McAllen area was considered a record. But today the number tops 300,000! Don't worry, there's always room for one more. More than 500 RV parks compete for snowbird tenants; some parks have several hundred spaces each. In the town of Mission, just southwest of McAllen, fewer than 100 RV parks accommodate more than 10,000 RVs. Yet the year-round population of Mission is only 25,000!

This floating population has become a political force to reckon with. Because Texas requires only a 30-day residence to become a legal voter, a significant number of folks register to vote as soon as they finish hooking up electricity and water to the motor home. These enthusiastic voters become involved in brisk political campaigning, providing swing votes to elect local officials and pass ordinances that affect their Winter Texan communities. You can be sure local politicians and city officials are responsive to the wishes of the Winter Texans. They aren't just retirees, they're *voting retirees!*

Organized Activities

RV parks of all descriptions abound, with variety to suit everyone's taste. Some are extremely plush, others plain. The fancy resorts routinely offer refinements like Olympic-size swimming pools, indoor shuffleboard, tennis, dance halls, libraries, pool rooms, sewing rooms, and other special halls for recreation and socializing. Even bare-bones parks usually have a rec hall to go with laundry facilities.

Like all RV facilities that cater to seasonal guests, these south Texas parks compete with each other by offering social activities and other amenities. They hold pancake breakfasts, ice-cream socials, square dances, and other events to get people mingling and having a good time. If the Winter Texans enjoy spending the season in one park, they are likely to return to the same park next winter. In addition, most visitors come from the Midwest, an area well known for amiability and informality. They quickly form social groups based on individual interests, activities such as bridge clubs, bicycling groups, and adult education classes.

Learning Spanish is a popular pastime, since Mexico is just across the river. People go in groups and have fun bargaining for treasures and practicing their new language skills. They travel by car, go in RV caravans, by chartered bus, or airplane. A high percentage of tourists you'll meet in Mexico, particularly in the northern part, are winter residents of the Rio Grande Valley on excursion. In the summer, when the sun turns Texas sidewalks into griddles, many permanent valley residents seek relief in the cool mountain towns of Mexico. Saltillo, Guanajuato, and San Miguel de Allende are favorite summer destinations, where thousands of North Americans convene to rent affordable apartments or small houses and renew friendships from the last season.

Restaurants in Mexico serve dishes that are unavailable in the United States. Wild game often appears on menus, items such as venison, dove, wild pig, and quail. Merchants in Mexico also benefit from this transfusion of greenbacks; retirees are viewed with gratitude and good will. Local police are instructed to be protective of the Winter Texans. Mexican businesses and city officials want nothing to discourage them from returning with more dollars!

Border Towns

Border towns are famous for being dreary places, with rundown shacks, high unemployment, and boarded-up storefronts. This picture was particularly true after the collapse of the Mexican economy and the demise of the Texas oil industry in the 1980s. When Mexico devalued the peso, merchandise on our side of the border became too expensive for Mexican consumers; they no longer crossed over to shop in U.S. stores. For a time, this was economically disastrous for American businesses that depend on cross-border commerce to stay healthy. Commerce has improved lately, since the Mexican government is holding on to the dollar-peso ratio. Once again prices on our side are more favorable for Mexicans, and shoppers are again patronizing U.S. stores. For many border areas, it's an up-again, down-again proposition.

However, the lower Rio Grande Valley's economy generally escapes these cyclical economic hardships. Businesses buzz with activity; restaurants and stores teem with customers. Everyone agrees that this prosperity is largely due to Winter Texans' cash. One bank reports that 20 percent of its deposit growth for the last six years is snowbird money. Another bank admits that one-third of its deposits come from transplanted and temporary Texans. The city of McAllen (one of the border towns) estimates that 25 percent of its winter sales-tax revenue comes from visitors. One bank flies a Canadian flag alongside an American flag to acknowledge the importance of the growing number of northern neighbors who winter here.

A final benefit of living here, one that is constantly pointed out by local boosters, is the low crime rate. Robberies, for example, are less than one-fourth the national average. As a temporary retirement area, we highly recommend the lower Rio Grande Valley. For those who can stand the heat, this is an excellent place for year-round retirement.

Brownsville   Brownsville is Texas's southernmost city. Its history began in 1846 when General Zachary Taylor established a military base—calling it Fort Brown—to back up our claim that the Rio Grande should have been the western boundary of Texas. Mexico took offense at this, however, insisting that the agreed-upon boundary was the Pecos River, *not* the Rio Grande River. This misunderstanding touched off the Mexican War of 1846–48. Once the war was underway, our diplomats realized that, logically, neither the Pecos *nor* the Rio Grande should mark the western edge of the United States. What else could it be but the Pacific Ocean? Stands to reason. After our troops captured Mexico City and explained the revised negotiating position (at gunpoint), Mexican diplomats reluctantly recognized the logic of our argument. Thus we ended up with not only the Rio Grande but also the states of California, New Mexico, Arizona, Nevada, Utah, and parts of Colorado and Wyoming.

Today, Brownsville is the Rio Grande Valley's largest city, with a population of around 105,000. Zachary Taylor's military outpost is now the site of the Texas Southmost College. Some of Fort Brown's facilities are in use today as school administration buildings. In addition to the college, the community is served by two excellent hospitals and several senior nursing homes.

The cost of living here is favorable despite unusually high utility rates. Low housing prices account for the difference, with sales figures fully 19 percent below national averages. That's partly because the floating retiree population returns home every summer—they don't buy houses and settle down for the entire year along the Rio Grande Valley. Supermarket prices are generally moderate, especially for locally grown produce, since this area is the country's top producer of winter vegetables. Year-round apartment and home rentals are inexpensive, although those rented just for the winter are predictably pricey.

Wages are low, as in most border areas, due in part to the availability of eager workers from Mexico who are willing to cross the river and do a hard day's work for minimal wages. Job competition means lower wages, lower costs of goods and services, and a lower cost of living for visitors. Even so, the large influx of winter visitors creates a cornucopia of seasonal jobs for retirees. Employers like to hire employees they won't have to lay off when the season ends; they'll be leaving anyway.

Just across the river is the Mexican city of Matamoros, a favorite shopping target for Winter Texans staying in and around Brownsville. Nightclubs, restaurants, gift shops, and stores of all descriptions compete for the Yankee dollar, although some prices on the Mexican side have been creeping toward Texas price levels. You'll hear praise for Matamoros dentists, whose work is said to be both inexpensive and high quality. Of course, the usual across-the-border doctors and medical clinics administer unorthodox treatment for diseases such as cancer and arthritis. Although the American Medical Association insists that unapproved remedies are worthless, many patients disagree. One man explained, "My doctor back home claims these Mexican clinics can't help my arthritis. Says I'm wasting my money. But he admits there's nothing *he* can do about arthritis, either. So, for a few dollars, I'm betting that the other doctor's wrong. I can't afford *not* to make the bet."

Another benefit of living along the international border is inexpensive prescription drugs purchased in Mexican *farmacias*. In Mexico—as in most foreign countries—many essential medications do not require prescriptions. Even though manufactured by the same companies that distribute in the United States and Canada, these drugs are significantly less expensive in Mexico. Just one example: A thirty-day supply of Enderal—a common medication for hypertension and heart irregularities—costs about a third to a half of what you would pay on the American side of the border. The Mexican government successfully controls drug prices and carefully monitors the sale of medications to prevent unfair profit-taking. (Is there a lesson here for our government?)

Only a 22-mile drive from Brownsville is South Padre Island, the 34-mile barrier island discussed previously. Gulf fishing, boating, and beachcombing are popular pastimes here and are very accessible to Brownsville residents.

Mission   "Home of Winter Texans" is one of the ways Mission advertises itself, but the town can't seem to make up its mind, because it also claims the title of "Home of the Grapefruit." It's said that Texas's first citrus orchard started here when mission priests planted trees in 1824 (hence the name Mission). The area is indeed famous for its groves of Texas Ruby Red grapefruit. In addition to the sweet aroma of citrus blossoms in December, residents enjoy a particularly colorful Christmas because of the abundance of poinsettias throughout town. The joyful theme of "Tropical Christmas" is celebrated with profuse displays of these colorful plants in public buildings, parks, and private homes.

The Mexican city of Reynosa sits across the river from Mission. A popular shopping place for valley residents, Reynosa offers much the same attractions as Matamoros. Some excellent restaurants here serve cuisine unobtainable in the United States, wild game, for ex-

LOWER RIO GRANDE VALLEY WEATHER						
In degrees Fahrenheit						
	Jan.	April	July	Oct.	Rain	Snow
Daily Highs	70	83	93	84	26"	—
Daily Lows	51	67	76	66		

LOWER RIO GRANDE VALLEY COST OF LIVING					
Percentage of	Overall	Housing	Medical	Groceries	Utilities
National Average	91	77	113	84	92

ample. As is the case in all the border towns, tourist cards or passports aren't required for visits of less than seventy-two hours unless you travel to the interior of Mexico.

Harlingen   About 30 miles from Brownsville, Harlingen is somewhat smaller, with a population of about 45,000. Like the rest of the Rio Grande Valley, Harlingen's population climbs dramatically during the winter. This city stands out because of its local beautification campaigns and recycling efforts, and thanks to the hard work of its citizens, Harlingen won the All-American City award from the National Civic League. Also, a recent survey by *Money* magazine ranked the city the twentieth best place to live in the United States.

This is an area of truck farms, orange groves, and more of the prized Texas Ruby Red grapefruit. With a year-round growing season, one crop or another is ready to be harvested at any given time of the year. Harlingen's appearance is similar to that of Mission, with palm trees, colorful bougainvillea, and poinsettias brightening the warm Christmas season.

Overall, Harlingen is a nice place for winter retirement even though it requires a longer drive for shopping in Mexico. A compensating attraction is a large greyhound racing park. (Dogs, not buses.) The city also boasts four PGA championship golf courses plus a twenty-seven-hole municipal course and several par-three layouts.

When comparing lower Rio Grande Valley housing and year-round rentals, Harlingen turns out to be the most economical of the towns mentioned here. Housing costs are among the lowest in the country. In early 1999, real estate prices were 23 percent below national norms.

El Paso   Just over four centuries ago, the first Europeans pushed their way north from Mexico and found an easy crossing, or pass, across the Rio Grande into what is now Texas's upper Rio Grande Valley. Early Spanish explorers named the crossing "El Paso del Norte." When Mexico relinquished claim to the crossing, the U.S. Army established a post here to protect American settlers from marauding Comanches and to oversee the growing business of international trade between Mexico and the United States. Over the ensuing years, El Paso grew from a dusty cow town into a modern city of more than 500,000, the largest city on the American side of the 1,933-mile U.S.–Mexico border.

That first military post established a continuing tradition of military presence in El Paso. Fort Bliss, in northeast El Paso, is the home of the U.S. Army Air Defense Center and contributes a huge payroll to keep the economy level. Military families and civilian support personnel live in all sections of the city and make the population very "middle America." When retirement time rolls around, military personnel quite naturally think of El Paso as one of their retirement possibilities. They remember the cleanliness and neighborliness of the city as well as the affordable real estate. Of course, being military, post-exchange privileges and medical facilities for retirees influence their final decisions.

El Paso has several good things going for it. First, the climate is mild, with summers far cooler than those of the lower Rio Grande Valley. You can usually get out in July or August and play a game of golf without risking sunstroke. Lower humidity and a 3,700-foot elevation makes a world of difference.

Another attraction for retirees is Ciudad Juarez, just across the Rio Grande. Juarez is more than just another border town like Reynosa or Matamoros; it is truly a city. It's even larger than El Paso, with an estimated population of nearly a million inhabitants. Juarez's downtown section, situated close to the border, is a bit grungy, with honky-tonks, bars, an occasional good restaurant, and the inevitable curio and souvenir shops. But when you get away from the old downtown section you'll find modern areas with broad boulevards, nice restaurants, and nice clothing stores, and, depending upon the state of the economy, shopping in Juarez can be an experience in bargaining. Some commodities are always cheaper across the border, particularly items like booze, instant coffee, and some grocery items. Many retirees make weekly forays across the border to take advantage of bargains. Produce sells at giveaway prices; unfortunately, you can't carry veggies across the border.

El Paso has a delightful way of blending Mexican and Anglo cultures, something that doesn't happen in the lower Rio Grande Valley. Instead of rigid social lines separating Anglo-Saxons and Hispanics, keeping a gulf between the United States and Mexico, you'll find a congenial mixture of Texas and Chihuahua. Radio and television announcers on both sides of the border often jump between Spanish and English, never missing a beat. Restaurant menus on both sides of the border do much the same. El Paso restaurants typically offer dishes like pozole or chiles rellenos, and Juarez restaurants are famous for steak-and-lobster dinners and Chinese food. Years ago, when I worked for the *El Paso Times*, my favorite lunch-break restaurant served a great chicken-fried steak. But instead of gravy on the steak, it came with chile con queso sauce!

American modern and old Mexican charm blend to give El Paso a distinctive character. The downtown's wide streets branch out in all directions, and Interstate 10 moves traffic quickly and efficiently through the center of the city. Commercial buildings are modern and crisp, avoiding the garishness and mirrored walls that seem to be in vogue elsewhere. As you move toward the outskirts of the city, you can't help but be impressed with El Paso's neatness and cleanliness. Most single-family neighborhoods favor brick construction, one-story homes, and neatly trimmed landscaping. Housing costs are 11 percent below national averages.

EL PASO WEATHER
In degrees Fahrenheit

	Jan.	April	July	Oct.	Rain	Snow
Daily Highs	58	79	95	78	8"	6"
Daily Lows	31	49	70	49		

EL PASO COST OF LIVING

Percentage of	Overall	Housing	Medical	Groceries	Utilities
National Average	95	86	94	99	83

In El Paso's newer sections, away from downtown, you'll find a proliferation of apartment buildings. Like many Texas cities that participated in the savings-and-loan jubilee, condo and apartment construction has been overly enthusiastic, resulting in an oversupply. You'll often spy billboards shouting out special deals to entice renters. Some apartments offer the first month's rent free, or free utilities for the first year, maybe a color television to bring you into the fold. The best part is the advertised monthly rates are affordable.

When asked, "Why retire in El Paso?" answers include mild weather and healthy, year-round outdoor activities. Besides golf, tennis, and jogging, less vigorous spectator sports include bullfights and horse racing across the river in Mexico. I asked an old friend why he and his wife chose El Paso over other towns where he'd worked, places like San Francisco or Fort Lauderdale, or why they hadn't moved back to their hometown in Connecticut.

He smiled wryly as he looked around the spacious, almost-new apartment. "You know what a place like this would cost us in Connecticut?" Before I had a chance to guess, he went on, saying, "At least $750 a month, that's what. A big chunk of my Social Security check would go to make the rent. We'd have to dig into savings every month to buy food. We wouldn't be able to enjoy life if we had to live like paupers."

His wife nodded agreement. "The secret to low-cost retirement is cutting back on housing," she emphasized. "Our rent and utilities here come to about $450 a month. That extra $300 covers groceries and other bills. Actually, we have no problem getting by on our Social Security checks."

Central Texas

San Antonio   It's difficult to think of San Antonio (pop. 935,000) as being in the south-central part of Texas, because it looks like west Texas to me. Only 28 inches of rain per year falls on San Antonio, compared to Houston's 45 inches or Port Arthur's 52 inches. Dry range country with thorny bushes starts not far from the city limits. Certainly, from here westward, we are looking at the kind of country one expects from the western United States, with brush, cactus, and sandy soil. If the "West" doesn't start in San Antonio, then where?

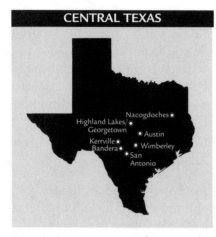

CENTRAL TEXAS

Nacogdoches
Highland Lakes/
Georgetown   Austin
Kerrville
Bandera   Wimberley
San
Antonio

When white men first came here, a Coahuilecan Indian village occupied the bank of a beautiful river, where present-day downtown San Antonio is located. The river, life-giving and crystal-clear, was shaded by large poplar trees ("alamo" trees in Spanish). The Indians called the river Yanaguana, or "refreshing waters." Unfortunately, the river didn't retain its pristine state once white men began using it to dump sewage and trash.

Today, this river is a symbol of San Antonio's fight against urban decay. The downtown river project is a textbook example of how to remedy central-core blight. The city completely transformed the river—which was little more than a weed-choked garbage dump a few years ago—and turned it into an elegant shopping and restaurant area. Soaring cypress and cottonwood trees grace the riverbanks, shading shops, restaurants, and hotels. Tourists and residents alike enjoy strolls, boat rides, and nightlife along the riverbanks. The project has revitalized San Antonio's entire downtown section. The Coahuilecan Indians would be proud of the way their river has returned to its "refreshing waters" status.

San Antonio's weather is a plus retirees constantly brag about. Summers are warm, with highs typically in the low 90s. Yet summer evenings are delightful, with temperatures dropping into the high 60s or low 70s—just right for shirt-sleeve evenings and for sleeping without the annoyance of air-conditioning. The humidity is moderate, so swamp coolers work efficiently and refrigerated air-conditioning isn't absolutely necessary. In the winter, temperatures rarely drop below 40 degrees at night, and afternoons are almost always in the mid-60s, even in the coldest months. For all practical purposes, there is no winter. Snow? Almost none; every three or four years San Antonio catches enough snow to measure, although in 1985 it snowed 13 inches! Rain? Just enough to keep lawns and shrubbery green.

SAN ANTONIO WEATHER					
In degrees Fahrenheit					
	Jan.	April	July	Oct.	Rain	Snow
Daily Highs	62	80	95	82	28"	—
Daily Lows	39	59	74	59		

SAN ANTONIO COST OF LIVING					
Percentage of	Overall	Housing	Medical	Groceries	Utilities
National Average	89	83	95	88	79

San Antonio, like Austin to the north, enjoys a low cost of living, about 11 percent below national averages. San Antonio ranks lowest of the top twenty-five U.S. metropolitan areas; low-cost utilities and real estate at 17 percent under national averages are partly responsible for this happy condition. Residential areas flourish on the fringes of the city, with new subdivisions popping up everywhere. Most newcomers prefer to live in the outer ring of newer subdivisions, near one of several large shopping centers. These areas have comfortably high levels of personal safety, as opposed to the inevitably higher crime rate found closer to a city's center.

Apartments and condo units are overbuilt, with rentals appropriately reasonable. One reason for the abundance of rentals is the enormous military population that is constantly on the move. A few years ago, developers sized up this market and decided to increase the number of rentals. With abundant savings-and-loan money available, apartments and condos sprouted far quicker than tenants.

Medical care here is awesome. The University of Texas Health Science Center is located here, with schools in medicine, dentistry, and nursing, and research programs in cancer, cardiology, and other problems endemic to the elderly. This is one of only six sites in the nation that is approved for patients to try experimental cancer drugs. The South Texas Medical Center, a 700-acre complex, encompasses eight major hospitals, clinics, laboratories, and a cancer research and therapy center. Also there's the world-renowned Burn Unit at Brooke Army Medical Center at Fort Sam Houston, which receives burn victims from all over the world.

Since its beginning as a Spanish presidio almost three centuries ago, San Antonio has maintained a military tradition. Four Air Force bases circle the city: Brooks, Kelly Field, Lackland, and Randolph, plus Fort Sam Houston, an Army post. Brooks Air Force Base is famous in military circles for having one of the finest medical facilities in the country. This alone is an attraction for military retirees and would bring them here even if San Antonio weren't such a nice place to live. Our understanding is that almost 70,000 service personnel and families live in the San Antonio area and at least twice that many retirees. This may well be the largest population of ex-military folks in the country.

Bandera   Not far from San Antonio, the little town of Bandera is a delightful place to investigate for retirement. Its population is less than a thousand, but it's too nice to ignore. It's become a retirement haven for San Antonio residents who are familiar with the area and probably will draw retirees from other parts of the country once Bandera becomes better known. Just a 26-mile drive from Kerrville, this community is one of the nicest, greenest, and most comfortable of all. Situated on the Medina River, surrounded by oak–covered hills laced with winding creeks, Bandera has long been a favorite of San Antonio residents as a weekend getaway.

The town's carefully preserved main street is pretty much the same as it must have appeared in the last century, recalling memories of the days back in the 1870s when Bandera was known as the "Cowboy Capital of the World." This was a staging area for Texas cowboys and their cattle herds to join up with drives traveling north along the Western Trail to Kansas and sometimes on to Montana. It's easy to imagine the *Lonesome Dove* crew moving their herd through here on their way north.

Texas Hill Country

The picture most of us have of West Texas is flat or rolling stretches of eternity, sparsely covered with prairie grass or low brush that extends to meet the distant horizon. Sometimes wheat replaces grass; occasionally a lethargic steer can be seen munching cactus. Nothing moves except the up-and-down rocking of oil pumps or perhaps a distant windmill. Texas flatlands do indeed flow pretty much undisturbed by mountains, except for the extreme western portion, where the Rocky Mountains march southward through Big Bend National Park.

This bleak picture is more or less accurate, with a notable exception: the Texas Hill Country. A geological formation known as the Balcones Fault has pushed the land a thousand feet above the surrounding plains, creating a mini-mountain range. This not only changes the geography of Texas, it also profoundly affects the state's climate. Moisture-laden breezes from the Gulf of Mexico can't easily lift over the Hill Country, so they release their rain on the southeastern part of the state and leave the western part arid. You can easily see this, for the great Southwestern Desert begins the other side of the Texas Hill Country.

This special part of Texas is a wonderland of large, limestone-cropped hills not quite large enough to be called mountains, mostly wooded and intersected by half a dozen clear rivers, spring-fed creeks, and lakes. Perhaps half a hundred small, friendly towns and cities are scattered through the lightly populated countryside, many of them holding great retirement potential. Because much of the Texas Hill Country is rocky, with high concentrations of limestone and caliche, the soil isn't suitable for extensive farming operations. Therefore, customarily the land is left in its natural state. Most acreage is covered by juniper thickets, wild cherry, gnarled oak, native pecan, and mountain laurel trees. Along the slow-moving rivers, magnificent cypress and elms shade the banks and provide cover for wild creatures. Cattle and sheep share the wilderness with white-tailed deer, turkey, javalina (wild pigs), and imported Russian boar.

The Texas Hill Country is as different from our usual view of Texas as can possibly be. Long considered one of the better living areas in the state, the region has been enjoying nationwide attention through retirement publications. One thing that makes it so different from other parts of West Texas is its year-round rainfall. The Hill Country receives more than 30 inches of rain each year, several times that of many Southwest locations. This accounts for its green, sometimes lush vegetation. The rain falls every month of the year, helping to keep things looking fresh.

Kerrville   Kerrville is often considered the "capital" of the Hill Country since it's the largest city in the hills and is centrally located among them. With a population of almost 19,000, Kerrville is the Hill Country's major shopping destination. Being close to Interstate 10, many residents find it convenient to commute to jobs in

San Antonio, about 45 minutes away. Thus Kerrville fulfills two roles: as a place to retire and as a bedroom community.

Kerrville shares in the Hill Country's panoramic views and is further blessed by the Guadalupe River flowing softly through the heart of town. Kerrville's location at 1,600 to 1,800 feet above sea level, the Hill Country's highest, contributes to its good climate, providing cooler summers and more clearly defined seasons than Austin or San Antonio. Local people are happy with July and August days, always several degrees cooler than the lowland cities. One source of retirees stems from those summer residents who later decide to move to the Hill Country when embarking on new careers as retirees.

Because of the area's growing population of retirees (almost 30 percent of county residents are over age sixty-five), many Kerrville social and business events focus on seniors. The local chamber of commerce is one of the few we've seen that really goes all out for retirees and deserves high praise. An interesting example is the annual Senior Job Opportunity Fair that the chamber of commerce conducts. This year local businessmen and more than 200 seniors joined together in a half-day seminar to explore employment possibilities. Together they worked out ways to create a large number of part-time and permanent jobs for retirees and supplied valuable employees for area businesses.

Kerrville holds a reputation as the Hill County's preeminent art colony. The picturesque surroundings naturally encourage artistic development and act as a magnet to draw working artists, many of whom display works in local galleries and boutiques. One of Kerrville's galleries, the Cowboy Artists of America Museum, is the nation's only museum whose exhibitions are restricted to America's Western and cowboy artists. Artistry isn't restricted to visual arts; there are also outdoor theater productions and a performing arts group that brings concerts and other live shows.

Another popular cultural presentation is the annual Kerrville Folk Festival, held in late spring. Residents and tourists enjoy eighteen days of musical events, which include original works performed by artists in an outdoor theater, evening concerts around campfires, and a songwriter's competition.

Camp Verde, 11 miles south of Kerrville, was the eastern terminus of a camel route that stretched all the way to Yuma, Arizona.

This was part of an experiment in overland transportation, an idea whose time has never quite arrived.

Wimberley   Wimberley is another Hill Country town that's been basking in the warm light of national publicity as a new discovery in retirement destinations. Its photogenic qualities make wonderful color layouts for magazines. This is where the clear, cool waters of Cypress Creek join the warmer waters of the slow-moving Blanco River, a place where large trees and old homes of native stone harken back to another era. This was a popular getaway during World War II, when rich folks from Houston and San Antonio didn't have enough gasoline to travel to their second homes in the Blue Ridge Mountains. So they built summer homes—"camp houses" as they called them—in Wimberley. When they retired, these summer places became permanent homes, thus starting a retirement trend. As a result, Houston transplants are well represented here. It's properly called a "village," because it's never been incorporated, and folks hereabout like it that way.

Wimberley is strategically located between Austin and San Antonio, not far off Interstate 35. The population here is a little more than 8,000, large enough for essential services, but Wimberley enjoys a small-town atmosphere, with low crime and friendly neighbors. Because it's only 12 miles to San Marcos, that's where most heavy-duty shopping is done, or 45 miles (about an hour) away in Austin. San Marcos is also the nearest place to purchase bottles of wine or liquor; local restaurants do serve wines and cocktails by the drink.

Although there is no Greyhound bus service, the county sponsors a service called CARTS, which takes disabled and senior citizens

HILL COUNTRY WEATHER

In degrees Fahrenheit

	Jan.	April	July	Oct.	Rain	Snow
Daily Highs	56	77	90	79	30"	2"
Daily Lows	36	57	74	59		

HILL COUNTRY COST OF LIVING

	Overall	Housing	Medical	Groceries	Utilities
Percentage of National Average	92	79	94	87	93

to medical appointments and even into Austin for shopping and special medical needs. A volunteer ambulance group takes emergency cases to the hospital in nearby San Marcos.

Wimberley sits at an altitude of 1,100 feet—twice as high as Austin—and therefore enjoys slightly cooler summers and a few inches more rainfall. Like other towns in this part of the country, snow is a rarity. Homeowners choose among properties on rivers or hills, on city-size lots or acreages, with homes selling for slightly under national averages. Nearby Woodcreek is a planned community with an eighteen-hole golf course, tennis courts, clubhouse, and other amenities. Rentals are almost impossible to find, since there are no apartments, just single-family homes.

A summer community tradition is an outdoor movie theater (bring your own chairs). The Blanco River, lined with huge old cedars and oak trees, passes one edge of town and intersects with Cypress Creek on the other. The rivers are crossed by one-lane bridges, which residents refuse to widen because that would mean cutting some beautiful cypress trees. The Blanco River's turquoise waters are excellent for swimming, tubing, fishing, and canoeing.

Austin   The capital of Texas, Austin sits 80 miles north of San Antonio on Interstate 35. Austin (pop. 470,000) is about half the size of San Antonio, but equally charming. Its downtown centers around an ornate state capitol and its extensive grounds.

Not as level as most Texas cities, Austin sits on the fringe of the Texas Hill Country and is surrounded by a circle of low hills. Unlike San Antonio, which developed from a haphazard grouping of trails converging at a river crossing, Austin began as a carefully planned city designed to be the state's capital. The downtown has an interesting mixture of modern and older buildings, creating an air of informality.

Austin is becoming widely known as a country music center, second only to Nashville. Not only country music, but everything from jazz to reggae can be heard in the clubs around the city, particularly on Sixth Street, the renovated nineteenth-century historic district. The city is also proud of its reputation as a cultural center in arts other than music. Museums, theaters, and art galleries are well attended throughout the city. A symphony, ballet, and lyric opera complement the cultural offerings. Medical services are more than adequate, with a dozen hospitals and numerous specialists in attendance.

AUSTIN AREA WEATHER						
In degrees Fahrenheit						
	Jan.	April	July	Oct.	Rain	Snow
Daily Highs	59	79	95	81	32"	1"
Daily Lows	39	58	74	59		

AUSTIN COST OF LIVING					
Percentage of	Overall	Housing	Medical	Groceries	Utilities
National Average	100	102	107	100	92

Austin is also known for its universities and colleges. The University of Texas at Austin is the largest in the state system. Adult education classes are widely available. Almost twenty golf courses are open to the public, plus another fifteen private clubs, the mild climate permitting fairway use throughout the year.

Real estate costs in Austin are above national averages by 2 percent, which may be explained by the large number of quality homes being sold in the many pleasant-looking neighborhoods on the fringes of the city. Popular retirement areas such as nearby Georgetown or San Marcos have similar housing selling for almost 10 percent lower.

Highland Lakes   Austin's outdoor recreation centers around the Highland Lakes area. This has long been considered one of the better retirement areas in the state. With 150 miles of water wonderland, a series of lakes stair-step down toward Austin. The lakes area offers abundant fishing and boating as well as wonderful scenery for retirement living. Buchanan Dam (pop. 3,800) is a small resort and retirement community that grew at the construction site of the lake by the same name. This is the largest of the lakes and also the highest. The altitude is 1,025 feet (about 500 feet higher than Austin), high enough to be cooler in the summer but not so high as to have heavy winter snows. Roads circle the lake, giving access to retirement homes, RV parks, and rental properties.

Another retirement possibility, Marble Falls (pop. 4,235) takes its name from the dam that created this particular lake. Sheer bluffs of limestone, granite, and marble encompass the lake at this point. Hunting, fishing, and camping are popular activities. White-tailed deer and wild turkey are said to be plentiful. Nearby Granite Moun-

GEORGETOWN COST OF LIVING					
Percentage of National Average	Overall 96	Housing 97	Medical 92	Groceries 99	Utilities 89

tain is the source of the distinctive pink-and-red granite used to construct the state capitol in downtown Austin. Other lakes in the area are Travis, Austin Town Lake, Canyon Lake, and Lake Georgetown.

Georgetown   With a population of a little over 15,000, Georgetown is proud of its history and delights in its wealth of Victorian architecture. The centerpiece is old, historic Courthouse Square, with antiques stores and boutiques. Residents take great care in the restoration and preservation of this historic town, with 180 homes and commercial structures designated as having historical significance. Some are now in use as restaurants and bed-and-breakfasts. Georgetown is about 30 miles from downtown Austin on the interstate, within commuting distance for those involved in Austin's high-tech industries.

As an indication of faith in Georgetown's future as a retirement location, the Del Webb Corporation is proceeding with one of its famous Sun City developments near here. Sun City Georgetown's 5,300-acre planned community features two scenic creeks meandering through fields of Texas wildflowers and stands of native pecans, walnuts, and majestic live oaks. Del Webb's first Texas venture, this will be an active retirement community designed for those age 55 and older.

Eventually, 9,500 homes will be built, with 45 percent of the land remaining as open space and natural areas. Four eighteen-hole golf courses are planned. Other recreational facilities will include swimming pools, tennis courts, and extensive hiking and biking trails.

Nacogdoches   This town may be located in central Texas as far as its north-south positioning goes, but really Nacogdoches is east Texas in spirit and environment. Here you'll find towering pines, rolling hills, vast blue lakes, cypress swamps, and Spanish moss as well as majestic plantation homes reminiscent of old Natchez and New Orleans. That shouldn't be surprising, since this was the first area of Texas to be settled by pioneers from Tennessee and Louisiana. Their new homes were duplicates of those they left behind. Since few Civil War battles were fought in Texas, war's destruction passed them by, leaving many buildings of historical interest intact for today's enjoyment.

Nacogdoches (pop. 28,744) is the oldest town in the area, for it was an Indian settlement for centuries before the earliest Spanish explorers passed by. DeSoto's troops stopped here in 1541 and were received hospitably by the city fathers of that time. Today's North Street is claimed to be the oldest public thoroughfare in the United States, since it was a major route connecting the Indian community of Nacogdoches with other Indian towns to the north. La Salle's expedition passed over that road in 1687, and Spanish friars established a mission here in 1716. An old Spanish stone fort still stands, now the campus of Stephen F. Austin State University.

The university has 12,000 students and contributes to the city's cultural atmosphere. Many retirees take advantage of the school's program of speakers, concerts, and drama presentations. Also important to retirees are two excellent hospitals and a senior citizens' treatment center.

The weather is typical Deep South: hot, muggy summers and mild winters. But one retiree said, "Great weather the rest of the year makes up for summer. We have flowers blooming until late November." This part of the country catches about 43 inches of rain a year, enough to keep things pretty and green without making it too soggy.

A couple of years ago Nacogdoches was named one of the top ten cities in the United States in which to live by *U.S. News and World Report*, so we had to visit to see if we agreed. We did. Something about this section of Texas feels right for retirement. Nacogdoches in particular seems to be vigorous, prosperous, and modern, with none of the run-down qualities that characterize some sleepy Texas towns.

NACOGDOCHES WEATHER						
In degrees Fahrenheit						
	Jan.	April	July	Oct.	Rain	Snow
Daily Highs	62	79	94	82	43"	—
Daily Lows	41	58	72	57		

The city seems to have just about everything a person would need, except nearness to a big city. Dallas is a three-and-a-half-hour drive, and Houston is two and a half hours to the south. Add another hour to get to Galveston's beaches.

Western Mountains
and Deserts

FROM NEW MEXICO TO EASTERN CALIFORNIA, from the Mexican border
to Colorado, the Southwest is a geological and scenic wonderland.
Distinctive, dramatic arrangements of earth, water, and sky blend
together, creating landscapes of unforgettable beauty. Sprawling,
forest-covered plateaus scarred by awesome canyons contrast with
endless expanses of sand, cactus, and sagebrush; great man-made
lakes sparkle like aquamarine jewels in stark red settings. Badlands,
with enormous monoliths, arches, and chiseled buttes, imitate
mythical cities while snowcapped peaks preside over all. This is what
draws retirees to the Southwest (in addition to snow-free winters).

It isn't all unspoiled natural paradise, however, because
modern cosmopolitan cities rise over the shards of ancient Indian
ruins and old ghost towns. In many areas, Anglo, Spanish, and Native American cultures blend to create a spicy potpourri of something distinctly Southwestern. Huge retirement developments with
golf courses and Olympic-size swimming pools (that look as if
they've been magically transported from Florida) compete with
small, comfortable localities of a few hundred homes.

The word *desert* incorrectly conjures images of Sahara-like sand
dunes and desolate sweeps of barren land. True, North American
deserts *can* be like that, but rarely are. Over eons, plants and animals
have adapted to living in dry country—even in places with 4 or 5
inches of rain per year. Trees and bushes survive on little water,
flourishing miraculously in a dry desert or mountain environment.
The first spring storm makes the desert bloom with an unforgettable explosion of colorful flowers and a profusion of green, all of
which disappear when the plants withdraw into their water-con-
serving mode for the summer. Some plants have developed tough
skins that prevent precious water from evaporating and thus stay
green year-round.

Animals, too, have adapted. An amazing variety of reptiles, mammals, and birds do perfectly fine in the desert. Some survive the fierce summers by conserving body energy during the heat of the day, then foraging and exercising in the cooler hours of the morning and evening. Other species developed patterns of migration, spending summers in northern or coastal areas where the weather is cool and damp, and then wintering in the pleasant warmth of the desert.

Therefore, it should come as no surprise that the famous species *Snowbirdus americanus* has also adapted to dry mountain and desert living. Some have adapted to full-time living in the desert, conserving body energy in air-conditioned homes and autos and by foraging at shopping malls or playing golf in the cooler hours of the morning and evening. Midday is for naps. Instead of developing tough skins that prevent precious water from evaporating, these creatures develop sun-tanned skins and sip cool drinks. Evaporation be damned!

Arizona and New Mexico are favorite winter destinations, although a growing number of retirees choose to live there year-round. Two things you can count on: summer heat and abundant winter sunshine. Phoenix averages 295 days a year of sunny or partly sunny days. Winters are gloriously warm, but daily summer temperatures average over 100 degrees! We can't have everything. Fortunately, relative humidity in Phoenix is as low as you can hope to find. This low humidity is why places such as Phoenix and Las Vegas are adding permanent residents like crazy, while parts of the Rio Grande Valley double in population each winter, only to lose it again in the summer.

Relative humidity is the key to desert and dry mountain environments. Humidity affects temperature by making it feel as if it is warmer or colder than it really is. Studies show that a 95-degree day in a place like Las Vegas (at 20 percent humidity) is perceived by the body as fairly comfortable. Yet a 95-degree day in Florida (at 75 percent humidity) would be felt as 115 degrees! No wonder people sit in front of their air conditioners in Florida!

The Southwest mountain and desert country was made expressly for snowbirds. When the first days of fall turn frosty in their hometowns, they pack up their golf clubs, tennis racquets, and suntan oil and head for the Southwest. Many mobile-home parks in places like Yuma, Arizona, report that 90 percent of their residents arrive in October and November and are gone by April.

The mobile home makes a perfect winter retreat for the snow-bird, inexpensive to buy and park. In hot areas, most parks reduce rents during the summer, making it convenient and affordable to leave your winter retreat sitting empty until next season. With low-maintenance desert landscaping, homes can be shut up for several months without the yard becoming shaggy. Cactus seldom requires mowing; rocks need little water.

All desert retirees, however, are not wanderers. Of those folks who buy conventional homes in places such as Phoenix and Las Vegas, only about 5 percent regularly travel to cooler climes for the summer.

Arizona

This is a state with scenic variety: evergreen-covered mountains; peaks with a foot of winter snow; deserts with forests of cactus; mineral-rich, shaded valleys; gently or rapidly flowing streams and rivers; and America's greatest natural wonder, the Grand Canyon. This is also a state with human variety: One-seventh of the United States's Native American population resides here. There are also generous numbers of Spanish speakers and newcomers from across the United States and Canada. Add to this the benefits of mild winters and a strong senior citizen political presence and support structure, and you have a state where retirement is a growth industry.

ARIZONA TAX PROFILE

Sales tax: 5% to 7%, food and drugs exempt
State income tax: graduated, 3.8% to 7% over $150,000
Property taxes: range between 0.8% to 1%
Intangibles tax: no
Social security taxed: no
Pensions taxed: private employer pensions taxed fully; government pensions receive $2,500 exemption; allows personal tax credits
Gasoline tax: 18¢ per gallon

Southern Arizona: Sonoran Desert Living

Arizona's southern towns are strongly flavored by both their social and geographical surroundings. First off, towns here are often just across the border from Mexico. This means that the charm of the

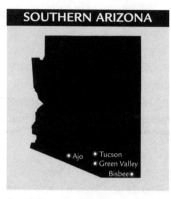

SOUTHERN ARIZONA

Ajo • Tucson • Green Valley Bisbee •

Spanish lifestyle is evident in local architecture, food, and language. This nearness to Mexico also allows for easy across-the-border day trips for shopping and touring (see the Rio Grande Valley section of the Texas chapter for more details). Secondly, the local Sonoran desert environment provides a mix of classic vistas of desert valleys and mountains with scenes of extensive irrigated croplands, one of the region's major industries.

Bisbee   When I first wrote about Bisbee, the town had just suffered a financial disaster. At one time completely furnished homes sold for as little as $500. Homes were sometimes abandoned with unlocked doors. By the time we visited, things had taken a turn for the better, with retirees coming in to buy the cheap real estate and to rebuild the town. Bisbee made a dramatic switch from an abandoned mining town to its newer role as a retirement "discovery."

Revisiting a few years later, we found even more retirees had selected Bisbee for permanent homes. This increase in retiree population encouraged even more activity in services and organizations serving retired people. Of course, this wave of bargain-hunting home buyers pushed selling prices up. But since prices started at an incredibly low level, real estate is still an excellent buy.

More than just a place of bargain housing, Bisbee's colorful history matches its picturesque desert-mountain setting. Tucked away in a canyon in the southeastern part of Arizona, only a few miles from the Mexican border, its narrow, winding streets present a classic style of mining towns of the late nineteenth century. The buildings are a mixture of authentic Victorian and Western mining camp, with brick and clapboard construction dating from the 1890s and even earlier. Because of its steep hills and ornate Victorian construction, people often describe the town as having a certain San Francisco atmosphere—without the cable cars, of course.

Once a wild, wide-open city of 20,000 miners, merchants, and adventurers intent upon making their fortunes, Bisbee's pace today is slow and quiet. Since the town is off the standard tourist track, relatively few visitors disturb the ghosts of yesteryear. A stroll through Bisbee's narrow streets is like stepping into the past. Night sounds are muted, and after midnight the streets are all but deserted. Yet, it's far from a ghost town. Retirees express great satisfaction with Bisbee's balance between leisure and recreation.

What happened to change Bisbee? Disaster struck quite suddenly, beginning in 1975, when Phelps-Dodge, the mining company that sustained Bisbee's economy, ceased operations. Panic struck the hearts of the canyon's households. Families began leaving in droves—sometimes abandoning their houses and furniture. If Bisbee hadn't been the county seat, disaster would have been total.

This collapse happened near the end of the "flower child" movement of the 1960s and 1970s. Word circulated through the underground that Bisbee was a great place to "be." Young adventurers, intellectuals, artists, and a few loafers floated into town on a wave of fading idealism. Some bought furnished homes from $500 to $5,000; others squatted in vacant houses.

When retirees heard about these bargains, a new wave of emigration to Bisbee began, yet some of the first wave didn't want to leave. These "kids" are now in their 40s and 50s, with graying hair, moving inevitably toward senior-citizen status. Fortunately for Bisbee, those who stayed were artists, writers, and intellectuals loaded with talent. Enough creative people stayed to give Bisbee the reputation and flavor of an artist colony. Today's population has stabilized at just over 8,000.

Be aware that the days of bargain homes are long gone. Of course, fixer-uppers can still be found, and satisfactory housing can easily be had for well under national averages. Remember that the really old, historic places can require a lot of remodeling to bring up to acceptable standards. Yet, for many people, renovating and rejuvenating an old house is enjoyable, a chance to allow artistic and creative abilities to run rampant. And, at the price you pay for an old home, you can afford to be creative!

A community college located a few miles east of town offers numerous activities for senior citizens. Several excellent restaurants, with authentic period settings, do good business. Bisbee even has a nine-hole golf course. Regretfully, I didn't see the golf course, and I often wish I had. I just can't imagine where they would find enough level ground, or enough grass, for even one green!

BISBEE WEATHER					
In degrees Fahrenheit					
	Jan.	April	July	Oct.	Rain	Snow
Daily Highs	60	80	96	82	4"	2"
Daily Lows	37	47	71	57		

Medical facilities are impressive for a small town: a forty-nine-bed hospital with eight full-time doctors and an ambulance service. Other medical professionals include five dentists, two optometrists, a chiropractor, and an osteopath. The town has a daily newspaper to keep up with local and national happenings.

The climate is excellent, since Bisbee is at a high enough altitude to keep summers pleasant and humidity low enough to make the winters brisk but not bitter. During our January visit the thermometer dropped into the 40s one night, yet we walked around town in light sweaters, feeling perfectly comfortable. Many summer residents come here from Phoenix and Tucson, fleeing the baking, 100-plus degree July-August season. One reason for the cooler summer temperatures is that the steep canyon walls cast early shadows across the town to block the afternoon heat of the desert sun. A sign painted prominently on one of the downtown business buildings proclaims that Bisbee has the best climate in the world.

Ajo   About 100 miles west of Tucson and 100 miles south of Phoenix is Ajo, another Phelps-Dodge mining town. Once a prosperous community of skilled miners and workers employed in the huge open-pit copper mine, the town boasted a population of more than 10,000 people. Its history dates to 1854 with the discovery of copper ore, but Ajo didn't really boom until new recovery methods were adopted after the turn of the century.

Suddenly, in 1984, the bubble burst—just as it did earlier in Bisbee. The mining company announced the closing of its mines and smelter operations. Caught without regular paychecks, the townspeople wasted no time in packing their belongings and leaving for greener pastures. The bustling town dwindled down to 2,800 residents, a skeleton of its former self.

Since most houses in town belonged to the mining company, used as employee housing, there wasn't a mass abandonment of dwellings as happened in Bisbee. But the company homes went on the real estate market as low as $13,000 for a two-bedroom home.

Privately owned properties also went for giveaway prices. A real estate broker said, "At one time we had 600 houses for sale. However, now all company-owned homes have been sold."

Even though distress sales have subsided and there aren't as many homes for sale today, Ajo's real estate market never fully recovered. Since retirees purchased most of these homes, the town has embarked upon a new career as a retirement center. Today, the population is reaching 8,000, about half retirees. "The nice thing about Ajo," said a retired couple, "is that we have a mixture of young and old. We have about 600 children in our school, and many young adults to balance out the social scene."

An oasis in the vast Sonora desert, Ajo sits near the edge of the 300,000-acre Organ Pipe National Monument. The town centers around a pleasant garden plaza with huge palm trees that were planted in 1917 when the copper company rebuilt the town. (Originally, Ajo was located elsewhere, but when copper was discovered underneath the town, the mining company promptly moved everything.)

Residents keep in touch with the world via cable TV (with about ten channels), a weekly newspaper, and daily delivery of the Phoenix and Tucson papers. An interesting transportation development is La Tortuga Transit, a rural-transportation bus project that connects the town with Tucson and points in between. A community health center is open daily from 8:00 A.M. to 5:00 P.M., with a doctor on call around the clock. Helicopter service is available for emergency hospitalization in either Phoenix or Tucson.

The weather is typical of the Arizona desert. The local chamber of commerce describes Ajo as "the place where summer spends the winter" or "the town where warm winters and friendly smiles await you." The chamber of commerce also claims that Ajo is noted for having the best climate in the country, with warm winters and continuous sunshine that other parts of Arizona cannot equal. Notice that the emphasis is on the *winter* climate. Since I've never been there

AJO WEATHER						
In degrees Fahrenheit						
	Jan.	April	July	Oct.	Rain	Snow
Daily Highs	66	82	100	86	6"	2"
Daily Lows	40	50	74	56		

in the summer, I can only go by statistics, but these tell us that it gets hot there.

Tucson   Sitting in a high-desert valley surrounded by mountains, Tucson's elevation of 2,375 feet guarantees an agreeable year-round climate. Its dry air and rich desert vegetation qualify it as one of the nation's finest winter resorts. Its 420,000 inhabitants make Tucson a moderately large city, and it is still growing. The fastest-increasing age group here is the over-sixty crowd, which used to account for 20 percent of the population but is now pushing 30 percent. Since it's the over-sixty group who are most likely to vote, it's no surprise that senior citizens get fair treatment in this city. The well-appointed Tucson Senior Citizens' Center clearly shows the attention that city politicians show retired people.

The University of Arizona, located in Tucson, greatly enriches the community's educational, cultural, and recreational life. Classes, lectures, plays, and concerts are an ongoing boon to retirees. The state's only opera company is based in Tucson, and a light opera company stages Broadway musicals.

Another favorable aspect of Tucson retirement is below-average housing prices. Buyers have a wide selection of neighborhoods ranging from inexpensive to out of touch with reality. The warm and pleasant winters don't demand much in the way of heating costs, but this will be offset by air-conditioning in the summer.

Tucson is also a popular place for mobile-home living. The newspaper's classified section usually has listings from mobile-home parks advertising spaces for rent, something rare in many metropolitan areas. A space in one of Tucson's adult mobile-home parks can often be found for less than $200 a month. The nicer ones charge more, with $250 considered a fairly high rent. Compare this with $350 to $400 in some cities and you'll understand what a bargain mobile-home living is in Tucson.

With so many mobile home parks to choose from, you would be well advised to do some shopping. Some parks are primarily for working people, and their interests and social lives are intertwined with friends who live somewhere else. Other parks have mostly retired folks, where you'll find plenty of activities and neighborly retirees. Visiting a park residents' meeting or attending one of the bingo sessions can tell you worlds about who your new neighbors might be.

TUCSON–GREEN VALLEY WEATHER					
In degrees Fahrenheit					
	Jan.	April	July	Oct.	Rain	Snow
Daily Highs	65	81	98	82	12"	2"
Daily Lows	38	50	71	56		

TUCSON AREA COST OF LIVING					
Percentage of	Overall	Housing	Medical	Groceries	Utilities
National Average	102	92	103	110	133

Tucson is also known for its organized retirement and adults-only complexes. With beautifully designed homes, shopping and medical facilities, and extensive sports centers, these complexes are small cities in themselves. One adult community, Saddle Brooke, calls itself the "youngest adult community" because it sets its lower age limit at forty-five instead of the usual fifty-five. Housing prices in these adult communities range from $100,000 to $280,000. These complexes typically feature eighteen-hole golf courses, shuffleboard, bocci and tennis courts, cardrooms, jogging tracks, exercise rooms, and, of course, the ubiquitous swimming pools.

Smaller, apartment-type retirement quarters are available in and around Tucson. They range from places where renters must be "active" to those offering "senior care" concepts, a euphemism for "nursing home." You'll also find the growing concept of life-care centers, in which apartments are provided for those who are still active, then rooms with housekeeping care, and eventually nursing care for those who need it.

The Armory Park Senior Citizens Recreation Center (in downtown Tucson) is a model of its kind. Senior citizens take an energetic part in running the center and have no trouble getting all the volunteer help they need. At any one time several hundred volunteers are on call as they try to use everyone's special skills. For example: Retired accountants and tax practitioners give free income-tax assistance. Others teach handicrafts such as jewelry making, crocheting, and painting. A senior citizens' housing authority high-rise is across the street from the center and another is planned, making it convenient for everyone to participate.

Green Valley　Located 25 miles south of Tucson on Interstate 19 and 40 miles north of Mexico, Green Valley is an unincorporated adult retirement community. It sits at an altitude of 2,900 feet at the foot of the Santa Rita Mountains (an Apache hangout in the olden days). Green River has more than 18,000 residents, a high percentage of them retired, living in an area 8 miles long and 2 miles wide divided by the interstate.

Complete facilities include a huge shopping center, which has a bowling alley. Three eighteen-hole public courses and two private courses, plus a couple of private nine-hole courses, satisfy that urge for hunting lost golf balls some retirees cannot shake. The rec center for Green Valley is quite comprehensive, with facilities for arts and crafts, sewing, lapidary, and photography. A swimming pool, Jacuzzi, sauna, and exercise room complete the recreational picture.

Green Valley has two highly rated nursing homes and a twenty-four-hour emergency clinic as well as two private clinics and a sixty-bed health care center. Tucson hospitals are 20 miles away. There is also a volunteer organization called Friends In Deed (F.I.D.), which assists seniors in sharing their lifetime experiences and skills with one another.

Central Arizona: Between Phoenix and Flagstaff

In between the urban centers of Phoenix and (much smaller) Flagstaff, you'll find small towns and high-altitude resorts and recreation areas where winter skiing, summer fishing, and year-round access to the outdoors are available. This forested, mountainous region is a classic Arizona retirement area, and it's home to the majority of the state's residents. Yet once you get off the main highways, you'll be as struck by the lovely, undeveloped landscape as we were.

CENTRAL ARIZONA

Flagstaff
Sedona
Prescott
Payson
Wickenburg
Sun City/
Phoenix

Phoenix and Vicinity   Located in the appropriately named Valley of the Sun, Phoenix is Arizona's largest city and also the state's capital. The city sprawls over miles of desert landscape, encompassing a wide variety of neighborhoods catering to all budgets and lifestyles. The metropolitan area is even larger than statistics would suggest, because more than 20 other cities begin where Phoenix ends. The sum is a bewildering number of possible retirement choices.

Retirees who relocate in the Valley of the Sun usually do so because of the more than 300 days of sunshine they can count on each year. Rarely will they be rained out at one of the area's more than 130 golf courses. All types of outdoor recreation are available year-round in the Phoenix area. You'll find tennis courts in almost every neighborhood, miles of hiking trails, and access to some of the country's best sporting events. Although this part of Arizona is famous for hot summers, you can always get outdoors to play tennis or golf in the morning or evening and stay indoors, in air-conditioned comfort, during the afternoon.

Sun City   We have investigated large, commercially developed retirement complexes all over the country, but the biggest we've seen is Sun City, near Phoenix. This one goes on and on, with more than 50,000 residents, the vast majority retired!

Most prospective buyers drove expensive automobiles and looked quite affluent. Many were from parts of the country where a $100,000 home would be a steal. According to a salesman, many buyers come from Florida, having given up on retirement that includes hordes of insects and rainy days. However, we didn't know whether to accept his word, because almost everywhere in the country we went, salespeople kept telling us that a big percentage of their clients came from Florida. On the other hand, in Florida, salespeople claimed their buyers were coming from Arizona!

After just one tour through the model homes, one feels tempted to buy immediately. The architecture is bold and imaginative (to match the payments), the furniture is top quality and luxurious. It's terribly easy to stand in the middle of one of these well-lighted and superbly furnished units and imagine how happy you might feel living there.

PHOENIX–SUN CITY WEATHER					
In degrees Fahrenheit					
	Jan.	April	July	Oct.	Rain	Snow
Daily Highs	65	83	105	88	7"	—
Daily Lows	39	53	80	59		

PHOENIX AREA COST OF LIVING					
	Overall	Housing	Medical	Groceries	Utilities
Percentage of National Average	103	101	114	104	103

Although we have reservations about single-generation living, the sales staff presented arguments in favor of it. One of the advantages of buying into a planned community rather than an ordinary neighborhood, they pointed out, is that you know that everyone in the development is about your age and you have a good chance to meet people who need to make friends as badly as you do.

Here you are assured that you won't be bothered by children or teenagers; the community insists upon restrictions against them. You must be over fifty, with no dependent children, to buy into the development. To further ensure against children, the residents continually vote against property taxes for schools. The result is no children and no schools—only adults. We were told that this has cut teenage vandalism and crime to almost nothing.

The major facilities at Sun City and Sun City West are eleven golf courses (four of them eighteen-hole layouts), a forty-acre recreation center, the 7,169-seat Sundome Center, a library, seven medical complexes, restaurants, banks, and seven other local recreation centers.

Wickenburg   About an hour's drive northwest from Phoenix, the town of Wickenburg is attracting retirees who don't want to accept the neatly arranged, orderly, and secure life of Sun City or the bustle of traffic-bound Phoenix. In small-town Wickenburg, they savor the tang of the Old West. The town has been famous for years for its guest ranches (they used to call 'em dude ranches), which go way beyond being simply ranches. They come complete with amenities such as swimming pools, tennis courts, and sometimes a golf course. Although guest ranches are still popular with tourists, the retirement emphasis is on small-acreage places where you can keep and ride your own horses.

Wickenburg has a population of 6,000 and is the shopping center for 20,000 in the area. Health care is adequate, with a thirty-four-bed hospital and many doctors in private practice. Fifty minutes of driving takes you to excellent Sun City hospitals, which specialize in and cater to problems of the elderly.

Land here is abundant and inexpensive, so lots are typically sold by the acre. You may keep horses in your yard if you care to; the local horse population is considerable. You can saddle up and go for a ride through open desert and brush country in almost any direction you care to ride. Since almost all of the surrounding land is owned by the federal Bureau of Land Management (BLM) nobody can interfere with your rides. You don't know how to ride horseback? No problem, local saddle clubs with friendly members will help you get started. The clubs organize numerous social activities centered around horseback riding, from afternoon rides for beginners to the grueling Desert Caballeros Ride for seasoned horsemen, who come from all over the country to participate.

This area is rich in minerals and was the site of a considerable gold rush back in the late 1800s. Several mines encircled the town, and millions of dollars worth of the glittering mineral were taken from the ground. Although most of the richest locations have been worked out over the years, enough remains to keep the local people busy prospecting and panning for gold that the old-timers may have missed. Not only gold: Other valuable minerals such as silver, copper, turquoise, mercury, nickel, and tungsten crop up within a 25-mile radius of Wickenburg. The town celebrates its Wild West past every February with Gold Rush Days, a weekend of rodeos, gold panning, and dressing up in period costumes.

Wickenburg has several mobile-home parks, with many units used only part of the year, their owners choosing to live elsewhere during the hot summer months. At one time it was possible to buy

WICKENBURG WEATHER						
	In degrees Fahrenheit					
	Jan.	April	July	Oct.	Rain	Snow
Daily Highs	63	79	103	82	11"	2"
Daily Lows	30	48	70	52		

a lot and install a mobile home, but nowadays this is frowned upon by the city council.

It does get hot in the summertime, with July and August posting highs of 100 degrees and above. But like most Arizona desert country, low humidity takes much of the sting from the high temperatures. Winter nights can be cold, with frost common, but daytime temperatures are quite pleasant, with shirt-sleeve weather being the noonday norm, and January highs averaging 63 degrees at midday.

Sedona Getting to Sedona from Flagstaff requires a slow, 27-mile drive down the Oak Creek Canyon road, one of the more scenic roads in North America. The pavement winds and twists through thick pine forests and gnarled oaks, with distant glimpses of deep gorges and arroyos embellished with enormous natural stone sculptures. Then, without warning, a broad canyon emerges, dramatically carved from colossal red sandstone walls. Fantastic shapes of spires, chimneys, and buttes never fail to bring sighs of amazement.

When you reach Sedona, the canyon broadens and drops into a wide amphitheater overshadowed by enormous red, pink, and orange rock formations. The rich greens of Arizona cypress, junipers, and Pion pines contrast dramatically with the red background framed by the deep blue Arizona sky—a sight not easily forgotten.

Even though this view of Sedona contained some of the most exciting scenery we had ever seen, there was something curiously familiar about it all. It was as if we had been there before!

Suddenly it hit us! We've seen this exact scenery in innumerable Western movies. Countless bands of Indians attacked wagon trains as they lumbered past the red rock formations. Stagecoaches surrendered so many strongboxes full of treasure that we half expected to see a posse arrive at any moment. We could almost smell the buttered popcorn from the concession stand.

Hollywood discovered Sedona and Oak Creek Canyon in the 1920s, beginning a relationship continuing to this day. With all this astounding scenery, it is quite understandable. Actually, it was Zane Grey who discovered Sedona artistically; he fell in love with the place, which inspired his popular novel *Call of the Canyon*. When Hollywood was ready to film it, Grey insisted that it be shot on location. Since that time hundreds of films and television commercials have used the dramatic rock formations as a backdrop. A local group called the Sedona Film Commission is engaged in promoting the area for more films.

Hollywood artists and technicians came so often that many decided to relocate; some still call Sedona home. This "Red Rock Country" has long attracted artists of all dimensions, who draw inspiration from the country's fantastic vistas.

The number of retirees who select Sedona as their home base is truly impressive. The head of the senior citizens' center estimates that around *40 percent* of the population are retired. "This makes for an interesting mix of retired folks, artists, New Age devotees, and businesspeople," he said.

Until recently the town was unincorporated, divided by county lines and governed by differing county ordinances. When Sedona officially became a separate town, a new energy of politics enlivened the community, with vigorous exchanges of opinion and political alignments. "We all have at least one thing in common," said the senior citizens' president. "We are all lovers of the outdoors." Living in Sedona, you couldn't be otherwise.

The town has around 10,000 residents, although the business district and facilities make the town seem much larger because of an additional 2,000 people in nearby communities. Tourism is big, and tourist money supports an unusually wide range of restaurants (thirty-five of 'em), plus two nine-hole and two eighteen-hole golf courses, as well as five tennis-club resorts. These are facilities that wouldn't be there were it not for tourist dollars.

Sedona surely is a place to cultivate latent talents or to appreciate the artistic talents of others. Sedona has between 200 and 300 resident artists, which accounts for the thirty-five art galleries and an exceptionally active community art center. Two theater groups present year-round performances, and there are several ad hoc performances by a senior citizens' center group. Another theater group presents outdoor performances on summer evenings.

A local arts and cultural commission tries to focus the efforts of all talented people in the community into interesting, year-round projects. The theater and music wing of the Artists and Craftsmen Guild presents programs ranging from jazz to the classics, and the arts center holds monthly art exhibitions to augment the many art galleries in town. Other highlights of the seasons are the two-day Hopi Artists Gathering, a sculpture show, the Native American Arts and Crafts Fair, and the Sedona

SEDONA WEATHER						
		In degrees Fahrenheit				
	Jan.	April	July	Oct.	Rain	Snow
Daily Highs	55	72	95	78	17"	9"
Daily Lows	30	42	65	49		

SEDONA COST OF LIVING					
	Overall	Housing	Medical	Groceries	Utilities
Percentage of National Average	105	116	108	113	98

Chamber Music Festival. In addition, internationally renowned musicians gather each fall to present Jazz on the Rocks, a day of musical celebration.

Camping, fishing, and hiking are exceptionally popular and accessible, because 77 percent of the countryside is government forest service land—open to everyone—and the wilderness begins at the edge of town.

A new medical facility was recently completed and there are other facilities nearby in Cottonwood and Flagstaff, 27 miles to the north (on the slow winding road). The area also has paramedics, ambulances, an outpatient health care center, and a medical evacuation helicopter. Also, an adequate number of doctors, dentists, and optometrists take care of residents.

Sedona has grown rapidly in recent years, with retirees and artists forming the bulk of new residents. As a result, property prices have kept pace with growth. This is not a place to look for bargain-basement real estate; views like this do not come dirt cheap. Some are expensive showplaces, constructed to take full advantage of the natural beauty of the panorama, but you'll also find less costly homes that do quite the same. Manufactured homes start at $45,000 and sell for up to $130,000; conventional homes on quarter-acre lots start at $125,000. One prestigious development asks $315,000 for its entry-level homes and $900,000 for its top-of-the-line places, with building lots starting at $160,000.

Expect to pay from $800 to $1,200 per month rent for a house and $500 for an apartment. In nearby Cottonwood, prices are considerably lower, with apartments going for $395 for a furnished two-bedroom with a pool.

Since growth has been recent, most construction is new and well maintained. People here understand the beauty and practicality of natural landscaping to blend their homes into Sedona's beauty (desert landscaping eliminates lawn mowing.)

The altitude at Sedona is 4,300 feet—that's 3,200 feet higher than Phoenix, only an hour and a half away by car, and 2,700 feet lower than Flagstaff, which is less than an hour away. This altitude means warmer winters than Flagstaff and cooler summers than Phoenix. (Some guidebooks list Sedona as being at a 4,400-foot altitude. Since the town slopes downward, it all depends upon where you measure.)

Prescott   Sedona's rival in Arizona mountain retirement is Prescott, a few miles to the southwest. Its setting is as spectacular as Sedona's but with a different flavor. Instead of desert scrub, cactus, and dramatic red rock formations, Prescott is surrounded by jagged peaks, sometimes snow-covered, and a forest of ponderosa pines (reputedly the largest in the world) overlooks the city. Prescott's movie-set panorama not only equals Sedona's, but its residents claim the weather is better as well; the four seasons are more sharply delineated. The elevation here is about 1,000 feet higher, which means cooler summers, with daily highs rarely climbing out of the 80s and dropping to the 60s every evening. On the other hand, winters are colder, with several snowfalls every year.

One of our visits to Prescott was in January, two days after a 3-inch snowfall. The sky was brilliant, most of the snow gone after two 60-degree afternoons, although it still looked pretty covering the ground among the ponderosa pines. We found housing prices somewhat lower than Sedona, with an abundance of rentals for those who want to try the area for a few months before making any decisions. This is an older town—founded back in the 1860s—and it has neighborhoods of Victorians and many areas of modest, smaller homes. Since the surrounding area is uneven, most homes are custom built, with few tract models constructed. For exceptional bargains in housing, nearby Chino Valley is the place to look.

Prescott likes to think of itself as a small town, but it's actually a good-sized place, with a local population of 35,000. In addition, it is the shopping center for 70,000 people. As such, it's able to provide a multitude of services for its citizens, including a museum, a concert hall, and a 110,000-volume library that would be the envy

PRESCOTT AREA WEATHER					
In degrees Fahrenheit					
	Jan.	April	July	Oct.	Rain	Snow
Daily Highs	51	68	90	74	13"	16"
Daily Lows	24	36	61	42		

PRESCOTT AREA COST OF LIVING					
	Overall	Housing	Medical	Groceries	Utilities
Percentage of National Average	100	116	108	113	98

of many larger cities. Yavapai College, a two-year institution, offers a non-credit "retirement college" with 900 students over the age of 62. There are also a liberal arts college and an aeronautical university in the area. Health care is above average here, with nearly one hundred physicians and surgeons and a 129-bed hospital. Several golf courses are part of the recreational scheme, along with hiking, camping, fishing, and horse trails. Should you be unable to control the urge, 7,600-foot Granite Mountain offers exciting rock-climbing opportunities.

Payson A third candidate for Arizona mountain retirement is Payson, located to the east of Sedona and Prescott. Sitting at about 5,200 feet, the same altitude as Prescott, Payson shares the same four-season climate. It also is bordered by the Tonto National Forest with its ponderosa–pine wonderland. Summers are pleasant, as you might expect in a high altitude; winters are mild enough for hiking, fishing, or horseback riding, with occasional snows for cross-country ski treks. The town of Payson is more heavily wooded than its competitors to the west.

Retirees here have plenty of kids their own age to play with. Almost 60 percent of the population is over 55 years of age. The chamber of commerce utilizes retirees, with twenty-nine volunteers

PAYSON WEATHER					
In degrees Fahrenheit					
	Jan.	April	July	Oct.	Rain	Snow
Daily Highs	59	78	95	80	13"	30"
Daily Lows	26	40	66	45		

working in the chamber office. "We couldn't operate without 'em," said the local chamber manager. Because of the older population here, the local hospital is in the process of enlarging and becoming a cancer treatment center for northern Arizona.

This is the place for outdoor sports, with the spectacular Mogollon Rim just a few miles to the north, where hunting, fishing, hiking, and sightseeing are legend. For indoor sports, a nearby gambling casino operated by the local Indian tribe brings revenues to the community as well as affording entertainment at the casino's 476 slot machines. A bus service connects the area with Phoenix, some 94 miles to the south.

Flagstaff   North of Sedona, and close enough to be a strong cultural influence, is the city of Flagstaff. At 7,000 feet in altitude, it receives full mountain winters averaging 97 inches of snow annually. Because of the high altitude and sunny days, the melt-off is said to be rapid. Summer highs seldom top 80 degrees, while nearby Phoenix cooks at over 100 degrees. Summer evenings are always cool, with low humidity taking the bite out of a brisk winter. Housing costs are higher than normal, but some terrific buys can be found out in the country, nestled in pine forests.

Flagstaff is a beautiful, modern city with lots of tall pines. The San Francisco Peaks here rise 12,670 feet and provide a breathtaking backdrop to the city. For the outdoor sportsman, fishing and hunting opportunities are without equal. A mid-size university and a symphony orchestra contribute to a cultural ambience under leadership of the Flagstaff Arts Council and its comprehensive performing–arts program.

FLAGSTAFF WEATHER						
In degrees Fahrenheit						
	Jan.	April	July	Oct.	Rain	Snow
Daily Highs	42	57	82	64	21"	97"
Daily Lows	15	26	50	30		

FLAGSTAFF AREA COST OF LIVING					
Percentage of National Average	Overall	Housing	Medical	Groceries	Utilities
	112	128	113	112	109

Western Arizona: Colorado River Retirement

After the wild Colorado River exits from the Grand Canyon, it heads south toward Mexico and the Sea of Cortez. Along the way, the Colorado is captured by a series of dams that provide peaceful lakes, contrasting nicely with the desert hills and shaded canyons that enclose the river.

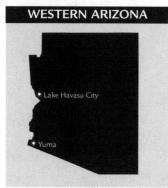

Along this stretch of waterway—from the Arizona town of Parker on the south to the Nevada town of Laughlin on the north—growing numbers of retirees and snowbirds settle in every winter. The numbers increase every year, with more and more buying homes and staying year-round. Places such as Lake Havasu have grown from small clusters of trailers and fishing shacks, with catfish and mallards as the only major attractions, into virtual cities with all the facilities needed for comfortable retirement.

Lake Havasu City   It all started when Robert P. McCulloch was flying over the area in search of a place to test his motors and spotted an abandoned Army Air Corps landing strip, which is now the airport of Lake Havasu City. Back in 1963, McCulloch purchased 16,630 acres of virgin territory on the Arizona side of the lake and began designing a city. At first the idea of relocating in an isolated desert town seemed outlandish, but gradually the notion took hold and folks began buying lots and building winter homes.

From these unpretentious beginnings Lake Havasu City has boomed to a city of more than 20,000 full-time residents. Houses and condos, trailers and mobile homes, and businesses and services of all descriptions appeared as if by magic. An estimated 6,000 to 8,000 winter residents swell the population and add to the general prosperity.

Despite all this growth, housing costs are generally lower than in other metropolitan areas of Arizona and markedly lower than comparable housing in southern California. According to the Lake Havasu Board of Realtors, single-family detached homes range in price from $45,000 to $400,000 (for golf-course sites), with an av-

LAKE HAVASU CITY WEATHER						
In degrees Fahrenheit						
	Jan.	April	July	Oct.	Rain	Snow
Daily Highs	68	85	104	90	3"	—
Daily Lows	42	55	79	62		

LAKE HAVASU CITY AREA COST OF LIVING					
Percentage of	Overall	Housing	Medical	Groceries	Utilities
National Average	104	89	110	112	111

erage selling price of $65,000. Townhouses and condominiums are available from $35,000. Apartments and home rentals are plentiful and available from $275 to $700 per month. Residential lots average around $9,000.

Because of the high number of retirees, the Lake Havasu area enjoys a more complete health–care system than ordinarily found in communities of similar size. A 99-bed acute-care hospital staffed with 35 physicians and a 120-bed nursing center serve the community. The hospital is in the process of expanding by 50 percent.

Mobile-home and RV parks dot the riverbanks, each with its own boat–loading ramp and nearby bait shop. By the way, boating and fishing aren't the only sports enjoyed in Lake Havasu. Several golf courses and at least one bowling alley will keep you active. A bustling senior center provides a dial-a-ride service in addition to the customary bridge games, arts, and nutrition facilities. A community college offers fee discounts to senior citizens, and some activities are coordinated with Arizona State University, including drama performances, concerts, and lectures.

Yuma   Yuma, the last of the Colorado River towns, anchors Arizona's southwest corner, where the mighty Colorado crosses into Mexico on its way to the Sea of Cortes. At this point, the river loses some of its majesty; much of its flow has been siphoned off along the way to irrigate truck farms, supply drinking water to dozens of communities, and make ice cubes for gambling casinos. A sleepy little desert town just a few years ago, Yuma's development can be described as explosive. Since 1980, its population increased by 35 percent to today's 60,000.

YUMA WEATHER					
In degrees Fahrenheit					
	Jan.	April	July	Oct.	Rain	Snow
Daily Highs	69	85	107	91	3"	—
Daily Lows	43	56	80	62		

YUMA AREA COST OF LIVING					
Percentage of	Overall	Housing	Medical	Groceries	Utilities
National Average	104	99	108	102	147

Only the center part, or "old town," shows evidence of its age and historic past. Everything else looks brand new. Originally described as "the great crossing place of a very wide and treacherous river," this was a trading center for early-day adventurers and settlers.

Because of its low desert altitude (only 138 feet), summers here are exceptionally hot. Throughout the year, residents expect just a little more than 3 inches of rain. Make no mistake, this is desert!

Yuma's winter population triples, as snowbirds from all over the country descend upon the area, bringing motor homes, trailers, and campers. But like the Rio Grande Valley area, Yuma convinces many snowbirds to nest for year-round retirement.

Many retirees take advantage of nearby Mexico for inexpensive prescription drugs, dental care, and experimental medications not yet approved in the United States (although most have been in Europe). A Marine Corps base is located in the city limits, sharing its runways with private and commercial aircraft. Residents are treated to an interesting display of Marine fighter jets and airliners alternating on take-offs. This base provides PX, commissary, and medical care for military retirees.

For gaming activity, Yuma Greyhound Park presents live dog racing and pari-mutuel betting on horses as well as greyhounds. Then there's the Cocopah Gaming Center, a tribal casino south of Yuma on Highway 95. For the academically inclined, a state college, a state university, and two private colleges fill educational needs.

Nevada

Because a high mountain range, the Sierra Nevada, extends along the California-Nevada border cutting off rain-bearing winds from the Pacific Ocean, Nevada is the driest of the Southwestern states. Extensive deserts cover most of the land, with most residents choosing to live in or near one of Nevada's major towns. In fact, more than half live in the vicinity of either Las Vegas or Reno. Most

rainfall occurs in the spring, at which time barren deserts become a riot of color with the blossoms of cactus, sagebrush, and wild iris.

Of all the Western states, Nevada most represents the Old West to me. Sparsely settled, yet growing with new settlers arriving daily, Nevada feels like a frontier, a place of new beginnings. Something about Nevada's wide-open spaces stimulates a spirit of adventure and go-for-broke attitudes. It's a place where string ties, boot-top jeans, and snakeskin boots feel like natural apparel, a place where you might even be tempted to wear a Stetson hat, confident you won't look downright foolish.

Perhaps a hangover from an era of frontier gambling and gold rushes, a definite atmosphere of excitement hovers over Nevada. Gambling casinos are everywhere, and slot machines are strategically located in gasoline stations, drugstores, and supermarkets. Sometimes you'll even find them in rest rooms—the gambling syndicates don't want to miss a bet. This is a state where lucky gamblers made a stake and lucky miners made fortunes. This is evident today: Prospecting for precious metals is a big hobby in Nevada. There's always that chance that the next rock you crack open with a hammer will expose a gleaming streak of gold. (I've broke open many a rock myself in Nevada.)

Nevada is the country's fastest-growing state, by the way, with a 5.4 percent increase in population every year. And there's plenty of room to grow, since 87 percent of the land is public property, owned by the United States Government. Newcomers aren't strangers here, because their neighbors come from all over North America, just as you do. In Nevada casinos, you'll notice that blackjack dealers, bartenders, and security guards traditionally wear name tags that tell you where they came from, sometimes without names, just their hometowns.

NEVADA TAX PROFILE

Sales tax: 6.5% to 7%, food and drugs exempt
State income tax: no
Property taxes: approximately about 1% of appraised value
Intangibles tax: no
Social security taxed: no
Pensions taxed: no
Gasoline tax: 23.5¢ per gallon

By the way, Nevada casinos set the odds so they can rake off 10 to 20 percent for overhead and profit. But state lotteries stiff you for 40 to 60 percent—sometimes even more. So, you really can't figure you're gambling when you buy state lottery tickets; you're being robbed.

But should you know that you, or your spouse, has a tendency to go overboard on gambling and succumb to the irresistible fever of chance, then forget Nevada. Go around it, fly over it, or go in the opposite direction. The round-the-clock excitement is just too much for some folks. They end up throwing their household money on the tables in increasing amounts in a desperate attempt to recoup their losses. The sad thing is that if they do hit a lucky streak and win a bundle the fever won't let them quit. They'll play until they are broke again.

On the other hand, many retirees handle gambling quite well, taking advantage of all the freebies and bargains the clubs offer to lure customers inside. Some never put even a nickel in the machines but have a great time anyway. Buffet tables laden with salads, entrees, and desserts offer unlimited visits for three or four dollars. Prime rib dinners can be as low as $5.50. Lounge entertainment with music, dancers, and comedians is free, although you're encouraged to buy a drink. Some casinos even present free circus acts, complete with animals, high-wire performers, and clowns.

Las Vegas   Sadly known as "Lost Wages" by chumps who've thrown the rent money across the gambling tables, Las Vegas is gaining a national reputation as much more than a gambling center. Today it is a virtual boomtown. About 60,000 new residents arrive yearly—a large percentage of them retirees—making this one of the fastest-growing cities in the country. To accommodate newcomers about 12,000 houses sprout up annually.

Because of this vigorous growth, retirees easily find part-time jobs at more than just minimum-wage. Casinos, restaurants, and other tourist businesses need part-time help, but the incoming industries and businesses siphon new residents from the labor pool, offering them full-time jobs. The area consistently leads the nation in employment growth.

As in Reno, casinos give special consideration to hiring senior citizens. The percentage of older employees is impressive. Well, except for the cocktail waitresses, that is, who tend to be young and buxom. This is certainly age discrimination, but then, you wouldn't care to run around scantily dressed, delivering drinks to a bunch of gamblers anyway, would you? (Personally, I look terrible in one of those frilly tutus with sequins.)

As you might suspect, housing activity has kept up with this influx of newcomers; in fact, it has more than kept up. From its inception, Las Vegas has tended to over-build; optimistic developers keep supply ahead of demand, keeping housing costs under control. Apartments are plentiful, with high vacancy rates. In short, Las Vegas housing isn't inexpensive, but neither is it prohibitive.

Many people who normally might choose Phoenix for retirement are trying Las Vegas instead. When asked why, they gave various reasons: No state income tax and proximity to southern California, however, headed the list. (Las Vegas is a five and one-half hour drive from Los Angeles, compared to Phoenix's seven and one-half hours. Before long, a privately financed super-train will link Las Vegas and southern California, moving millions of visitors at a fan-

LAS VEGAS WEATHER						
In degrees Fahrenheit						
	Jan.	April	July	Oct.	Rain	Snow
Daily Highs	56	77	104	82	4"	1"
Daily Lows	33	50	76	54		

LAS VEGAS AREA COST OF LIVING					
Percentage of	Overall	Housing	Medical	Groceries	Utilities
National Average	107	97	125	115	87

tastic 250 miles per hour!) Other taxes in the state are low, because about 50 percent of all state tax revenues come from the resort, tourism, and casino industry. Because of this easy income, Nevada doesn't need taxes on corporate or personal income and its property taxes are among the lowest in the West.

All those questioned about their choice of Las Vegas as a retirement destination included weather in one form or another. Make no mistake, summers in Las Vegas are hot, yet those who retire here maintain that they love it that way.

Because of low humidity and absence of freezing weather, mobile homes are quite practical. Inexpensive evaporative coolers do a fine job during the warm months. Mobile-home parks present a wide choice of options, from inexpensive to super-luxurious. During the winter, RV parks fill with fugitives from cold weather, who, as expected, depart for cooler climes come the summer. But, unlike in some desert cities, retirees in Las Vegas form a steady year-round population as opposed to the floating second-home group found around Lake Havasu.

Las Vegas has several active senior citizens' groups as well as the usual volunteer organizations like R.S.V.P. Local newspapers run regular features covering news and activities of interest to retirees. Because this is a city instead of a town, senior citizens' centers aren't small and intimate as you might expect in a smaller place, but they certainly offer a wide range of activities to keep active folks busy and happy.

Reno   Although Las Vegas and Lake Tahoe try to be as formal and glitzy as possible, places like Reno tend to be more informal and relaxed. Except in some of the newer Reno hotel-casinos, neckties and cocktail dresses are rare; Western wear—cowboy hats, ornate boots, and string ties—are seen about as frequently. This is changing in Reno to some extent, since the Las Vegas–Atlantic City gambling corporations are attempting to duplicate their luck in Reno. New elaborate and classy casinos are sprouting like magic, but I suspect this will have little effect upon the Reno of the non-tourist.

Reno is an old town in a picturesque setting with a backdrop of snow-fringed peaks looming in the distance. This is a town proud of its rowdy gold- and silver-mining past—demonstrated by its deliberately preserved old-West atmosphere. Originally, Reno's major business was supplying the booming mining camps that flourished nearby. About the time the mines played out, a new industry arose in the form of quickie divorces. Reno divorces were once considered the only practical way to go for an uncomplicated marriage dissolution. As other states liberalized their divorce laws, legalized gambling became the leading industry. Ironically, today Reno has become a quickie *marriage* center, with wedding chapels scattered around town like fast-food restaurants, and marriages in Reno outnumber divorces by a ten-to-one ratio.

Although Las Vegas construction imitates southern California modern style—stucco, sprawling ranch houses, and tile roofs—Reno prefers old-fashioned houses built of honest red brick. The older neighborhoods are of solidly built, no-nonsense homes, a settled, mature city. Las Vegas is an Eastern-style glamour girl, adorned with mink and diamond bracelets; Reno is pure Western, a cowboy with a string tie and blue jeans.

Yet Reno also offers twenty-four-hour entertainment and glitter. Folks here are proud of Reno's self-bestowed title of "The Biggest Little City in the World." But there's something hometown about the downtown gaming tables that escapes Lake Tahoe, Las Vegas, and Laughlin. This hometown feeling was deliberately cultivated when gambling was legalized during the Great Depression. Harold Smith, the founder of Harold's Club, decided to go after local money instead of depending upon tourists. He instituted the practice of giving free drinks and double odds on crap tables. He cashed paychecks without charge and tried to make people feel at home. Harold's Club also started the practice of preferential hiring of local people and senior citizens. Retirees work at

RENO WEATHER						
In degrees Fahrenheit						
	Jan.	April	July	Oct.	Rain	Snow
Daily Highs	45	63	91	70	7"	24"
Daily Lows	20	29	48	31		

RENO AREA COST OF LIVING					
Percentage of	Overall	Housing	Medical	Groceries	Utilities
National Average	110	117	123	109	95

everything from dealing blackjack to making change.

As a retirement center, Reno is one of our favorites. Because of the large number of retirees, the level of services for senior citizens is exceptionally high. Retiree clubs and organizations are unusually active. Thirteen apartment complexes specialize in assisted housing for the elderly, handicapped, and disabled. In addition, there are three, large, full-service retirement facilities. Private programs such as Meals on Wheels and Care and Share are active, as are several run by the government. There's a senior citizens' employment service, and a senior citizens' law center provides free assistance with wills, Social Security, leases, and things of that nature.

The cost of living is not cheap, but compared to many urban locations, it is reasonable. With the adjoining city of Sparks, the population is about 180,000, making it a good-size city. The Reno area has all the facilities necessary for good retirement: hospitals, colleges, cultural events, and community services.

Some choose Reno retirement for excitement, but everyone likes its extraordinary climate. The 4,440-foot altitude and very low humidity keep the weather pleasant year-round despite its apparent low temperatures. For those who cannot stand hot summer weather, Reno is perfect. Expect to enjoy about 300 sunny days a year here. Even though July and August temperatures usually approach 90 degrees by mid-afternoon, you will sleep under an electric blanket every night; the thermometer always drops into the 40s. Even in the middle of winter the high temperatures are about the same as summer lows!

A light jacket or sweater feels warm in this dry climate, even when the temperature is below freezing. I am always surprised to walk out of a casino in my shirtsleeves, feeling perfectly comfortable, and then notice a thermometer announcing that it is 38 degrees! Air-conditioning is unknown in residential properties, and low electricity rates keep winter heating bills within a reasonable range.

Lake Tahoe   A short drive from Reno up a wide, four-lane highway is a beautiful, bustling area in a forested lake setting that many consider a prime retirement place. This is South Lake Tahoe, a sprawling community that straddles the line between Nevada and California. Well known for luxurious hotels and gambling casinos, Lake Tahoe is also celebrated for beauty; it sits next to one of the most gorgeous lakes in the world. Mark Twain had this to say about

Lake Tahoe in his book *Roughing It*:

> Three months of camp life on Lake Tahoe would restore an Egyptian mummy to his pristine vigor and give him an appetite like an alligator. I do not mean the oldest and driest mummies, of course, but the fresher ones. The air up there in the clouds is very pure and fine, bracing and delicious. And why shouldn't it be? It is the same the angels breathe. Lake Tahoe must surely be the fairest picture the whole earth affords.

Snow is an important part of Tahoe's winter. If there isn't at least a 6-foot pack on the ski slopes, skiers feel cheated. From anywhere in the area it is a matter of minutes to a ski lift, a joy to those who enjoy the sport. The snow typically falls in isolated, heavy storms that dump up to 3 feet in one night; then the weather turns sunny for days or weeks until the next snow. From my perspective, the best thing about Lake Tahoe snow is that it takes only a twenty-minute drive to be out of it. You can be skiing at Incline Village in the morning and wandering through Carson City in shirtsleeves that same evening.

Why would folks consider retiring here? "Living here is like being on permanent vacation," says a friend of mine who owns a lakefront cottage near North Shore. Like many residents, he bought his home several years ago, in anticipation of retirement. He rented out his place by the day or week at premium rates to regular visitors—vacationers, skiers, and gamblers—and by the time he was ready to retire, a good portion of his retirement home had been paid off. The deductions and depreciation as a rental also helped ease his tax burden. Long-term rentals, however, are usually available at rates one would expect to pay in most California urban areas. That can be expensive and worth it only if you cannot consider living anywhere else because you love Lake Tahoe so much. Many people living here feel just that way.

New Mexico

With its inventory of scenic deserts, lush forests, and high mountain ranges, New Mexico clearly lives up to its nickname: Land of Enchantment. The state has a dry to partly dry climate not particularly different from other arid Southwestern regions. A combination of low humidity, high altitude, and abundant sunshine makes this a pleasant and healthy place to live. Summer days are hot, but nights in New Mexico are always cool. Many localities commonly find that temperatures may register 90 degrees on a sunny day and then fall to 50 degrees in the evening. Although daytime air-conditioning may be popular in some areas, most of the time you'll sleep under blankets at night. Rainfall varies from 8 inches per year in some places to as much as 24 inches in some mountainous areas. Yearly snowfall ranges from almost nothing to as much as 300 inches near Ruidoso.

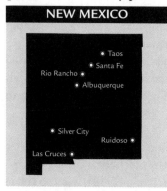

NEW MEXICO

- Taos
- Santa Fe
- Rio Rancho
- Albuquerque
- Silver City
- Ruidoso
- Las Cruces

About a third of New Mexico's residents consider themselves to be Hispanic and are quite proud of their heritage. Early Spanish explorers and colonists were the first white settlers in this area. The founders were farming and building towns and villages in New Mexico a full generation before the first Pilgrim ever set foot on Plymouth Rock. By the way, don't make the mistake of calling New Mexico Hispanics "Mexican Americans" or you'll run the risk of dirty looks and sarcastic replies. After all, some Hispanic families were living here more than three centuries before there even was a Mexico! People here converse in an archaic form of Spanish, the cultured manner of speaking

NEW MEXICO TAX PROFILE

Sales tax: 5% to 6.25%, no exemptions
State income tax: graduated, 1.8% to 8.5% over $41,600; can't deduct federal income tax
Property taxes: about 7%
Intangibles tax: no
Social security taxed: no
Pensions taxed: excludes up to $8,000, depending on income level
Gasoline tax: 16¢ per gallon, plus possible local taxes

that was in vogue back in the sixteenth and seventeenth centuries; some words in their vocabulary wouldn't be understood in Mexico. They've been isolated so long that their customs, cooking, and worldviews are very different from those of Mexico. And, although New Mexico shares a border with Mexico, no highways, railroads, or connections with Mexico exist along the desolate southern frontier other than one minor border crossing at Columbus. Historically, Mexican immigration (legal and illegal) bypassed New Mexico, moving into California, Arizona, or Texas instead.

Las Cruces   Las Cruces, the largest town in southern New Mexico, is forty-five minutes away from El Paso via Interstate 10. Like some other cities along the Rio Grande, Las Cruces is rapidly attracting retirees. Even though the town is small compared to nearby El Paso (62,000 inhabitants), it offers plenty of amenities for its senior citizens. New Mexico State University is located there, complete with a theater and even a symphony orchestra. Community participation in the university's cultural and entertainment events is a definite plus. Shopping is more than adequate, with El Paso nearby for anything not available in Las Cruces. Medical care here is exceptional, with one of the best-equipped hospitals in the state, the 286-bed Memorial Medical Center.

Nestled in the fertile Mesilla Valley, which draws irrigation water from the Rio Grande, the city is in the center of a prosperous farming district, producing cotton, pecans, and chili peppers. Mountains rising to over 9,000 feet surround Las Cruces and block some of the northern winter winds to produce a mild, low-humidity winter. Summers are warm, similar to El Paso's, although the large amount of irrigation raises the summer humidity somewhat. Its mild weather permits fishing year-round in nearby Elephant Butte and Caballo reservoirs. Las Cruces has two public golf courses and a private country club. Eighteen lighted tennis courts make for comfortable play on hot summer evenings.

Las Cruces is an unusually attractive setting with a distinctive, Old West pueblo character. Apparently, city planners try to channel architecture toward the pueblo style of Santa Fe, with soft, earthy tones. Yet Las Cruces has avoided a regimented, stiff adherence to

LAS CRUCES WEATHER					
In degrees Fahrenheit					
	Jan.	April	July	Oct.	Rain	Snow
Daily Highs	59	79	96	76	9"	3"
Daily Lows	27	42	63	44		

LAS CRUCES COST OF LIVING				
Percentage of	Overall	Housing	Medical	Groceries	Utilities
National Average	101	111	96	101	97

this style, permitting pastels and bright colors to break up the muted earth tones. We looked at a display of exceptionally imaginative homes of elegant, Old West style. They were set on landscaped low-maintenance lots that incorporated natural shrubs and cactus. We guessed the price at $250,000 and were surprised to learn the asking price was just over $100,000. A buyer's market prevails.

Albuquerque   High in the desert, sitting on the east bank of the Rio Grande at an altitude of over 5,000 feet, Albuquerque is a fast-growing retirement area. Its combination of high altitude, dry air, and mild temperatures is exactly what many people look for in a place to live. The thermometer rarely hits 100 degrees and almost never sees zero. With afternoon humidity typcially 30 percent, the weather seems even milder than charts might indicate. July's (the hottest month) average highs of 90 degrees always drop into the 60s at night.

A scant 8 inches of rain falls per year, which means lots of brilliant, sunny weather. And the best part is that the winter months of December and January are the sunniest. It's a two-season year, with about 11 inches of snow expected every winter. It doesn't stick around for long, though, because winter days usually hit 50 degrees by noon. Muggy days and long, drizzling spells are just about unknown in Albuquerque. Summers can become quite dry, however, causing the mighty Rio Grande to dwindle to a muddy trickle. Once when Will Rogers was giving a talk in Albuquerque, he cracked, "Why, you folks ought to be out there right now irrigating that river to keep it from blowing away!"

Albuquerque's biggest drawback is that its name is difficult to spell. The problem with spelling started in 1706 when the Spanish Duke of Alburquerque decided that this spot, where the old Camino Real crossed the Rio Grande, would be a great place to have a town named after himself. But when they put up the city limits sign, somebody left an *r* out of his name. And schoolkids have had trouble spelling it ever since. (Shouldn't there be at least one *k* somewhere in Albuquerque?)

The city has taken pains to preserve its historic sector. Preservation was possible partly because the coming of the railroad in 1880 moved the "downtown" away from the original plaza, thus sparing it from development. Today the area, now known as Old Town, offers fine restaurants and shops and maintains the historic

ALBUQUERQUE WEATHER					
In degrees Fahrenheit					
	Jan.	April	July	Oct.	Rain	Snow
Daily Highs	47	71	93	72	8"	11"
Daily Lows	22	39	65	43		

ALBUQUERQUE AREA COST OF LIVING					
Percentage of	Overall	Housing	Medical	Groceries	Utilities
National Average	101	103	100	103	96

flavor of the Old West. Venerable adobe buildings and museums cluster around the Duke of Alburquerque's village.

The downtown section is clean, modern, and prosperous-looking. Everything seems polished and tastefully designed. A pedestrian mall completes the picture of a pleasant city center. The rest of the metropolitan area is also quite pleasant, with many homes designed in an adobe style and lots of huge shade trees in the older areas of town.

The metropolitan hub of New Mexico, Albuquerque is also a high-technology center of the Southwest. As such, it attracts people from all over the country to work and live there. The University of New Mexico (enrollment 25,000) accounts for much of the rich cultural offerings of the city. There's a full calendar of lectures, concerts, drama, and sporting events, as well as numerous classes of interest to senior citizens.

Skiing is great, with more than eleven facilities within striking distance. Sandia Peak (15 miles northeast of Albuquerque) has lifts that rise over 10,000 feet. Hunting, fishing, prospecting, and rock-hunting are all great outdoor pastimes. But all outdoor activities don't require going into the wilderness. Horse-racing fans will find seven racetracks in New Mexico, with the season starting in January at The Downs at Albuquerque.

Rio Rancho   As an example of Albuquerque retirement away from the city congestion, let's look at Rio Rancho, twenty minutes from downtown Albuquerque and forty-five minutes from Santa Fe. It's a comfortable, safe area of mixed new and older homes. Originally started as a mail-order retirement scheme to sell parcels of worthless desert landscape, Rio Rancho targeted New Yorkers, and as a result, many residents come from that state. Some folks were skeptical about the project, but they were surprised when it actually took off, and it hasn't stopped since. Today, about 40,000 people live on ranch land that twenty-five years ago supported less than 200 cows. Rio Rancho is one of the fastest-growing communities in the country. Although many retirees are buying new and older homes here, a recently opened Intel Company facility is bringing high-tech workers from all over the world. It's a great place for retirees, but it's basically a multi-generational community.

With a twenty-seven-hole golf course and a panorama of the Sandia mountains in the distance, Rio Rancho is a blend of Southwest desert and middle-class suburb.

Santa Fe   Fifty-nine miles northeast of Albuquerque, the town of Santa Fe sits like an antique jewel in the picturesque Sangre de Cristo mountains, perched at an altitude of 7,000 feet. A sense of history pervades the streets and byways of this oldest capital city in the United States. Settled in the year 1610, Santa Fe was a bustling town and commercial center ten years before the Pilgrims set foot on Plymouth Rock! Santa Fe has been a capital city for more than 375 years.

Here, you'll find the oldest private house in the United States and the oldest public building in the country, the Palace of the Governors. This building became General Kearney's headquarters in 1846, when his troops captured Santa Fe during the Mexican War. Incidentally, this was the first foreign capital ever captured by U.S. armed forces.

Santa Fe is not only a town steeped in history and culture, and

SANTA FE WEATHER						
	In degrees Fahrenheit					
	Jan.	April	July	Oct.	Rain	Snow
Daily Highs	40	60	78	62	15"	33"
Daily Lows	19	35	57	39		

SANTA FE COST OF LIVING					
Percentage of	Overall	Housing	Medical	Groceries	Utilities
National Average	113	142	103	103	85

its residents work hard at keeping it that way. Strict building codes insist that all new construction be of adobe or adobe-looking material; all exteriors must be in earth tones. This preserves the distinctive Spanish pueblo style for which Santa Fe is famous. Occasionally one sees a home that was built in the days before zoning codes, and the blue or white building sticks out like the proverbial sore thumb. At first the shades of sand, brown, and tan can seem a bit somber, but, after a while, one grows to appreciate the way they complement the setting.

Along with tourism and retirement, artistic endeavors are one of Santa Fe's prime industries. Art impacts the everyday lives of Santa Fe residents, with hundreds of painters, artists, and craftspeople doing their thing and almost 200 galleries exhibiting their treasures. The old plaza in the heart of the city is usually lined with street artisans displaying jewelry, paintings, leather goods, and all kinds of quality artwork. Local Native Americans bring intricate silver and turquoise jewelry to sell in the plaza. A highly regarded opera company performs in a unique outdoor theater. Fortunately, Santa Fe's weather seldom interferes with the performances, since only about 15 inches of rain falls a year. A year-round calendar of events includes concerts by the Orchestra of Santa Fe, the Chorus of Santa Fe, the Desert Chorale, and the Santa Fe Symphony, as well as Native American festivals and celebrations. Numerous theater and drama presentations come from the New Mexico Repertory Theatre, the British American Theatre Institute, the Armory for the Arts, the Santuario de Guadalupe, the Community Theatre, and the Greer Garson Theater. There's even a rodeo every summer. Of course, the thoroughbreds race at famous Santa Fe Downs from May to Labor Day.

"When I get up in the morning, I know there's going to be sun," said a man who retired in Santa Fe after living most of his life in northern Illinois. "It makes a big difference in my life." Santa Fe is almost tied with Albuquerque for sunshine; almost 300 days a year are guaranteed to be at least partly sunny. Santa Fe gets more rain, though, and there's three times as much snow, about 33 inches annually. This keeps Santa Fe greener. You'll find a true four-season year with very pleasant summers. Be prepared to wear a sweater on summer evenings; the temperature typically drops to below 50 degrees at night.

Folks who can afford to buy a second house anywhere they like tend to buy one here. That should tell us something about Santa Fe's quality. The problem is that Santa Fe has such a reputation as a retirement and artist center that outsiders have bid up real estate to an unusual level. "It's getting so we natives can't afford to live here anymore," lamented one hometown resident. Yet, housing is curiously mixed in price. Generally, it's more expensive than Albuquerque, particularly for nicer housing. But there are also some inexpensive places. Several high-end developments are under way, at least one with its own private golf course. A couple of attractive, full-care retirement residences are located in Santa Fe, one without any endowment or entrance fees; but there could be a waiting list. An active senior citizens program, Open Hands, offers services and an opportunity to volunteer for satisfying and worthwhile community projects.

Taos   Farther up the road from Santa Fe, in the heart of the Sangre de Cristo Mountains, is the delightful town of Taos. Bustling village, quiet retreat, art colony, ski resort—these are but a few of Taos's many faces. Its fifty-five art galleries and numerous art programs hint at the large number of artists in residence. One drawback could be cold winters; however, the dryness takes the bitterness from the cold. Summers are cool, with air conditioners unheard-of.

Compared to Santa Fe, housing is less costly, and the lifestyle is a bit more casual. Taos seems to be more for seriously artistic folks rather than for wealthy summer residents. Don't expect to find rock-bottom prices here, however, because Taos is a popular place. Few properties list for under $100,000, with $150,000 and up more common. There are retirement complexes here; one, Plaza de Retiro, is located just 3 blocks from historic Taos Plaza, within walking distance of shopping, churches, restaurants, and other facilities. It sits on six acres, with many facilities: a dining room, a library, and activities rooms as well as a ten-bed licensed health care facility.

Ruidoso   Ruidoso bursts upon travelers as an absolute surprise; it's a setting you don't expect to find in New Mexico. Almost magically, the landscape changes from dry desert covered with brush and patches of carrizo grass into a gorgeous, winding river canyon graced with majestic evergreens perfuming the breezes. Cool mountain air and lush vegetation make Californians imagine they're at Lake Tahoe. Easterners might recall Maine forests or Canadian mountain vistas.

Of course, this isn't news to West Texans; they knew about the Ruidoso Upper Canyon for decades, as an excellent place to escape blazing Texas summers. The crystal-clear river cascading through the tree-shaded canyon made for a wonderful escape and family fun. Summer cabins sprang up among the large ponderosa pines and along the small river. By the way, *ruidoso* in Spanish means "noisy," an apt description of the sound of cascading water.

With the opening of the racetrack at Ruidoso Downs in 1947, people started thinking of Ruidoso as a resort instead of merely a summertime mountain getaway. More than thirty years ago, the Mescalero Apache tribe, with the help of a Texas oilman, developed a ski run high up on Apache Peak, a part of the Mescalero reservation. They called it Ski Apache and established Ruidoso's second career as a winter resort. The 12,000-foot ski run immediately attracted the attention of ski buffs from all over the country. This is the southernmost place to ski in the Southwest, and because of its exceptionally high location, skiing lasts long after many other areas have closed down, providing some of the best warm-weather powder skiing in the world. The January 1994 issue of *Ski* magazine rated Ruidoso as one of the ten best ski towns in which to live.

Skiing did more than simply bring tourists and increase employment opportunities; it brought visitors and allowed them to observe the area under winter conditions as well as summer. Visitors were pleasantly surprised to discover relatively mild winters here and to learn that fall and spring are delightful seasons as well. This launched Ruidoso upon yet another career as a center for year-round residence and retirement.

Summer cabins were enlarged and larger homes started springing up for both retirees and working families. This continuing growth provides employment for even more new residents and encourages more businesses to open. Today Ruidoso has blossomed into a pleasant town of about 7,500 inhabitants and is still growing, with the county population pushing 12,000. The area supports many more shops, stores, restaurants, and businesses of all kinds than you might expect of a town this size. Since Ruidoso draws visitors and tourists all year long, small businesses flourish, and you'll find an astonishing selection of excellent restaurants serving almost any kind of cuisine imaginable, from French to Chinese, from prime rib to Indian squaw bread. According to local business owners, the only slow time is in April, when they manage to squeeze in their vacation time. April, by the way, is an excellent time of the year to investigate Ruidoso as a retirement destination. You'll not only find less traffic and off-season rates for motels, you'll experience Ruidoso's spring, one of its best seasons.

The tall forest makes a proper setting for Ruidoso real estate, with homes shaded by a thick green canopy, casually located in a somewhat hodgepodge way. Elegant homes can sit next door to small cottages, log cabins, and, often, mobile homes. The higher end of the housing scale, at the northern edge of town, is also at the highest elevation. Trees are higher here, as are selling prices.

Silver City   For a thousand years the area around Silver City has been a source of valuable minerals. Early Native Americans mined outcrops of copper to fashion ornaments and spear points. In the 1790s Spanish miners worked the copper deposits, loading the ore on the backs of burros and hauling it south into Chihuahua for smelting. But Silver City itself wasn't established until returning California forty-niners discovered silver ore a few miles north of the present town site. This kicked off a typical mining–boom scenario, with a tent city being replaced by substantial brick buildings and optimistic expansion.

Western-history buffs might be interested that Silver City is where the famous outlaw Billy the Kid grew up, went to school, committed his first crime, was arrested for the first time, and made his first of several escapes from jail. Billy the Kid's first arrest was for robbing clothes from a Chinese laundry when he was fifteen. Had to start somewhere.

Silver City's 6,000-foot altitude provides cool, dry weather and beautiful, forested mountain vistas. With a population of 12,000, Silver City is large enough to supply most services, but still small enough to escape big-city crowding, crime, and pollution.

The town's architectural style clearly reflects the time of its development. Downtown buildings are influenced by the town's ranching and mining background, rich with Victorian brick buildings so popular in Western mining towns during the last century. In

SILVER CITY WEATHER						
In degrees Fahrenheit						
	Jan.	April	July	Oct.	Rain	Snow
Daily Highs	47	65	87	69	14"	21"
Daily Lows	18	36	60	40		

fact, Silver City's historic district boasts the largest concentration of Victorian homes in southern New Mexico.

The presence of Western New Mexico University takes Silver City out of the category of an ordinary mining town and is responsible in part for inspiring a fast-growing artist colony in Silver City. An astonishing number of galleries, studios, and workshops welcome art lovers, either regularly or by invitation.

Outdoor enthusiasts will find much to do within a short distance from Silver City, which is surrounded by the 3.3-million-acre Gila National Forest. Five fishing lakes offer good catches of bass and crappie, and there are rivers and streams with trout. Five tennis courts and an eighteen-hole golf course augment the ten parks and two swimming pools in Silver City.

Affordable real estate is one of the attractions that draws retirees here. In nearby Tyrone, the Phelps-Dodge company decided to move some of its company housing by marketing the workers' homes as retirement locations. Homes were refurbished and sold starting at $40,000. Now that these are gone, executive housing is going on the block, starting around $100,000.

Colorado

When you think of deserts and mountains, Colorado has to figure big. The state's highways cross the most impressive mountains on the continent, so high that some folks have trouble breathing; several passes climb over 10,000 feet. When folks do catch their breath, the mountain scenery immediately takes it away again. From legendary old mining towns to ultra-modern cities, from farmlands to forests, Colorado has a lot to offer the retiree. Many part-time re-

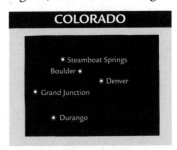

COLORADO

- Steamboat Springs
- Boulder
- Denver
- Grand Junction
- Durango

COLORADO TAX PROFILE

Sales tax: 3% to 7.5%, food and drugs exempt

State income tax: 5% of federal taxable income; can't deduct federal income tax

Property taxes: average 1% of purchase price

Intangibles tax: no

Social security taxed: half of benefits are taxable for higher incomes

Pensions taxed: excludes first $20,000; double deduction for taxpayers over 65

Gasoline tax: 4¢ to 10¢ per gallon

tirees love the state for its wonderfully refreshing summers, and full-time retirees like the reasonable housing and mild winters of some areas.

Grand Junction   Earlier, we discussed economic disasters that turned out to be bonanzas for retirees. Here's another story. During the late 1970s, encouraged and subsidized by the government, oil companies began experimenting with the enormous oil shale deposits of Colorado and Wyoming. Thousands of workers flocked there to help develop this potentially valuable natural resource.

Grand Junction participated in this welcome economic boom. New houses and apartments went up like mushrooms after a rainstorm. All this new building still wasn't enough, so Exxon, one of the larger companies, was forced to enter the construction business to provide housing for its employees. Among other things, Exxon developed a flat mountaintop, a place called Battlement Mesa, into a spiffy housing development. The company constructed 684 residences, complete with a multi-million-dollar recreation center.

Suddenly, the bubble collapsed. Slumping oil prices had made it too expensive to squeeze petroleum from the shale. Grand Junction remembers this date as Black Sunday. By the end of a year, almost 8,000 workers lost their jobs. Almost as quickly as they came, they began leaving. Knowing they hadn't even a prayer to make payments, many simply walked away from their homes. They couldn't even *give* the properties away because they owed more money on the mortgages than the current market value of the properties. The few buyers who were in the market waited for foreclosure and then

GRAND JUNCTION WEATHER

In degrees Fahrenheit

	Jan.	April	July	Oct.	Rain	Snow
Daily Highs	36	65	94	69	8"	25"
Daily Lows	15	38	64	41		

GRAND JUNCTION AREA COST OF LIVING

Percentage of	Overall	Housing	Medical	Groceries	Utilities
National Average	102	107	104	104	85

bought from the banks at bargain prices. As in Bisbee and Ajo, the workers who lost their jobs suffered both financially and from their shattered hopes for the future.

The businesspeople who survived realized that the solution to the problem lay in attracting industry with a stable financial base, something not subject to boom and bust like petroleum. Economic incentives such as free land for new and expanding industries were offered. At the same time, they began concentrating on a special business, one that's clean, doesn't pollute the air, and brings in an obvious source of steady income: the retirement industry! Exxon began to market its deluxe Battlement Mesa complex as a retirement community. Nearby towns, such as Parachute, Palisade, Fruita, and Clifton, joined in the movement to attract retirees.

Their efforts were successful. Gradually, the economy recovered, due in large measure to retiree money. Surplus homes were eventually purchased, and the population began rising once more. According to a real estate broker, about 50 percent of today's buyers are retirees from out of state. Although homes are selling at the national averages nowadays, retirees are still coming.

Grand Junction is the largest city in western Colorado, located in a broad valley in the high plateau country west of the Rocky Mountains. Its name came from its location near the junction of the Colorado and Gunnison rivers (the Colorado was originally called the *Grand* River). Grand Junction is the center of an urban area of some 82,000 people, although the town itself has a comfortable population of 33,000. Shopping malls, a senior citizens' center, and excellent health care are among the attractions. An abundance of sunshine and a mild winter that permits year-round golf and tennis adds to its desirability for retirement.

Denver   The largest city for many miles, Denver is a very interesting place from the perspective of a retiree. At first glance it would seem to be a horrible place to winter, what with a yearly snowfall of 60 inches! But that's only part of the story. Yes, it can snow a foot or more overnight, but within a couple of days, it's all gone, and you're basking in 65-degree sunshine! Even in the coldest months, afternoon temperatures average 43 degrees. Snow doesn't have a chance to stick around. Furthermore, the dryness of the air makes you think it is far warmer than it really is.

DENVER WEATHER					
In degrees Fahrenheit					
	Jan.	April	July	Oct.	Rain	Snow
Daily Highs	43	61	88	67	15"	60"
Daily Lows	16	34	59	37		

DENVER AREA COST OF LIVING					
Percentage of	Overall	Housing	Medical	Groceries	Utilities
National Average	108	126	123	105	88

Denver is a clean place, with pleasant, tree-shaded residential areas and loads of inexpensive apartment buildings. Most homes are built of brick, especially the older ones. According to a common story, an early-day mayor owned a brick factory, so he passed laws that all homes must be constructed of brick. Maybe it's not true, but the brick construction does add a special touch to Denver's architectural flavor.

A few years back, the most impressive thing about the city was its real estate prices. For a while the daily newspapers ran a sixteen-page supplement every Sunday full of HUD repossessions. Condos were offered at $15,000, three-bedroom brick homes for $40,000. This was the most depressed big-city market we found anywhere in the country. The reasons appear to be twofold: First, the shale oil boom had inflated new construction, and, second, the savings-and-loan industry (or racket?) had been disbursing construction loans and financing homes, apartments, and office buildings for anyone who asked.

During our latest visit, we were astounded at the turnaround. Today homes are selling at 26 percent over national averages. A drawback here (as in many urban areas) is the high number of youth gang-related shootings, but this kind of crime rarely affects seniors and is restricted to the inner-city neighborhoods where you aren't likely to locate in the first place. Most people choose to live in the delightful suburban areas far from downtown.

Boulder   A growing retirement trend is movement to college towns. Even if they haven't the slightest interest in continuing education, retirees often find that a university influences a community, serving as an exciting source of entertainment and cultural stimulation. Many of these social and cultural activities wouldn't exist without the school's presence. You don't have to be a registered student to attend lectures and speeches (often free) given by famous scientists, politicians, visiting artists, and other well-known personalities. Concerts ranging from Beethoven to boogie-woogie are presented by guest artists as well as the university's music department. You can attend the school's stage plays, Broadway musicals, and Shakespeare productions with season tickets that cost less than a single performance at a New York theater. Some schools allow senior citizens the use of recreational facilities and access to well-stocked libraries.

Therefore, without hesitation, I highly recommend Boulder as one of the better examples of university retirement locations. In addition to the University of Colorado at Boulder's intensely active college atmosphere, Boulder's immediate surroundings are as beautiful as you could imagine. It's about 27 miles northwest of Denver, with the Flatiron Mountains and snow-covered peaks looming in the background and Rocky Mountain National Park just minutes away. This wonderfully cosmopolitan city of 83,000 inhabitants is the home of the University of Colorado. The university, students, and faculty impact the city's environment in many pleasant ways, carrying the institution's intellectual excitement into the community as a whole.

The school's influence is most obvious in the city center where you can stroll along the renovated downtown pedestrian mall known as Pearl Street. This vibrant historic preservation district is the focal point of the city, its traditional heart and soul. Mimes, jugglers, and musicians mingle with the crowds, adding a touch of magic to the scene, something you'd expect to find in San Francisco or Paris rather than Colorado. All generations mix here to meet for coffee, read a newspaper or magazine, or perhaps browse a bookstore or a boutique. Pearl Street offers a great selection of good restaurants, art galleries, and specialty shops of a variety and quality seldom seen in downtown areas of today's cities. Pearl Street is the site of continual activities, formal and ad hoc, the site of art festivals, practicing musicians, birthday celebrations, a place for people-watching and relaxing. In short, downtown Boulder is a user-friendly, enjoyable place to visit.

The University of Colorado encourages retirees to enroll in

BOULDER WEATHER						
In degrees Fahrenheit						
	Jan.	April	July	Oct.	Rain	Snow
Daily Highs	41	66	88	70	17"	90"
Daily Lows	17	45	57	40		

BOULDER AREA COST OF LIVING					
Percentage of	Overall	Housing	Medical	Groceries	Utilities
National Average	118	155	108	117	86

classes for credit or as auditors. But for those who don't feel up to total immersion in the university's curriculum, an extraordinary senior center operated by Boulder Housing and Human Services gives classes in everything from papermaking to computers. They even offer sailboat instruction on Boulder Reservoir and day trips to archaeological sites and theaters in Denver. Coupled with an active volunteer program, this is one of the better senior programs we've seen.

Boulder's winter looks bad statistically—that is, if you consider snow bad—because Boulder catches even more snow than Denver! December and February receive the heaviest blankets of the white stuff, but like Denver, it doesn't hang around for long; daily temperatures climb high enough to get rid of it quickly. Most days of the year can be spent walking, biking, or pursuing outdoors activities. Summer makes amends by providing gloriously sunny and comfortable days.

The cost of living here is about 18 percent above national averages, mostly because of the high cost of housing, which is 55 percent above average. The last several years have seen a spectacular increase, with home prices up more than 25 percent since 1993.

Durango   Tucked away in a horseshoe of the San Juan Mountains in the southwestern corner of the state, Durango has been the gateway to southwestern Colorado's natural riches for more than one hundred years. Indians and fur traders, miners and prospectors, ranchers and railroad engineers alike passed through Durango on their way to seek their fortunes. Many found that Durango itself was the treasure they sought. Two million acres of national forest surround the city and provide countless places for outdoor recreation, with hunting, fishing, and hiking opportunities galore.

Although the town is relatively young—established little more than a century ago—the Four Corners Region where it's located boasts evidence of ancient glories. Two thousand years ago, this was home to a mysterious aboriginal culture known as the Anasazi (the Ancient Ones). For some unknown reason the Anasazi abandoned their sophisticated, several-storied apartment buildings and left the area to the next wave of inhabitants, the Ute tribes, who arrived a couple of centuries later. They were there to welcome the Spanish, who explored the region in the 1500s.

The town of Durango got its start in 1880 as a depot and roundhouse location for the railroad, and grew rapidly into a town of 2,000 residents just a year later. Before long the fledgling town boasted twenty saloons and 134 businesses. Today the population is 15,000 and still growing. Retirees make up a good percentage of the inhabitants; almost 30 percent are age 62 or older. The business community and residents recognize the treasure of the original buildings constructed by Durango's pioneers that are still in use today. Parts of downtown have been named by the Colorado Historical Society as a national historic district, bestowing Durango with Victorian splendor and elegance.

Residents like the town because it's a pleasant and peaceful community with a below-average crime rate and above-average quality of living. A 6,500-foot elevation ensures a four-season climate with bountiful snowfall in the town, yet not so high an altitude that temperatures don't rise above freezing every winter day. With 85 percent solar exposure, snow removal is seldom a problem. You're also guaranteed cool summer evenings without the need of air-conditioning.

Because Durango sits all by itself near the Four Corners area, by necessity it's become a self-contained little city. As Will Rogers once said, "Durango's out of the way and glad of it." Shopping needs are met by commercial development in and around Durango. Turn-of-

DURANGO WEATHER					
In degrees Fahrenheit					
	Jan.	April	July	Oct.	Rain	Snow
Daily Highs	41	62	85	67	19"	71"

the-century hotels and commercial buildings abound in the business district, and an unusually high number of good restaurants serve a variety of cuisines. The year-round tourist business encourages upscale establishments, to the benefit of year-round residents.

Durango is also gaining recognition as an artist colony. In addition to several well-known painters, half a dozen writers of fiction and nonfiction make this their home as well as do a number of essayists, freelancers, and poets. Three galleries here are nationally recognized for quality Native American arts, Navajo weavings, jewelry, paintings, and sculpture.

Skiing at Purgatory Ski Resort, 26 miles away, is reputed to be among the best in the country. Nine lifts and 250 inches of snow account for the resort's impressive increase in ski hours. Although the resort has record snowfall, it also has record blue-sky days, which makes for great downhill fun.

The cost of living here is slightly below national averages, and real estate prices possibly slightly higher than in some other Colorado locations. The reason for this is that there are fewer lower-end starter homes than elsewhere. Contractors prefer to build more upscale places, since they sell well.

Steamboat Springs   You say you love winter? You can't wait until ski lifts start running? Maybe Steamboat Springs is your town. Snuggled in a high valley at 6,700 feet, the town's alpine climate features low humidity, warm summer days, and cool, crisp nights. It also features winter snow—from 170 to 450 inches! Most of that is on the slopes, thank goodness.

This is a charming, upscale place for those who enjoy delightful summers and abundant outdoor winter sports. While its winter "champagne powder" skiing brings winter sportsmen from all over the country, Steamboat Springs enjoys wonderful summer weather, just what you might expect from its Rocky Mountain setting. Even in July and August, temperatures rarely climb out of the 80-degree range, and every evening they drop into the 50s.

STEAMBOAT SPRINGS WEATHER						
In degrees Fahrenheit						
	Jan.	Apr.	July	Oct.	Rain	Snow
Daily Highs	30	52	82	60	26"	60"
Daily Lows	01	24	41	24		

The town's name came from a mineral spring that made a chugging noise that sounded like a steamboat to the early fur trappers who passed through the area. More than 150 mineral springs are found nearby, supplying medicinal waters for modern-day residents' hot tubs and baths at the public swimming pool.

Abundant wild game and rivers teeming with fish encouraged settlement, and the development of the town as a ski resort brought Steamboat Springs to its present population of about 7,000 inhabitants. Its early development is evident in the well-preserved Victorian homes and substantial brick business buildings that date from the late 1800s. Folks who've moved here recently say they appreciate the change from the hectic, crime-plagued lifestyle of big cities.

Although it sits on U.S. 40, a major east-west highway, Steamboat Springs is somewhat isolated, being 157 miles from the nearest big town (Denver). However, express shuttles to Denver airport plus frequent shuttle flights from the local Yampa Valley Regional Airport keep folks in touch with big-city civilization (if they need that sort of thing).

Of course, the major recreational drawing card here is skiing. Steamboat Springs bills itself "Ski Town USA," and has produced more Olympic skiers than any other other U.S. town. With twenty lifts, 108 trails and a 3,600-foot vertical rise to 10,500 feet, this area is recognized as one of the best in the country. The season runs from Thanksgiving to Easter each year. Snowmobiling, sleigh rides, and back-country skiing are also enjoyed.

This is not a place to look for bargain real estate; it's an upscale area and property offerings show this. This higher-priced real estate pulls the overall cost of living up as well. Condos are big here, and practical, because they can be turned into rentals for any time you're someplace else.

Utah

Utah is the most desert-like of all the Western states, with seemingly endless stretches of barren land. Sometimes alkaline flats stretch as far as the eye can see; occasionally, the landscape is crusted with a pavement-like salt surface. The Great Salt Lake, actually an inland sea, has water

UTAH

• Salt Lake City
• Provo

• Cedar City
• St. George

so loaded with salt that most ocean fish would die if they tried swimming there.

In contrast, the state also boasts the most spectacular mountain scenery in the country, perhaps in the world. Southern Utah, with Zion and Bryce Canyon national parks to take your breath away, competes with Capitol Reef and the Canyonlands areas for sheer desert and mountain beauty.

Although these areas are beautiful beyond description, most are *not* places I would consider for retirement! In the first place, most are in isolated areas with just a few scattered farms and an occasional rural village. Second, small-town Utah can be a lonely place indeed for those of you who are not Mormons. In fact, my main reservation against Utah as a place to retire is its closely knit society that centers around religion and church activities. Among themselves, the people are wonderfully warm and loving, with deep concern for one another's welfare. But even converts tell me of discrimination because they were not born into the church. An indication of how religion permeates Utah life is that 90 percent of the state's politicians are active members of the Mormon Church.

UTAH TAX PROFILE
Sales tax: 5% to 6.25%, drugs exempt
State income tax: graduated, 2.25% to 7.2% over $3,750; federal; income tax partially deductible
Property taxes: average 0.8% of market value
Intangibles tax: no
Social security taxed: half of benefits taxable for higher incomes
Pensions taxed: excludes up to $7,500, depending on income level
Gasoline tax: 19.5¢ per gallon

Having said this and emphasizing that this is strictly my opinion, I can also say that many non-Mormons tell me that they haven't found religion much of an obstacle. "It's only a problem if you let it be a problem," said one newcomer to St. George. Most larger towns are pleasant-looking and have affordable property. Salt Lake City is an exceptionally clean and prosperous city. We have friends who live there (Mormons, of course) and who swear by its four-season climate and invigorating, clean air.

Salt Lake City In 1847 Brigham Young led a band of Mormons westward across the plains and mountains in search of freedom from religious persecution. When the travelers looked down from mountains overlooking the valley of the Great Salt Lake, Brigham Young announced that this was the Promised Land where they would live. They set to work tilling the soil that same day, and began transforming the dry and desolate land into beautiful, well-planned Salt Lake City.

The capital of Utah and one of the largest cities in the Rocky Mountain region (pop. 170,000), Salt Lake City is also the world capital of the Church of Jesus Christ of Latter-day Saints. It sits in a valley bordered to the north and east by mountains, near the southeastern shore of the Great Salt Lake.

At first the city's growth depended on the inflow of Mormon converts from Europe and America. Later, industrial and business expansion attracted many "gentiles," or non-Mormons, who now make up almost half the population. This makes for a more cosmopolitan community than is found in most areas of Utah.

In the center of the city, surrounded by beautiful grounds, are the chief buildings of the Mormon Church. Other buildings of note in the city are those of the University of Utah, the state capitol, the city and county building, the museum, the exposition buildings, and two former residences of Brigham Young. In Temple Square is the Sea Gull Monument; at this point the altitude is 4,400 feet. Most neighborhoods are clean and well kept, with reasonably safe conditions.

The overall cost of living in Salt Lake City is slightly above average, helped in part by exceptionally low utility costs (almost 20 percent below average). Housing costs, however are 10 percent above average.

SALT LAKE CITY WEATHER

In degrees Fahrenheit

	Jan.	April	July	Oct.	Rain	Snow
Daily Highs	37	61	93	67	15"	58"
Daily Lows	20	37	62	39		

SALT LAKE CITY AREA COST OF LIVING

	Overall	Housing	Medical	Groceries	Utilities
Percentage of National Average	102	110	105	106	80

Provo   Located about 40 miles south of Salt Lake City is the city of Provo, which recently received top rating as a place to retire by *Money* magazine. Provo is also the home of Brigham Young University, one of the largest private universities in the country. Most towns with high ratings for personal safety and low crime rates are small places, with populations around 20,000 to 30,000. So with 92,000 inhabitants, Provo is unusually large to rank so high on the FBI's charts for personal safety. Salt Lake City, by the way, ranks quite low in personal safety. This is puzzling, because folks who live there claim it's exceptionally safe. There must be some factor that causes this anomaly, but I've been unable to discover it.

St. George   The largest city in southern Utah, St. George works hard to attract retirees and has acquired a strong reputation as a retirement community. It consistently receives top recommendations from national magazines and retirement guides as a place to retire, often ranking number one in the West.

Conveniently located on Interstate 15, a little more than two hours' drive from Las Vegas, St. George isn't as isolated as it might seem. The city's population of about 30,000 is large enough to provide adequate services, and the community stands on its own commercially.

St. George's picturesque surroundings are some of the more dramatic of any retirement destination described in this book. Stark red cliffs loom over the town, sometimes rising vertically from residents' back yards. You get the feeling that you're living on the set of a Western movie. In its own way, St. George is as spectacular as Sedona, Arizona, although on a smaller scale.

ST. GEORGE WEATHER						
In degrees Fahrenheit						
	Jan.	April	July	Oct.	Rain	Snow
Daily Highs	54	76	101	80	11"	5"
Daily Lows	26	44	66	45		

ST. GEORGE AREA COST OF LIVING					
Percentage of	Overall	Housing	Medical	Groceries	Utilities
National Average	102	101	96	107	95

A combination of beauty, relatively mild winters, and great golfing draws more retirees from outside Utah than do other Utah communities. This is important for non-Mormons, because outsiders dilute the religious majority, and newcomers won't be so likely to feel like outsiders. In fact, St. George has twenty-four community churches besides those of the Mormon faith. These range from Roman Catholic to Jehovah's Witness, with five Baptist churches, an Episcopal, Lutheran, Presbyterian, Methodist, and several I've never heard of. Of course, the majority of the residents are Mormons, but it looks as if there's plenty of room for others.

Settled in 1861 by 309 Mormon families, St. George was transformed from a forbidding alkali flat into a livable town in the space of a decade. Some of the original homes survive and are treated with reverence by local residents. Included is the house where Brigham Young spent a few of his last years. Streets are wide and tree-lined, and homes are as neat and orderly as Brigham Young would have wished.

Cedar City   This small university town of 17,000 offers many advantages for retirement living. Sheltered in the foothills just a few miles from some of the most spectacular landscapes in the world, Cedar City combines the cultural atmosphere of an active university with some of the best skiing and outdoor sports to be found anywhere. The 5,800-foot altitude guarantees a vigorous, four-season climate. According to residents, there are usually four good snowfalls every winter, but warm afternoons and plenty of sunshine make quick work of melting them away.

Cedar City is located on Interstate 15, which gives it easy access

CEDAR CITY WEATHER						
In degrees Fahrenheit						
	Jan.	April	July	Oct.	Rain	Snow
Daily Highs	54	76	101	80	11"	5"
Daily Lows	26	44	66	45		

CEDAR CITY COST OF LIVING					
Percentage of National Average	Overall	Housing	Medical	Groceries	Utilities
	93	77	91	106	77

to St. George, 52 miles south, and to Salt Lake City, 270 miles north. Las Vegas is little more than three hours away. You might expect a small city like Cedar City to be safe, and it is, exceptionally so. According to our calculations, only a few cities in the United States have lower crime rates than Cedar City.

Because of an exciting variety of cultural presentations, Cedar City calls itself the "Festival City." Now in its twenty-sixth season, the Shakespeare Festival is famous throughout the West and draws fans from far and wide. Running from the last week in June through Labor Day, each year Southern Utah University presents four Shakespeare plays plus another stage play and a musical. Another interesting festival is the yearly Jedediah Smith High Mountain Rendezvous. This follows an old-time Western theme, assembling trappers, traders, and mountain men for a nostalgic festival of frontier contests and camaraderie. Southern Utah University's campus is the focus of many other community events such as music festivals, ballet, and the Utah Summer Games.

CHAPTER 8

California

THERE ARE DEFINITE DIFFERENCES BETWEEN FOLKS who live in the extreme western part of the nation and those who live in the East, Midwest, and South. The reasons for the differences are partly historical and partly environmental. Personalities and worldviews vary with each section, and sometimes the differences are subtle.

Folks who live in the southern portions of the United States are, by tradition, rural and outdoor-oriented. Midwesterners share much of the Southern tradition, yet their larger cities, larger farms, and industrially developed environments, plus a history of Eastern immigration and Eastern ideas, distinguish them from Southerners.

On the other hand, the Eastern mindset is shaped by closely packed cities, little open space, and an orientation toward business and industry. In heavily populated areas, the friendliness and hospitality of the South and Midwest just aren't possible.

The West Coast has a comparatively short history, and with the exception of a few Native Americans, it is composed principally of "newcomers" from every part of the country and the world. The population is mixed and so are their personalities. Southern hospitality mixes with Northeastern reserve, and the love of open spaces mixes with a love of the city. The result is a multifaceted, laid-back lifestyle.

Yes, the West Coast has earned a reputation for being laid-back. So, what's wrong with kicking back and enjoying life? I'm convinced you'll live longer and enjoy life more. We have friends in Connecticut who think nothing of commuting an hour and a half each way to work. That's almost two extra working days a week, or ninety working days a year, spent staring out a train window! On the other hand, most Californians complain bitterly if their commutes are longer than twenty minutes (except for Los Angeles, where businesspeople spend their spare time parked on the freeways).

Another East-West difference is the attitude toward education. Western community colleges and adult education are accessible and liberally patronized by senior citizens. Many universities waive fees for those over age sixty-five, welcoming them and their potential contributions to the system.

A friend who moved west after spending most of his life in New York City once told me,

> A big difference I see between East Coast and West Coast living is a sense of space and belonging. That is, in New York I always felt that I *belonged* to a certain neighborhood, and I felt perfectly comfortable there. When I went elsewhere, I felt almost as if I were intruding—that I *didn't* belong. But in the West, I don't feel this restricted sense of neighborhood. *Everywhere* belongs to me, and I don't feel out of place no matter where I am.

Two factors account for this. One is the historical fact that the West Coast is still in the process of being settled; people have no deeply ingrained sense of neighborhood. Western families tend to live in one house for short intervals, and when they can afford to upgrade their lifestyles they trade for a more expensive home in another neighborhood. They seldom develop deep roots, binding friendships, or loyalty for one locale; the new one is always better than the last.

The second factor is the environmental circumstance of so much open land. Much of it actually does belong to everyone. A huge percentage of Western lands is in nationally owned forests, deserts, and mountain slopes. Unlike the East Coast where just about every acre is fenced and posted as private property, most Western land is public and open for anyone to enjoy. Almost 50 percent of California and Oregon belongs to the U.S. Government. Nevada is 85 percent federally owned and Arizona, 44 percent. Compare this with only 3.8 percent in New England, the Eastern Seaboard, and the Midwestern states.

Openness means more than forests and deserts. The ocean also belongs to the people. Unlike the Atlantic and Gulf shores, where property owners own the beach in front of their homes and can post no-trespassing signs, Pacific beaches belong to everyone. By law, property owners must provide public access to their beachfront properties; their ownership extends only to a certain distance above the high-tide line. You can stroll along any beach you please, secure in the knowledge that it is as much your property as anyone's.

Weather

Because West Coast weather is mild and generally pleasant year-round, people tend to find outdoor things to do. Most live within a few hours' drive of excellent ski country or uncrowded beaches. They can enjoy snow sports in the afternoon, then drive down the mountain to swim in a pool or relax in a hot tub the same evening. Outdoor living is the hallmark of Westerners.

The West Coast offers the most amazing smorgasbord of retirement choices imaginable. Choose from mountain communities with Alpine winters, deserts that look more like the Sahara than the Sahara, farmlands that remind one of Iowa, rugged coasts as pretty as the Spanish Mediterranean, and beaches as smooth as Hawaii's (albeit with colder waters). Within an hour or so of most retirement locations you can be hunting deer, fishing for trout, or trolling for salmon. From a rustic cabin deeply isolated within a redwood forest you can drive for thirty minutes to an art museum, the theater, or an ocean beach. From a city home you can drive twenty minutes to a wild and scenic wilderness. Almost any ecological, environmental, or climatic feature can be found on the West Coast.

Yes, some California locations have smog and air pollution at least as bad as I've seen in many Eastern cities. (Los Angeles has dramatically cleaned up its act over the last two decades, however.) But most of the state enjoys pristine, clear air.

What about water? Isn't the West always in a drought of some sort? Not really. Some mountain areas in California consistently get so much rain it's ridiculous—more than 60 inches a season, and that's nothing compared to parts of Oregon and Washington—while places not far away in the desert are lucky to see a couple of inches all year. But as a general rule not much rain ever falls in the summer. In the mountains you might catch some summer rain, and even thunderstorms, but elsewhere you can pretty much count on leaving your waterproof hat at home when golfing, fishing, or hiking. This arrangement is perfect for tourists and retirees, but it is a little difficult for farmers—no rain during the growing season, and too much rain when they don't need it. Fortunately, an irrigation system remedies this situation, permitting California to be one of the most productive of all the farming states. Another nice thing about the weather here is a low relative humidity. This means gentler hot days, more comfortable cool days, and far, far fewer bugs such as cockroaches.

Along the ocean, temperatures vary little between winter and summer. It is pleasant year-round from San Diego to Vancouver. Granted, the farther north, the cooler the temperatures, but they remain remarkably stable regardless of the season. This is due to the chain of low, coastal mountains that runs along the entire West Coast, from Washington's Puget Sound to San Diego. This ridge separates the coast from the inland valleys and prevents the cool Pacific air from sweeping eastward.

A natural "air-conditioning" system occurs when the sun heats up the inland valley air. This warm air rises, creating low pressure that then draws air from the ocean across the coast and over the mountains to cool things off. If it weren't for this occurrence, the coast would be as hot as the interior valleys. In the winter, the air currents are stable and the cooler air stays offshore, allowing both beaches and inland to bask in the sunshine. Often the "heat waves" of the coastal lands occur in November, with 80 degrees common, as opposed to the 70-degree days of August.

Therefore, the coastal towns are for those who don't like air-conditioning and also hate freezing weather. Los Angeles is a bit different, since the mountains are farther from the coast and the sun heats the entire coastal plain. However, the ocean breeze performs somewhat the same natural air-conditioning function. That's why Los Angeles has such pleasant weather: warm in the winter but rarely extremely hot in the summer. This climate is exactly why so many people live there.

Through the coastal valleys north, across the San Joaquin and Sacramento valleys, through Oregon and Washington, the climate patterns are similar: hot, sunny summers and mild winters. The farther north, the cooler the summer weather and the greater likelihood of a touch of snow in the winter. But all along the coast, rain comes in the winter. This causes a strange switch in seasons. Unlike the green eastern summers, things turn brown in the summer, sometimes by the first of June, and then brilliant green in November, when the rains begin to fall. This is agricultural land, lush when irrigated. The people living here enjoy a mild climate and snow-free winters.

On the other side of the valleys is yet another range of mountains, high and forbidding. These run almost in an unbroken chain from the Canadian Rockies to the Andes in South America. On the slopes and foothills of these mountains is a third climate system. It was along this uplift, in California's Sierra Nevada range, where the early-day miners found gold and settled during the West's infancy. After a brief flurry of mining activity, the area was almost deserted. Much of it is rolling country, forested with hardwood and pine. Cold-water rivers teaming with trout tumble their way from the mountains on the way to the ocean. Folks who live here like the mild four seasons and the rustic, forest atmosphere plus the knowledge that big-city convenience is a short distance away.

High mountains, deep snow, ski lifts, and tall trees characterize the next level of Western living. The high Sierra, with crystal-clear air and brisk mornings, attracts a special breed of retirees. These folks either are not afraid of snow or they are not afraid to admit they hate it and leave every winter; in some places the snow level reaches 12 feet. But summer in the Sierra is beautiful: warm and sunny with cool evenings (and a wood fire). To be perfectly honest, most of these homes are shuttered for the winter while their owners travel in RVs to snow-free climes or move to their alternate digs on the Colorado River or the Pacific shore.

The last type of ecosystem is the desert. This is found in great abundance on the other side of the tall mountains and in both the southern and northernmost sections of the West. In eastern Washington and Oregon, Nevada, Utah, Colorado, California, Arizona, and New Mexico, uncountable square miles are desert country. Many people think of desert as searing hot stretches of sand dunes. Some low-altitude desert country can fit that description. But high desert country can be as bitterly cold and uninhabitable as Alaskan tundra, although most falls somewhere between these extremes.

Earthquakes

Shortly after Los Angeles's 1994 Northridge earthquake, I was traveling through south Georgia on a research trip. The director of a local chamber of commerce—as soon as she found out I'm from California—asked the inevitable question: "Aren't you afraid of earth-quakes?" And, typically, she added, "Why, I would be scared to death to live there!"

The truth is, like most Californians, I simply get a mild thrill of excitement whenever the room starts shaking. Why? Because we're used to them and know that the chances of this being the "big one" are extremely remote. After more than forty years in California, the worst earthquake I've been in did little more than rock the chande-liers. But for sheer terror, I can't imagine anything worse than a tor-nado. Unlike earthquakes, there's no such thing as a *mild* tornado. Furthermore, killer tornadoes outnumber mild earthquakes a hun-dred to one.

When I explained this to the Georgia lady, she argued, "But with tornadoes, you get plenty of warning on television. Earth-quakes happen without any warning at all."

Now, I have to admit that's quite true. There is absolutely no way to predict an earthquake, although at least twice a year, news-papers quote self-styled experts who predict the "big eight-pointer" is coming within the year. Whenever a newspaper runs short of news, a page editor digs up the latest "expert opinion" to fill empty columns. After the forty years I've lived here, though, earthquake warning headlines somehow lose their edge.

Anyway, after I'd finished that day's interviews, I returned to my motel room in a driving rainstorm. As I watched the evening news, the storm gained fury. Suddenly, a message flashed across the bottom of the screen! "Tornado Warning for Landfill County!" My heart began pounding furiously.

I snatched up a road map and tried to locate Landfill County. Sweat popped out on my brow, and my hands trembled so that I couldn't read the map. The wind grew even more ferocious. Sleet began pecking at the window panes ominously. I just knew that at any moment a black twister was going to rip the motel into confetti, shred my body into machaca, and scatter my credit cards to the four winds. (Just my luck, I'd paid for the motel room in advance.) Yet I still couldn't find Landfill County on that blasted map!

In desperation, I tried to remember what you're supposed to do during a tornado. Let's see—hide in the basement? No, motels don't have basements. Stand under a door? No, no, that's for earthquakes. Crawl under the bed? Yukko! Too many ugly dust balls. Then a hor-rible truth flashed into my mind, accompanied by a flash of lightning outside: The main purpose of a tornado warning is to scare the bejeezels out of you! It worked.

Fortunately, nothing happened to me, my motel, or my credit cards that night, but you can be sure that I slept fitfully indeed, cringing with every crash of thunder. Now, an earthquake is a different situation. In ninety-nine out of one hundred earthquakes, there are a few seconds of adrenalin rush and it's over. People don't have time to become frightened. Thank goodness we *don't* get earthquake warnings!

Tragically, the next morning's newscast revealed that a series of tornadoes killed forty-two people in Kentucky, Alabama, and Georgia. News coverage was brief, since there's nothing unusual about tornado rampages. The important story of the day was whether Arkansas would beat North Carolina. But, if forty-two people had been killed in a California earthquake, the networks would have been filled with footage of the damage, interviews with witnesses, and hours of rehashing the event.

Unlike tornadoes and hurricanes, which, thankfully, California also doesn't have, earthquakes kill or injure relatively few people. Property suffers the most damage, with shakers generally trashing construction that wasn't entirely stable in the first place. To sum up, tornadoes have killed 4,625 people since 1917; hurricanes have killed 12,376 since 1900. Yet, the total number of Californians killed by earthquakes in the twentieth century is less than 700, and that's including the Big Mama of 1906.

Crime

When I first moved to California I expected to be threatened by bikers in black leather jackets brandishing switchblades. I worried about getting run over by cops and robbers as they routinely chased each other around city streets exchanging gunfire. Television and violent movies prepared me for the worst. Before long I realized that the reason California crime scenes appear so often on television is because California is where movie and television crews shoot their films. If Omaha were to become the motion picture center of the continent, that's where we'd see criminals. We'd be watching shows like *Streets of Omaha* or *Nebraska Crime Series*.

Of course California has crime; there isn't a place in the world that doesn't. What might surprise you is many California towns rank as the safest in the nation. Looking at the FBI crime statistics and comparing town for town, we've found California is just as safe as most other states!

I feel secure in California, not only in smaller towns and cities, but also in big places such as Los Angeles and San Francisco where crime rates are obviously high. (Of course, I'm careful about which neighborhoods I visit!) In my years of living in California I've never been robbed, mugged, or threatened with a weapon. Well, yes, my wife was involved in a mugging once, but the police made her return my money. (Just joking. My wife would *never* return the money!)

Kooks and Weirdos?

"California, fountainhead of fruitcakes and nuts," was how one Easterner put it when he explained why he had never visited California and had no intention of ever doing so. It's true that the state has been the source of some rather spacey ideas. Back in the 1920s and 1930s, religious cults and movements started here and spread over the country. The 1940s brought us beatniks—mild-mannered intellectuals who sat around coffeehouses sipping red wine and reciting bad poetry. They aroused the nation's indignation primarily because beatnik men wore goatees before it was deemed fashionable, and lady beatniks often lived with, rather than married, their lovers before *that* became fashionable. In the 1960s and 1970s, the "love generation" spawned hippies, starting in San Francisco and spreading across the nation.

Eventually these fads, like most fads, faded away. Today, you have the yuppie movement, with an intense pursuit of high-paying jobs, expensive automobiles, and designer clothes. (Frankly, I preferred the beatniks.) California is also a major center of computer technology, where the famous Silicon Valley turns out new inventions daily. As a result, the state attracts a steady stream of bright, innovative newcomers.

Californians are not slaves to fad and fashion as people tend to believe. We don't rush out and buy clothes simply because some magazine dictates that this year's fashions must be different. Few restaurants require ties, because California men seldom wear them. Women can wear slacks, blue jeans, or fancy dresses for any occasion. On the other hand, when I travel back East I have to remember that folks there dress differently; so I must remember to pack my only suit, some dress shirts, a tie—even socks of matching colors, if I can find them.

Comfort and Affordability

Are there really affordable places in California, without smog and without horrendous traffic? Places with hunting and fishing for the men and quality living for the women? A four-season climate? The unqualified answer: Yes!

Contrary to popular stereotype, California is not all palm trees, movie stars, and surfers. Much of the state, particularly the northern part, is almost Midwestern in character. Small towns set in national forests or in the wine country are pretty much like small towns everywhere when it comes to cost of living and lifestyles. The northern California coast is as different from southern California resort and surfing areas as New England towns are from Florida beaches.

CALIFORNIA TAX PROFILE
Sales tax: 7.2% to 8.5%, food and drugs exempt
State income tax: graduated, 1% to 11% over $207,200 ($25,000 at 8%); can't deduct federal income tax
Property taxes: vary widely, depending on when home was purchased and locality; typically from 1.5% to 1.75%
Intangibles tax: no
Social security taxed: no
Pensions taxed: all
Gasoline tax: 18¢ per gallon, plus possible local taxes and state sales tax

California's glamorous cities are well known, places such as Santa Barbara, San Diego, and San Francisco. We'll discuss them later, of course; it would be neglectful of our duty to do otherwise. But let's first start with some retirement possibilities generally unfamiliar to folks from other states.

California Deserts

Although many commonly think of California as surfing beaches, Hollywood, and redwood forests, the majority of California is desert or semi-desert. After all, that most famous of all U.S. deserts, Death Valley, is in California. The great Mojave Desert covers a good portion of southern California and continues up the eastern portion of the state.

Traditionally, California deserts are divided into two classifications: high desert and low desert. As you would expect, the higher country has colder winters and more pleasant summers. However, "colder" winters doesn't mean continual freezing weather; it means that when cold winds blow from the north, it gets cool enough to freeze the hair off a bald mouse. But most of the time, whenever it's sunny, daytime temperatures climb to either shirtsleeve or light sweater weather.

CALIFORNIA DESERT

Palm Springs

Victorville and Apple Valley are examples of high-desert locations that draw retirees. They mostly come from the Los Angeles area, attracted here by the low crime rates, cheap land, and wide open spaces. Since few folks outside of California actually retire in high-desert country, the discussion here covers mostly low-desert towns, although Yucaipa almost falls into the high-desert category.

Overall, California desert living may not be as affordable as living in other Western desert states, but for some folks money is less of an issue than locale. And for many retirees, California remains the land of their retirement dreams, no matter the cost.

Palm Springs   When people speak of Palm Springs they could mean any of a half-dozen towns scattered along Interstate 10 from Palm Springs to Indian Wells. Playground of millionaires, movie stars, and other rich and famous types, Palm Springs is synonymous with "class." Well-known personalities—such as Bob Hope, Bing Crosby, Jerry Ford, and a host of others—have made golf fans aware of the great, year-round golf courses. When people with enough money to live anywhere in the world choose the Palm Springs area for their homes, there must be something special going on!

Sheltered in the lee of the rugged San Jacinto Mountains, with abundant water, Palm Springs is verdant and livable year-round. Green landscaping, huge palm trees, and manicured golf courses convert the desert into a botanical wonderland. The area supports more golf courses than most cities have supermarkets, ninety-three in all, although many are private, belonging to residents of the surrounding developments.

Winters are as delightful here as summers are hot. As one real estate salesperson put it, "Which is worse, a low-humidity, hot summer—or an icy, freezing winter?" (As I work on my notes, it's the middle of January here in Palm Springs. I am outdoors—barefoot, wearing shorts and no shirt—listening to radio reports of 18-below-zero storms savaging the Midwest and Eastern states, with snow-drifts deeper than my pool!)

Instead of snowstorms, Southern California deserts have wind-storms. One reason for Palm Springs's popularity is that nearby mountains block most of this wind. The farther south from the in-terstate, the more protection.

A drive through expensive neighborhoods can be over-whelming: one street after another competing for the title of the fanciest and most opulent. Shopping centers that look as if they were built for sultans or nobility offer any kind of luxury item you can afford (and many that you can't). Clean desert air and a rugged mountain backdrop give Palm Springs an aura of pristine beauty combined with regal affluence.

The curious thing is, although this is one of the more expensive retirement areas in the country, it's not necessarily out of reach for folks with moderate incomes. Most residents are *not* rich; they work for wages and can't afford a super-expensive lifestyle. The main in-dustry is support services: restaurants, stores, hotels, or gardening for wealthy families, and other jobs of that nature. Wages for grocery clerks or waiters are seldom so high that they drive up the housing market. Palm Springs real estate is an either-or thing: either you can't afford high payments, or you're rich and you don't give a damn!

The fanciest homes are found in adjoining towns, places such as Rancho Mirage, Palm Desert, or Indian Wells. Yet interspersed with these exclusive enclaves are affordable neighborhoods for ordi-nary wage-earners and retirees, often just a few blocks away. Mobile-home and RV parks also provide moderate-cost alternatives. Some are elegant, complete with golf privileges; others are more plain, with competitive rates.

PALM SPRINGS AREA COST OF LIVING					
Percentage of National Average	Overall 112	Housing 103	Medical 136	Groceries 113	Utilities 143

During a research trip to Palm Springs in early 1994, we noticed an unusual number of foreclosure sales and HUD offerings. To our surprise, prices of homes, condos and country-club residences had *dropped* since our previous visit. We looked at a small two-bedroom condo within walking distance of downtown Palm Springs for $44,000 (a HUD repo). $100,000 would buy a three-bedroom place in a "gated" development (with a twenty-four-hour guarded entrance, almost always with pool and tennis, often with golf). How about $130,000 for a luxury place on a private, eighteen-hole golf course? Even though we visited during the high tourist season, apartment and condo rentals were affordable, with many vacancies.

It turned out that the Palm Springs real estate market had been trashed by a downturn in Los Angeles's economy. When defense industry jobs dry up, when lucrative businesses go bankrupt, and when high-paid executives go on unemployment, the first things to go are the yacht and the Palm Springs condo.

At that point, we made an earnest recommendation to readers to invest in Palm Springs real estate. Unfortunately, we didn't follow our own advice. Today the going prices of homes and condos have recovered to pre-bargain levels. By August of 1997, the median home sale price had risen from about $100,000 to $167,000. However, two years later it had dropped to $150,050. This shows that Palm Springs real estate prices are not prohibitive—in fact, only a few points above the national average.

Palm Springs is without a doubt our favorite desert location in terms of winter weather, luxury, and prestige. While it's more expensive than some other places discussed in this book, it's also more affordable than many people think. The key is finding housing that won't break your budget. After that, everything falls into place.

Gold Country

In 1847, in a part of Mexico called Alta California, a group of workers labored to construct a sawmill on a rushing stream that flowed down from the Sierra Nevada range. This was in the north-central part of what was to become California, near what is now Sacramento. As they dug into the river's bank, one man noticed something curious in his shovel's blade. Sparkling metal pebbles mixed with the gravel. Gold!

This event touched off one of the most exciting chapters in

United States history. News of the discovery spread; the rush was on. People came by covered wagon and horseback; some sailed around Cape Horn to join in a frenzy of prospecting. Eager miners attacked streams with gold pans and sluice boxes to fill their pockets with gold nuggets. Gold deposits were so rich that miners called the area the "Mother Lode."

CALIFORNIA GOLD COUNTRY

Dunsmuir
Fall River Mills/
Burney
Chico
Paradise
Grass Valley/
Nevada City
Amador
County

Within a short span of time, rude mining camps became towns and then small cities. Paved streets, brick buildings, theaters, and businesses flourished, creating replicas in miniature of Midwestern and Eastern towns of that era.

When gold claims finally played out, gold miners drifted on to other enterprises. Some moved to fertile California valleys to seek fortunes as growers. Others settled in the growing coastal cities. When miners moved away, Mother Lode towns became virtual ghost towns. Luckily, this abandonment preserved many old mining towns in time-capsule form, fascinating pictures of life as it was during California's romantic past. Because of low-cost housing and pleasant environments, these are now great places for retirement.

Gold Country is about as far from the usual California image as you can get. Its collection of old mining towns, with narrow streets and buildings of native stone and brick, harmonize perfectly with the green-clad mountain backdrops. The state jealously preserves the sites as a charming part of California's past, the country of Brett Harte, Mark Twain, and John Fremont.

From rolling hills studded with black oaks and manzanita to the majestic peaks of the Sierra Nevada, the Mother Lode encompasses a unique scenic wonderland. Here you find not only a true four-season climate, but variation on the seasons, depending on the altitude you choose. From mild winters and warm summers in Jackson and Angels Camp to deep snowpack and cool summers in Lake Tahoe, you have a complete selection of climates and seasonal colors. Trout streams are well stocked, with rare golden trout waiting to be hooked in higher lakes.

GOLD COUNTRY AREA COST OF LIVING					
Percentage of National Average	Overall 109	Housing 96	Medical 113	Groceries 112	Utilities 117

The Mother Lode encompasses a 300-mile stretch of rolling-to-rugged country that runs from Downieville in the north down to Coarsegold in the south. It takes in nine counties: Madera, Mariposa, Tuolumne, Calaveras, El Dorado, Placer, Nevada, Sierra, and Amador. Then, 100 miles to the northwest, another area of historic gold-mining towns spreads across several more counties: Butte, Siskiyou, Tehama, Shasta, Trinity, and Lassen.

By the way, the forty-niners didn't get *all* the gold. They left enough to keep hundreds of weekend prospectors and amateur miners working at their dredges and sluice boxes. With most of the countryside designated public land and national forest, you'll have ample opportunity to try your luck if you wish. A favorite family outing is to take a picnic lunch and a couple of gold pans and spend the afternoon working one of the many creeks and streams that traverse hills covered with oak, pine, and cedar. Some people do quite well, but you can expect them to be very close-mouthed about where they found their private bonanzas. Others are ashamed that they can't locate much gold, and they lie about how much they find. That's what I do.

Amador County   As an example of the Gold Country, let's look in detail at one location in the center of the Mother Lode. Amador County straddles historic Highway 49, which runs along the route of the trail that once connected the busiest of the mining towns from north to south. One of the richest gold-mining districts, Amador County accounted for more than half of all the gold harvested from the Mother Lode. Here are found such fascinating towns as Jackson, Sutter Creek, Volcano, Fiddletown, and Plymouth. Drytown, now a wide spot on Highway 49, was once not so small or so dry. At its prime, the mining camp boasted twenty-seven saloons. That was before it drew the attention of indignant prohibitionists, after which it earned the title of Drytown.

Loaded with relics of the past, each of these towns takes pride in maintaining and restoring its historic old buildings. Jackson, the largest town in the county, is an intriguing mixture of old and new, with the downtown preserved in the tradition of the gold rush days. Brick and stone buildings line narrow streets, adorned with iron shutters and wrought-iron balconies in the style of the mid-1800s. Yet, the newer outskirts have modern ranch-style homes as California-looking as you might expect to find anywhere. Like other Mother Lode towns, Jackson is proud of its restored old brick and Victorian frame houses, with all the modern conveniences added. Housing costs are below national average, and far, far below what you would pay in the larger California cities. Because of very mild winters, mobile homes are practical. You can choose from five mobile–home parks in the county.

Highway 88, the trans-Sierra route, cuts through Jackson on its way east across the mountains at Carson Pass and down into Nevada. Highway 88 was once designated as the country's most scenic highway by *Parade* magazine. It winds through Pine Grove and Volcano, past Inspiration Point, Maiden's Grave, and Tragedy Springs, just to name a few historical sights along the way. This route was once called the Carson Emigrant Trail because of its popularity with gold-seeking settlers.

In more mountainous western locations, climate varies with altitude, and the altitude varies wildly in Amador County. Lower elevations start at 200 feet and climb all the way to more than 9,000 feet. Magnificent views of snow-covered peaks, mountain lakes, and meadows are everywhere. With low summer humidity, even the warmest days are comfortable. Winters are short and mild (January highs average 56 degrees), and the area enjoys a true spring and colorful fall season.

When I asked Marcia Oxford of the Amador County Chamber of Commerce why she thinks retirees are moving there, she replied: "It *must* be attractive here; almost 50 percent of our population consists of retirees. Because of the geographical diversity, people can live in the rolling foothills, in the pines and evergreens, or higher in the snow country. We enjoy four distinct seasons, the air is clean, and there's a wonderful, warm small-town care and friendliness that we all enjoy."

Grass Valley/Nevada City   Other popular retirement towns are found to the north of Jackson, places like Grass Valley and Nevada City, which are a bit more sophisticated and offer a more cosmopolitan charm than Jackson. The area teems with a sense of history and abundant natural beauty. Gold Rush architecture with white church steeples and Victorian buildings is shaded by century-old sugar maples and liquidambars that early settlers brought with them from the New England states. Thousands of miners came here in the 1800s—this was one of California's richest gold-producing regions—and today retirees are finding their personal bonanzas in quality living.

The towns of Grass Valley and Nevada City sit in the foothills of the Sierra Nevada Mountains, at an average elevation of 2,500 feet. The surroundings vary from rolling hills to rugged peaks, with plentiful forests of oak, pine, cedar, and fir. Residents enjoy four gentle seasons, with homes perched above the fog line, yet below the heavy snow line.

Grass Valley is the larger town, with almost 10,000 residents, and nearby Nevada City adds another 3,000. Conveniently close to Interstate 80, trips to Reno (ninety minutes) or Sacramento (one hour) or San Francisco (three hours) are a piece of cake for those who crave action from time to time. Many dynamic cultural activities are available right here, however, including classical music festivals, concerts, and theater productions. Several theater companies entertain with productions almost year-round. A community college is the latest addition to the cultural scene.

For outdoor recreation, the region is filled with lakes, streams, parks, campgrounds, and hiking trails. Winter skiing is only an hour away at half a dozen resorts, and the short drive makes returning home after a hard afternoon's skiing less of a chore. Summers see very little rainfall, so you'll have plenty of sunshine to accompany you on fishing trips and picnics. There are four golf courses—one public and three private.

Nevada City, by the way, has an exceptionally active senior center, with plenty of activities and volunteer opportunities galore. The Gold Country Telecare network keeps folks in touch by phone for problem solving, assistance, and counseling. Telecare volunteers

AMADOR–GRASS VALLEY WEATHER						
In degrees Fahrenheit						
	Jan.	April	July	Oct.	Rain	Snow
Daily Highs	54	62	85	71	40"	5"
Daily Lows	35	38	54	44		

are available for seniors who can't afford to hire someone to fix a leaky faucet or to repair porch steps. Legal and tax questions are covered by other volunteers and still others make sure seniors don't miss shopping, recreational activities, or an appointment with the dentist. Medical care is excellent, with a nonprofit hospital with a 124-bed acute–care facility offering state-of-the-art diagnostic, surgical, and therapeutic equipment.

Scattered around the countryside are any number of smaller communities, historic places such as Rough and Ready, Gold Run, or Colfax, away from town but only a few miles from shopping. Before you settle on a gold-mining location, you must see 'em all!

Paradise   About 100 miles to the north of Amador County, the Feather River yielded another rich harvest of shining metal. Scattered above the canyon on a place called Nimshew Ridge, a collection of little villages and mining camps sprang up, with vivid names such as Dogtown, Toadtown, Poverty Ridge, and Whiskey Flats. At Dogtown (now Magalia) a prospector uncovered a fifty-nine-pound gold nugget back in 1859. Several nuggets weighing up to nine pounds each turned up later, but after the Dogtown nugget, everything else seemed anticlimactic.

Apparently, folks grew tired of explaining why they lived in Whiskey Flats or on Poverty Ridge, so they agreed to form one town and call it something more romantic: "Paradise." Thousands of modern-day retirees believe they've found their paradise here. Forty-nine percent of the residents are older than fifty-five.

Paradise and nearby Magalia share a particularly scenic location. Heavily forested, sitting at an altitude of 2,000 feet, the area is below the snow belt, yet above the Sacramento Valley's smog level. (There isn't really that much smog in the valley except when farmers burn the rice fields every fall.) This higher altitude also means summer temperatures ten degrees lower than the valley floor below.

Being below the snow belt doesn't mean that Paradise is snow-free. Around these parts, higher elevations (more than 4,000) are generally covered with snow most of the winter. When winter rains fall on Paradise, it's a good bet that it'll be snowing in Stirling City, some 20 miles away and a thousand feet higher. But, when conditions are right, Paradise's rain turns to snow. At this altitude, snow doesn't come down in small flakes and particles, it forms large puffs the size of golf balls. Very soft and fluffy, it piles up incredibly fast.

What might be a 4-inch snow in Stirling City becomes 12 inches in Paradise or Magalia. Oldtimers tell of 3 feet of snow falling overnight. This type of snow melts quickly, however, as soon as the sun warms things up. Even in the coldest months, afternoons are usually warm enough for a light sweater to feel comfortable, and golf courses are open year-round.

Contractors take care to build homes without disturbing the trees any more than necessary. Building lots are large, usually a quarter to half an acre, sometimes several acres, and houses are scattered so that it's hard to believe there could be 40,000 people living in the area. With low housing density and lots of forest, Paradise is a sanctuary for wild animals, since hunting is prohibited in town. Deer and raccoons saunter about town insolently, as if they were taxpayers.

Adequate shopping facilities, with several tastefully done centers, make for convenience. Cable TV is available and so is that ultimate mark of civilization, home pizza delivery. A drawback is that Paradise lacks both public transportation and intercity bus service; an auto is necessary.

As a normal response to a large retiree population, health care is unusually good. There's a 109-bed hospital, two convalescent hospitals, three medical care centers, and several residential-care and guest homes. This large population of retirees means lots of organized activities and clubs. In addition to the usual AARP organization, there is a Golden Fifties Club, a Retired Teachers Association, a senior singles club, and a couple of senior citizens' political action coalitions.

Paradise-Magalia is a peaceful and safe place, ranking seventh highest in our safety research. Many of the local cops, like the retirees, are from Los Angeles. When Paradise organized its own police force, the city recruited in Southern California. One ex-L.A.P.D. officer said, "What a difference! Here I spend my time helping people instead of dealing with criminals. In Los Angeles it was always 'them against us.'"

PARADISE WEATHER						
In degrees Fahrenheit						
	Jan.	April	July	Oct.	Rain	Snow
Daily Highs	52	71	92	85	45"	18"
Daily Lows	32	45	61	48		

Because almost half the population lives on fixed incomes, housing costs and rents haven't been pushed to the ridiculous highs of some other parts of California. Home prices start at around $60,000 for a modest place to over $200,000 for something with a spectacular view of the Feather River Canyon below Nimshew Ridge. Because of the large number of absentee owners, rentals for two- to three-bedroom homes are plentiful and rents affordable. Mobile homes on landscaped, residential lots are particularly good bargains, and sometimes are difficult to distinguish from conventional housing.

Chico   In contrast, only a twenty-minute drive from the mountain city of Paradise is the flatland city of Chico, another excellent retirement location. Although its population is about the same as Paradise's, the two places are a world apart. Chico is a typical Sacramento Valley town, with live oaks and huge ash trees shading quiet streets on topography as flat as a table.

The thing that lifts Chico above most small, agriculturally centered valley towns is its university and vibrant academic timbre. Precisely because of the town's laid-back atmosphere, away from the distraction of big-city life or surfing beaches, Chico State University is preferred by many California parents when helping their kids select a school. Like all California state universities, Chico State encourages senior citizen participation with free and reduced tuition rates. Cultural events, such as concerts, plays, lectures, and foreign films are plentiful and, more often than not, free.

Many good home buys in Chico are found in older neighborhoods and in some more recent developments on the edge of town. Typical construction is frame with stucco finish, favored because of its resilience in earthquakes. (A brick building tends to crack and suffer damage; a frame house simply twists and rolls with the shaking.) Because of the university, housing prices are higher than in ordinary Sacramento Valley cities, and inexpensive rentals are either snatched up by students or are located in student neighborhoods where stereo music is commonly played at a volume that blisters wallpaper.

Retirees living in Chico point out the advantage of being close to the mountains—good fishing, hunting, and camping. A short drive takes you to the natural beauty and the recreational opportunities of the Feather River Canyon wilderness. Skiing is enjoyed at

CHICO WEATHER						
In degrees Fahrenheit						
	Jan.	April	July	Oct.	Rain	Snow
Daily Highs	54	73	98	79	22"	1"
Daily Lows	36	44	59	47		

Inskip, about forty minutes away, and some of the best striped bass in the West are caught in the nearby Sacramento River. Incidentally, fishermen haul monster sturgeon from this river, many fish tipping the scale at more than 200 pounds! Since sturgeon is a game fish and not sold commercially, few people have ever tasted a succulent steak from one of these large creatures. It's like no other fish you've ever tasted—as firm as lobster and as juicy as a filet mignon, yet with a flavor closer to frogs' legs than fish.

Chico weather, as in all Central Valley towns, is both a blessing and a drawback, depending on your opinion of how hot summers should be. You can find days on end with temperatures approaching 100 degrees. Balance that against the warm, seldom-frosty winter days, and I believe Chico's weather comes out a winner. After all, when the summer gets going, that's the time for you to get going for the nearby mountains for a picnic beside a cool stream or a day's prospecting and panning for gold in the Feather River.

Dunsmuir   The Sacramento River, which passes through Chico on its way to San Francisco Bay, has its origins farther north, past Redding and beautiful Lake Shasta, in the mountains not far from the town of Dunsmuir. Dunsmuir sits in a canyon, overlooked by ridges covered with Christmas-tree pines and segmented by streets that climb steeply from river bottom to the interstate highway above town. The town enjoys a spectacular year-round view of snow-covered Mt. Shasta in the distance. This ancient volcano is one of the highest peaks on the continent and offers some pretty fair skiing at a place called Snowman's Hill.

Dunsmuir is an old town, with few homes newer than fifty years old. A sense of history permeates the old-fashioned downtown section and its one main street. Here the bus station is still called the "stage stop" by older residents, and the Greyhound bus is called the "stage." Although some mining went on in the area, Dunsmuir originated as a roundhouse and repair service for passing trains, providing fuel and water for the locomotives and food for the dining cars.

DUNSMUIR WEATHER						
In degrees Fahrenheit						
	Jan.	April	July	Oct.	Rain	Snow
Daily Highs	50	53	90	68	30"	18"
Daily Lows	30	36	58	39		

With the decline of steam engines, the original purpose of the town faded. Some railroaders moved away when they lost their jobs; others retired and stayed there. Thus began a continuing tradition of Dunsmuir as a retirement location. When the railroaders left, the bottom dropped out of the real estate market, which didn't have far to drop, since property was always quite reasonable. Retirees found this an ideal location, with great fishing, economical living, a gorgeous view from the front porch every morning, and unforgettable sunsets.

Lurking trout, sometimes large native ones, tempt the fisherman to the shores of the Sacramento River. Wild blackberry bushes on the banks yield delicious makings for cobblers, should the fish not be biting that day. The river has recovered nicely from a horrendous pesticide spill a couple of years past. Once again the odor of rainbow trout frying for breakfast fills the morning air.

Because Interstate 5 bypasses the town by a quarter-mile, the pace along the town's main street is leisurely and unhurried. Dunsmuir's northern location and 2,300-foot elevation ensure at least a couple of good winter snowstorms. Since I spent one winter here working on the old *Dunsmuir News,* I can attest that snow here is of a special sort—soft, fluffy, and pretty (as long as you don't have to shovel the blasted stuff). But it does pile up quickly. The canyon turns into a billowy white winter fantasyland for a day or two, until a warm rain clears it all away.

Fall River Mills/Burney One last example of Gold Country retirement is called the Intermountain Area and nestles between the Sierra Nevada and the Cascade mountain ranges in the northeast corner of California. This is just one of many such picturesque and unspoiled areas of the state with inexpensive living. The highway east from Redding winds past several abandoned mines as it makes its way to the towns of Burney and Fall River Mills. Today, gold mining is no longer an economic force,

FALL RIVER MILLS–BURNEY WEATHER						
In degrees Fahrenheit						
	Jan.	April	July	Oct.	Rain	Snow
Daily Highs	40	74	91	69	40"	25"
Daily Lows	28	47	68	46		

having been pushed aside by wild-rice farming in Fall River Mills and lumber mills in Burney.

Tall Douglas firs shade Burney's streets and homes. A recent forest fire devastated large tracts of forest, but firefighters heroically stopped it before it could damage the town. Twenty miles away, in a sharply different terrain, are Burney's sister towns of Fall River Mills and McArthur. The panorama in these towns is a wide, grassy valley circled by tree-clad mountains. A remarkably clear stream (the Fall River) wells up from the depths of a volcanic formation a few miles away and collects the waters of a dozen sparkling trout streams as it meanders through the valley. The views are enhanced by Mt. Lassen (10,466 feet) to the southeast and by majestic, snowcapped Mt. Shasta (14,162 feet) to the northwest.

"Fall River Mills," I hear you saying. "Never heard of it. Why would anyone want to live there?" Well, you've heard of one of Fall River Mills's earlier residents: Bing Crosby. With all of the country to choose from, Bing bought a ranch there as a place to raise his boys. (Another Hollywood personality owns the ranch now; I won't say who, because local people don't like to bring attention to the town that way.)

Bing's favorite sports were golf and fly-fishing. The superb trout streams throughout the Intermountain Area satisfied the latter interest, but Bing could not survive without golf. This explains the existence of a beautiful eighteen-hole championship golf course located just west of Fall River Mills on the main highway. It's reputed to rank among the top fifty courses in the United States. The unique layout of the course poses a challenge to professionals and amateurs alike. Amenities include a restaurant, a clubhouse, and a pro shop, with other facilities planned for the future.

Between these two towns you'll find most of the services available in a city, yet the towns cling to an away-from-it-all atmosphere. Burney has a bustling "downtown," complete with shopping district; Fall River Mills is scattered over several miles of highway and ends at an even smaller town, McArthur. Even though the nearest city of any size, Redding, is an hour's drive away, the Intermountain Area is self-sufficient, with shopping centers, banks, restaurants, and a hospital.

Those looking for low-cost living would be hard-pressed to find a better bargain. Three-bedroom houses sell for as little as $65,000 in Burney. Since land is inexpensive, small lots are rare. Fall River Mills property is priced a bit higher due to a recent real estate shortage. In a small place like this, just a few buyers can create a scarcity.

The Mountain Senior Center, located in Burney, is a complex consisting of single-family homes and one-bedroom apartments situated within easy walking distance of shopping and medical facilities. It also features a park, community center, and RV storage, all designed for use by people age fifty-five or older. Free bus transportation is also available to seniors throughout the Intermountain area for special needs.

The waterways of the Intermountain Area offer many varieties of fishing. Choose from deep, cold lakes or mountain streams for bass and trout; try the warmer waters for catfish and crappie. Lakes Britton, Eastman, Fall River, Baum Crystal, and Iron Canyon are a lure to all types of fishermen. With a short drive to the northwest, fishermen will find other hot spots on Bear Creek, Medicine Lake, McCloud River, and others. Two wild trout streams—Hat Creek and Fall River—offer trophy trout to the dedicated fly-fisherman or those fishing with artificial lures. (Live bait is prohibited.)

Northern California Coast

The northern California coast is highlighted by the urbanity and sophistication of the San Francisco Bay area. But the City by the Bay shouldn't be your only stop on a tour of this area's retirement possibilities. After you cross the Golden Gate Bridge going north, Highway 1 winds through some of the most peaceful and rural landscapes to be found anywhere. The towns are small, neighborly, and uncrowded. The only large town on the California stretch of coast is Eureka, the next "metropolitan" area being the Coos Bay–North Bend area in Oregon. Several picturesque villages sit along the coast, interspersed with forest and grazing land, sleepy and laid-back, just as they should be. Small, family-owned wineries and their tasting rooms make for interesting visits. If you are looking for discos, beach parties, and tourist traps, you are much too far north.

NORTHERN CALIFORNIA COAST

Eureka/Arcata

Mendocino/ Fort Bragg

San Francisco

Along this coast the traditional industry has always been lumbering, which appears to be in a permanent state of depression all over the West. The second industry is fishing, much of which is done by amateurs or people just out for fun. Since neither industry is hiring workers, jobs are scarce and younger people are leaving for the cities. That means housing is affordable. The moral of this story is, if you need to work part-time to make ends meet, forget about the northwest coast. If you can satisfy your need for work through meaningful volunteer jobs, you will do just fine.

If you are members of that class that hates hot summers and cold winters, you've come to the right place. Frost is all but unheard-of, with 40 degrees just about as cold as it ever gets in January. Highs in January in Eureka, for example, average 53 degrees; but the July and August highs rarely top 70 degrees! Compare that with *your* town's average July temperatures. Every night of the year you will sleep under blankets; an air conditioner would be a waste of money. On the other hand, since lows are never subfreezing, many homes don't have central heating systems, depending upon a wall furnace or fireplace for comfort.

California's Napa Valley wine-producing country and its delightful little towns and villages are great for retirement. People choose places like Calistoga, Healdsburg, or St. Helena, just to name a few. For quality living at moderate costs, the Napa–Sonoma region merits closer investigation. But there's a lesser-known wine country—just as pretty, less crowded, and not far away—on the Mendocino Coast, with the Pacific Ocean on one side and the low coastal mountains on the other.

San Francisco   Even folks who don't care for California fall in love with this fabulous city of cities located on beautiful San Francisco Bay. No other city I've seen—anywhere I've ever visited—compares with it for breathtaking scenic vistas, restaurants, architecture, cultural ambience, and excitement. If you haven't guessed it by now, I'll admit that this is my favorite city in the whole world.

It's a great place to visit, and anyone who passes up a chance to spend some time here is missing a wonderful experience. Although I generally recommend against retirement in a large city, in the case of San Francisco, I'll have to make an exception. Not for just anyone, mind you, because it's expensive, it's crowded, and has unsafe neighborhoods. But the excitement of San Francisco, its sophisticated ambience, and glamorous setting make it all worthwhile, for some folks anyway.

The "City"—as it's called hereabouts—is composed of neighborhoods, each distinct and sometimes radically dissimilar from the others. Our favorite activity is exploring these neighborhoods (or districts). Cow Hollow is so different from the nearby Marina district that you can tell where you are just by the types of restaurants. Chinatown, Japantown, the Fillmore, the Financial district, the Mission district, Fisherman's Wharf, Potrero Hill, Twin Peaks, the Tenderloin, Castro Street, Pacific Heights, the Western Addition, the Sunset district—all these places are special to San Franciscans. Each has its distinctive flavor and color, sometimes even a different language. You'll encounter Irish enclaves, where in pubs you'll hear a strong brogue spoken over glasses of Guinness stout; other areas where Italian or Spanish is the lingua franca; and of course, Chinatown, with its myriad of restaurants, shops, and mysterious alleyways.

Restaurant exploration is a favorite pastime here. In the Mission district you can order *papusas,* enchiladas, empanadas, gallo pinto, and even a hamburger or pizza. Chinatown has my favorite: dim sum breakfasts with shrimp rolls, steamed dumplings with quail eggs poached over the tops, *char siu, hoc gau, siu mai,* and on and on. (Okay, I also admit that restaurants are a major factor in my evaluation of San Francisco neighborhoods.)

San Francisco's suburbs are exceptionally high-quality places for retirement, but only for those who can afford the high cost of housing. The nicer neighborhoods are costly, but enjoy higher levels of personal safety. Rents are also steep, but not in proportion to the cost of buying property. For example, we have friends who live in a lovely home with a marvelous view of the bay. The value of the property is $550,000, yet it rents for only $1,800 a month. Although this

SAN FRANCISCO WEATHER					
In degrees Fahrenheit					
	Jan.	April	July	Oct.	Rain	Snow
Daily Highs	56	63	71	70	20"	—
Daily Lows	42	47	54	51		

SAN FRANCISCO AREA COST OF LIVING					
Percentage of	Overall	Housing	Medical	Groceries	Utilities
National Average	125	199	115	113	100

may sound like a formidable rent, it amounts to a 3.2 percent return on an investment of $550,000. Even municipal bonds pay bigger returns than that, which leads me to question the wisdom of real estate investment here.

In short, unless you can afford to pay $1,200 a month or more, San Francisco is best visited rather than chosen as a retirement location. If the idea of high rent doesn't put you off, the City by the Bay is an excellent place for a six-month or longer adventure in dining, theater, museums, and walking tours. However, when choosing an apartment, make sure a garage parking space is included. Otherwise you will spend your six months looking for a parking space.

My personal preference for quality retirement in this area is in the southern portion of the San Francisco Bay, places like Los Gatos or Saratoga (which ranked number *one* in our safety research). On the edge of the Santa Cruz mountains, with wooded hills, even some redwood groves, these offer some of the prettiest home settings with a climate at least ten degrees warmer than San Francisco. When the coast is fogged in, you can be sure of sunshine in Los Gatos and the Santa Cruz mountains. To get to the City from here requires about a fifty-minute drive, and getting to the ocean beaches in Santa Cruz takes about twenty-five minutes.

Mendocino/Fort Bragg   The Mendocino Coast is accessed only by a slow, two-lane coastal highway; most casual tourists and hurried travelers choose to travel inland, along multi-lane, high-speed Highway 101. This leaves the towns along the coast untouched by those who aren't specifically interested in enjoying the special ambience of this area.

Founded in 1852 as a mill town, Mendocino started with a Cape Cod flavor that has been carefully preserved. This is a community of artisans, which accounts for the many art galleries and boutiques in the town. It's a small place, unincorporated, with approximately 1,100 residents, although more than 8,000 live in the surrounding area. The village sits high on a bluff, surrounded on three sides by the Pacific Ocean. Hollywood filmed several motion pictures here, taking full advantage of Mendocino's picturesque setting.

Popular with tourists and those looking for beautiful seascapes, the basic business here deals with art in one form or another. Mendocino is popular with those looking for quality living in a rural, cool (but not cold) climate. Housing prices are not as inexpensive as you might expect; well-off San Franciscans like their weekend homes here. Single-family homes of two to three bedrooms range from $175,000 to $378,000. Rentals vary from $600 on up. Expect to pay $1,200 rent for a place with a gorgeous view. But when you leave the immediate vicinity of the town center, prices drop considerably.

Ten miles north of Mendocino on Highway 1 is the working community of Fort Bragg, a lumbering and fishing community of more than 6,000 residents. A no-nonsense business section makes Fort Bragg the place where people come for necessary services and shopping. It's an exceptionally clean and attractive place, more modern in appearance than Mendocino. Several local performing-arts companies produce concerts, stage plays, musicals, and revues. San Francisco Symphony musicians join local musicians for the Mendocino Music Festival in July.

Housing costs are in line with local wages, thus less expensive than Mendocino. Both communities are attracting retirees as well

MENDOCINO–FORT BRAGG WEATHER						
In degrees Fahrenheit						
	Jan.	April	July	Oct.	Rain	Snow
Daily Highs	53	54	64	63	39"	1"
Daily Lows	41	44	52	49		

as artisans, many coming from the San Francisco and Los Angeles areas.

Eureka/Arcata   This is another area that owes its origins to the gold rush. In 1850 its location on Humboldt Bay made it ideal as a port to supply mines east in Trinity County. Eureka flourished overnight as gold seekers poured into the port fresh from San Francisco. Arcata, on the north side of Humboldt Bay, was also founded in 1850. Brett Harte put in a brief stint as editor at a newspaper here until some local toughs took exception to his writing. He hopped a steamboat for San Francisco, where he achieved fame for his tales of life in the mining camps.

After the gold fields played out, prospectors stayed and looked for steadier work as fishermen, farmers, and lumberjacks. The stately redwoods became the backbone of the economy in the late 1800s. Victorian homes built of almost indestructible redwood lumber grace the landscape of Eureka and the surrounding communities. These old homes are showcases for now-forgotten arts of carpentry. Since many early settlers were lumber barons, you can imagine the care and attention to detail with which the artisans constructed the homes. For this reason, the town has been declared a State Historical Landmark.

Humboldt Bay fishing highlights Eureka's economy nowadays. More than 300 fishing vessels call this home port and land more rockfish, crab, oysters, and shrimp than any other place in California. Strolling along Eureka's quaint Old Town waterfront is a favorite activity, breathing in the fresh sea air, watching boats returning with catches of salmon and tasty Dungeness crab.

Although its population is less than 30,000, Eureka is the center, culturally and commercially, of another 45,000 residents in the immediate urban area. Approximately 86 percent of Humboldt County's 117,000 population lives within a 20-mile radius of Eureka. The famous Redwood Empire forests begin near the

EUREKA–ARCATA WEATHER						
In degrees Fahrenheit						
	Jan.	April	July	Oct.	Rain	Snow
Daily Highs	53	55	61	60	39"	—
Daily Lows	42	44	52	48		

edge of town and climb the mountains beyond and into the Trinity Alps, with backdrops as high as 6,000 feet. Although this is primarily a mountainous region encompassing six wild and scenic river systems and stands of majestic redwood groves, Eureka itself is located on a level coastal plain. Eighty percent of the county is forested public lands.

The weather here, typical of beach towns along the coast north to Washington, is a place for retirees who hate the thought of hot, steamy summers or icy, frigid winters. Except for more rain in the winter months, there's little difference in the weather year-round. A sweater feels comfortable almost every evening of the year, and noonday weather is seldom, if ever, hot enough to make you sweat. Air-conditioning is something people here read about. Winters are mild enough that many homes heat with fireplaces or woodstoves. Many older houses have fireplaces in every room. Annual rainfall here is around 38 inches, a lot for California but much less than most Midwestern and Eastern cities. Snow shovels are as unnecessary as air-conditioning.

Located on Highway 101, a main north-south artery, the Eureka area also has an airport with regional carriers for short flights to San Francisco and other important local cities. The airport is located a few miles north of Arcata, about 15 miles from Eureka, and is served by a shuttle bus.

Three excellent hospitals serve the area, one each for Eureka and the neighboring communities of Arcata and Fortuna. Arcata's hospital can boast that its staff makes house calls, since they operate a home-care service for those who need ongoing treatment outside the hospital. The service is carried out by registered nurses, home health aides, and physical therapists under the direction of a physician.

The Eureka Senior Center, housed in an old grammar school building, is one of the most extensive and comprehensive we've seen. From classes such as arts and crafts to an Alzheimer's day-care center, the services are superb. The Retired Senior Volunteer Program counts on more than 700 retirees who contribute their skills and interests in service to the community.

Fishing, of course, is a favorite sport here, with salmon, albacore, and Dungeness crab to catch. With generally benign weather, some kind of fishing, crabbing, or clamming is possible all year. For those who get seasick, the country immediately behind the town, continuing 100 miles or so, is full of great trout streams. Deer, river otters, herons, and other wildlife are plentiful, for much of the Coast Range and inland Klamath Mountains are jealously preserved as wildlife areas.

Nearby Arcata (pop. 17,000) is the home of Humboldt State University, one of the area's economic mainstays. With a good reputation as a serious school, the university is also the source of many cultural and intellectual events open to the public. In addition, there is the College of the Redwoods, a two-year school, and Eureka Adult School, with many community locations. The academic atmosphere complements the old-fashioned, Victorian atmosphere of the area, a place where mountains, forest, and blue Pacific all come together.

Along this northern coast, all the way to Washington state, low wages and living costs are the rule. As a result, housing is quite reasonable—probably as low as you might expect to find anywhere on the West Coast. It's not difficult to find homes selling for $60,000 or less. For $75,000 and up you can buy a new place. We looked at several Victorians—our favorite going for $94,000, had high ceilings, a claw-foot bathtub, an antique wood cookstove, and three bedrooms. Mobile homes are located away from the city's residential sections and seem to be in abundant supply, because they sell at very reasonable prices. In the countryside, many place mobile homes on spacious wooded lots. Except for Arcata, where students compete for housing, rentals are readily available.

A place famous for Victorians is Ferndale, a short drive south of Eureka. Started in the late 1800s as a prosperous dairy center, the early settlers built some splendidly ornate homes that became known as Butterfat Palaces. Even though the town is a tourist attraction, it's mostly a "stop-for-lunch, look around and get-going-again" sort of tourism. Retirees find it a place to stay. Ferndale, like the other towns around Eureka, preserves a small-town atmosphere of neighborliness. Bed-and-breakfast places are popular.

The Southern California Dream

When most folks think about California, they conjure images of Hollywood, surfboards, swimming pools, and convertibles. They picture southern California towns like Santa Barbara, Beverly Hills, or San Diego with broad, palm-lined boulevards, pastel-colored mansions, and ultra-modern apartment buildings. Easterners imagine southern California as a place to fantasize over, not a practical place to live.

Although some of these images are indeed true, hundreds of thousands of retired folks will tell you they wouldn't consider living anywhere else. Don't misunderstand: This is not a place to look for bargain living; most southern California locations are not cheap places to live. In many neighborhoods, Los Angeles home prices are sixty-one percent higher than national averages! Yet, there are some excellent southern California communities where housing is comparable to many parts of the country—not next door to movie stars, but certainly in pleasant, safe neighborhoods.

SOUTHERN CALIFORNIA

San Luis Obispo
Pismo Beach
Santa Barbara
Los Angeles
San Diego

Southern California living costs aren't out of line; after all, groceries, clothing, automobiles, and such cost about the same no matter where you live. Competition for consumer business keeps prices competitive in the Southland (as folks here like to refer to their home). You'll find the Los Angeles area always has among the lowest gasoline prices in the state. And, because the climate is mild to warm, neither air-conditioning nor heating costs make drastic dents in the budget.

Why do people keep coming to southern California? Primarily because of the weather, but also because of the wide variety of things to do and sights to see. Places like Los Angeles and Santa Barbara owe much of their early growth to retirees coming to visit and to stay. Land promoters used to run cross-country passenger trains with free tickets just so retirees could investigate southern California as a retirement haven. When the unsuspecting retirees were hooked on the lovely orange–grove dreamland, the slick promoters would sell them building lots for as much as $175 per parcel and then a house for an additional $3,000—places that wouldn't sell for much more than $375,000 today. Unscrupulous!

San Diego   San Diego, with a population of well over a million, is an excellent example of a city in transition from old to new. The downtown section, once rather ordinary and deteriorating—as most U.S. cities are lately—has been transformed into an exciting, welcoming city center. Trees, landscaping, and careful planning are doing the trick.

The attraction here is the superb weather—statistically, San Diego has the best climate in the continental United States. It never freezes or snows, and it rains a scant 11 inches a year, just enough to keep shrubbery and flowers fresh. A constant breeze from the Pacific pushes heat into the desert and nullifies cold snaps. There is no smog or air pollution, and little need for air-conditioning. This results in less use of utilities and lower bills.

The San Diego area has an unusually large percentage of retirees. There are more than 100 senior citizens' organizations, with membership totaling over 100,000. Numerous life-care centers and seniors-only apartments and housing complexes are scattered around the region.

The big drawback with San Diego is expensive housing, some of the costliest in the nation. The median price of a single-family home is almost $190,000. Selling prices of homes are inflated, rents are costly, and mobile-home parks are scarce and ridiculously expensive; many have been converted to commercial use, with tenants forced to look for other nonexistent parks. The inflated cost of

SAN DIEGO AREA WEATHER

In degrees Fahrenheit

	Jan.	April	July	Oct.	Rain	Snow
Daily Highs	65	68	76	75	9"	—
Daily Lows	48	55	65	60		

SAN DIEGO AREA COST OF LIVING

Percentage of National Average	Overall	Housing	Medical	Groceries	Utilities
	127	161	123	123	104

keeping a roof over your head drags the overall cost of living index up as well.

Like Los Angeles, however, it isn't necessary to live in the city itself to enjoy the weather and ambience. At the eastern edge of San Diego the country turns into desert hills, with dramatic boulders and rock formations garnished with cactus and desert brush. Within easy shopping distance from San Diego are the towns of El Cajon, Alpine, Lakeside, and several other smaller communities. Land is far less expensive and lots tend to be spacious, sometimes large enough to keep horses. Riding trails take off in all directions to wander through the empty mountain country. Although housing is less expensive, the tradeoff is warmer summers and cooler winters.

From your suburban home you can run into San Diego to enjoy professional sports: the San Diego Chargers, the Padres, the Hawks, or the Andy Williams PGA Open. San Diego State brings collegiate football as well as the usual artistic presentations, and the San Diego Opera, Theater, and Symphony are nationally renowned.

As an example of a nearby retirement location, El Cajon (pop. 86,000) maintains a separate identity, self-contained as far as retirement living is concerned, yet only 15 miles via interstate to downtown San Diego. Senior citizens account for about 19 percent of El Cajon's population and enjoy numerous services provided by the East County Council on Aging and Grossmont Hospital. Two other hospitals are there, including a Kaiser Foundation facility.

For those who like dry, warm weather, El Cajon is a good prospect for retirement. It isn't all that hot, either. According to the U.S. Weather Bureau, the maximum temperatures for July average 88 degrees (at only 28 percent humidity), and January high temperatures average 67 degrees. How does that compare to your summer weather?

Northeast of San Diego about 30 miles is the town of Escondido (pop. 80,000). The climate is similar to El Cajon's—dry and pleasant—but it is situated in rolling, grassy country. Low mountains loom in the background, and ranches and homes on acreage lots dominate the outlying areas here. Many homes have horse stables. Houses and condos rent for considerably less here than in San Diego, and homes sell for 25 to 50 percent less than similar homes in the city. Escondido offers most amenities retirees demand: a hospital, an excellent senior service center, a community college, and adult education programs that are free to those older than sixty.

Los Angeles   This is where the southern California dream started. Retirement became big business back in the 1880s when promoters began capitalizing on its ideal climate. From that time on, retirement remained big as the town grew larger and larger. But Los Angeles didn't simply grow larger, as most cities do; it grew quite unpredictably, spreading out in this direction and that, until the result is a city that looks different and is different from any other major city in the world.

Recently an Argentinian couple came to visit us. We met them at the Los Angeles airport and treated them to a sightseeing tour. They were excited at the opportunity of finally seeing fabulous Los Angeles. But after an hour of driving around, they became puzzled. "But where is the city?" they asked. "We were expecting tall buildings. Everything here is small!" We drove through Hollywood, Beverly Hills, and all the other obligatory areas, and they found few places that matched their image of what Los Angeles should be. To them, a real city should resemble Buenos Aires, Paris, or New York. There should be tall, elegant apartment buildings, graceful skyscrapers, fancy restaurants with sidewalk cafes, and all the metropolitan delights that combine to make a real city. Instead they found single-family homes and one- and two-story commercial buildings. The occasional tall building seemed lonely and out of place.

In most large cities of the world land is at a premium, far too valuable to waste on lawns and landscaping. Buildings start at the sidewalk and rise as high as possible. When room is left over for a lawn, it is placed *behind* the house and jealously guarded for the family's personal use. To be sure, the Los Angeles city center does have a group of high-rises, but they are for commerce, not for people to live in. They stand out like lost visions, mistaken attempts to create something impossible: a real city.

There is, of course, a downtown section, but it isn't the same as in other big cities. People don't go downtown for Christmas shopping or to seek out those special restaurants as they do in New York, San Francisco, or Buenos Aires. People avoid the central downtown and go to the nearest shopping mall instead. Like satellites, a garland of smaller cities surrounds Los Angeles. Each features its own "downtown" focus, which could be a giant shopping mall, and in turn each is surrounded by even smaller shopping centers and neighborhoods.

LOS ANGELES WEATHER						
In degrees Fahrenheit						
	Jan.	April	July	Oct.	Rain	Snow
Daily Highs	65	67	75	74	12"	—
Daily Lows	47	52	63	59		

LOS ANGELES–LONG BEACH AREA COST OF LIVING					
Percentage of	Overall	Housing	Medical	Groceries	Utilities
National Average	126	155	115	114	120

This ring of small towns is where retirement is best considered, not in Los Angeles proper. The FBI crime charts show that some of the towns circling Los Angeles are quite safe. Hermosa Beach, Agoura Hills, and Redondo Beach, for example, rank in the top levels of personal safety. People who live here seldom if ever venture into less safe zones; they have no reason to do so.

There are so many delightful communities here that it's impossible to list them. If the weather here is a strong enough magnet, it's worth spending time driving and looking from Capistrano in the south to the San Gabriel Mountains to the north or out to the desert-like settings in the east as far as San Bernardino. By the way, the smog problem disappears as you leave the Los Angeles Basin, as does the population density. Nice mobile-home parks are increasingly plentiful the farther you travel from Los Angeles.

The area's superb year-round climate makes outdoor recreation practical, with golf, tennis, and swimming available in most every neighborhood. Wilderness areas are but one or two hours' drive from city hall. Gold panning in the San Gabriel Mountains, skiing and trout fishing at Lake Arrowhead and Big Bear, or rock-hounding in the desert—all these and more are available. Fishing off the piers, jogging, walking, or loafing on the beaches add another facet of outdoor recreation: The ocean can be enjoyed to the limit. Sailboats and fishing craft can be berthed at numerous places along the coast.

Those who locate away from the city will find that Los Angeles itself offers cultural advantages found only in big cities. World-famous art galleries, museums, and symphonies are easily accessible, as are theaters, universities, and all types of senior activities. It's a great place for short visits. Most satellite towns have community colleges and none are very far from a state university branch.

The Los Angeles area is not an inexpensive place to retire, yet it doesn't have to be prohibitive. Everybody here isn't rich; it takes some shopping to find a comfortable niche, a place where housing prices aren't off the wall. Nothing here is cheap, but compared with San Diego or Santa Barbara, real estate can be reasonable. But it's important to look beyond housing prices here; the quality of a neighborhood is far more important than affordability. The bottom line around Los Angeles is: If you can't afford to live in a safe neighborhood, forget it.

Santa Barbara   Santa Barbara started as a retirement center when wealthy people from Beverly Hills and Hollywood "discovered" it early in the century. Movie stars—whose income was matched only by real estate developers and other money-heavy people—found Santa Barbara the ideal place to get away from it all. Maintaining a weekend house in Santa Barbara, which would later become one's retirement home, became the thing to do.

Santa Barbara is indeed a lovely setting, set on a narrow coastal plain and overshadowed by the tall San Rafael Mountains. Miles of prime beaches line the coast. With typical southern California flair, the newly rich built mansions and lavish homes overlooking the beaches, in the town, and up the sides of the mountains. Stucco Spanish and Moorish palaces with red-tiled roofs and swimming pools soon made Santa Barbara a re-creation of Beverly Hills dreams. No expense was spared in construction or landscaping. Decorative trees and plants from all over the world graced mansions and even ordinary homes. Today this landscaping has matured into a virtual arboretum.

The tradition of costly housing has endured over the years. Although Santa Barbara is one of the highest-quality retirement areas we've looked at, it is also one of the most expensive. The local newspaper shows most two- and three-bedroom houses renting for more than many retired couples earn. A few places can be found for around $1,000 a month, but they are described as "cottages" or "charming" (translation: cramped). Most house rentals fall into the $1,300 to $1,700 range. At $1,700 a month, that means $20,400 a year just for rent. In Montecito, a small neighborhood on the southern edge of the city, rents range from

SANTA BARBARA AREA COST OF LIVING

Percentage of National Average	Overall	Housing	Medical	Groceries	Utilities
	116	140	125	109	100

a low of $2,400 to $5,900 a month ($5,900 computes to $70,800 a year, not counting gas, electricity, and an occasional meal). Even studio apartments (translation: one room and a hot plate) rent for $500 to $600. We didn't have the heart to ask how much it costs to purchase a home.

If you are one of the lucky persons who can afford this kind of housing cost, you will find that Santa Barbara is a marvelous place for retirement. Its major university is a source of cultural and intellectual stimulation, and it has excellent services for senior citizens. Seven senior centers serve the community.

Santa Barbara is my favorite southern California town to visit, and I've always suspected I'd like living there as well. If it sounds good to you, don't let my assessment of the real estate situation scare you away. If you look hard enough, you can usually find something affordable, if not in the city of Santa Barbara itself, then in the more reasonably priced towns nearby. For example, if you drive north through Santa Barbara, you'll end up in the community of Goleta. This unincorporated area is contiguous with Santa Barbara, but rather less stylish and much more affordable. You'll find both retirees and families here, enjoying the lower cost of living while taking advantage of all this lovely area has to offer.

Pismo Beach/Five Cities Area   Once the butt of many Jack Benny jokes, Pismo Beach is today having the last laugh. People are discovering that it's a very pleasant place to spend a vacation, plus it's a great place to retire. Located about 200 miles north of Los Angeles, Pismo Beach has a population of around 6,000. It's just one of five adjoining towns spread along the beach and near-inland areas that gives the Five Cities its name. (By the way, the word *pismo* comes from the famous pismo clams that at one time seemed to almost pave the long stretches of sandy shoreline.) Pismo Beach is a typical example of smaller beach-retirement towns on the California coast.

Until recently, the favorite sport here was digging into sand at low tide in search of the large, succulent clams. Both locals and tourists still do, but today's clam diggers aren't like the crowds of a few years ago. Too many clam forks have thinned the mollusk population considerably. But clams are still there for the persistent, however, and fishing is still great from the long pier that juts out past the surf (no license required). Bottom fish such as ling cod, red snapper, and sand dabs are favorite catches. Fishing and clamming are year-round sports. Boat launching facilities are available at nearby Avila Beach, just north of the Five Cities.

Pismo Beach is one of the few places along the California coast where it is permissible to drive a motor vehicle onto the sand, and there are several ramps that give access to the beach. Huge, undulating sand dunes are meccas for four-wheel-drive vehicles and dune buggies. Converted Volkswagens, Jeeps, and other souped-up contraptions zip up and down the dunes like motorized roller coasters (away from the more quiet beach crowd, of course). Another favorite beach activity is horseback riding. A couple of stables rent horses for leisurely rides along the surf line. Golf is popular, with several courses in the area.

The loosely connected communities that together comprise the sprawling, lightly populated Five Cities area are Shell Beach, Oceano, Grover City, Arroyo Grande, and Pismo Beach itself. Arroyo Grande is away from the beach, but it is the largest (pop. 11,000) of the Five Cities and is considered part of the "metropolitan" area (pop. 30,000). Housing is naturally more expensive along the cliffs or anywhere an ocean view fills your picture window.

Until recently the Five Cities area was considered one of the best real estate buys on California's Central Coast. One reason for this was the exodus of workers who labored on the nearby Diablo Canyon nuclear–power project when the facility was completed. Real estate was a glut on the market for a while. But a wave of popularity and economic growth soon boosted prices to the level of similar California locations. New developments with up-scale housing

PISMO BEACH–FIVE CITIES AREA WEATHER						
In degrees Fahrenheit						
	Jan.	April	July	Oct.	Rain	Snow
Daily Highs	64	68	72	74	13"	—
Daily Lows	43	48	53	51		

have been competing with large, luxury homes. This isn't to say this is now an expensive area, just that prices are back to "normal" for California. A nearby place where real estate is a bargain, at the moment, is Avila Beach. This is due to an environmental disaster, when it was discovered that an oil-pumping facility had polluted the land under the beach. The government is in the process of completely removing the oil-soaked sand and replacing it with clean material. In the meantime, the downtown area—where tourists and residents used to enjoy a beautiful beach—is fenced off and non-functional. Real estate is at a rock bottom. However, within a year or so the restoration work will be complete, and presumably property prices will once again rise to normal.

As you might expect, where there are large numbers of retired folks, you will find active senior citizens' organizations. Pismo Beach supports several organizations, ranging from grandmothers' clubs to a singles' club for people older than sixty. You'll find an active R.S.V.P. chapter, Meals on Wheels, and a senior citizens' ride program—plus plenty of opportunities to get involved in volunteer projects.

San Luis Obispo   Just a 15-minute drive north of the Five Cities is the university town of San Luis Obispo, with a population of nearly 40,000. The school sponsors a multitude of cultural events, such as plays, lectures, and concerts, many free to senior citizens. One of San Luis Obispo's most popular sites is Mission Plaza, a place for special events such as the Mozart Festival and the Central Coast Wine Festival. (Locals consider the "Central Coast" to be anything between Santa Barbara and San Luis, whether on the coast or a few miles inland.) We consider San Luis Obispo one of the real charmers of the Central Coast. It is a beautiful place to live, with a viable downtown, and property costs are below average for California.

The relaxed, intellectual atmosphere generated by the presence of California State Polytechnic University makes San Luis Obispo a pleasant retirement location for those who don't *have* to be able to walk to the beach (yet the ocean is only a 13-mile drive from the town). The advantage of living away from the shore is more sunshine and more comfortable evenings, which can be shirtsleeve weather rather than the typically cool, sweater affairs in nearby Pismo Beach.

As in other university towns, San Luis Obispo enjoys a vibrant combination of services and facilities that satisfy tastes and requirements of students and retirees alike. Interesting yet affordable restaurants, bookstores that stock more than just best sellers, and foreign and award-winning movies that other towns would never think to present are just a few of the items that retirees say they like about living here.

San Luis Obispo, being a much larger community than the Five Cities area, naturally offers more senior citizens' activities. From bowling leagues to golf tournaments, the sports sector is covered. Woodcarving, folk and square dancing, lectures, and all sorts of social activities are there for your participation.

CHAPTER 9

The Pacific Northwest

OREGON AND WASHINGTON OFFER a dramatic collection of varied landscapes providing a broad range of choices for retirement living; there's something here for everyone. Rugged seascapes and coastal mountains contrast nicely with inland valleys and fertile plains. High mountain passes of the Oregon Cascades resolve into the lava beds and the ponderosa pines of the high desert, then into the magnificent waterfalls and cliffs of the Columbia Gorge. You can test your luck with salmon, steelhead, sturgeon, or bottom fishing—from the banks of a river, an ocean boat or in a sunny forest glade. The nice thing is that the overwhelming majority of acreage in the Pacific Northwest is publicly owned, with national forests and deserts open to everybody for hiking, camping, and general outdoor enjoyment.

The conventional image of Oregon and Washington is that of a place of continual rain, where long-term residents develop duck feet and where ducks wear galoshes. I admit that I once believed this myself. Years ago, when I accepted a job by telephone on a newspaper in Pasco, Washington, my expectations were of green, verdant mountains towering over lush river valleys with misty waterfalls and leaping trout. There are, of course, scenes in the Northwest exactly like that. But when I arrived in Pasco, I discovered that particular part of Washington is practically treeless! As far as the eye can see, it's rolling hills of wheat, scrub grasses, and an occasional, thirsty-looking sagebrush.

An interesting thing about Washington and Oregon weather is that places 50 miles apart can have climates and topography so different it's hard to believe you're in the same state. The extreme eastern parts are high mountain country, with tall evergreen trees, harsh winters, snow-covered peaks, and great skiing. The central portions have scanty rainfall—about half that of Kansas—with a mild four-season climate and light snowfalls. The Pacific coast catches enough rain to keep everything perpetually green—even though it may snow occasionally. The ocean moderates temperatures far inland, since the warm Japan Current flows by the coast, sending temperate breezes inland and keeping freezing weather to a minimum. With a steady, year-round mildness, the climate approaches perfection for those who detest hot, sweltering summers. All but the higher elevations escape the Montana-like winters you might expect at this latitude. There's even a conifer and fern rain forest on the Olympia Peninsula, the only one in the Northern Hemisphere. Annual rainfall here is as much as 140 inches!

Despite Washington and Oregon's reputation for rain, statistics show that Olympia, Washington, has about the same yearly rainfall as Orlando, Florida (51 inches), and Portland, Oregon, averages 37 inches of rain each year, about the same as Buffalo, New York (except that Buffalo also receives 92 inches of snow). Rainfall in places like Ashland or Grants Pass is around 30 inches a year or less—about the same as San Antonio, Texas and only half as much as most parts of Florida.

Having defended Oregon's weather so strongly, I must admit that sometimes it feels like Oregon gets much more rain than statistics indicate. This is because rain tends to fall gently upon the landscape here, slowly, mostly in the winter, and over long periods of time while it builds up the accumulated totals. And, along the coast, low clouds can hang around for days upon end, even when it isn't raining, giving the impression of dampness.

Just a few years ago, some of the best housing bargains in the country were to be found in Washington and Oregon. The economy was staggered by the near-collapse of fishing and lumbering, and already reasonable prices tumbled. The states were losing population as families moved away to find employment.

This has changed dramatically, with local economies booming and real estate prices on the rise. The more popular towns have seen housing costs rise far beyond the national norm. A great deal of this increase is due to the immigration of people looking for pleasant places for retirement.

Oregon

When it comes to taxes in Oregon, I must rely on the old cliché of "good news and bad news." The good news is Oregon has no state sales tax. But the bad news is property taxes are high to make up the deficit. The good news: A state referendum sent outraged property owners to the polls to vote a reduction in property taxes to a maximum of $15 per $1,000 valuation, with a prohibition against raising assessed values to make up for lost revenue. The bad news: Voters didn't notice that the prohibition applied only to commercial property; private homes could be (and were) reappraised. It turns out that the tax reduction proposition was the brainstorm of business property owners. Eventually, the good news should be that the reassessment loophole will be closed, because property owners are really outraged now!

> **OREGON TAX PROFILE**
>
> Sales tax: no
> State income tax: graduated, 5% to 9% over $5,000; federal income tax deductible to 7% on $25,000 and over
> Property taxes: because of a ballot "reform" measure, property tax rates go down every year while assessments go up; there's no way to predict future rates; current rate may be about 1.6%
> Intangibles tax: no
> Social security taxed: no
> Pensions taxed: $5,000 exemption for government pensions or low income; private fully taxable
> Gasoline tax: 24¢ per gallon, plus possible local taxes

Oregon's Inland Valleys

As it traverses the state north to south, Interstate 5 travels through a string of exceptionally desirable retirement locations, from Ashland near the California border to Portland on the Columbia River at Oregon's northern edge. From our point of view, this entire region offers more of what retirees say they want than any other part of the nation. Yet few people outside the West Coast ever hear much about this part of the country. Californians, of course, have heard of it—much to Oregonians' chagrin—and they come here with open checkbooks, snapping up bargain retirement homes like alligators on a chicken ranch. Of course, this pushes up prices.

The landscape changes quickly as you cross into Oregon from California. Suddenly everything looks green, even in the middle of summer when most of California turns golden tan. Tall pines cloak the hills, and meadows are lush with grass; there are cows standing knee-deep in clover. It's easy to imagine the early pioneers' amazement as their covered wagons rumbled along the Oregon Trail to California. We understand why so many of them stayed right here!

Although rainfall in most inland valley locations averages only 25 to 37 inches, enough moisture falls in the summer to keep things fresh. Without heavy frost in winter to kill the grass, fields are greenest in December through March, because that's when more rain falls.

The operative climate word here is "mild." Although an occasional light snow may fall, it seldom stays around more than a few hours because of warm afternoon temperatures. January lows are typically around 30 to 40 degrees, with highs of 50 to 60 degrees. Since it rarely freezes, few homeowners bother to insulate their water pipes. A recent cold snap caught them by surprise, however, giving plumbers scads of overtime work.

Outdoor recreation is accessible year-round. Golf courses never close; fishing is possible in all seasons; bicycling and walking will lure you outdoors to do healthy things instead of watching television. Summers are mild, with average highs in the 80s, although July and August do have their share of over 100-degree days in the inland valleys. These are tempered by a low, 38 percent relative humidity.

Ashland/Medford   These two cities are about fifteen minutes apart along Interstate 5. They share a pleasant countryside of gently rolling hills, with sporadic remnants of the thick forests that once covered the area. Rich farmland and dairy farms spread out beginning at the edges of the towns. Off in the distance, about 30 miles to the east, the forest-covered mountains of the Cascade Range are sometimes covered with snow in the winter, with Mt. McLaughlin rising majestically in white-frosted splendor. To the south, another 30 miles distant, is Mt. Ashland, which dominates the Siskiyou Mountain Range. Skiing is available there from Thanksgiving through April, with up to twenty-two runs operating (snow permitting). Elk, deer, and other wildlife abound in the area.

With thirteen lakes only a short drive in any direction from Ashland and Medford, recreational activities are abundant.

Medford (pop. 46,000) and Ashland (pop. 17,000) are traditional retirement choices not only for Californians but for folks from all over the country who appreciate a blend of culture, year-round outdoor activities, and affordable housing costs. Medford is the commercial center, Ashland its academic counterpart. This area enjoys a very low crime rate, with Ashland ranking in the top 25 percent of towns nationally in personal safety. Here, you'll find small-town living combined with city conveniences.

Ashland is often chosen for retirement because of the enriching cultural atmosphere of Southern Oregon State College. It's also the site of a nationally acclaimed Shakespeare festival. This has expanded from a once-a-year event into a year-round production in three theaters, with contemporary theater and other popular entertainment in addition to classic presentations.

A few miles west of Medford is the historic town of Jacksonville, site of another famous festival. The ongoing Britt Festivals are the oldest outdoor music and performing–arts festivals in the Northwest. Five events featuring world-class artists are presented each summer. Concertgoers combine theater with picnics, sipping wine and sampling cheeses while they relax and listen to classical music, jazz, and bluegrass or watch ballet and light opera.

Once the site of a major gold strike, Jacksonville lost its chance to become the largest town in southern Oregon back in 1883 when the Oregon & California Railroad pushed its tracks northward. When the railroad requested a $25,000 "bonus" to place a station in Jacksonville, the city fathers unwisely refused to pay. Instead, the station was built at a crossroads called Middle Ford. Middle Ford shortened its name to Medford and grew while Jacksonville languished. In some ways this was fortunate, because "progress" passed the town by, saving its historic old buildings from the bulldozer.

Jacksonville's shady, tree-lined streets, 130-year-old brick hotels, commercial buildings, and restored Victorian homes assured its designation as a National Historic Landmark Town in 1966. Antiques stores, boutiques, and interesting restaurants line the main street, while quiet residential neighborhoods are set back from the commerce. Except for during the festivals, Jacksonville is basically quiet, a place many folks have selected for retirement. The surrounding countryside and north toward the community of Gold

ASHLAND–MEDFORD WEATHER					
In degrees Fahrenheit					
	Jan.	April	July	Oct.	Rain	Snow
Daily Highs	45	64	91	69	20"	8"
Daily Lows	30	37	54	40		

Hill are perfect for horses, with pastures and breeding ranches spaced at frequent intervals.

Grants Pass/Rogue River   Downriver towards Grants Pass, the scenic Rogue River flows through several small towns and communities where retirement is a pervasive theme. Mobile-home parks and cozy-looking houses sit in close proximity to the river, allowing sportsmen to enjoy record steelhead and salmon fishing just a few yards from their back doors.

Eight miles to the south of Grants Pass is the city of Rogue River (pop. 6,000), a delightful little community sitting where Interstate 5 and the Rogue River intersect. Quiet streets, shaded by mature trees, provide inexpensive homes, condos, and small apartments for those who prefer to be within walking distance of stores and the library. To the east, a vast countryside of small farms and forested homesites captivates the get-away-from-it-all crowd.

The river wends its way downstream to Grants Pass, a traditional retirement area for Southern Californians. With about 17,000 people living within the city limits, Grants Pass supports enough commerce to take it out of the realm of a small town. Yet it is surprising how often residents drive forty-five minutes to Medford for heavy-duty shopping.

Houses in town are predominantly older frame buildings, mostly single family, neat, well cared for, and affordable. Newer houses tend to be away from downtown, built on an acre or so, with trees and natural shrubbery planted as low-maintenance landscaping devices. As in the case in the Rogue River area, a great number of retirees choose to retire out in the more rustic places. Oregon becomes mountainous at this point, with forests and rugged hills covering much of the landscape. A fifteen-minute drive from Grants Pass's downtown takes you to wonderfully secluded and wild-looking properties where you will be plagued by deer eating your flowers and black bears raiding your garbage cans.

GRANTS PASS–ROGUE RIVER WEATHER						
In degrees Fahrenheit						
	Jan.	April	July	Oct.	Rain	Snow
Daily Highs	47	69	96	69	28"	4"
Daily Lows	32	40	56	42		

The Grants Pass retirement community is exceptionally active, engaging a large number of volunteers in worthwhile programs. This is important, because without sales-tax revenue, Oregon has little money to spare for senior services. If some things are to happen, they must be done with volunteer labor. Since part-time jobs are exceptionally competitive (due to low employment levels), those who need meaningful work to feel fulfilled will have plenty of opportunities. Isn't it a good feeling to know that at least *somewhere* people still consider you vital and dynamic?

After the river leaves Grants Pass on its way to the ocean, the going gets rough. White–water enthusiasts who have braved rapids all over the world will tell you that rafting Oregon's Rogue River is the ultimate white–water experience because of the river's incredible beauty. Congress designated it as the first of the nation's protected rivers under the Wild and Scenic Rivers Act of 1968. Here is where Zane Grey chose to build his home and to write many of his famous Western novels. Many scenic descriptions in his books were inspired by the picturesque Rogue River country. Moviemakers have found inspiration as well, with Hollywood crews making the trek to Grants Pass to take advantage of the scenery.

Eugene/Springfield   Located halfway up the state, this area catches 40 inches of rainfall a year, half again as much as in the southern part of the state. This ensures that the twin cities of Eugene and Springfield stay green all year, but it's still below rainfall averages in the Midwest and South. Spring, summer, and fall are gorgeous.

The biggest "industry" here is the University of Oregon, with an enrollment of nearly 16,000 students. Like Ashland, university life and the excitement of learning and culture spill over into the community. Ongoing schedules of lectures, concerts, plays, and sports offerings, many of which are free, provide a constant source of interest for the retirement community. The Hult Center for the Performing Arts houses two theaters: a concert hall and a playhouse, which feature plays, concerts, and performances by local, regional, and national talent.

Eugene's business center features a large pedestrian mall for pleasant shopping convenience. Toward the outskirts, a surprisingly large mall presents about any kind of shop or store imaginable. As a university town, Eugene's residential streets are restrained, with plenty of older homes providing housing for students and retirees alike at reasonable prices. However, this is one of the places that have seen phenomenal increases in real estate. Homes that once sold for $120,000 are today going for $160,000. Across the river in Springfield, housing costs are usually about 10 percent lower, and its downtown makes up for lack of size with extra charm. By the way, Springfield supports one of the best senior centers we've encountered in Oregon or anywhere, for that matter. Facilities are excellent, the staff dedicated, and retirees unanimously pleased with their center.

The weather here is mild enough for senior citizens to enjoy the outdoors all year. On the average, only fifteen summer days a year reach or exceed 90 degrees. Much outdoor activity centers around the Willamette River, which runs through Eugene and Springfield, providing trout fishing, picnicking, miles of bicycle trails, and river walks. For ocean fishing, clamming, and beachcombing for driftwood or Japanese glass fishing floats, Pacific beaches are just a 90-minute drive west through beautiful low mountain country and the Siuslaw National Forest. A short drive in the opposite direction is the Deschutes National Forest, crowned by the Mt. Washington and Three Sisters wilderness areas. To the north, similar towns suitable for retirement await your investigation, places such as Corvallis,

EUGENE–SPRINGFIELD WEATHER

In degrees Fahrenheit

	Jan.	April	July	Oct.	Rain	Snow
Daily Highs	46	60	82	65	40"	6"
Daily Lows	33	34	50	41		

EUGENE–SPRINGFIELD AREA COST OF LIVING

	Overall	Housing	Medical	Groceries	Utilities
Percentage of National Average	108	120	119	102	84

Albany, and Salem (Oregon's capital). Some of the state's best trout fishing can be enjoyed toward the east, after a scenic drive to the Diamond Lake area.

Salem   Sometimes called the "Cherry City," Salem is known for flowering orchards in the surrounding countryside. Fertile soil brings bountiful crops of strawberries, raspberries, pears, filberts, and walnuts. The region is becoming known for wine, especially pinot noir, riesling, and chardonnays.

Salem is the third-largest city in Oregon, with a population of 118,000, and its appearance gets a double boost from being both the site of Oregon's state capital and the home of Willamette University. These institutions help keep the downtown alive and thriving. A great deal of commerce and business is generated by both entities. The city has one of the best libraries we've ever seen, not only for its book collection, but also for the public conference rooms available for residents to use for meetings, classes, lectures, and social events. The library is one of the focal points of the community for many retirees, a place to meet people and make friends.

As you might expect of a state capital, the downtown center is vibrant, with nice restaurants, shopping, and excitement in the air, yet with an informality not expected in a capital city. During our last research trip to Salem, a retired couple invited us to one of the local microbreweries for a snack. The place is famous for good hamburgers in addition to its home-made beer. While we were ordering our hamburgers, a couple walked in and sat at the table next to us. They turned out to be Oregon's governor, John Kitzhaber, and his wife, Sharon. Both were dressed casually; he wore his "trademark" blue jeans, sport coat, and tie. Our friends exchanged pleasantries with the governor, and we returned to our conversation. By the way, Governor Kitzhaber is a good friend to retirees. He is a medical doctor and the architect of Oregon's unique health-care program, which is often mentioned as a possible health-care model for the nation.

SALEM WEATHER						
In degrees Fahrenheit						
	Jan.	April	July	Oct.	Rain	Snow
Daily Highs	46	62	84	65	40"	6"
Daily Lows	34	38	51	42		

Salem is more than a one-university town. Besides Willamette University (a quality private school with 2,500 students), there's Chemeketa Community College, with a wide variety of adult educational programs to serve the surrounding area, and Western Baptist College, a private coeducational school that's been in Salem for more than forty years. Nearby is Western Oregon State, located 17 miles west of Salem at Monmouth.

Although most of the countryside around Salem is flat, conforming to the Willamette River's meandering course at this point, some beautiful residential areas are on hilly to almost mountainous tracts. These hills are wooded and have a rustic, country feeling, even though they are only fifteen minutes from the center of town. In these neighborhoods, homes are designed to blend with the forest setting.

Portland   Reno, Nevada, bills itself as "The Biggest Little City in the West"; Portland turns this around, claiming the title of "The Biggest Small Town in the West." And it is big, with a million people living in its urban area; the city limits alone include about half a million in population. Portland's influence spreads from the foothills of Mount Hood to the plains of the Coast Range, covering a four-county area.

Portland works hard to maintain its small-town atmosphere and its second motto, "City of Roses." Fortunately, the city's founding fathers incorporated a large number of parks, some quite large, which contribute to a feeling of uncrowded spaciousness. Rolling hills and lots of shade trees extend this feeling into Portland's neighborhoods.

PORTLAND WEATHER

In degrees Fahrenheit

	Jan.	April	July	Oct.	Rain	Snow
Daily Highs	44	60	80	64	37"	6"
Daily Lows	34	41	56	45		

PORTLAND AREA COST OF LIVING

	Overall	Housing	Medical	Groceries	Utilities
Percentage of National Average	113	123	123	109	81

Unlike many American cities, where shopping malls have destroyed downtowns by luring consumers into the suburbs, Portland has managed to keep its central core alive and well, a pleasant place to visit or shop. During the 1970s the city built a transit system and instituted a system of free public transportation in a 340-block downtown area, known as "Fareless Square." A combination of pedestrian-only streets and free buses makes shopping downtown Portland a pleasure. Well-preserved buildings, upscale shops and restaurants, and good law enforcement complete the picture of a "small-town big city."

Because Portland's climate, sophisticated setting, and hilly picturesqueness are reminiscent of San Francisco, Portland draws many retirees from that area. Coming here from one of the most expensive parts of the country is a pleasant surprise for ex-San Franciscans. Lovely Victorian homes, which would cost a fortune where they came from, can be purchased for California tract-home prices. (You realize, of course, that some California tract homes can be expensive.) At least one San Francisco publisher and several authors we know of have made the switch to Portland from "Baghdad by the Bay."

The Dalles/Hood River   The drive up the Oregon side of the Columbia River from Portland is another scenic marvel. A half-dozen historic little towns space themselves along the way, with the huge river flowing past, carrying fishing boats, cargo barges, and windsurfers. Two places in particular make wonderful retirement locations: Hood River (pop. 17,000) and The Dalles (pop. 11,000).

The Dalles received its name from French Canadian voyagers who used to "shoot the rapids" here instead of tediously unloading their boats and dragging them around the narrow rapids (which are now buried beneath the dam). The French used the word *dalle* to refer to a place where waters were constrained between high rock walls. They called this exciting stretch of river la *grande dalle de la Columbia*, "the great rapid of the Columbia." Those traveling the Oregon Trail who floated downriver to this point had to portage

THE DALLES–HOOD RIVER WEATHER						
In degrees Fahrenheit						
	Jan.	April	July	Oct.	Rain	Snow
Daily Highs	42	60	90	63	37"	5"
Daily Lows	31	38	52	41		

around the rapids for the final leg of the trip. Others arrived with their wagons and either had to build rafts and float their belongings downriver from this point or detour inland around Mount Hood. Some weary travelers decided to give it up and settle in The Dalles, making it one of the earliest towns in the state. Later on, steamboats made their way up the Columbia as far as The Dalles—the trip taking twelve hours and the fare $1 round-trip.

Today The Dalles is the center of a thriving agricultural region, with wheat fields and orchards fringing the town limits. It's definitely dry here, with less than half the rainfall of Portland, just 100 miles downriver. The Dalles catches about 14 inches of rain (about the same as Los Angeles) and a couple of inches of snow two or three times each year. Summers are warm, often in the 90s, but it's a dry heat, with lots of breeze off the river, and almost no rain during July and August.

In the historic downtown shopping district, streets run parallel with the river, full of substantial brick buildings of late 1800s vintage. The town center seems to be active and spared from traffic by the interstate that bypasses The Dalles. Most major shopping retailers are represented on the edge of town. Residential neighborhoods climb the rather steep hillside behind the town, each street enjoying panoramic views of the Columbia River Gorge and Dallesport Peninsula. At the very top, the Columbia Gorge Community College and the large Sorosis Park command the final view across the river into the state of Washington.

Residential neighborhoods are almost sitting on streets that stairstep up the steep hillside. Most homes, therefore, enjoy great views of the river and of the state of Washington in the distance. Residential neighborhoods vary from elegant to economical, something for every pocketbook.

Hood River   When it was settled in 1854, early residents called the community Dog River, but under pressure by housewives the name was changed to Hood River. This was one of the first places along the Oregon Trail where pioneers found enough rain to grow some of the same kinds of crops they were used to back East. Some of the first things planted were apple trees and strawberries. Today the region is famous for pear and apple orchards.

It's interesting how just a little distance between The Dalles and Hood River (22 miles) makes a real difference in the climate. Hood River gets 30 inches of rain and lots more snow than The

Dalles. This extra precipitation makes a big difference in the vegetation as well. Everything is green, even through the summer, and more lush. Still, Hood River gets less precipitation than Portland, or about the same as Des Moines or Detroit.

The downtown business center, varying from 1 to 3 blocks wide, follows along the river. It seems to be holding up well against the heavy shopping competition on the highway leading out of town. Several interesting restaurants and historic buildings with specialty stores draw downtown shoppers. Residential neighborhoods close to the town center vary from comfortable to not-quite-elegant, and most older homes are shaded by large trees. The newer homes away from downtown can be quite upscale and command great views of the Columbia River. Many places, either up or down the river, combine views and acreage. Behind Hood River, ascending the mountain slopes toward Mt. Hood, a series of small communities and towns adds to Hood River's regional population—such places as Odell, Dee, and Parkdale.

Oregon Coast

A wonderful, often overlooked, retirement area is found along Washington and Oregon's Pacific coast. North along Highway 101, an inviting string of small towns dot the shore, starting with Brookings, just across the California state line, to Astoria, on Oregon's northern border and on up to Washington's Grays Harbor.

Ask people who retire along this picturesque stretch of coast, and they'll most likely give "wonderful year-round climate" as a major reason for their decision. Forget about air-conditioning and snow shovels. Since it seldom freezes, sweaters or windbreakers are the heaviest winter clothing required. Because midday temperatures rarely top 75 degrees, folks here sleep under electric blankets year-round.

However, it's this stretch of Pacific Coast that earns Oregon and Washington a reputation for being rainy. Gold Beach is perhaps the wettest of all, with almost 80 inches per year. Most of it falls in the winter; it would fall as snow somewhere else. The summers are often sunny and dry, although low clouds are also common. This is a great place for part-time retirees, those seeking to escape Arizona's scorching July and August or Florida's muggy summers.

Overcrowding? Coast residents have plenty of elbow room. Along Washington and Oregon's 500-mile stretch of Pacific coastline you'll only find about twenty towns plus a scattering of villages. Most have between 1,000 and 5,000 friendly residents. The only cities are Coos Bay, Astoria, and Aberdeen, and they are just barely large enough to be called cities. Most beaches are deserted, with unrestricted public access guaranteed by state law. Five or ten minutes' drive inland takes you to a low mountain range, the Cascades, with thousands of square miles of wilderness—almost all publicly owned, or in national forest.

Good fishing, both ocean and river, is another plus. Steelhead, chinook salmon, and rainbow trout lurk in streams flowing from nearby mountains. Clamming, crabbing, and whale-watching are popular activities. The open countryside is perfect for camping, picnicking, or beachcombing as well as golf and horseback riding. White-tailed deer are plentiful, and you might see an occasional black bear or cougar. A large proportion of beachfront is dedicated to public parks and campgrounds, in the midst of the most beautiful seascapes to be found anywhere in the world.

Brookings/Harbor   Just across the California line are the twin towns of Brookings and Harbor. An estimated 30 percent of the population here are retirees. That seems like a low estimate, because retirement is big business along this coast.

Residents love their unusually mild climate, optimistically referring to the area as Oregon's "banana belt." There's some justification, since flowers bloom all year; about 90 percent of the country's Easter lilies are grown here. Rhododendrons and azaleas bloom wildly in the late spring, and an Azalea Festival is held every Memorial Day. Let's face it, bananas don't grow well at all in this banana belt.

When we asked one man why he chose the Brookings–Harbor area for retirement, he invited us into his small travel trailer for coffee. "This is my home," he said proudly. "It's only 25 feet long, but it's all I need as a bachelor and fisherman. My rent is $100 a month, and this trailer cost me $2,800. Paid more than that for my boat. So here I am, gettin' by on my government money and goin' fishin' anytime I care to, which is almost every day."

Like all Oregon coastal towns, Brookings and Harbor have plenty of things for retired folks to do, both organized and do-it-yourself. The main problem, as far as I am concerned, with these smaller towns is the distance from large shopping centers. People who live here insist there's an adequate supply of hardware stores, grocery markets, and the like, but I suppose some of us are spoiled and want huge selections of everything.

Gold Beach   The mighty Rogue River empties into the ocean at Gold Beach. A road follows its course for a few miles inland, passing many retirement places favored by fishermen who prize the steelhead and salmon that pass their doors every day. Some folks just can't choose between ocean or river fishing. They have to have both. Behind the town stretches mile after mile of forested wilderness, with trout, steelhead, and salmon streams and deer hunting.

Gold Beach has an interesting history. It derived its name from an incident that started a frantic gold rush back in the forty-niner days. A prospector passing through the area discovered a small quantity of gold mixed in with beach sand. He panned a tiny bit of color and casually mentioned the fact to some other miners. As the word spread, the story expanded until gold–mining camps all over California and Oregon fluttered with news of a place where the ocean's waves deposited nuggets of gold in the sand, the beach strewn with riches, there for the gathering. Mining camps in California's Mother Lode all but emptied as miners frantically rushed to the "gold" beach.

Actually, gold is rather common on Oregon and California beaches, usually found in black streaks of magnetite sand mixed in with beach terraces. The problem is that it is very fine and difficult to separate from the coarser sand. Back during the Great Depression, when many people had nothing else to do, a lot of gold was gleaned from the beaches, but it was tedious work.

The gold stampede in Gold Beach was short–lived, but some miners, tired of jumping from place to place in search of riches, decided to retire from gold panning and settle down. They started the first retirement community on the Oregon coast. The tradition continues today, with retirement becoming a significant industry.

Single-family homes, cottages, and mobile homes are the general rule, with people living in multi-generational communities rather than strictly adult developments. A small hospital with an emergency room takes care of Gold Beach's medical needs.

As you drive north along the Oregon coast and catch a glimpse of the coast at Port Orford, you will see the ultimate picture-postcard scene. Dramatic rock formations jut from the sea, catching the force of waves, sending spray flying, and then the swells continue on to become gentle breakers on the sandy beach. Beaches here are known for semiprecious stones such as agates, jasper, and jade as well as being places to look for redwood burls. Both Port Orford and Bandon (27 miles up the road) are truly retirement communities. A local real estate broker claims that 68 percent of his clients are retired.

Bandon   The town of Bandon (pop. 1,600) deliberately cultivates a "quaint" atmosphere, with period restaurants, art galleries, ceramic studios, and small shops of every description. It's gained a reputation as an artist colony. The local chamber of commerce coordinates activities for retirees, with monthly dinners, art shows, and an annual cranberry festival.

One of Bandon's more popular attractions is a floating dock that extends out into the water, especially for catching Dungeness crabs. Eager fishermen drop baited crab traps to the bottom and wait for fat crabs to scurry inside. Then, with quick hand-over-hand pulls, up comes the trap, often with half a dozen or so tasty crustaceans, each weighing a pound or two. The market price, last time we went crabbing, was almost six dollars a pound!

Because views are so spectacular here, oceanfront property is scarce and expensive, with homes commonly selling for as high as $300,000. However, if a seascape is not essential in your choice of homes, away from the ocean's edge and up nearby rivers you'll find homes selling for as little as $100,000.

Florence   Florence isn't that much different from its neighbors, but we like it because it's only 60 miles to Eugene, with its

OREGON COAST WEATHER						
In degrees Fahrenheit						
	Jan.	April	July	Oct.	Rain	Snow
Daily Highs	53	54	62	58	65"	1"
Daily Lows	41	44	51	48		

larger-city shopping, university, and excellent cultural and entertainment opportunities. Housing here is a good value; the cost of living is low, and personal safety is high. Excellent senior services and a helpful chamber of commerce make Florence an easy place to settle into for retirement.

An interesting phenomenon along the coast is the large number of freshwater lakes. Groundwater flowing from the mountains tries to find its way to the ocean, but sand dunes trap the water in low-lying areas to form freshwater lakes sometimes just a few hundred yards from the ocean. Within a few miles of Florence, the Oregon Fish and Wildlife Department stocks two dozen lakes with game fish. Some are loaded with cutthroat trout and restricted to barbless hooks, flies, and lures. No bait is permitted. Other lakes feature prize-winning bass and still others are reserved for sailboats. Homes built on the shores of these lakes offer dramatic views at bargain prices.

Astoria   The second-largest town on the coast, Astoria (pop. 15,000) sits at the northern edge of the state, where the mighty Columbia River empties into the Pacific. Hilly and verdant, Astoria is fortunate to have many picture-book Victorian homes.

This was the site of John Jacob Astor's fur trading post back in 1811; within a few decades, Astoria developed into a thriving seaport. The affluence of that time shows today in the stately Victorian homes scattered about the town, imparting a formal but comfortable visage to Astoria. Its small-town atmosphere is affirmed by an exceptionally low crime rate, ranking in the top 15 percent in the United States for safety. Astoria doesn't face the open ocean; it fronts a large bay where the mighty Columbia River empties into the Pacific. The water expanse is so large it seems like the ocean, however. Nearby beaches are famous for long-neck clams (you have to dig fast to catch 'em) and Dungeness crab for delicious cioppinos. Portland is a two-hour drive for those who need a "big-city fix" once in a while.

ASTORIA WEATHER						
In degrees Fahrenheit						
	Jan.	April	July	Oct.	Rain	Snow
Daily Highs	47	56	68	61	70"	5"
Daily Lows	35	40	52	44		

Seaside   Sixteen miles from Astoria, just north of Tillamook Head, the charming town of Seaside (pop. 5,600) commands a stretch of miles and miles of wide and sandy beach—all accessible to the public. Seaside is the quintessential beach community, and is Oregon's oldest seaside resort. The town's focus is on its historic oceanfront promenade and its centerpiece, the famous Turnaround at the end of Broadway, a large, circular promenade at the center of beach activity.

Summer is the hectic tourist season, and one lady volunteered, "We love the state of peace and serenity during the winter months. We have plenty of fun activities, but we don't miss the excitement of families coming to enjoy the ocean and beaches as in the summer."

Seaside's Providence Hospital operates a twenty-four-hour emergency clinic, and for major medical crises they fly patients to Portland by helicopter in less than thirty minutes. According to local people, the medical care here is excellent.

Oregon High Country

On the other climatic extreme, let's look at places that not only enjoy four seasons, but experience true-blue winters as well. The town of Bend, for example, averages 46 inches of snow every year. That's less than Albany (New York) with 65 inches or Flagstaff (Arizona) with 97 inches, but it still seems like a lot to me!

OREGON HIGH COUNTRY

Sunriver/Bend

Klamath Falls

Many retired folks point to their winter season as one of the things they *like* about living here. "It took a while to get used to driving on snow," said one lady who had lived most of her life in Monterey, California. "But after a couple of days, I was out there with the best of 'em."

Sunriver/Bend   An example of retirement for active folks is a development like Sunriver. About a twenty-minute drive from downtown Bend (pop. 20,000), Sunriver is a self-contained resort community of 3,300 acres. About 1,300 homes have been built there, ranging from nice to ultra-deluxe. More than 650 condominiums are scattered throughout the property, with undeveloped forest serving as green belts. A shopping mall and full complement of services make the community nearly self-sufficient.

The interesting thing about the layout of the resort is that each house has plenty of land separating it from the next, so even condos don't seem crowded. Hiking paths and 80 miles of paved bike trails pass by each living unit. Two eighteen-hole golf courses, twenty-six tennis courts, two swimming pools, hot tubs, stables, and a racquet club provide summer sports for active retirees. Winter sports are skiing at nearby Mt. Bachelor and cross-country skiing over the hiking trails and golf courses.

Of the 1,500 full-time residents, better than half are retired, most from other states. Retired couples are even more strongly represented among the many part-time owners. They spend part of the year there—whichever is their favorite season—and rent their property for other seasons. A close family friend owns a house there, but spends most of her time in Monterey, California. "One of the advantages of owning," she says, "is that if my kids don't want to use the place in the winter ski season or for summer golf, I just call the management company and they generally find tourists who are happy to pay $90 a day for my place." The winter ski tourists and the summer fishing and golf enthusiasts just about cover our friend's payments. This is done through one of several management companies that advertise the rentals, collect the rent, and clean after each tenant leaves.

Something that needs to be stressed about places like Sunriver: They aren't full-service retirement communities. Sunriver isn't a place where you can expect doctors to visit or home-care workers to look after you. Instead, this is a place for active and alert people; the kind who won't mind an average of 2 feet of snow during winter or who might like to try cross-country skiing. Why is this any different from places in Idaho and Montana? Because, despite the snow, the Oregon High Country doesn't get the severe low temperatures, and spring comes earlier and fall stays longer.

SUNRIVER–BEND WEATHER						
In degrees Fahrenheit						
	Jan.	April	July	Oct.	Rain	Snow
Daily Highs	37	56	84	62	10"	46"
Daily Lows	18	30	54	34		

The city of Bend is also a place for retirement, particularly for those who would rather not put as much money into housing or who need to be closer than a twenty-minute drive to major shopping or medical services. However, real estate prices are not truly bargains, due to the pressures newcomers place on the market. Bend manages to blend urban sophistication with a relaxed quality of life. It brims with city parks and activity. Within thirty minutes of town, folks can enjoy a choice of nine golf courses, some of the best alpine and Nordic skiing in the Northwest, and white-water rafting or rainbow trout fishing on the Deschutes River.

Klamath Falls   An overlooked retirement area, but not over-looked by bargain-hunting California retirees, is Klamath Falls. About 18 miles from the California border, Klamath Falls offers a high-desert climate similar to Bend, some 137 miles to the north. Fishing and hunting are great, with camping, nature trails, and sailing on the huge Klamath Lake providing a full range of outdoor activities. Landlocked salmon and steelhead grow to outstanding sizes. Local fishermen claim that the average trout taken from the water measures 21 inches. (Would local fishermen lie?)

The climate is dry, with 280 days of sunshine and crisply cold winters. There's far less snow and cold in Klamath Falls than in Bend, but winters are really winter.

The big drawing card for most retirees (besides excellent trout fishing) is affordable real estate. Housing prices are as low as any-where we've investigated, and considering the quality of the area, it's perhaps one of the best buys in the country. Another economic benefit here is an unusually low cost of utilities, more than 25 percent below national averages. This helps offset higher heating bills in the winter.

KLAMATH FALLS WEATHER						
In degrees Fahrenheit						
	Jan.	April	July	Oct.	Rain	Snow
Daily Highs	38	59	85	64	14"	12"
Daily Lows	22	33	54	36		

Washington

Oregon has traditionally attracted more West Coast retirees than Washington; however, this is changing. More and more retirees are traveling just a little farther to investigate Washington. The state's electronics and aerospace industries are bringing skilled workers from all parts of the country to join the steady stream of Californians who have been jumping over Oregon to land in Washington. They are pleased to find pleasant living conditions, a mild climate, and moderate housing costs.

Worthy of special mention is Washington's philosophy on state income taxes: it's one of the few states in the country that does not collect income taxes! Furthermore, it's one of those states with laws prohibiting other states from placing liens to collect taxes owed to that other state. Another good idea here is property tax breaks for the elderly. Under state law, seniors age sixty-one and older with incomes under $26,000 are entitled to a full exemption from special assessments, and those earning less than $18,000 can be exempt from a portion of regular property taxes.

WASHINGTON TAX PROFILE
Sales tax: 6.5% to 8.2%, food, drugs exempt
State income tax: no
Property taxes: average 1.8% of assessed value; exemptions for those 62 and over.
Intangibles tax: no
Social security taxed: no
Pensions taxed: no
Gasoline tax: 23¢ per gallon, plus possible local taxes

The most popular retirement locations are found in high-quality towns near Seattle and on Puget Sound's network of bays, coves, straits, and inlets. Because so much of Washington's coastline is in Puget Sound, the total land fronting on the sea is almost twice as long as Oregon's. This large mass of water moderates temperatures, which rarely drop below freezing or rise above 80 degrees.

Places like Shelton, Sequim, and Port Townsend share Seattle's climate and scenic beauty but also offer the benefits of small-town living. Equally charming are the communities set on islands, large and small, in and around the sound, among them Whidbey Island, Fidalgo Island, and the San Juan Islands. These quaint coastal towns nestled in forests of Douglas fir remind us of New England fishing villages. One drawback is that both Olympic National Park and the

San Juan Islands attract tourists by the thousands, which can mean waiting in line for several hours to board a ferry during the summer and on weekends year-round.

All around Puget Sound, however, the cost of living is relatively high. In some places, especially the San Juan Islands, it can be extremely high. More affordable living can be found farther south in seaside communities such as Grayland and Long Beach on the Pacific coast.

Seattle Area   Seattle offers all the advantages of a large city, as well as all the disadvantages. Its setting, between Puget Sound and Lake Washington, with magnificent mountain views in all directions, helps make it one of the more beautiful cities in America. Lofty evergreens shade its parks and suburbs, which blend into the surrounding forest. Its location, on the water and sheltered from Pacific storms by the mountains of the Olympic Peninsula, keeps winters mercifully mild and summers pleasantly cool. There is an all-pervasive community spirit such as is found in few other major cities. As you might expect from a big city, crime rates are a little higher than in surrounding communities, but for an urban area the safety factor here is reassuring. Most local neighborhoods in Seattle are as safe as you can find anywhere.

It's the high-quality towns near Seattle or on Puget Sound's network of bays, coves, straits, and inlets that makes this such a great retirement choice. Places like Bellingham, Burlington, or Olympia—to name just a few—share in Seattle's climate and scenic beauty, but also offer the benefits of small-town living. Anacortes, for example, located on a peninsula jutting out into the bay, enjoys one of the lowest crime rates in the country. Edmonds is another attractive area, sitting between Seattle and Everett; its downtown is right on the water, with a beach and ferry terminal at the end of the main shopping street.

The San Juan Islands, in the northern portion of Puget Sound, are one of the scenic wonders of the entire country. Real estate prices

SEATTLE AREA WEATHER						
In degrees Fahrenheit						
	Jan.	April	July	Oct.	Rain	Snow
Daily Highs	44	57	75	60	39"	7"
Daily Lows	35	41	55	46		

SEATTLE COST OF LIVING					
Percentage of	Overall	Housing	Medical	Groceries	Utilities
National Average	112	123	142	110	78

are a bit high here compared with some of the other island complexes nearby, but the quality lifestyle possible here makes it worthwhile. Whidbey Island, another favorite retirement area, has the advantage of being accessible by highway bridges rather than ferry boats.

Bainbridge Island   One of Seattle's most exclusive suburban neighborhoods, Bainbridge Island is linked to the peninsula by a highway bridge and to Seattle by a ferry route. Here you'll find many gracious homes secluded on large estates hidden from casual view by stands of evergreens. The 48-square-mile island is home to 17,500 people, of whom nearly half commute to Seattle on a daily basis. Another island connected to the peninsula, Vashon Island, has a part bucolic, part artsy population of 10,000 and is linked by ferry to Tacoma.

The most intriguing communities on the peninsula are those farthest from the ferries that carry commuters to the urban side of the sound. Poulsbo, a waterfront community 16 miles north of Bremerton, got its start in the 1880s as a fishing village of Norwegian immigrants. The Scandinavian heritage lives on along the town's main street, now filled with art and craft galleries, antiques shops, and waterfront cafes, as well as in annual events ranging from the Viking Fest in May and the Midsommarfest in August to a traditional lutefisk dinner in October and the Christmastime Yule Fest. Hartstene Island, connected by bridge to the southeastern corner of the Kitsap Peninsula, has forests, beaches, and meandering roads that provide access to hundreds of residences concealed deep in second-growth forest.

Olympia   Olympia, the capital of Washington, is the kind of dignified, clean, not-too-big city that every state capital should be. So many people here work for the government that the city's shops, sidewalks, and parks are almost deserted during regular business hours. During rush hours and weekends it's best to stay home.

The Olympia area is home to about 22,000 senior citizens. Since 1980, the over-sixty-five population has grown by 53 percent—almost double the area's overall population growth rate. Retired military personnel who discovered the area while stationed at nearby Fort Lewis or McChord Air Force Base account for a sizable segment of Olympia's active senior community.

Temperatures are generally mild, though Olympia gets considerably more rain and fog than Seattle and other Puget Sound communities farther to the north. It usually doesn't rain very hard, but it rains often, with an average of 230 cloudy days a year, with more than a trace of rain on 147 of those days and fog on 75 of them.

Shelton   An easy drive from Seattle, the town of Shelton (pop. 7,600 people), is the county seat and only incorporated town in rural Mason County. Traditionally a bedroom community of Olympia, commuters enjoy the county's only stretch of four-lane highway to the city. The area is known as the "South Sound." As a place to stay home and enjoy the quiet, peaceful little Shelton and Mason County have a character that is completely different from the Olympia area.

Shelton sits on the edge of Oakland Bay, a saltwater inlet not much wider than a river. Its town center dates from the 1850s when it was a logging camp, but today it boasts dozens of historic buildings dating back to the era between World War I and the Great Depression. (In Washington that's historic; in Boston, that would be recent history.) Then, as now, it provided shopping, banking, schooling, and other services for many smaller logging camps, farms, and fishing villages scattered throughout the area. Even today, two-thirds of Mason County residents live in rural areas away from Shelton. An interesting aspect of the population here: Two Indian tribes, the Skokomish and Squaxin Island people, live on separate reservations within a few miles of Shelton.

Bremerton/Kitsap Peninsula   Bremerton, the site of the Puget Sound Naval Shipyards, is directly across Puget Sound from Seattle. The 40,000 population here is predominantly military personnel and their dependents, being the site of western Washington's largest military base. Bremerton itself clearly lacks the Pacific Northwest charm that lures retirees to the Puget Sound region. However, within a few minutes' drive of the dock where ferries arrive from Seattle, you'll find custom-built homes and vacation cabins hidden along rustic unpaved country lanes that wind through the forests of the Kitsap Peninsula.

In fact, nowhere else in the region will you find so many secluded woodland homes and homesites so close to a major urban area. Many retirees on the Kitsap Peninsula first discovered the unique area while stationed here in the military. A large number of houses here are used as weekend getaways by Seattle residents. Eventually they plan to use their places as retirement homes, either on a full-time or part-time basis. The marvelously scenic ferry ride from Bremerton to downtown Seattle takes about fifty minutes—not bad when you consider that it takes just as long to get downtown from many Seattle suburbs such as Edmonds, Lynnwood, or Bellevue.

Port Townsend   Port Townsend, with its carefully preserved Victorian architecture and magnificent vistas of sea and glacier-clad peaks, may well be Washington's prettiest town. As the original shipping port on Puget Sound, it prospered from the 1860s to the 1890s. Because the architecture of this epoch has been carefully preserved, the entire town of Port Townsend has been designated a National Historic Landmark. Sitting on the northwesternmost tip of the Olympic Peninsula at the mouth of Puget Sound, Port Townsend is just remote enough from the Seattle metropolitan area to be out of the question for commuting to the city.

PORT TOWNSEND WEATHER						
In degrees Fahrenheit						
	Jan.	April	July	Oct.	Rain	Snow
Daily Highs	44	59	76	61	49"	4"
Daily Lows		33	41	53	45	

Because of brisk tourist trade in season, Port Townsend has become home to many artists, crafters, and bed-and-breakfast innkeepers. In the off season, the town slows down so much that many locals migrate south to sunnier, livelier climes until spring.

Port Townsend has been described a split-level town. A neighborhood of stately Victorian homes and churches surrounds the ornate courthouse, overlooking the water from atop limestone cliffs as much as a hundred feet high. At the foot of the cliffs, red-brick buildings preserve the memory of bygone days when Port Townsend was reputed to be the roughest seaport on the West Coast. Then the commercial district around the docks was filled with saloons and bordellos; today they have been replaced by restaurants and art galleries.

The oceangoing ships of former times are gone. Some of the old docks have decayed away to leave only stubs of pilings standing in rows far out into the water, ideal perches for seagulls and pelicans. At the center of the old waterfront is the modern Washington State Ferries dock. There is no direct service from Port Townsend to Seattle; car ferries run frequently to Whidbey Island, where an 18-mile drive takes motorists to another ferry that carries them to the mainland at Mukilteo, an Everett suburb about an hour by interstate north of Seattle. In other words, a trip to the city can take all day. In the summer, a private ferry company offers daily passenger service to the San Juan Islands from the same docks.

Living and housing costs in Port Townsend are similar to those in most other communities on the Olympic Peninsula.

Sequim   Sequim (pronounced "Skwim") has a reputation as Washington's top retirement haven. Hundreds of older newcomers move to Sequim each season, contributing to phenomenal growth: The area population has risen from 4,000 residents a decade ago to 25,000 today. Less than 15 percent of the populace lives in Sequim's small town center; the rest live in suburban and semi-rural areas of the surrounding Dungeness Valley. Approximately half of area residents are over age sixty-two.

The main factor accounting for Sequim's rise to retirement mecca status is the weather, which has earned the area its nickname, the "Banana Belt." More than any other western Washington community, Sequim is protected from foul weather by the rain shadow of Mount Olympus, the massive peak 30 miles to the southwest. The town receives approximately the same annual rainfall as Los Angeles, and the sun shines 306 days a year. Average annual rainfall increases 1 inch per mile going west from Sequim, and almost as much going east.

Although Sequim lacks the architectural charm of other nearby towns, notably Port Townsend, the downtown area has a growing number of antiques shops, as well as galleries that show the work of artists and crafters who make their homes in the area.

Seafood gourmands prize the local Dungeness crabs. The sunshine factor makes Sequim a great place for gardening. Flowers, vegetables, and fruits thrive and sometimes reach prodigious size. Several raspberry and strawberry farms in the area let you pick your own baskets of berries in season for a small charge. Area growers sell their produce at the Sequim Farmer's Market every Saturday during the summer months.

Port Angeles The largest town on the Olympic Peninsula, Port Angeles (pop. 17,500) is the main gateway to Olympic National Park. This fact alone makes it an appealing choice for nature lovers. Besides limitless hiking trails and unparalleled wildlife watching, the park has special programs that provide volunteer opportunities for senior citizens.

Port Angeles itself is a busy town that stretches along the waterfront. Its two parallel main streets, and the downtown area small enough for walking, are complete with turn-of-the-century architecture in need of a fresh coat of paint. A long waterfront park has paved hiking trails and well-groomed woodlands. Growth has been slow and steady, so residential areas contain a mix of older and contemporary homes.

Homesteaders came to the mountain valleys around Port Angeles long before the creation of the national forest and national park, so the fringe areas around the park are a patchwork quilt of federal and private land. You'll find houses of every description, from rustic log cabins to contemporary custom-built homes, many

PORT ANGELES WEATHER						
In degrees Fahrenheit						
	Jan.	April	July	Oct.	Rain	Snow
Daily Highs	44	54	67	57	49"	—
Daily Lows	36	40	51	44		

of them secluded miles in on unpaved forest roads. The area's rural residents actually outnumber the population of Port Angeles itself.

Recreation and hiking enthusiasts will find hundreds of miles of trails of every length and difficulty in Olympic National Park. The park is also one of the best places in Washington for wildlife viewing. The Port Angeles area is also a great place for saltwater and freshwater fishing, with four public boat launches inside the city limits. Favorite catches are black-mouth salmon and halibut. Clams, crabs, and shrimp are also abundant in offshore waters. Anglers cast in dozens of nearby rivers and lakes for steelhead, cutthroat, and rainbow trout. Fishing charters and river float trips are available in season.

Whidbey Island   Whidbey Island was known as a retirement area long before the first senior citizen thought of moving to Sequim. Langley, a residential community on the southwest shore of the island, is nicknamed "Port of the Sea Captains" because it has been a favorite retirement spot for mariners for more than a century.

Measuring 55 miles from north to south, Whidbey Island is the longest island in the United States—a distinction it gained in 1985 when the U.S. Supreme Court ruled that Long Island, New York, was actually a peninsula. It has the advantage of being accessible by highway bridge, but only from the north. Frequent ferries carry vehicles and passengers from terminals on the island to both Mukilteo, north of Seattle, and Port Townsend on the Olympic Peninsula.

Whidbey Island is predominantly rural in character, with three towns and a scattering of tiny villages along the protected coast that faces the mainland across Skagit Bay and the Saratoga Passage. The biggest town on the island is Oak Harbor, with a population of 15,000, including many personnel from nearby Whidbey Naval Air Station; however, the county seat of Island County (Whidbey Island, that is), is little Coupeville, an old-fashioned, Victorian-era port town of 1,300. For the most part, Whidbey Island residents live on small dairy and truck–produce farms nestled in the fir trees that line a seemingly endless labyrinth of nameless little paved roads.

Whidbey Island is the place to go if the ultimate in peace and quiet is your goal. Any kind of excitement is highly unlikely here; in fact, retirees we've talked to in such laid-back places as Sequim, Port Townsend, and Anacortes dismiss the prospect of life on Whidbey Island as "too boring." Boredom gives way to congestion on sunny weekends and during the summer months, when day-trippers from the Seattle area arrive as fast as the ferries can carry them and clog the island's only highway with bumper-to-bumper traffic bound for Deception Pass State Park and other popular recreation areas.

Bellingham If any area of the northwestern Washington coast can claim to be "undiscovered," it is Whatcom County, which stretches along the Canadian border from the Straits of Georgia shoreline to the crest of the North Cascades.

The population center of Whatcom County is Bellingham, a city of 68,000 people located 18 miles south of the Canadian border. The setting, on a series of hills along Bellingham Bay, is as spectacular as the most romantic of Pacific Northwest daydreams. Many neighborhoods and parks have beautiful views of the San Juan Islands across the water to the west, and just a few miles to the east rises 10,775-foot Mount Baker in all its glacier-clad majesty. Although Bellingham is situated just off Interstate 5, a mere ninety-minute drive north of Seattle, it's historic charm has never been overwhelmed by the growth boom that has transformed other cities to the south.

Over the years, Bellingham has developed an intriguing cultural mix. Through much of the twentieth century, the town's economy depended mainly on Canadians from Victoria and Vancouver, British Columbia, who came south to buy U.S.-made goods duty-free. Though the North American Free Trade Agreement is gradually eliminating import tariffs between Canada and the United States, you still see about as many British Columbia license plates as Washington ones in shopping mall parking lots. As the site of Western Washington University, Bellingham has a college student population of nearly 11,000. It is also one of the favorite communities in Washington among aging hippies and enlightenment seekers. Smaller neighboring villages retain distinctive Dutch and Scottish influences from early settlement days. In addition, about 5,000 Lummi and Nooksack Indians make their homes on two nearby reservations.

Senior residents find that it's hard to get bored in Bellingham.

The exceptionally active senior center offers more than sixty classes, health programs, and social events each week. Additional activities are offered by AARP and the Older Women's League (OWLS). Whatcom County Senior Services sponsors low-cost boat, train, and bus trips to destinations throughout Washington, Oregon, and even Alaska. Independent-living apartments including dinner, transportation, and social activities are available at the Willows Retirement Community near St. Joseph's Hospital.

Pasco/Kennewick   Earlier in this chapter I poked fun at Pasco because of its dry, desert-like surroundings. Actually, it's a highly productive wheat-producing area and has grown immensely over the years since I worked there. Most neighborhoods are new here, a consequence of fast growth during the past two decades, and an overall prosperity is evident.

Although Pasco may not live up to the damp and green expectations most folks have of Washington, there are certain advantages to living in the eastern part of the state. Besides being a place that actively seeks retirees, the Pasco–Kennewick–Richland area offers great real estate prices and an interesting climate. Even in the coldest part of winter, when the temperature dropped to 20 degrees in the morning, I could be fishing that same afternoon on the Columbia River bank, in my shirtsleeves. Like rain, snowfall here is slight; it didn't snow at all the winter we lived in Pasco. Sunshine was plentiful and being outdoors was a pleasure year-round. A low-humidity summer rounds out the weather picture.

Fishing for salmon and sturgeon are favorite outdoor sports.

PASCO AREA WEATHER						
In degrees Fahrenheit						
	Jan.	April	July	Oct.	Rain	Snow
Daily Highs	37	64	89	65	16"	6"
Daily Lows	20	35	53	35		

PASCO-KENNEWICK COST OF LIVING					
Percentage of	Overall	Housing	Medical	Groceries	Utilities
National Average	99	99	127	100	73

VANCOUVER WEATHER						
In degrees Fahrenheit						
	Jan.	April	July	Oct.	Rain	Snow
Daily Highs	44	60	80	64	37"	6"
Daily Lows	34	41	56	45		

Vancouver   Although in the state of Washington, just across the Columbia River, Vancouver is essentially part of Portland's metropolitan area, a bedroom community, so to speak. Yet the city stands alone in several respects. For one thing, its commercial centers are self-sufficient and residents don't think in terms of "downtown" being in Portland; Vancouver has one of its own, thank you. Residential neighborhoods here tend to have larger lots and smaller home prices. The most significant difference, though, is in taxes. As we have discussed, the state of Washington doesn't collect state income taxes, yet also provides substantial property tax relief to low-income senior citizens. However, the state does have a sales tax. Vancouver residents handle this quite well; they simply cross over the mighty Columbia to sales-tax-free Oregon to make their major purchases, much to the dismay of the state of Washington and Vancouver merchants.

The Vancouver Parks and Recreation Department presents an awesome array of services and programs for seniors. Its Marshall Luepke Center offers a series of tours that would put a travel agency to shame.

Upriver on the Washington side of the Columbia are several delightful little towns strung along a winding, scenic road. Camas, Washougal, and Skamania are close enough to the city for convenience but not so close as to feel overwhelmed by it. The river's bank rises from the waterline, with streets forming tiers that provide scenic views for the towns' homes. There's an exceptionally peaceful air about this stretch of river, a combination of woods, meadows, and steep hills that invites retirement.

Hawaii, Anyone?

HAWAII! THE VERY NAME CREATES EXCITEMENT. Visions of swaying coconut trees, blue Pacific surf, and sandy beaches paint tantalizing
pictures of idyllic retirement. Yet, most folks push these visions
aside as frivolous daydreaming. The common belief is that Hawaii is
only for the filthy rich. There's a lot of truth in that, for Hawaii can
be extremely expensive, particularly in the area of housing. In some
neighborhoods, million-dollar homes are not unusual.

But the interesting
thing is that living in
Hawaii doesn't have to be
super-expensive. The vast
majority of Island resi-
dents are not rich and do
not live in million-dollar
mansions. The fact is, if
you can afford to live on a
comfortable scale in your
hometown, without wor-
rying about watching your expenses, chances are you can do okay on
one of the Hawaiian islands. Of all the places we researched for this
book, Hawaii surprised us the most. You can't live just anywhere,
and you'll have to make tradeoffs in your lifestyle, but you needn't
be a millionaire to retire in Hawaii.

Hawaii is pricey; tourists can vouch for that. The first thing
you'll hear them say when they return from their three-week vacation is, "My God, but it's expensive over there! Everything costs
twice as much!" But as a retiree you won't be living like a tourist.
You'll be bargain shopping, just like local residents.

When we asked one couple how they managed to retire in Honolulu—in a $600,000 home on a $25,000-a-year retirement income—

the wife replied, "Just do as we did. Buy your home thirty-three years ago for $20,000 on the GI Bill, for $500 down." She makes it sound so easy. But for most of us, it's a case of being thirty-three years too late and $600,000 short. Furthermore, even if you're accustomed to living in a $600,000 home on the mainland and can afford to buy one in Honolulu, you'll be disappointed in its quality because the *average* sales price for Honolulu homes is $650,000. A comparable place in Florida might sell for $90,000.

Inflated real estate is the major culprit in sending Hawaii's cost of living soaring above the palm trees. In the Waialae/Kahala area (where my friend has the $600,000 house) the median price is $1.6 million! The topper: Many homeowners don't own the land their homes are standing on; it's leased ground!

Are wages so high that local people can afford expensive housing? No. Although employment is probably at the highest in the nation, wages are surprisingly normal. In fact, a common complaint on the island of Oahu is that many people need to work two jobs to survive. Then, how can local people afford to buy houses? Most of them can't. If they didn't buy twenty years ago, and have scads of equity, chances are they'll never be able to afford even a median-priced home. The same conditions found in San Francisco, Scottsdale, and Washington, D.C., exist in Hawaii, only on a more exaggerated scale.

HAWAII TAX PROFILE
Sales tax: 4%, drugs exempt
State income tax: 2% to 10% over $20,500; can't deduct federal income tax
Property taxes: residents over 60 receive $80,000 exemption; over 65, $100,000; taxes about 0.7% on assessed valuation
Intangibles tax: no
Social security taxed: no
Pensions taxed: no
Gasoline tax: 41.6¢ per gallon, plus local taxes from 8.8¢ to 16.5¢

The interesting part about all this is the lack of for-sale signs around the neighborhoods. Instead of taking their profits, most people are sitting tight. A longtime resident said, "Sure, I could make a big profit on my home, but I would either have to dump the profit back into another house or else I'd have to move away. I'm staying right here!" I know of one working-class family who did sell; they took their profits to Oregon, where they bought a much larger home, invested in a money-making restaurant, and banked a half-million dollars. But they miss Hawaii!

Two conditions account for the super-inflation of Hawaiian real estate. The first is obvious: Hawaii's an exceptionally desirable place to live; the more people move here, the higher the demand for homes. Second: Real estate is continually pushed higher because of the depressed dollar on the world market. Investors from other countries see our dollars and our properties as incredibly cheap bargains. During our last visit, Honolulu newspapers told of an investor from Japan who rented a limo and cruised about town looking for for-sale signs. Every time he found one, he sent his secretary inside to purchase the house at whatever the asking price. They were so cheap (to him) that he bought 123 homes in a little more than one week, never bothering to get out of the limousine.

With this kind of pressure on the real estate market, prices are going to stay high. Therefore, Honolulu is not a retirement option for folks without a great deal of money to invest in a house or a high enough income to pay monthly rent of $3,000 without shuddering. Today, about the only mainlanders who can afford Hawaiian real estate for retirement are those lucky folks who bought a $20,000 house thirty years ago, and can cash it in today for $300,000. Yes, there are places in the islands where that amount will buy a nice place.

The real estate market on the islands we visited was very dynamic, climbing steadily upward. At the time of our research, many areas of the mainland were undergoing slumps in the real estate business, with prices dropping. The Hawaiian reaction seemed to be a slowdown in sales, but very little if any dropping of prices. We visited many open houses and saw enthusiastic potential buyers at every one.

After retirees buy a piece of island property, they tend to start wheeling and dealing, trading up or down, sometimes even going into the real estate business themselves. All the salespeople we talked with had come over as tourists or retirees in the not-too-distant past and before long found themselves selling Hawaii property to other tourists. In fact, we were so caught up in our research that we came very close to buying a lovely condo on the Big Island! Fortunately, at the last moment we remembered our oft-repeated admonition of *try living here before you buy,* and we demurred.

Tips on Locating

A friend who has lived on Oahu for nearly thirty years gave us a few tips on where to locate and what to look for.

First of all, don't be too anxious to have a house directly on the beach. It's wonderful to hear that wind and surf through the bedroom window, but that same wind blows sand and moisture into the house. Sand damages carpets and damp salt air speeds corrosion and mildew. You'll soon grow tired of scraping green mold off your shoes and painting your house with salt-proof paint.

Another caution is not to get too close to those steep-walled mountains that jut almost straight up from the Hawaiian coastal plains. It isn't that they might fall, it is that the steep mountains deflect the trade winds, leaving homes in the shelter of the mountains without cooling breezes. To make matters worse, the mountains cut off the sunshine and never give the houses in the shadows a chance to dry out completely. Finally, the difference in rainfall can be dramatic, just within a distance of a few hundred yards. It can average 40 inches of rain a year away from the mountain shadows, but up to a hundred next to the mountain.

Speaking of rain, although it may rain normally in most neighborhoods—say 30 inches a year—a couple of miles away, up in the mountains, it could rain 400 inches a year. An exceptionally heavy series of rains can quickly turn certain low-lying neighborhoods into lakes. A tipoff is when many homes are built on tall pilings. You could be buying a home in a drained swamp that returns to that state periodically. Even though your home may be built high enough to miss water damage, your car and anything left at ground level can be hurt.

Another thing to watch for is single-wall construction, very common in older homes. This construction means only one layer of wood between you and the outside world; there isn't any wallboard or insulation. This permits free passage of outside noise and conducts the sun's heat into interiors. The tipoff that a house is single-wall is vertical plank construction with a horizontal board running along the wall, just under window height. Later building codes prohibit this kind of fabrication. Single-wall isn't necessarily bad—with Hawaii's balmy weather, insulation isn't crucial—it is just an indication of inexpensive construction and justifies a lower sales price.

What is bad is any evidence of termites. It isn't the flying types that are dangerous, just those that live in damp ground. A friend who lives on Oahu claims termites can totally destroy a house in a matter of weeks. Apparently, this is one of the reasons houses are commonly built on pillars—to prevent the hungry little rascals from sneaking their tunnels into your floors and walls.

Yes, rents are high on the islands. If you want a condo for a week or two, expect to pay at least $150 a night for something nice— $75 on the Big Island where everything is less expensive. For a longer stay, a condo might cost from $1,500 to $1,900 a month. Since so many folks use their condos during the winter and want to rent them out during the summer, however, rents are considerably lower in the off-season. Because so many non-residents own property, there is rarely a shortage of rentals, whether long or short term. If you rent in a non-tourist area—a working-class neighborhood, if you will—the story is again different. If landlords want to keep their places rented, prices have to be competitive and in line with what the tenants can afford to pay.

Caution: Fee Simple versus Leasehold

The history of Hawaiian real estate is very tangled and complex. Because early European settlers grabbed as much acreage as they could and turned it into sugar cane and pineapple plantations, land is scarce and considered very valuable. Landowners, rather than selling the land, prefer to lease it for periods of sixty or more years. Every thirty years or so, the lease comes up for renegotiation. Therefore, you may own your house, but someone else owns the land. This arrangement is called a *leasehold*. If you own the property outright, it's called *fee simple*.

The differences between leasehold and fee simple are very important. We've heard some absolute horror stories concerning leaseholds. One person told of having a $400-a-month leasehold, and upon renegotiation discovered that the lessor wanted $12,000 a month from then on! We understand that the government is trying to control abuses like this, but it's quite important to know what kind of lease you are signing. Another problem is that when a leasehold has less than thirty years remaining, banks are hesitant to finance the property. So, although your purchase could be financed without a problem, you may run into trouble when you get around to selling.

Is Hawaiian Retirement Practical?

Because of our personal prejudices, making recommendations on retirement in Hawaii is difficult. We love the climate and we've had very positive experiences dealing with the local people. We've never seen a place where smiles appear so spontaneously and seem so genuine.

The fact that we enjoy the islands doesn't mean others will like them. A friend who moved to Honolulu a few years ago—not for retirement, but in search of a job—painted a different picture of life on the islands. She said, "Yes, if you spend your time with other retirees, and if your dealings with the local people are as a customer or client, you will love the place. But as a worker, I've encountered resentment and even prejudice, simply because I am an outsider. They feel I am taking a job away from a Hawaiian." Her experience is personal, but should be considered if you are thinking of part-time jobs during your retirement.

One problem that comes with living on an isolated island is that you may become *rock-happy*. This is akin to cabin fever or going stir-crazy. It happens when you start feeling confined, when you realize there is no getting away, and that a three- or four-hour drive in any direction will put you right back at your garage door. People claim that the sickness sets in after about three years of bliss.

Folks who have lived here for long periods of time claim the only cure for being rock-happy is a trip to the mainland. One of the most popular flights is to Las Vegas. Apparently, the mind is soothed by vast expanses of gambling casino, fields of green-felt tables, and cocktail waitresses swaying in the background like coconut trees on the windward coast. Apparently, those who can afford to make periodic trips to the mainland often don't care whether they go or not. It's those who *cannot* afford to leave the "rock" who get the rock-happy sickness the worst.

Another aspect to our view of retirement in Hawaii is that we've lived in a fairly high-cost-of-living part of the country for many years. We're used to high housing costs. What we might view as economical or affordable housing may contrast sharply with someone who is used to far lower costs. Because we can afford it doesn't mean everyone can.

Therefore, our conclusions are favorable. Although Honolulu and the island of Oahu might be out of range for us, other places—

particularly the Kona area of the Big Island—would suit us as places where we could retire. Our philosophy of retirement involves keeping a home base and spending time elsewhere, depending upon the season. We will surely be spending at least some of our time on the islands, perhaps renting a condo or townhouse during the off-season.

Grocery Prices

You may well expect prices to be higher in Hawaii, since most goods have to be brought in by ship or airplane. When vacationing tourists visit Honolulu, they often rent condos for a week or two and do some of their own cooking to cut expenses. When they return they'll say, "We couldn't believe the price of groceries! They're double the cost at home!"

And it's true; if you shop in the tourist areas, food items can easily cost twice as much or more. At a corner deli in Waikiki, a head of cabbage was priced at $3.75 and a dozen eggs at $4.00. Other sundries were similiarly tagged. If you check only prices around the tourist hotels, you'll wonder how in the world islanders can afford to feed themselves.

Obviously, folks who live in Hawaii year-round won't be shopping in tourist-oriented enterprises. Just as you shop for the best prices where you live, islanders patronize ordinary supermarkets, far from the hotel strip. The surprising thing is how close to mainland prices groceries are—at least on the three islands where we did our research. We visited four large supermarkets to compare prices: a well-known chain store on the windward side of Oahu; the same chain supermarket in Kaanapali, Maui; the largest market in Waimea, Hawaii; and a supermarket a few blocks from the tourist area of Kona, Hawaii. We found price variations among these stores on identical items, but no more than you might find between stores on the mainland. The closer to tourists' condos, the wider the variation.

Although some items were considerably more expensive in Hawaii, the surprising thing was that so many items were not much higher or about the *same* as on the mainland! What happened to the extra costs of shipping? Products such as mayonnaise, coffee, and ice cream were priced about the same as back home, as were things like paper goods, soap, and pasta. Meats, which we expected to be sky-high, turned out to be *less* than at our neighborhood supermarket!

Some items, however, are much more costly in Hawaii, particularly eggs, milk, and fresh vegetables. That milk is expensive is understandable. Land that isn't already planted in pineapple and sugar cane is so expensive that devoting it to dairy cattle would be unprofitable. But the curious thing is the high cost of fresh vegetables. They cost far more than at home, often twice as much or even more. This was particularly true on Oahu and less so on Maui and the Big Island (Hawaii). One would imagine that Hawaii's lush fields and fertile backyards should yield such a high volume of quality produce that people would be almost giving food away. But that isn't the case.

Part of the problem is that some fruits and vegetables don't do well in warm, tropical climates; others suffer from a Mediterranean fruit fly infestation that Hawaii has never been able to overcome. That I understand, but what about vegetables such as lettuce, cabbage, and broccoli? Whatever the reason, high prices prevail at the supermarket. Pineapples are the one item that seems to be cheap (and high quality).

When we returned to the mainland, we visited our local supermarket in California to compare prices. Our conclusions are that the Hawaiian grocery bill needn't be a barrier to living in the islands. By shopping shrewdly and planning meals around weekly specials, we feel that we could keep our grocery bills to within 10 to 15 percent of our California budget.

Clothing prices seemed to be pretty much the same as on the mainland. How could this be? Because like so many products that we used to make in America, most wearing apparel is now manufactured in Asia. Shipping costs to Hawaii are lower, since it's closer to the factory.

The same is true of automobiles. It costs less to ship a Honda to Honolulu than it does to ship a Mitsibushi to Minneapolis. Furthermore, since the islands have very few miles of highway, cars tend to last a long time. If it weren't for rust and corrosion related to salt-water breezes, autos would probably never wear out. As it is, many old clunkers are still running around happily carrying their owners on short runs to the beach.

Gasoline is one item that costs much more than on the mainland. Since you cannot drive very far without returning to the same spot, however, gasoline shouldn't be a crucial portion of your budget.

The Bottom Line

If you are the type who likes to put down roots, and if you need to own property, and if you want to live in an idyllic climate and, finally, if you can afford a large investment in real estate, then you must investigate the Hawaiian Islands. If you like warm winters and the sight of palm trees swaying in the breeze, yet you can't afford $250,000 for a condo, perhaps Florida is a better choice for you. It isn't Hawaii, but no other place in the world is.

Oahu

The best-known islands of the Hawaiian archipelago are Oahu, Kauai, Maui, and the Big Island of Hawaii. But in reality, these make up only a small portion of the Hawaiian Islands: 132 islands, shoals, atolls, and reefs stretch from tiny Kure, more than 1,500 miles away, to Loihi, an undersea mountain next to the Big Island that is still building. One day Loihi will be Hawaii's newest island. For all I know, there may be a promoter selling lots on Loihi, so please be cautious.

The secret to living on Oahu is simple: you don't *have* to live in Honolulu. In fact, that's a place I'm not sure I'd choose for a residence even if property were cheap! Too many cars crowd the streets, too many tourists fill the beaches, and too many high-rise hotels line the avenues.

Just thirty-five to forty-five minutes from the hustle and bustle of Waikiki Beach are some lovely communities that have all the attributes of small-town U.S.A. The Kailua and Kaneohe areas are good examples, with almost no buildings over two stories high and single-family homes the norm. Each has a population of more than 30,000. You'll find exceptionally low crime rates, light traffic, and friendly neighbors. Beaches are seldom crowded—often empty, in fact—in sharp contrast to the elbow-to-elbow tourists on Waikiki beaches. The bonus is a year-round climate that is as nearly perfect as can be found anywhere in the world.

Homes here sell for considerably less than Honolulu prices; they're not cheap, but not too much more expensive than similar quality mainland neighborhoods. A comforting note: If you do invest in Hawaiian real estate, the odds are overwhelming that you can get your money back (plus profit) later, should you return to the mainland.

Drive another twenty minutes and prices drop even lower. On Oahu's north shore the median price for homes is around $300,000, and for condos, $140,000. Now, we are approaching the ballpark for many mainlanders. For folks living in many parts of California, these prices sound normal. Don't misunderstand; I'm not suggesting that these homes are inexpensive or are superb buys. A house for under $300,000 is often located in a neighborhood where I'd feel uncomfortable living. Too many homes are flimsy, single-wall construction and sit on leased land.

How is it possible then, to retire in Hawaii without being wealthy? Remember, I said you could live *modestly*. By modestly, I don't mean wearing high-neck bathing suits with long drawers, but modestly as in wearing bathing suits with patches on the seat.

To test living on Oahu on our normal budget, my wife and I felt that $750 a month was about as much rent as we would like to pay; that's what a small apartment rents for in our California hometown. We quickly found a place called Punaluu on the North Shore. It was a one-bedroom condo right on the beach with a swimming pool, off-street parking, and a secure building. The monthly rate was $750. Had we wanted to buy the condo, it was listed at $125,000. The neighborhood was quiet, with a couple of grocery stores located within walking distance (plus a convenience store on the premises) and near long stretches of semi-private beachfront. (All Hawaiian beaches are open to the public.) About 40 percent of the condo owners live here year-round; the rest spend the winter months here and rent out their units for the rest of the year. Rents vary between $600 and $950, depending upon the amenities and views. Although we had a rental car, bus service is excellent. Those who live here part of the year have automobiles and store them in reserved parking spaces with waterproof covers when they are staying on the mainland.

Living in the condo as if we owned it and shopping in local markets gave us an insight as to what it would be like to actually live on Oahu as retirees. We got by just fine on about what we would have spent living at home under similar circumstances. Well, we probably would have rented a larger place on the mainland and

HONOLULU WEATHER					
In degrees Fahrenheit					
	Jan.	April	July	Oct.	Rain	Snow
Daily Highs	80	83	87	87	23"	—
Daily Lows	65	69	73	72		

dined at more upscale restaurants. But the gorgeous weather and lovely beaches nearby balanced out our lifestyle, probably on the plus side.

Maui

Maui is the second largest of the islands and is famous for its marvelous beaches and fantastic views. A few years ago, Maui was a haven for those seeking tropical splendor at cut-rate prices. Property was cheap and the living was easy. Hippies and counterculture refugees from bourgeois boredom passed the word: "Like, Maui is where it's at, man!"

Things have changed. Somehow, the word must have gotten out to the bourgeoisie, because they've invaded Maui with a vengeance—fully equipped with plaid polyester shorts and matching golf clubs. With their middle-class values they also brought higher prices, which forced many counterculture folks to go tripping off to discover new island paradises.

Kapalua/Kaanapali   Most retirees—and mainlanders in general—prefer the western coast of Maui. The luxury areas of Kaanapali Beach and Kapalua are particularly popular, with elegant condos, hotels, and expansive golf courses around every bend in the road. Ritzy shopping centers, art galleries, and restaurants instill feelings of awe in the most blasé shoppers. The beaches are tops, and the islands of Molokai and Lanai make a wonderful backdrop for sunsets.

We felt fortunate that we had studied Honolulu real estate prices before coming to Maui, because that made Maui property seem reasonable. We stayed at a condo in Kaanapali Beach, a two-bedroom affair with a great view of the ocean. Humpback whales were arriving after their annual voyage from Alaska, and they were leaping from the water in spectacular expressions of joy that the trip was finally over. A couple in a nearby condo had also just arrived from Fairbanks, Alaska, for their winter migration, and although they weren't leaping for joy, they obviously felt like it!

Based on Oahu prices, we estimated the cost of the condo to be at least $500,000. We figured that any offer less than that might be grounds for calling the police. To our amazement, the owner informed us that a unit like that could be purchased for less than $350,000—furnished, no less. A few weeks earlier this would have sounded like a lot of money, but now it seemed like a steal. You would have to see the luxurious layout to realize what a bargain one of those condos was.

In our forays to the supermarket to supply our condo's kitchen, we found groceries a bit cheaper than on Oahu, but not remarkably so. Vegetables, eggs, and milk were expensive, just as we had expected.

Lahaina A couple of kilometers to the south is the historic whaling village of Lahaina, a place praised by Melville, Mark Twain, and other famous people over the years. The picturesque old buildings are a natural attraction for artists and photographers. Art galleries and numerous artists at work with easels are common sights. Condos and homes are less expensive here, some selling in the neighborhood of $150,000, although we did look at one place for $475,000—nice but way out of range for most mainlanders.

Lahaina has a very comfortable feeling, but the downtown center suffers from steady streams of tourists wandering around buying souvenirs. The town of Maalea, a bit farther south, is another comparatively inexpensive place. There we found a beautiful two-bedroom condo, right on the beach, selling for $225,000 and a one-bedroom unit for $175,000. These units are usually placed in the hands of rental agents when owners travel elsewhere. A rental agent swore that she could keep them rented at an 85 percent occupancy rate for $125 a night.

On the "south coast" (still on the western side of the island) are Wailea and Makena, with a good share of expensive places. With the islands of Lanai and Kahoolawe across the water, it is a magnificent place for Hawaii's legendary sunsets. Long stretches of beach and spectacular surf make this a favorite with mainlanders.

The Big Island

It was here, on the Big Island of Hawaii, that the Polynesians first came ashore, probably landing on Punaluu Beach on the southern end of the island. All around the island you can discover traces of the ancient Hawaiian civilization. Petroglyphs, temple mounds, and burial grounds recall the days of the Hawaiian monarchy, from the time before the Europeans entered the picture.

Hawaii is called the Big Island for good reason; with 4,038 square miles, about twice as large as all the others put together, it's about the size of Connecticut. And the Big Island hasn't stopped growing! In an awesome display of nature, lava from the Kilauea volcano has added hundreds of acres of land surface since its eruption a few years ago. The growth continues daily. As the lava flow pushes into the ocean to build more land, it also destroys homes and buildings that lie in its path.

Hawaii is famous for these "drive-in" volcanoes. You can usually drive to where the molten lava moves down the volcano's side and crosses the highway. You can park, walk over to the lava flow, and take pictures of the glowing, taffy-like material as it moves toward the sea at 2,000 degrees Fahrenheit.

This process of land building started aeons ago when a crack in the ocean floor some 18,000 feet below the water's surface opened and began oozing molten lava onto the ocean bottom. It grew ever higher, pouring magma down its sides until the crater's mouth finally broke through the surface of the water and began preparing for an onslaught of tourists. The process of discharging melted basalt continued until the volcano reached its present height of almost 14,000 feet *above* the ocean's surface. Some claim that if you measure from the ocean floor to the snow-covered top of Mauna Kea, it becomes the highest mountain in the world.

Our Favorite Hawaiian Island

Of the islands we visited, the Big Island is, without a doubt, our favorite. You'll find almost every climate and topography imaginable, from tropical rain forests with lush, jungle-like vegetation to deserts and snow-covered peaks. On the Kona coast, where most retirees settle, rainfall is about 40 inches a year—about the same as a typical Midwestern U.S. location. Yet at the Kona airport, just a few miles north, only 10 inches of rain falls each year. This lower rainfall doesn't mean water shortages as it might on the mainland, because about 400 inches a year falls in the mountains, just a few miles to the east. This water flows in underground streams and is tapped by wells. At the other extreme, Hilo (on the eastern coast) gets more than 140 inches, and residents claim that some years the rainfall measures more than 200 inches!

During the winter months you can ski the slopes of Mauna Kea in the morning; travel through sugar cane plantations, desert, and cactus land during midday; go scuba diving in the afternoon; and watch glowing rivers of red lava flow in the evening. Because traffic is light and the roads are good, all these activities are possible with a minimum of hassle.

Notice that I said the Big Island has *almost* every climate and topography imaginable. It seriously lacks something other islands are famous for: beaches. In fact, it has almost *no* beaches! This singular lack clearly makes the Big Island unattractive to many Hawaii fans, especially those whose idea of an ideal holiday is lying on warm sand and soaking up sunshine. On the island of Hawaii, most of the coast is black, jagged lava rock. You can spread your towel on the lava, but you won't be comfortable lying back and enjoying the sun.

Beaches are scarce here because the Big Island is the newest of the islands. Just a few millions of years old, Hawaii is still in the process of becoming an island. The coastlines are twisted rivers of lava rock that have flowed into the ocean; waves and water action haven't had time to break the rock into fine grains of sand. In a few places the lava has disintegrated into black sand—sometimes green or red, depending upon the chemical composition of the lava—but regular old Malibu-type sand is rare. Instead of waves lapping against sand, the ocean usually hits boulder-sized black rocks or sharp, formidable cliffs.

At first, it might seem that a lack of beaches should be a drawback. But there are two major benefits. The first is that the surf and views are truly spectacular, with blue-green waves crashing incessantly upon the black cliffs and jagged boulders. The sounds and sights are infinitely more exciting than the quiet ripples of Waikiki Beach or the leeward side of Maui.

The second benefit is that this scarcity of beaches also means a scarcity of surfers, beach bums, and disco maniacs. Tourists and retirees come to the Big Island for kinder, gentler forms of entertainment. The end results are highways without heavy traffic and lots of empty country. As a matter of fact, this enormous piece of land has a population of only 117,000. Honolulu has more than that along one street. The island's largest and only city is Hilo, with a mere 47,000 residents. The rest are in towns and villages.

Another result is the age composition of the tourists and residents. Without surfing, discos, and other things that attract youngsters, the Big Island has a quieter, more reserved feeling. Your next-door neighbor is more likely to be your age; your dinner companions will not be youngsters. Hotels are quieter, and more folks live here year-round instead of coming for a hectic, fun-packed vacation.

Hilo   The quiet, laid-back atmosphere of the Big Island and the lightweight population of tourists are some of the charms of Hilo. Another big plus is the affordability of housing. When you hear people say that Hawaiian real estate is out of sight, you can be sure they aren't talking about the eastern side of Hawaii.

The city of Hilo, for example, boasts of housing prices that compare favorably with all but the most inexpensive places in the United States. You can buy a four-bedroom home on an acre of ground for $100,000. A three-bedroom place can be found for $80,000, or a country cabin on three acres for $45,000. A one-bedroom apartment with a view of the ocean rents for $350 a month, a studio apartment for $285. Any number of homes are listed for rent in the local newspaper at rates from $250 to $750 a month.

I'm not saying I would prefer living in Hilo to the other side of the island. It is a neat, clean city, with many interesting, historic buildings (reminiscent of Lahaina on Maui), and some absolutely gorgeous homes and townhouses adorn the coast. But it rains too much for me. As a Californian, I am used to zero rainfall during the summer months, so I don't think I could adjust to an average of 11

HILO WEATHER						
	In degrees Fahrenheit					
	Jan.	April	July	Oct.	Rain	Snow
Daily Highs	80	80	83	83	128"	—
Daily Lows	63	65	68	68		

inches a month. Obviously, the folks who live in and around Hilo would disagree with me, since about half the entire island's population chooses to live here. Except for Kailua–Kona and Waimea—both with under 10,000 population—most other towns on the Big Island barely qualify as villages.

Kailua–Kona This is our favorite part of the Big Island as well as the attraction for most other retirees. Yes, you'll find tourists—droves of them—but the scene isn't nearly as hectic as on Oahu or Maui. The panorama is typically Hawaiian and tropical, with palms, broad-leaf plants, and flowers everywhere. Lovely homes, condos, and townhouses command views of the coast and few have either air-conditioning or heaters; neither are really needed.

In short, Kailua–Kona has everything you need for Hawaiian retirement (except beaches) with an added bonus: reasonable housing costs. For $150,000 or less, you can find a very livable condo or townhouse with swimming pools, tennis courts, and a view of the ocean—a place that would cost $450,000 in Honolulu. It's true that you can find something less expensive in or near Honolulu, but would you be happy living in a poor man's home near a rich man's neighborhood? I wouldn't.

We looked at many places, mostly condos or townhouses, and we tried to stay in the below-$150,000 range. There were two reasons for this. First, that seems to be the average price range, and second, these are the easiest to rent, should you decide to live here part-time. These places rent for $65 to $75 a night; several reliable companies specialize in handling short-term rentals. Often the condominium's office is set up like a hotel desk, with the manager renting condos for the owners. (The fee varies from 10 to 20 percent of the rental.) With the nearby Kona Hilton renting rooms at $140 a night, the $65 rate looks great to tourists who want more than just a hotel room.

In early 1991, when we visited Kona, there were more than 130 condos or townhouses on the market, ranging from $65,000 for a studio without an ocean view to $399,000 for a deluxe three-bedroom place right on the ocean. There were nine one-bedroom places with ocean views selling for $79,000 to $99,000 and several two-bedroom condos under $150,000. The median price of a one-bedroom condo was around $140,000. Compare that with a $230,000 median price for Honolulu, and you'll see why we like Kona.

Waikoloa/Waimea   Farther up the coast, a series of super-expensive golf/country club projects are sprouting. My impression is that they are being built by Japanese investors and may be designed for tourists from Japan. Although they are beautifully designed, they are not only expensive but also are isolated from the rest of the island. That may not mean much to a golf nut, however, whose main interest is finding the best courses to play, and these new courses are said to be superb.

But inland a bit, at an elevation of 1,000 feet, is Waikoloa. This also has dry weather, which, combined with the altitude, boasts one of the finest climates on any of the islands. This is a fairly new condo and townhouse project, and it is well laid out. We looked at several places right on the golf course that were selling for under $150,000 for two-bedroom units. There's a shopping center and all the amenities nearby.

Normally, I would say Waikoloa would also be too isolated, except that the town of Waimea is only 16 miles away. Even though Waimea is so close, its rainfall patterns are remarkably different. I believe it gets close to 30 inches a year, which is enough to make wonderfully lush farming and ranch country. In some ways, Waimea looks like a prosperous farm town in the Midwest. It has less than 5,000 inhabitants, and it isn't tourist oriented at all. Single-family homes are the norm, with tidy yards and comfortable-looking neighborhoods. It's at a higher altitude and enjoys an almost temperate climate, with springtime every day of the year.

Most homes are in the $200,000 to $250,000 range, with some as low as $175,000 for a three-bedroom place. When we were there, an older five-bedroom, two-bath place on acreage was offered at $149,000, and a two-bedroom, two-bath place at $140,000.

Appendix:
Chamber of Commerce and Senior Agencies

Alabama

Advantage for Retirees
P.O. Box 250347
Montgomery, 36125

Anniston
P.O. Box 1087
Anniston, 36202

Auburn/Opelika
P.O. Box 4007
Opelika, 36831

Blount County
P.O. Box 87
Oneonta, 35121

Dothan
P.O. Box 638
Dothan, 36302

Enterprise
P.O. Box 577
Enterprise, 36331

Eufaula
P.O. Box 697
Eufaula, 36072

Evergreen
100 Depot Square
Evergreen, 36401

Gadsen
P.O. Box 185
Gadsen, 35902

Gulf Shores
P.O. Drawer 3869
Gulf Shores, 36547

Jasper
P.O. Box 972
Jasper, 35501

Ozark
308 Painter Avenue
Ozark, 36360

Pelham
P.O. Box 324
Pelham, 35124

Scottsboro
P.O. Box 973
Scottsboro, 35768

Arizona

State Department of
  Economic Security,
  Aging, and Adult
  Administration
1789 West Jefferson
Phoenix, 85007

Ajo
P.O. Box 507
Ajo, 85321

Apache Junction
P.O. Box 1747
Apache Junction, 85217

Casa Grande
757 North Marxhall
Casa Grande, 85222

Bisbee
P.O. Box BA
Bisbee, 85603

Bullhead City
1251 Highway 95
Bullhead City, 86430

Green Valley
P.O Box 566
Green Valley, 85614

Lake Havasu
1930 Mesquite Avenue #3
Lake Havasu City, 86403

Payson
P.O. Box 1380
Payson, 85547

Prescott
P.O. Box 1147
Prescott, 86302

Sedona
P.O. Box 478
Sedona, 86336

Sun City
P.O. Box 1519
Sun City, 85372

Tucson
P.O. Box 991
Tucson, 85702

Wickenburg
P.O. Box Drawer CC
Wickenburg, 85358

Yuma
P.O. Box 10230
Yuma, 85364

Arkansas

Arkansas State
P.O. Box 3645
Little Rock, 72203

Bull Shoals
P.O. Box 354
Bull Shoals, 72619

Camden
P.O. Box 99
Camden, 71701

Fayetteville
P.O. Box 4216,
Fayetteville, 72702

Heber Springs
1001 West Main
Heber Springs, 72543

Hot Springs
P.O. Box 6090
Hot Springs, 71902

Little Rock
101 South Spring Street,
  #200
Little Rock, 72201

Mena
524 Sherwood Avenue
Mena, 71953

Mountain Home
P.O. Box 488
Mountain Home, 72653

California
Department on Aging
1600 K Street
Sacramento, 95814

California State Chamber
  of Commerce
P.O. Box 1736
Sacramento, 95808

Amador County
P.O. Box 596
Jackson, 95642

Arcata
1062 G Street
Arcata, 95521

Bakersfield
P.O. Box 1947
Bakersfield, 93303

Chico
P.O. Box 3038
Chico, 95927

Crescent City
1001 Front Street
Crescent City, 95531

Desert Hot Springs
P.O. Box 848
Desert Hot Springs, 92240

Escondido
720 North Broadway
Escondido, 92025

Eureka
2112 Broadway
Eureka, 95501

Fall River Mills
P.O. Box 475
Fall River Mills, 96028

Fortuna
P.O. Box 797
Fortuna, 95540

Garberville
P.O. Box 445
Garberville, 95440

Indio
P.O. Box TTT
Indio, 92201

Jackson
P.O. Box 596
Jackson, 95642

Monterey
P.O. Box 1770
Monterey, 93942

Mt. Shasta–Dunsmuir
300 Pine Street
Mt. Shasta, 96067

Ojai
P.O. Box 1134
Ojai, 93023

Oroville
1789 Montgomery Street
Oroville, 95965

Palm Springs
190 West Amado Road
Palm Springs, 92262

Pismo Beach
581 Dolliver Street
Pismo Beach, 93449

San Diego
402 West Broadway
Suite 1000
San Diego, 92101

San Luis Obispo
1039 Chorro Street
San Luis Obispo, 93401

Sun City
P.O. Box 656
Sun City, 92386

Yucaipa
P.O. Box 45
Yucaipa, 92399

Colorado
Colorado State
1860 Lincoln Street, #550
Denver, 80296

Boulder
P.O. Box 73
Boulder, 80302

Denver
1445 Market Street
Denver, 80202

Durango
P.O. Box 2587
Durango, 81302

Grand Junction
360 Grand Avenue
Grand Junction, 81501

Steamboat Springs
P.O. Box 774408
Steamboat Springs, 80477

Florida
Florida State
P.O. Box 11309
Tallahassee, 32302

Apalachicola
57 Market Street
Apalachicola, 32320

Boca Raton
P.O. Box 1390
Boca Raton, 33432

Boynton Beach
639 East Ocean Avenue,
  #108
Boynton Beach, 33435

Bradenton
P.O. Box 321
Bradenton, 33506

Cocoa Beach
400 Fortenberry Road
Cocoa Beach, 32952

Daytona Beach
P.O. Box 2475
Daytona Beach, 32115

Ft. Myers
P.O. Box 9289
Ft. Meyers, 33902

Ft. Walton Beach
P.O. Box 640
Ft. Walton Beach, 32549

Gainesville
P.O. Box 1187
Gainesville, 32602

Jacksonville
P.O. Box 329
Jacksonville, 32202

Key Largo
105950 Overseas Highway
Key Largo, 33037

Key West
P.O. Box 984
Key West, 33040

Kissimmee
1425 East Vine Street
Kissimmee, 32744

Lakeland
P.O. Box 3607
Lakeland, 33802

Leesburg
P.O. Box 490309
Leesburg, 34749

Marathon
12222 Overseas Highway
Marathon, 33050

Melbourne
1005 East Strawbridge
   Avenue
Melbourne, 32901

Miami
1601 Biscayne Boulevard
Miami, 33132

Naples
3620 North Tamiami Trail
Naples, 33940

Ocala
P.O. Box 1210
Ocala, 32670

Orlando
P.O. Box 1234
Orlando, 32802

Panama City
P.O. Box 1850
Panama City, 32402

Palm Coast
Star Route Box 18-N
Bunnell, 32110

Pensacola
P.O. Box 550
Pensacola, 32593

Pompano Beach
2200 East Atlantic
   Boulevard
Pompano Beach, 33062

Port Charlotte
2702 Tamiami Trail
Port Charlotte, 33952

Sarasota
1819 Main Street
Sarasota, 34236

St. Augustine
1 Riberia Street
Augustine, 32084

St. Petersburg
P.O. Box 1371
St. Petersburg, 33731

Sun City
1651 Sun City Plaza
Sun City, 33573

Tallahassee
P.O. Box 1639
Tallahassee, 32302

Winter Haven
P.O. Drawer 1420
Winter Haven, 33882

Georgia
Department of Human
   Resources
Office of Aging
878 Peachtree Street NE
Atlanta, 30309

Brunswick-Golden Isles
   Chamber of Commerce
4 Glynn Avenue
Brunswick, GA 31520

Dahlonega
101 South Park Street
Dahlonega, 30533

Habersham County
P.O. Box 366
Cornelia, 30531

Rabun County
P.O. Box 761
Clayton, 30525

Savannah
P.O. Box 1628
Savannah, 31402

Thomasville
P.O. Box 2036
Thomasville, 31799

Valdosta
P.O. Box 790
Valdosta, 31602

Hawaii
Hilo
202 Kamehameha Avenue
Hilo, 96720

Honolulu
735 Bishop Street
Honolulu, 96813

Kahului
(Maui Chamber of
   Commerce)
26 North Puunene Avenue
Kahului, 96732

Kentucky
Bowling Green
P.O. Box 51
Bowling Green, 42101

Murray
P.O. Box 190
Murray, 42071

Louisiana
Alexandria
P.O. Box 992
Alexandria, 70821–3217

Baton Rouge
P.O. Box 3217
Baton Rouge, 70821

DeRidder
P.O. Box 309
DeRidder, 70634

England Oaks
1008 B Norman Drive
Alexandria, 71303

Houma
1700 Street Charles Street
Houma, 70361

Lafayette
P.O. Box 51307
Lafayette, 70505

Leesville
U.S. Highway 171
Leesville, 71496

Natchitoches
700 Front Street
Nachitoches, 71457

Toledo Bend
Janell Ross
15091 Texas Highway
Many, 71449

Mississipi
Council on Aging
421 West Pascagoula Street
Jackson, 39203

Biloxi
P.O. Box 1928
Biloxi, 39533

Clinton
P.O. Box 143
Clinton, 39060

Columbus
P.O. Box 1016
Columbus, 39703

Gulfport
Mississippi Beach
  Retirement
P.O. Box 569
Gulfport, 39502

Hattiesburg
P.O. Box 751
Hattiesburg, 39403

Madison
P.O. Box 544
Madison, 39130

Natchez Retiree Partnership
P.O. Box 700
Natchez, 39121

Oxford
428 North Lamar Boulevard
Oxford, 38655

Picayune
P.O. Box 448
201 Highway 11 North
Picayune, 39466

Tupelo
117 North Broadway
Tupelo, 38801

Missouri
Missouri State
P.O. Box 149
Jefferson City, 65102

Columbia
P.O. Box 1016
Columbia, 65205

Osage Beach
P.O. Box 193
Osage Beach, 65065

Nevada
Nevada State
P.O. Box 2806
Reno, 89505

Division for Aging Services
1665 Hot Springs Road,
  Suite 158
Carson City, 89710

Carson City
1900 South Carson Street
Carson City, 89701

Lake Tahoe
P.O. Box 7139
Lake Tahoe, 89449

Las Vegas
711 East Desert Inn Road
Las Vegas, 89109

Pahrump
P.O. Box 42
Pahrump, 89041

Reno
P.O. Box 3499
Reno, 89505

New Mexico
Albuquerque
P.O. Box 25100
Albuquerque, 87125

Carlsbad
P.O. Box 910
Carlsbad, 88220

Las Cruces
Drawer 519
Las Cruces, 88004

Rio Rancho
1781 Rio Rancho Drive
Rio Rancho, 87124

Ruidoso
P.O. Box 698
Ruidoso, 88345

Santa Fe
P.O. Box 1928
Santa Fe, 88061

Silver City
1103 North Hudson Street
Silver City, 88061

Taos
P.O. Drawer 1
Taos, 87571

North Carolina
Division of Aging
693 Palmer Drive
Raleigh, 27626

Asheville
P.O. Box 1010,
Ashville, 28802

Brevard
P.O. Box 589
Brevard, 28712

Chapel Hill
P.O. Box 2897
Chapel Hill, 27515

Durham
P.O. Box 3829
Durham, 27702

Henderson
330 North King Street
Hendersonville, 28793

Pinehurst/Southern Pines
P.O. Box 458
Southern Pines, 28388

Raleigh
225 Hillsborough Street
Suite 400
Raleigh, 27602

Sanford Enrichment Center
1615 South Third Street
Sanford, 27330

West Jefferson
P.O. Box 31
West Jefferson, 28694

Winston-Salem
P.O. Box 1408
Winston-Salem, 27102

Oklahoma
Oklahoma State
4020 North Lincoln
    Boulevard
Oklahoma City, 73105

Bartlesville
P.O. Box 2366
Bartlesville, 74005

Grand Lake o' the
    Cherokees
104-B West Third Street
Grove, 74344

Tallequah
123 East Delaware Street
Tallequah, 74464

Oregon
Ashland
P.O. Box 1360
Ashland, 97520

Astoria
P.O. Box 176
Astoria, 97103

Bandon-by-the-Sea
P.O. Box 1515
Bandon, 97411

Bend
63085 North Highway 97
Bend, 97701

Brookings
P.O. Box 940
Brookings, 97415

Eugene
P.O. Box 1107
Eugene, 97440

Florence
P.O. Box 26000
Florence, 97439

Gold Beach
1225 South Ellensburg, #3
Gold Beach, 97444

Grants Pass
P.O. Box 970
Grants Pass, 97526

Klamath Falls
401 Plum Street
Klamath Falls, 97601

Medford
101 East Eighth Street
Medford, 97501

Portland
221 NW Second Avenue
Portland, 97209

Roseburg
410 SE Spruce
P.O. Box 1026
Roseburg, 97470

Salem
220 Cottage Street, NE
Salem, 97301

The Dalles
404 West Second
The Dalles, 97058

South Carolina
State of South Carolina
P.O. Box 11278
Columbia, 29202

Aiken
P.O. Box 1708
Aiken, 29802

Charleston
P.O. Box 975
Charleston, 29402

Cheraw
221 Market Street
Cheraw, 29520

Columbia
P.O. Box 1360
Columbia, 29202

Georgetown
P.O. Box 1776
Georgetown, 29442

Hilton Head
P.O. Box 5647
Hilton Head, 29938

Myrtle Beach
P.O. Box 2115
Myrtle Beach, 29578

Summerville
P.O. Box 670
Summerville, 29484

Tennessee
Chattanooga
1101 Market Street
Chattanooga, 37402

Clarksville
P.O. Box 883
Clarksville, 37041

Crossville
P.O. Box 453
Crossville, 38555

Texas
State of Texas
300 West Fifteenth Street,
    #875
Austin, 78701

Aransas Pass
452 Cleveland
Aransas Pass, 78336

Austin
P.O. Box 1967
Austin, 78767

Brownsville
P.O. Box 752
Brownsville, 78522

Corpus Christi
P.O. Box 640
Corpus Christi, 78403

Fredericksburg
106 North Adams
Fredericksburg, 78624

Galveston
2106 Seawall Boulevard
Galveston, 77550

Georgetown
P.O. Box 346
Georgetown, 78627

Harlingen
P.O. Box 189
Harlingen, 78551

Kerrville
1700 Sidney Baker Street, #100
Kerrville, 78028

Marble Falls
801 Highway 281
Marble Falls, 78654

McAllen
P.O. Box 790
McAllen, 78501

Nacogdoches
P.O. Box 631918
Nacogdoches, 75963

Port Aransas
P.O. Box 356,
Port Aransas, 78373

Port Isabel-Padre Island
213 Yturria Street
Port Isabel, 78578

San Antonio
P.O. Box 1628
San Antonio, 78296

Wimberley
P.O. Box 12
Wimberley, 78676

Utah
Cedar City
P.O. Box 220
Cedar City, 84721

Salt Lake City
175 East 400 South, #600
Salt Lake City, 84111

St. George
97 East George Boulevard
St. George, 84770

Virginia
Department for the Aging
700 East Franklin Street, 10th Floor
Richmond, 23219

Charlottesville
P.O. Box 1564
Charlottesville, 22906

Hampton
6 Manhattan Square
Hampton, 23666

Washington
Bellingham
P.O. Box 958
Bellingham, 98227

Bremerton
P.O. Box 229
Bremerton, 98337

Olympia
P.O. Box 1427
Olympia, 98501

Pasco
P.O. Box 550
Pasco, 99301

Port Townsend
2437 East Sims Way
Port Townsend, 98368

Seattle
1301 Fifth Avenue, #2400
Seattle, 98101

Sequim
P.O. Box 907
Sequim, 98382

Vancouver
404 East Fifteenth Street, #11
Vancouver, 98663

Index

Index
To Places